THE BEAU MONDE

Dr Hannah Greig is Reader in 18th-century British history at the University of York. Before joining York, she held fellowships at Balliol College, Oxford, and the Royal College of Art. She is also well known as a historical advisor for film, television and theatre. Her credits include the feature films *The Duchess* and *The Favourite*; and television series such as *Death Comes to Pemberley, Jamaica Inn, Poldark, Gunpowder, Sanditon* and *Bridgerton.*

Praise for *The Beau Monde*

'Hannah Greig . . . tackles the challenge posed by her title *The Beau Monde*, head on, wrestling with it, taking it apart, even adding a dense but deeply researched 'supplementary essay' on the uses and meanings of the term. All this pays off, for her vivid and playful book tantalizes us . . . Greig moves with faultless poise through the London scenes that she has so carefully and memorably anatomized'

Anthony Fletcher, *TLS*

'The pages of Greig's work sparkle with lush descriptions of jewels, clothing and colourful pictures of elite life . . . Readers seeking a meticulously researched exploration of the world of the beau monde won't be disappointed.'

BBC History magazine

'A fascinating study . . . If you remember Michael Heseltine being dismissively described by Alan Clark as a man who bought his own furniture, you will find Greig's thoughtful account of its 18th-century equivalent a great read.'

Times Higher Education Supplement

'*The Beau Monde* is diligently researched and the footnotes are full of matter.'

Norma Clarke, *Literary Review*

'Meticulously researched and beautifully illustrated, including merciless satirical drawings of the time, *The Beau Monde* is a fascinating spin round this most colourful period.'

The Lady

'This book, beautifully illustrated throughout, encapsulates the quest for power and exclusivity in a changing world.'

Discover Your History

'Ms. Greig's work is an absorbing cultural and political history of aristocratic Georgian England.'

Austenprose Blog

'A sparkling and iconoclastic debut. Hannah Greig rescues belles and beaux from celebrity biography to restore a dynamic social universe, charting the rise of a new social leadership in the wake of the glorious revolution—forged by fashion, and remade in town every single season.'

Amanda Vickery, author of *Behind Closed Doors: At Home in Georgian England*

'an impressively researched and wide-ranging account of the social and cultural practices of 18th-century Britain's 'fashionable' aristocratic elite'

M.H. Markus, *CHOICE*

'I suspect that it will succeed in gaining a wide readership—deservedly so, because it manages to combine readability (Greig has a keen eye for lively quotation and telling details) with subtle and important scholarship.'

Bob Harris, *English Historical Review*

'there is much to commend here. The wealth of manuscript material mined in the course of the book's production is impressive. Greig's use of a variety of household accounts helps to illustrate some keen observations.'

Robin Eagles, *History*

the BEAU MONDE

Fashionable Society in Georgian London

HANNAH GREIG

OXFORD
UNIVERSITY PRESS

OXFORD
UNIVERSITY PRESS

Great Clarendon Street, Oxford, OX2 6DP,
United Kingdom

Oxford University Press is a department of the University of Oxford.
It furthers the University's objective of excellence in research, scholarship,
and education by publishing worldwide. Oxford is a registered trade mark of
Oxford University Press in the UK and in certain other countries

First published 2013
First published in paperback 2020

Impression: 1

Published in the United States of America by Oxford University Press
198 Madison Avenue, New york, NY 10016, United States of America

British Library Cataloguing in Publication Data
Data available

Library of Congress Cataloging in Publication Data
Data available

ISBN 978–0–19–965900–5 (Hbk.)
ISBN 978–0–19–886118–8 (Pbk.)

Printed in Great Britain by
Bell & Bain Ltd., Glasgow

ACKNOWLEDGEMENTS

While this book matured from Ph.D. to publication I have taken it to a number of institutions, where it has been shaped by countless discussions, new research avenues, revisions, and reflections. Although not all of that work has made the final cut, I am incredibly grateful to those who have helped me along the way.

No historian can complete their research without financial support. I have benefited enormously from awards from the Arts and Humanities Research Council who funded my MA, Ph.D., and some additional postdoctoral work under various different grant schemes. An Isobel Thornley fellowship at the Institute of Historical Research and a visiting studentship to Yale University provided essential early backing, funding the final year of my doctoral studies. Finishing my thesis at Yale was especially formative. There I found firm friends as well as inspiring sources. Subsequently, postdoctoral fellowships at the Royal College of Art; the Paul Mellon Centre; Balliol College, University of Oxford; the Yale Centre for British Art; and Chawton House have provided me with invaluable access not only to research resources, but also to stimulating company, comfortable accommodation, and, not infrequently (and most memorably at Balliol), enjoyable dinners. Most recently, the history department and Centre for Eighteenth Century Studies at York has provided me with a welcoming scholarly home. I am indebted to my students for their difficult questions; to my genial colleagues for their warmth and intellect; and especially to the department and university for precious research leave that enabled me to finish this project. Over the years the research contained in this book has been aired at many seminars and conferences. I am grateful to all those patient audiences and particularly the Institute of Historical Research's 'Long Eighteenth Century Seminar' where I cut my teeth as a graduate student and learnt so much about the period from its members.

This book rests on manuscripts held at numerous libraries and local archives. These keepers of valuable historical resources deserve to be better known and far better funded. I am grateful to the following for granting permission to consult and quote from their manuscripts and special collections: Bedfordshire and Luton Records and Archives Service, Birmingham City Archives and Heritage Service, Birmingham University Library Special Collections, Borthwick Institute University of York, Brynmor Jones Library University of Hull, Derbyshire Record Office, Hampshire Record Office, Hertfordshire Archives and Local Studies, Huntingdon Library and Archives, John Rylands Library University of Manchester, Keele University Library, Kent History and Library Centre, Leicester Record Office, London Metropolitan Archives, North London Collegiate School Library, Nottinghamshire Archives, Southwark Local Studies Library, Suffolk Record Office, University of Nottingham Special Collections. My thanks also to the University of Chicago Press and Yale University Press for allowing me to republish research that forms a part of Chapter 4 and Chapter 5 which was first published in two essays: ' "All together and all distinct": Public Sociability and Social Exclusivity in London's Pleasure Gardens *c.*1740–1800', *Journal of British Studies*, 51/1 (January 2012) and 'Dressing for Court: Sartorial Politics and Fashion News in the Age of Mary Delany', in Alicia Weisberg-Roberts and Mark Laird (eds), *Mrs Delany and her Circle* (New Haven: Yale Centre for British Art, Yale University Press, 2009).

It is, though, to the many individuals who consist of my colleagues, friends, and family that I owe the most. This book would never have been completed (and it might never have progressed beyond an early proposal) without support from my agent, Rachel Calder, and from OUP's patient and brilliant editors, Luciana O'Flaherty and Matthew Cotton. Anonymous readers have helped me refine my ideas in very significant ways and I thank them for their insight and collegiality. Over the years I have gathered helpful suggestions, supporting references, and critical comments from many fine scholars, including Helen Berry, Clarissa Campbell Orr, Jonathan Conlin, Penelope Corfield, Brian Cowan, Inge Daniels, Margot Finn, Alex Goodall, Amanda Goodrich, Nicholas Guyatt, Frances Harris, Joanne Innes, Catriona Kennedy, Lawrence Klein, Peter McNeil, Jane Moody, Miles Ogborn, Morna O'Neill, Kate Retford, John Styles, Miles Taylor, William Weber, Susan Whyman, and Kate Williams. I am especially indebted to Giorgio Riello for reading more than his fair share of pages whilst wading through a messy early draft, and to Faramerz Dabhoiwala for sage advice at the eleventh hour.

One academic, though, has read more, provided more references, and asked more questions than anyone else: Professor Amanda Vickery. It was my great fortune to benefit from her exemplary Ph.D. supervision and, since then, Amanda has remained a mentor, colleague, and dearly loved friend. Her energetic wit, inspirational cleverness, and unswerving support deserves more than a written acknowledgement. She has readily shared her unpublished research, introduced me to countless references and stories, furnished me with make-up for TV appearances, shown me the ropes in radio interviews, and given far more of her time and knowledge than duty ever required. I am greatly indebted to Amanda. I trust she knows this book comes with a deep curtsey and much more gratitude besides.

The final stages of researching and writing this book coincided with the big life changes of births, deaths, and marriages. I am fortunate, then, to have this public context in which to express my love and thanks to my late father, Ken, my late mother, Hazel, and my brothers, Duncan and Bruce, for all they have done. Given her passion for historic textiles, I am pleased that my mother approved the final cover, even though (to my deep regret) she did not see the book in print. The arrival of my resilient son, Douglas, just as this book was due for completion, and his rocky start to life put such a run on family resources that these final words would never have been put to paper without the exceptional support provided by my family. In this context too I must include our most recent friend, Isla Simpson-Sedgwick, who entertained Douglas long enough for me to finish the remaining edits.

Last but absolutely first is the debt I have incurred to Quintin Colville. Acting in turn as skilled reader, editor, and well-mannered critic, his careful eye and considered opinion have transformed this text. At the same time, his cooking, childcare, love, and confidence have sustained and transformed this author. All told, even though we have recently navigated challenges we could never have imagined, Quintin somehow still found the reserves and patience to help me tidy up this book. I don't know how he has done it. My dedication is, of course, to him.

CONTENTS

LIST OF ILLUSTRATIONS

[A]mong the many descriptions which ingenious writers have given of places and people comparatively insignificant, no complete account has yet been written of the fashionable world. It is true, that our poets and caricaturists have honoured these people with a great share of their notice, and many particulars, not a little edifying, have been made known through the medium of these admirable publications. It is also true, that our prose-writers have occasionally cast a very pertinent glance over this fairy ground.... But after all that has been done towards exhibiting the manners and unfolding the character of this splendid community; much remains to be done; for though certain details have been well enough handled...a complete and systematic account of the fashionable world is still a desideratum in cosmography.

The Fashionable World Displayed (1804)

'The brilliant vortex'

There was no coming out...redy cut and dryed a fine woman, 'twas
not possible to be aqquented with the world or made fitt to converse
with the Beau Mond.

(Gertrude Savile, in her diary, 1727)

Le beau monde: people of fashion

(*A New Dictionary in French and English*, 1769)

Men and women of fashion are supereminently [*sic*] distinguished
from those of no fashion...whom no-body knows.

(James Adair, *Essay on Fashionable Diseases*, 1790)

Each autumn, throughout the 1700s, London's West End was transformed. Previously quiet squares were crowded by servants, tradesmen, and their traffic. The double doors of the largest houses, unused
for the summer months, were unlocked and the shutters above them
were swung open. Inside, rat traps were secreted in dark corners and
ornate beds were fumigated to kill bugs. Housekeepers pulled dust
sheets from fine furniture that was then inventoried, scrutinized for
damage, and, where necessary, re-upholstered or replaced. New things
modish and modern, perhaps a clock, a telescope, or a Chippendale
chair, were delivered and unpacked. Candlesticks and dinner services,

scuffed from hard use the previous year, were sent to goldsmiths to be painstakingly and expensively re-gilded. If a family tree boasted a new title (gained through marriage, service, or patronage) then engravers deftly edited the heraldic crests etched on all equipment, from tea-spoons to wine coolers, to reflect the promotion. Maids were vetted, as were cooks, footmen, and grooms, most hired on weekly rolling con-tracts. Trusted stewards re-established accounts, deferred payments, and settled old bills with the chandler, grocer, confectioner, wine mer-chant, jeweller, stationer, doctor, hairdresser, tailor, milliner, and draper. And, finally, as town carriages were rolled out from the mews to be washed clean of summer dust, pedigree horses were judiciously selected by the stable manager, so that the prize vehicle might be drawn by up to six thoroughbreds, all black, bay, or grey, according to the penchant of the owner. Once the steward, housekeeper, and servants had readied the house, their employers journeyed to the capital with the first frost, channelling in from country estates between October and January. Cold weather, noted one eighteenth-century woman, 'brings up all the Fine folks on the Wing [to London] flocking like half-frozen birds into a Farm-yard, from the terror...of another fatal month's confinement snowed-up in the country'.[1]

For them, the business and pleasures of the coming months were varied. Strategic political alliances and social networks needed to be established or rewoven, and hectic rounds of visits, excursions, and balls were planned to forge such connections. Season-long subscriptions for opera and theatre boxes were secured, appropriate concert series identified, and guest lists decided for weekly 'at home' assemblies. Of course, London was also a pool of potential suitors for young lords and ladies coming of age. Prospective spouses were therefore diligently researched and courted. A family's political, genealogical, and finan-cial fortunes might be secured by a shrewd match or devastated by an impulsive misalliance. All such transactions had to be completed by

June or early July. Once spring turned to summer, the carriages conveyed their occupants back to roost at their regional seats, to attend to provincial responsibilities, or to take the waters at a popular spa resort. Every autumn, however, the tide of visitors returned.

At the root of this sometimes frenzied activity was one central ambition: to secure or reaffirm membership of a new elite—the beau monde. Coined in the 1690s, rarely used by the 1840s, and near obsolete today, the Frenchified phrase 'beau monde' once enjoyed widespread English usage.[2] From late seventeenth-century plays to early nineteenth-century novels, from manuscript letters to monthly periodicals, from satirical poems to popular ballads, 'beau monde' was used to capture a social phenomenon specific to the period: the emergence of an urban, primarily metropolitan, 'world of fashion'. The precise criteria that denoted membership of the beau monde were endlessly debated. To be fashionable in the eighteenth century was not merely to be modish or trendy. Rather it was 'a mysterious talisman' and an 'invisible standard' involving pedigree, connections, manners, language, appearance, and much else besides.[3] This 'standard' was also known as 'ton', an anglophone application of the French noun for 'tone'.[4] For the prolific essayist Lord Chesterfield, fashion and ton constituted the 'certain je ne scay quoy [sic]' that defined the beau monde and 'which other people of fashion acknowledge'.[5] In a similar vein, another commentator declared confidently that ton meant 'the exact and invariable pursuit of everything that is fashionable, polite and elegant, as established in the most brilliant circles'.[6] Members of the eighteenth-century beau monde therefore laid claim to what might be described today as the 'it' factor: an elusive yet exclusive form of social distinction.[7]

Those who emerged as recognized leaders of London's fashionable world consisted primarily (although, arguably, not always exclusively) of high-ranking members of the peerage and their immediate relations. At its heart, if not at its peripheries, the 'world of fashion' comprised an elite within an elite, a subsection of the most elevated social ranks who successfully combined the securities of title and wealth with urban-based social and cultural authority. In this regard, their pre-eminence represented no revolution. The basis of their prestige, though, was rooted in new qualifications, including fashion, consumption, and public display. Whereas coronets and country seats had long stood as the most visible markers of social distinction, in eighteenth-century London, 'fashion' and membership of the beau monde held sway. It is this new 'fashionable' urban culture and its associated systems of social prestige and exclusivity that this book explores (Figure 1).

Although often caricatured as consisting of little more than a circus of marriage market flirtations, pleasure seeking, and luxurious consumption, a yearly relocation to London was fundamentally a serious endeavour. At its core were parliamentary politics and the business of government. After the 1690s, new constitutional stipulations ensured that the Houses of Commons and Lords met for regular annual sessions in the capital for the first time in parliamentary history. It was this unprecedented political timetable that initially lured the titled and wealthy to the metropolis. The catalyst for this change had come in 1689 when the reigning monarch, James II, was ousted by his daughter Mary and her Dutch husband William of Orange. This change of monarchy was one of revolution rather than ordinary succession, for James II was alive and well when he was forced to flee the country. Designated in its own time as the 'Glorious Revolution' (but also referred to as the English Revolution of 1688–9), the Protestant William and Mary jointly replaced the Catholic James II. Their claim was supported by a major cohort of the ruling nobility who were alarmed by James II's extensive pro-Catholic measures and his arrogant disregard for parliament's authority.[8] The nature and impact of the revolution has been variously characterized by historians as an

FIGURE 1 *The Beau Monde in St James's Park*, Louis Phillippe Boitard, *c*.1749–50.

aristocratic coup; a brake on change; the restoration of an old order; a Dutch invasion; and, most recently, a violent, modern revolution.[9] For the purposes of this study, the significance of 1689 resides in more prosaic but still vital transformations, most notably the rise and redefinition of parliamentary authority that followed in its wake.

The terms of the revolution settlement itself brought few formal constitutional changes. In theory, after their accession William III and Mary enjoyed the same traditional prerogatives granted to their predecessors. In practice, however, a new parliamentary infrastructure evolved in the revolution's aftermath. William III's foreign policy agenda had a marked impact on the character of the emerging polity. England had not fought a lengthy continental campaign for centuries but, deploying English resources to challenge France's continental expansion, William III plunged the nation into protracted European conflicts. Fighting major wars demanded major financial resources and, after 1689, the only route to substantial revenue was through parliament, who kept a tight hold on the royal purse and on the national financial interest. Whereas James II had simply dissolved parliament when it had challenged his initiatives, William III had no choice but to summon parliament year after year in order to fill the war chest his foreign policy required.[10] The change was dramatic. Between 1679 and 1688, parliament had met just five times, conducting brief business on 171 disjointed days, and passing only a few hundred bills. Between 1689 and 1698, it met for eleven sessions, undertook business for around 1,300 days, and passed over 800 bills. For the first time in its history, parliament met annually and continued to do so, without fail, thereafter.[11]

It was this yearly meeting of parliament, most often between November and June, that brought the titled to London and created the concept of 'the season'.[12] Much more, however, followed in their wake. With the politicians, courtiers, and office-holders came their entourages of relatives and households. Service, commercial, and entertainment industries flourished to meet the demand of this well-heeled and influential influx of seasonal residents. Opera and theatre performances, exhibitions, concerts, all manner of social pleasures, and, not least, shopping and other forms of commercial transaction were part and parcel of a flourishing London culture.[13] The reputed temptations of the metropolis were legion. 'I can but think London is a kind of mistress; dissolute in principles, loose in practice and extravagant in pleasure,' Anne Ingram, Viscountess Irwin, wrote teasingly in a letter to her father.[14] None characterized the appeal of the burgeoning London season more crudely than General Mostyn in a well-known quip to the Duke of Newcastle: 'tired of worsted...I took a run to London last Saturday to fuck somebody in silk.'[15]

Colourful rhetoric aside, it is important to recognize that this metropolitan shift in the lifestyle of the ruling elite was not just understood as an excuse to indulge in the capital's myriad pleasures. Nor was it solely a practical solution to the increased load of parliamentary business. In a less tangible but nonetheless significant sense, an elite metropolitan presence became seen as essential to good government. The visibility of powerful lords in London would, it was hoped, act to counter any tyrannical ambitions harboured by the crown. The responsibilities of landholding, rural paternalism, and local governance remained highly valued and critical to perceptions of the balance of power; but coming to London, residing in the capital, and participating in a central parliamentary body was now also understood and prioritized as a critical component of a balanced constitution.[16] Therefore, rather than evidence of the elite's dereliction of duty, extensive stays in the metropolis and the very concept of 'the season' were reframed as important components of noble obligation and modern government.

This is not, of course, to say that London had never seen a procession of titled figures before the 1690s. The increased use of Whitehall Palace by the monarchy in the sixteenth and early seventeenth centuries had created a fledgling season, encouraging the nobility to trek to the capital in pursuit of the court. Consequently, many high-ranking peers invested in substantial metropolitan residences to accommodate their families during their London stays.[17] With the exception of Somerset House (built in 1547), there are now few remnants of the private palaces that once ranged along The Strand, each with substantial frontages facing north and grand water gates opening to the busy Thames. At the time, though, such bold signs of relocation caused consternation. Fearing that grandees were neglecting their local duties, and that traditional forms of localized, paternalistic interaction were under threat, Tudor and Stuart monarchs issued a series of proclamations commanding the elite to stay in the provinces.[18] Stern royal commands never completely stemmed the flow of aristocratic traffic to London, but they evoke a contemporary suspicion about the metropolis exerting too great an influence over the nation's powerbrokers. Perhaps more significant than legislative attempts to lessen urban migration was the simple fact that the irregularity of parliamentary sittings and the uncertainty of the court's routine (both beholden to royal whim) ensured that the length and timing of metropolitan stays was difficult to predict. As a result, although elite investment in London life certainly increased during the sixteenth and seventeenth centuries, the concept of a 'season' only took what now seems a fractured and preliminary form.

Evidence of the growing importance of the London season during the eighteenth century can be found in the architectural changes of the period. The capital had experienced recent and rapid growth. In 1550, it had been a comparatively modest city of around 75,000 residents, far smaller than most of the major European centres. By 1700, its population had swelled to around 575,000, making London the largest city in Europe, almost three times the size of Naples, with only Paris coming close with a population of 510,000. By mid-century, London extended to 750,000 inhabitants, and one in six of the English population were either living in the capital or had done so at some stage in their life.[19] Many districts became more densely built and grew to accommodate new residents. By far the most marked expansion, though, occurred in the north-west quarter, with the creation of what was known in the eighteenth century as 'the town' district of London and during the 1800s became more popularly known as the 'West End'. From the early

1700s, a plethora of new squares and streets pushed the capital's parameters westward. Bloomsbury Square, Golden Square, St James's Square, and Soho Square were already occupied by the turn of the century. These were followed in the 1720s and 1730s by Hanover Square, Cavendish Square, Grosvenor Square, and numerous other impressive developments that filled the available space between Holborn in the east through to Hyde Park in the west. Another wave of building later in the century brought Manchester Square, Portland Place, and yet more Georgian squares and terraces (Figure 2).

The Honourable Frederick Robinson (second son of the politician Thomas Robinson, 1st Baron Grantham) marvelled at the changing

FIGURE 2 *View of Hanover Square*, Robert Pollard and Francis Jukes, 1787. The engraving is dedicated to Francis Godolphin, Marquess of Carmarthen, and taken 'from a drawing in his collection'. The view looks south. St George's Church (which still stands today) can be seen in the distance.

appearance of the West End and the speed of its expansion. Writing from London to his elder brother Thomas, then a diplomat in Madrid, he sketched the capital's changing appearance in the late 1770s: 'I walk'd a few days ago into Norfolk Street and found [it] so spruc'd, clean'd & adorned that I scarce knew it again, indeed I could not conceive it capable of so much improvement.'[20] 'There are extensive new buildings streets and squares near Bloomsbury all upon the Duke of Bedfords ground,' he reported on another day.[21] 'In Manchester Square, the Duke has built a large house to perpetuate his name, beyond this there is a circus, or crescent, for it is not far enough advanced to say which. I shall not be surpriz'd if we live to see the Haymarket upon Highgate Hill,' he predicted.[22] To contemporaries, London was a place of improvement, innovation, and such a rapidly evolving townscape that even the most established resident could lose his way in the maze of recently laid, and newly paved, streets.

This burgeoning West End, or 'town', enclave was the heartland of the season, accommodating its political infrastructure, including the court at St James's and parliament in Westminster, as well as its major social institutions: the theatre, opera, clubs, coffee houses, and concert venues. Characterized as the more leisured counterpoint to the older, mercantile 'city' in the east, it was specifically the 'town' rather than the capital as a whole that was said to accommodate the beau monde. 'The people of fashion,' Lord Chesterfield pronounced, were 'those who set the fashions and who give the tone of the dress, language, manners and pleasures to the town'.[23] Or, as *The Man of Pleasure's Pocket Book* (1780) sniffed, 'the brilliant vortex' of the beau monde 'is never to be met with on the eastern side of Temple bar, where the tar of Thames Street and the tallow of Blow-bladder-street contaminate the air'.[24]

It was in this comparatively small pocket of the capital that a seasonal elite collected. The Honourable John Ward (later 4th Viscount

Dudley and Ward) felt the essential criterion for his London home was to be within 'a stones throw of the House [parliament], the Opera and the Park—that is the three chief places of gentlemanly resort'.[25] In the 1720s, over half of the heads of households resident in Hanover Square were members of the peerage. When land belonging to the Duke of Grosvenor was developed in Mayfair from the 1720s, 69 per cent of the first tenants of Grosvenor Square were titled. In St James's Square, peers occupied twenty of the twenty-three addresses, and this picture of dense concentration of privilege repeated itself within other new squares throughout the century.[26]

This is not to suggest that the 'town' was an impenetrable patrician ghetto. Rate books and income tax records reveal retailers, artists, and craftspeople living in close proximity, and servants inevitably made up a substantial proportion of occupants in even the most exclusive quarters and prestigious residences.[27] Yet, withstanding such diversity, the pronounced congregation of titled personnel in London's western quarter is striking. Furthermore, although risk-taking speculators laid out the properties and squares, the ground they developed was leased from landed freeholders looking to exploit well-placed metropolitan estate assets. From Bedford Square to Grosvenor Square, these connections were trumpeted in street names that celebrated the grandee who owned the soil.[28] For the first time, a substantial proportion of the ruling elite resided in a compact geographical area for a significant period of the year. The West End became, as historical geographer Peter Atkins has put it, a 'container of frighteningly concentrated power'.[29]

As well as clustering in the new squares, a number of leading grandees established more substantial dynastic properties in the West End. The massive developments that had formerly lined The Strand were systematically abandoned and demolished as their owners invested instead in new builds at more fashionable addresses further west.[30] Devonshire House on Piccadilly had first been acquired by the Duke of

Devonshire in 1698, and was then rebuilt by his heir after it was devastated by fire in the 1730s. The remodelled town palace had a frontage that was the length of an urban terrace, with eleven front-facing windows. Screened by an equally substantial brick wall, the property garnered little architectural praise (it was likened by one contemporary commentator to an East India Company Warehouse), but its size alone made an impressive statement (Figure 3).[31] In 1765, the ambitious Earl of Shelburne acquired a partially completed property on its own plot near Berkeley Square from the disgraced Lord Bute, and there created a grand and modish residence designed by Robert Adam.[32] Chesterfield House, Spencer House, and Melbourne House were all similar new projects from the 1700s.

Such imposing properties are usually cited as the exception to a broader rule that the eighteenth-century nobility made do with terraced living and multi-year rentals. Indeed, the apparent ordinariness of urban properties long led historians to presume, as Sir John

FIGURE 3 *Devonshire House*, Benjamin Green and Samuel Green, 1761.

Summerson surmised in his study of Georgian London, that 'members of the aristocracy were not interested in their town dwellings to anything like the same extent as their country dwellings'.[33] The survival and preservation of country mansions, however, has left a disproportionate legacy that obscures the contemporary value the elite placed on their London residences.[34] Household account books testify to the vast sums required to support a metropolitan house. The Duke of Bedford, for example, kept over forty servants in London throughout the year— regardless of whether he was in residence or not—at the cost of over £860 per year, or £70 per month (approximately equivalent to £120,000 per year or £8,250 per month today).[35] This was only the beginning of an urban bill, for servants were cheap. Although a highly skilled pastry chef might name his price and long-serving housekeeper could command a comfortable £10 per annum living, the average maid or footman was often lucky to take home £3 a year.

Other household commodities were far more expensive than the help. In the 1760s, sundry household bills for food and drink delivered to the Duke of Newcastle's London house regularly ran to £350 per month between January and May (equivalent to £41,000 per month today), before dropping to a comparatively modest £70 during the summer once the season was over.[36] When George John Spencer, Viscount Althorp, inherited the title and estate from his father, 1st Earl Spencer, the moveable contents of Spencer House in London, encompassing everything from chairs to silver toast racks, were valued at £10,553 (approximately £724,000 today): a figure well in excess of the £8,000 that contemporaries crudely estimated to be the average annual income enjoyed by peers.[37] In 1798 the £29,285 valuation of the contents of Devonshire House in Piccadilly significantly exceeded the £22,321 estimation placed on the contents at Chatsworth, the family's seat in Derbyshire.[38] Surviving sections of interiors and examples of furniture commissioned specifically for London properties point to the attention paid to spectacle and detail. The gilded 1750s music room of Norfolk House and Northumberland House's red spangled glass drawing room from the 1770s (both now on display at the V&A) betray the architectural ostentation and drama that lay behind seemingly uniform and relatively modest exteriors (Figures 4 and 5).[39] Vast sums, then, were dropped on urban residences that were to be occupied for only part of the year. Moreover, the ability to maintain a part-time residence in London itself advertised substantial rural and regional assets. In this regard, the power and prestige of the country seat was reflected in its urban counterpart. Town houses may have been built on a far smaller scale than a peer's regional headquarters yet nonetheless, expensive, glittering, and gilded, they represented a massive new investment in metropolitan life.

FIGURE 4 The music room from Norfolk House, St James's Square, 1748–56.

FIGURE 5 Model of the drawing room at Northumberland House, showing the dramatic effect of its opulent red glass interior. The room was designed by Robert Adam in the 1770s for the Duke and Duchess of Northumberland.

It was against this background of urbanization, political change, and seasonal migration that the beau monde evolved. This book uses 'beau monde' to refer to the cohort of privileged individuals who enjoyed public prominence within the framework of the London season.[40] Many tried to master its requirements, and many failed. Take Gertrude Savile, for example, whose diary entries throughout the 1720s tell of her frustrated attempts to gain acceptance. In September 1721, following a month spent in London and Bath, the 25-year-old Gertrude returned to her family home of Rufford Abbey in Nottinghamshire, and there reflected on her social station. Gertrude was, theoretically, well positioned. Her brother and guardian, Sir George Savile, a man eighteen years her senior, was an affluent baronet, major landowner, and, from 1728, a member of parliament. She was related through her late father to the famous politician George Savile, 1st Marquess of

Halifax (a key player in William III's post-Glorious Revolution govern-
ment), and was named after his second wife, Gertrude Pierrepont.
Furthermore, Gertrude Savile enjoyed close acquaintance and regular
correspondence with a range of influential peers including Lady
Castlemaine, the Duchess of Rutland, Lady Oxford, and Captain
Stanhope (later 4th Earl of Chesterfield).

Yet, despite her pedigree and eminent connections, Savile struggled
to infiltrate the glamorous society that shimmered in such close proximity. 'There was no coming out...reddy cut and dried a fine woman,'
she lamented in her diary, 'twas not possible to be made aqquented
with the World...or fit to converse with the Beau Mond [*sic*].'[41] In particular, cripplingly shy and deeply depressive, she found the beau
monde's public profile and practised sociability impossible to manage.
At 30, she decided to stop her miserable and unsuccessful quest for
social acceptance. 'What should I do any more in Publick,' she wrote
despairingly in November 1727.

> No! I'll strive no more against the Stream. The World was not made for
> me, nor I for the World. I have but two things to choose. One, to show
> myself a disagreeable and ridiculous figure...the other to hide myself
> and let people invent what they please for reasons for my particularity.
> The latter I must choose; I can no longer support the first.[42]

Savile's personal sense of exclusion was further heightened by her conviction that others in her extended family and networks of acquaintance
had adopted the mantle of 'fashion' with ease. It was with considerable
resentment that she noted her cousin's ability to participate in the fashionable world. 'Tis what I woud wish to coppy out,' Savile confessed, 'she
is only completely fit for the World (diametrically my opposite).'[43]
Although Savile's diary entries are unusual for their candour, she was
only one of the many contemporaries who felt unable to access London's
beau monde: a metropolitan circle defined by the complex and shifting
requirements of 'fashion' (Figure 6).

FIGURE 6 *Following the Fashion*, James Gillray, 1794. Juxtaposing a 'town' lady of St James's on the left with a 'city' woman of Cheapside on the right, the caption reads: 'St James's giving the Ton, a Soul without a Body; Cheapside aping the Mode, a Body without a Soul.'

Searching for a definition of the beau monde in 1755, Lord Chesterfield posed the following question: 'who are they, what are they and what makes them people of fashion?'[44] Savile's embittered diary entries supply us with the beginnings of an answer. For her, the beau monde was both a community with which she was not 'aqquented' and a lifestyle that she could not master. It was not a vague or insubstantial rhetorical device, but something she could witness, a visible community of contemporary individuals and a fixture on the London scene.[45]

Notably, although being 'fashionable' in eighteenth-century London was widely deemed to involve credentials other than inherited wealth and rank (the mysterious air of 'ton'), its most visible participants were often peers. A bias towards title is readily apparent in contemporary newspaper reports that traded on the comings and goings of the fashionable world. The London newspaper *Bell's Weekly Messenger*, for instance, carried a regular column in the 1790s emblazoned 'FASHIONABLES' in large type, under which marriages, deaths, social events, other news, and also condemnatory gossip pertaining to the capital's 'fashionable' figures were reported.[46] The register of names it featured is suggestive. Within surviving issues published between 1 May 1796 and 16 December 1798, 68 per cent of the names cited were either members of the royal family or members of the peerage, their wives, or heirs.[47] A further 24 per cent were younger sons with close peerage connections, often MPs (including, for example, William Pitt and Charles James Fox) or office-holders in the military, church, and legal professions. To be sure, a smattering of parvenus also featured. Sir James Hoare of the Hoare banking dynasty, lawyer William Garrow, opera star Michael Leoni, and an heiress to a West India planter all got a mention.[48] But these were the rare exceptions that proved a more privileged rule. The vast majority of individuals cited in *Bell's* fashionable register (no less than 92 per cent) either possessed an aristocratic title or were closely related to someone who did.

It is such titled members of London's beau monde that feature in this book. In this regard, I apply a comparatively narrow working definition of 'beau monde'. This is not to suggest that the linkage between beau monde and the titled elite was in any way absolute. As English literature scholar Gillian Russell has revealed, leading actresses, successful courtesans, favourite artists, and fortunate families grown unthinkably rich in a generation from the profits of business and trade were sometimes cited as members of fashionable society.[49] I would argue, though, that their numbers were consistently small in comparison to the proportion, and relative social power, of titled figures.[50]

As this begins to suggest, this book deals with a tiny minority of the eighteenth-century population. Historians often rightly stress just how unrepresentative titled society was of eighteenth-century Britain as a whole. Throughout the entirety of the 1700s, a mere 1,003 men held peerages and represented the British titled nobility in its most formal definition.[51] To this miniscule body we should add siblings, spouses, and children, whose number significantly swells the ranks. Yet only a proportion of this somewhat larger community of titled families embraced the high profile and public lifestyle associated with membership of the beau monde. Fashionable society was not commensurate with the peerage in its totality or simply the nobility in a new guise. Many patricians looked upon the fast-living metropolitan culture of fashionable society with disdain, preferring instead the quiet comforts of a country seat and the responsibilities of rural paternalism or intellectual pursuits and a life of the mind. Others aspired to join London's world of fashion but were thwarted by limited financial resources, were refused entrance on the basis of their political sympathies, or, as the final chapter reveals, suffered exile from the beau monde in the wake of socially unacceptable behaviour. Any attempt to create too rigid a register of members would belie the potential fluidity of fashionable society and the fact that it was made and remade season by season. In general terms, this book deals with an exclusive group within an already select society, a community that can be roughly estimated as consisting of a few hundred individuals in any one year, and most probably no more than three or four thousand over the century as a whole.[52]

Throughout this study I use 'beau monde' interchangeably with the phrases 'fashionable elite' and 'metropolitan elite'. All are shadowy descriptions, but the latter two have been selected to give definitional clarity to the former. The figures who populate this study were 'elite' in that the majority boasted both inherited title and extraordinary wealth, but the additional quality of being 'fashionable' was the elusive *desideratum* that further distinguished them. Those deemed fashionable participated in what was known in the eighteenth-century as the 'public' world, and a fashionable status was won through strategic public performances in a round of interconnected urban spaces including the court and parliament, pleasure gardens, theatres, and private homes. Within the boundaries of this metropolitan stage, a fashionable profile depended on many things. Public demonstrations of political allegiance, kinship networks, marital associations, and material exhibitions were all crucial; the right speech in parliament, the right guests to dinner, the right family linkages, the right goods in your home, the right carriage at your door, and the right twist on your cravat. Generally speaking, however, London's beau monde was defined more by its group identity than by the personal assets of each individual. It was the cultivation and display of interpersonal connections and networks rather than merely the ownership of property that underpinned what it meant to be a member of London's 'world of fashion'. Traditional expressions of social rank continued to inform these more innovative definitions of social position. Yet, unlike title which might be held for a lifetime and which passed through generations regardless of the possessor's changing fortunes, membership of the beau monde was won or lost within a decade, a few years, or even within a single season.[53]

Unsurprisingly, this high-profile fashionable world was a source of fascination and also concern in the century's burgeoning press. Its members became the subject of popular prints (both celebratory and satirical), and were represented by name in plays, poems, and other cultural media (Figures 7, 8, and 9). This combination of exclusivity and publicity has led to the eighteenth-century beau monde being invoked in a number of recent cultural histories as a nascent form of modern celebrity culture.[54] Such attributions certainly have some conceptual value. In many ways, the notion of 'celebrity culture' has a

FIGURE 7 *Characters in High Life, Sketch'd at the New Rooms, Opera House,* James Gillray, 1795. Gillray routinely included portraits of fashionable figures and recognizable metropolitan locations in his caricatures. Here, for instance, he depicts Mary Isabella, Duchess of Rutland, and her daughter at the opera. Included in Figures 8 and 9 are Georgiana, Duchess of Bedford; Albinia, Countess of Buckinghamshire; Lady Archer; Charles James Fox; and the Prince of Wales.

FIGURE 8 *Lady Godina's Rout—or—Peeping-Tom spying out Pope-Joan, vide Fashionable Modesty*, James Gillray 1796. A 'rout' was an eighteenth-century term for a fashionable evening assembly, usually held at a domestic residence.

similar ambiguity to 'beau monde'. It can be applied both in sneering contempt and as a sober description of a visible phenomenon. It is widely accepted that 'real' celebrities feature in our celebrity culture, although precisely what underpins their celebrity status is not always clear. Is celebrity conferred by virtue of a quality innate to the individual (be it talent, wealth, power, or personality), or is it in the gift of an audience (whether the press or a wider public)? To be 'celebrated' implies some form of social distinction and exclusivity, for a celebrity must be distinguishable from the rest of a crowd, but the basis of that distinction belies easy quantification. Not least, the comparative exclusivity of the celebrity world can be variously determined, or the lack of exclusivity derided, depending on where each analyst draws the line.

FIGURE 9 *Modern Hospitality—or—A Friendly Party in High Life*, James Gillray, 1792.

These same conceptual problems are evident in the eighteenth-century notion of a beau monde. We should be wary, though, of presuming too close a correlation between a distant and distinctive eighteenth-century culture and our own.[55] The beau monde was period specific, forged at a moment of social and political change which created a culture and set of conditions peculiar to the 1700s. The coinage of colloquial and ultimately short-lived eighteenth-century terms (such as beau monde and a whole range of attendant words and phrases including ton, bon ton, haut ton, and fashion) testifies to an intense contemporary preoccupation with the new ways in which social status and elite power were interpreted and projected in the metropolis.[56]

By focusing specifically on the elite experience of the London season, this study is geographically limited to the metropolis, and even more particularly to London's West End. This is not, however, to imply that the streets from The Strand to Hyde Park were the limits of the beau monde's horizons. After all, migration and social movement was a defining feature of the world of fashion. At the end of each season, fashionable society returned to their country seats or marched on to leisure towns such as Bath, Brighton, and Scarborough, which flourished in consequence of their fashionable appeal. As John Owen (a former gentleman's tutor turned vicar) noted in his 1805 pamphlet *The Fashionable World Displayed*, such continuous movement made it hard to tie 'the world' to fixed coordinates:

> [The Fashionable World] can scarcely be treated as having any peculiar or exclusive locality. They are not, it is true, absolute wanderers like the tribes of Arabia, nor are they regular settlers, like the convicts at Botany Bay; but movable and migratory to a certain degree, and to a certain degree stationary and permanent, they live among the inhabitants of the parent country, neither absolutely mixing with them nor yet actually separated from them. This paradoxical state of the people renders it not a little difficult to reduce their territory within the rules of geographical description....[T]he only rule of any steadiness with which I am acquainted, and which chiefly relates to the metropolis, is that which prescribes a western latitude.[57]

Nor was it only provincial British resorts that were claimed as part of the beau monde's broader terrain. Europe too was presumed to be a magnet for the fashionable world. Elite families funded expensive and lengthy grand tours as a formative part of a young heir's aristocratic education; and exposure to continental courts, culture, and a network of European grandees was actively encouraged. 'Every woman past thirty that really lives a Paris life among the French and understands the language...will prefer Paris to London,' declared Caroline, Lady Holland, after visiting Paris in 1764.[58] Thirty years earlier, Lady Hertford (wife of Algernon Seymour, Earl of Hertford) sent her new maid to Paris to learn how to dress and cut hair according to the latest fashion.[59] The very choice of the phrase 'beau monde' emphasized its essential 'foreignness'. For critics, such pronounced foreign influences and engagement with continental society were worrisome. If the nation's powerbrokers adopted French fashions, mimicked Italianate manners, imported continental performers, and craved all manner of products from abroad where then, the censorious voices complained, would British cultural development, British strength, and, indeed, Britishness itself, reside? Some of these contexts (particularly the contemporary discourse about the power of French influences on the 'world of fashion') have received considerable treatment elsewhere.[60] A full analysis of fashionable society's extra-metropolitan and European arenas or of the rhetoric targeting those continental influences lies beyond the scope of this book. Instead, this study is concerned with the cultural life of the beau monde as expressed within and through the London season, the 'western latitude' of the fashionable world.

My analysis of the beau monde extends across the eighteenth century, drawing on materials from the 1690s through to the early 1800s. To a certain extent these chronological parameters are defined, quite simply, by the lifespan of the terminology itself. As a concept, 'beau monde' did not transcend time and place but dovetails with the period described by historians as 'the long eighteenth century'. Broadly speaking, the lifecycle of London's beau monde was therefore defined at one end by a more autocratic court system before the 1690s and, at the other, by a more formal and de-politicized version of 'society' that developed some time after the 1830s.[61] This is not to suggest, though, that the intervening period was unvarying and that the beau monde remained unchanged throughout the 1700s. A sequence of 'hot spots' can be identified when the nature and form of fashionable life was placed under pressure or even sustained assault. The creation of new peers by Queen Anne in the 1710s, and by Lord North and William Pitt in the second half of the eighteenth century, for instance, generated extensive debate about what constituted 'elite' status and 'true' nobility. For some commentators, fashionable society, with its apparently shadowy regulations for access, was also culpable in diluting and denigrating the pedigree of 'The Quality' at the top of the social ladder. Repeated and protracted wars with France triggered anxieties about the 'Frenchified' nature of London's beau monde, and generated widespread condemnation of elite reverence for foreign modes. Pronounced attacks on elite morals from the 1770s often singled out the perceived weaknesses and excesses of fashionable society as symptomatic of broader aristocratic failings. As a number of scholars have argued, these condemnations of fashionable society represented important precursors to the agitation for political reform that was to follow. Vices such as adultery, gambling, and duelling—all regarded as representative of the corrupt moral code of the fashionable elite—came under particular fire.[62] Such criticisms were not simply a case of 'aristocratic' excess being rebuked by a 'bourgeoisie' or a concerted effort to impose reforming 'middle-class' values on an unreformed elite. Nor can they simply be read a response to the French Revolution. Rather there was, from around the 1770s, a gradual 'cultural transformation' and move towards moral reform driven by the elite themselves.[63]

Identifiable moments of change, however, also involved more than shifts in rhetoric and a politicized late eighteenth-century targeting of fashionable society. Pronounced and fundamental changes in the infrastructure and operation of the beau monde are equally evident. The relationship between the beau monde and the royal court, for instance, altered from generation to generation, as threats of invasion by the exiled Stuarts intensified and subsided, and as competing court units periodically clustered around the monarch and his heir. Most visibly, the social sites frequented by London's fashionable society underwent a marked alteration as innovative and more varied leisure resorts opened, including Vauxhall pleasure gardens in the 1730s and new subscription venues such as the Pantheon in the 1770s. In this regard, the urban infrastructure that underpinned the society and culture of the beau monde itself evolved and changed over time. In response, though, London's fashionable elite altered their own practices to extend or defend their status and prestige. The picture that this begins to present, therefore, is one of noticeable but gradual change rather than dramatic ruction. The amalgam of 'modern' cultural authority and well-established inherited privilege that comprised the beau monde was, unsurprisingly, clothed in continuity.

However, the particularly vociferous attacks on the beau monde that marked the closing decades of the eighteenth century and the early 1800s shifted the terrain. Political writers from Thomas Paine to Charles Piggott took issue with the divisive ramifications of elite culture, arguing that social, political, and economic progress was hampered by exclusive systems based on inherited privileges and interpersonal connections rather than merit. Even the innumerable, so-called 'silver fork' or 'society' *romans-à-clef* novels of the early 1800s were read and reviewed by contemporaries not simply as frivolous romps through high-society life, but as thinly veiled critiques of London's inherent systems of social distinction, from politics to opera attendance to subscription assemblies. 'The exclusive system', wrote Archibald Alison, a writer for *Blackwood's*, '[that] has now, like a leprosy, overspread the land, is one of the chief causes of that hatred of the Aristocracy.'[64]

The following chapters piece together the strategies of distinction that demarcated the metropolitan elite and stratified eighteenth-century London, exploring the new social world and elite identity encapsulated by the beau monde. This study scrutinizes the 'world of fashion' to understand the connections that structured it, the practices that defined it, and the roles, responsibilities, and experiences of its most rarefied members. By recovering the prestige system that operated in the eighteenth-century metropolis, it explores how the potentially anonymizing and democratizing experiences of metropolitan life were met with new notions of social exclusivity that stigmatized interlopers and maintained the public coherence of a prominent beau monde.

The chapters in the first half of the book look at the different ways in which the beau monde's particular brand of social distinction was formulated and projected in eighteenth-century London. Chapters 1 and 2 focus on the key criteria contemporary commentators associated with life in the beau monde, namely ostentatious consumption and fast urban living. Chapter 1 ('Leading the fashion') analyses the relationship of the beau monde to fashion and the material expression of an exclusive identity. Chapter 2 ('Life in the town') explores the role of sociability, social display, and the beau monde's relationship to urban space. Chapters 3 and 4 then focus on the relationship between fashionable society, the royal court, and parliament, examining the institutions that structured the beau monde's metropolitan priorities. This group of chapters, therefore, shares a concern with the urban infrastructure that shaped the 'world of fashion', recovering how a new group identity was constructed.

The closing chapters focus on 'the people of fashion', exploring the beau monde's collective membership and its boundaries, considering its internal divisions (particularly gendered divisions), as well as the experiences of those on its periphery. Chapter 5 ('Beauties') examines the ways in which fashionable femininity was defined and the codes of conduct to which women were expected to adhere, asking why and with what intention women of the beau monde were routinely labelled as 'beauties' and what 'beauty' meant in that context. The final chapter ('Exile and fraud') considers how the blurred boundaries of the world of fashion were policed. It tracks the fate of high-profile fashionable figures exiled for their misconduct, and retrieves contemporary scandals surrounding conmen who feigned fashionable membership and titled acquaintances—with varying degrees of success—for fraudulent ends.

In undertaking the research for this book, I have endeavoured to move beyond the multifarious satirical representations of elite excess to engage instead with a wide range of sources: from personal papers to museum collections, business records, plays, poems, essays, periodicals, and more. Unpublished manuscript material forms the core of this endeavour, and this study combines the use of major collections of family papers (such as the Althorp, Blenheim, Portland, and Strafford papers in the British Library, and the Wrest Park Papers in Bedfordshire record office) with lesser-known and fractured collections held at local record offices around the country. However, it makes no claim to be exhaustive. The eighteenth-century nobility left in their wake a paper mountain rather than a paper trail, preserving their personal archives as a matter of routine. For the historian of non-elite individuals and experiences, the great challenge is to find evidence enough to piece together a lost and hidden world. In contrast, for the historian delving into the gilded society at the top of the social ladder the challenge is to select appropriately from an overwhelming mass of extant material.

In order to avoid the pitfalls of stereotyping, miscellaneous materials surviving in local record offices, and short spans of correspondence from figures making passing reference to the lifestyles of the beau monde, have been used alongside larger collections representing the prominent fashionable figures routinely targeted in contemporary exposés. In addition, personal diaries and memorandum books, pocket books, household and personal bills, and other ephemeral manuscript evidence—as well as material culture from jewellery and silverware to costume—have been mined to shed light on fashionable society from a range of perspectives. Together, they reveal the London-based experiences of figures from across the eighteenth-century peerage, from newly promoted figures nearer the bottom of the patrician hierarchy (such as the Earl of Strafford in the 1710s) to nobles of more elevated and established lineage (such as the dukes of Grafton, the dukes of Portland, and their wives and families). Archives with a substantial thread of metropolitan-oriented records predominate, as these suggest a particular investment in the London season on the part of their creators. Unsurprisingly, then, the majority of individuals who feature here enjoyed annual access to permanent London residences (whether built by their order, purchased from a speculator, or secured on long-term rental) rather than occupying short-term, season-long leases. It should be noted that many of those who participated in fashionable London society and who enjoyed the greatest security in its ranks were also often the wealthiest landholders, although no line has been drawn in this study according to estate size or value.

Many of the characters these varied resources bring to life have already had their histories repeatedly narrated. For Terence Hanbury White, writing in the 1950s, the late eighteenth century was 'The Age of Scandal'.[65] Writing at a particular political and post-war moment, his vision of late eighteenth-century Britain was suffused with salacious chatter, flirtatious duchesses, errant dukes, misdemeanours, and mistresses, underwritten by confident wealth, rolling acres, and Britannia's sovereignty over the waves. What White identified as the 'peculiar flavour' of this era has become big business in recent years. Colourful stories of gambling, adultery, high spending, and fast living in London's 'world of fashion' have attracted enthusiastic chroniclers, and scores of biographies have been quick to glamorize its lords and ladies.[66]

However, this popular imagining of 'Georgian' hedonism tends as much to conceal as illuminate the world it describes. By moving away from an individual, biographical format and focusing on the fortunes of a group, this book looks for an alternative approach. It takes as its focus the high-profile culture that has so attracted biographers, and that is so richly portrayed through contemporary caricature, surviving artefacts, and other cultural legacies. Yet, its aim is not to narrate a rollicking history of high living, nor is it to present a neo-Georgian celebration of aristocratic indulgence. Although often grossly ostentatious and relentlessly pilloried, the culture of the 'beau monde' was much more than an expression of elite frivolity. It was a new manifestation of social distinction and a new form of social leadership, one oriented to the changing conditions and contexts of the period.

1

Leading the fashion
'A most brilliant shew'

I humbly request that you will not permit the present century to slip
through your fingers, without informing us WHAT is FASHION? I
have been in pursuit of a solution to this question for many years and
have never been able to succeed. I have looked backwards and for-
wards, to the right hand and to the left, and I cannot find out what is
this same thing called Fashion. I have looked into Johnson's Dictionary, but I might as well consult the Pilgrim's Progress. I have stolen a
few minutes from a very fashionable company, to put this question
to you. I am told this company consists of fashionable people, yet I
see nothing among it that can enable me to say what Fashion
is.... —your Humble Servant IGNORAMUS

(*St James's Chronicle*, 11 December 1800)

The characterization of London's beau monde as matchless masters
of fashion is an arresting feature of eighteenth-century commentary. Whether celebrated or decried, the representation of this metropolitan set as the 'world of fashion' was commonplace in both pictures
and print. Commentators debated the precise criteria that bought
access to its ranks, but all concurred that the beau monde was best
defined as the 'people of fashion' whose material goods, social practices, and cultural preferences were without question 'quite the fashion'.[1] The linkage between beau monde and fashionability was certainly

conspicuous, but what did the accolade of fashion mean in this context and how was it won?

In modern usage, fashion is broadly accepted as designating modishness, newness, and the latest style. It is often, although not exclusively, aligned to a clothing industry that can respond rapidly to changing vogues. Fashion is something that we can purchase and it is presumed to be the powerful motor behind the operation of the market.[2] In the eighteenth century, however, the concept of fashion was, in certain contexts, understood very differently. As Adam Smith explained in his *Theory of Moral Sentiments* (1759): 'Fashion is rather different from custom... [it] is not the fashion which everybody wears, but which those wear who are of a high rank or character, 'As long as they continue to use this form,' he further explained, 'it is connected in our imaginations with the idea of something that is genteel and magnificent... As soon as they drop it, it loses all of the grace which it had appeared to possess before.'[3] For the eminent Enlightenment economist, fashion was, in essence, aligned to social position. It was associated specifically with the accoutrements and material preferences of those of 'high rank or character' and was defined, he implied, not necessarily by form or fad but rather more simply by ownership and attribution. Or, as radical writer Charles Pigott sneered dismissively in his 1795 pamphlet *The Rights of Nobles* (a polemical glossary outlining the inequities of political power), fashion is merely 'whatever prevails among the great'.[4]

In this etymology, then, fashion was defined more by its affiliation to particular people, and by extension to those people's possessions, than by the fundamental material characteristics or modishness of certain desirable products. This is not to suggest that fashion in this eighteenth-century derivation had no material form, for it was widely asserted that the consumption preferences of the 'world of fashion' had a number of distinguishing features. Indeed, it was a well-worn cliché that metropolitan life triggered a vain obsession with personal show and a crippling addiction to consumables. Critical and satirical comment claimed that the elite were frittering away fortunes on gewgaws and foreign goods and that, for many, fashion was little more than a passion for gross excess. Mary Barber's 1735 poem 'An Unanswerable Apology for the Rich', for instance, catalogued the extravagance of a newly married peer, listing the lavish 'essentials' for which he was compelled to shop:

> The good Castalio must provide,
> Brocade and Jewels for his Bride,
> Her toilet shines with Plate emboss'd,
> What Sums her Lace and Linen Cost!
> The Cloathes that must his Person grace,
> Shine with Embroidery and Lace,
> ...He's an Oeconomist confest,
> But what he buys must be the best,
> For Common use a Set of Plate,
> Old China, when he dines in State,
> A Coach and Six to take the Air,
> Besides a Chariot and a Chair,
> All these important calls supply'd,
> Calls of Necessity not Pride.[5]

Barbar's poem was but one of a multitude of published commentaries, satires, and broadsides that rebuked the consumer strategies of the fashionable world. Notably, the moral of such messages often targeted aspirants, warning society at large against being seduced by fashion's surface glitter. For instance, the perils of mimicking such ostentation were routinely parodied in caricatures of simple country folk returning from a jaunt to town unrecognizably and inappropriately *à la mode*, and in cartoons that showed mercantile citizens rendered vulgar and ridiculous in their quest for fashionable things (Figure 10). While such commentary attests to the complexity of ideas and anxieties surrounding the power of fashion in the period, approaching the meaning of

Our wise Forefathers would express
Ev'n Sensibility in Dress;
The modern Race delight to shew
What Folly in Excess can do.

What is this my Son Tom.

The honest Farmer, come to Town,
Can scarce believe his Son his own;
If thus the Taste continues Here,
What will it be another Year!

London, Published by R. Sayer & J. Bennett, N.º53 Fleet Street, as the Act directs 11 June 1774.

FIGURE 10 *What is this my Son Tom*, anon., 1774.

fashion from the perspective of satirical commentary can only take us so far. A more nuanced understanding of how fashion structured the beau monde, and also of the cultural value of high-end goods in configuring the 'world of fashion', must be drawn from the more direct study of material display within fashionable society itself.

A remarkable series of letters from the 1710s between Thomas Wentworth, Earl of Strafford, and his wife Anne provides a starting point for exploring what fashion actually meant to fashionable society.[6] As will be discussed, the Straffords were newcomers to London society and, in consequence, their correspondence (extending to over 200 letters) offers a uniquely detailed roadmap to its codes. The Straffords' preoccupations about London fashion reveal the key categories of goods prioritized by the beau monde, the exclusive world the Straffords hoped to enter. Unsurprisingly, the possessions foregrounded in their endeavour were ostentatious, showy, and similar, in that regard, to the forms pilloried by satirists. Yet what also emerges from an analysis of the Straffords' consumer choices is that it was not simply the material characteristics of certain goods that contributed to their value. Instead, it was the access to social networks they communicated that determined their worth. In this regard, it was the life of an object after purchase—its application, use, and attribution to particular owners—rather than just its allure at the point of sale, which denoted its relationship to fashion and its appeal to the beau monde.

In 1711, the recently married Earl and Countess of Strafford were ambitious newcomers to metropolitan society (Figure 11). The only daughter of wealthy shipwright Sir Henry Johnson, the new countess had brought an impressive dowry but no inherited title of her own to the marriage. Her alliance with Thomas Wentworth, formerly Lord Raby and recently created Earl of Strafford, catapulted her into the peerage,

FIGURE 11 *Thomas Wentworth, Earl of Strafford, and His family,* Gawen Hamilton, *c.*1732.

but their joint access to the beau monde was not a given. Indeed, the Wentworth family was precariously positioned in the new order ushered in by the Revolution of 1688–9. The Earl of Strafford's mother, Isabella, Lady Wentworth, had served as a lady of the bedchamber to James II's queen. Her husband was a nephew of the infamous royalist

1st Earl of Strafford, a courtier tried and executed in 1641 for his role as chief adviser to Charles I. Such family associations and close ties to the dethroned Stuarts would have met with suspicion by Thomas's generation, in the context of fears that Jacobites (supporters of the exiled Catholic James II) might challenge the progress of a Protestant succession.[7] Thomas Wentworth, however, displayed different allegiances from his royalist Catholic ancestors. In 1688, aged 16, he had presciently enrolled as a soldier under William III, to fight on behalf of the Dutch 'saviour king' and so demonstrate his loyalty to the new regime. In the late 1690s, he left his beloved army to pursue a more courtly and diplomatic career. Thomas Wentworth first succeeded to the peerage as Baron Raby in 1695, inheriting the title from a cousin who died without issue. Significantly, however, although Thomas laid claim to the title, his uncle bequeathed the majority of his wealth and the family estate of Wentworth Woodhouse to another nephew, Thomas Watson, son of Lord Rockingham.[8] In consequence, the ambitious Thomas Wentworth was left with a title but lacked the appropriate financial resources or property to support it. By the time of his lucrative marriage to Anne Johnson in September 1711, he had bought a country estate to add land to his title, he had served as an ambassador in Berlin, and was now in post as ambassador to The Hague. The same year he was created Earl of Strafford in recognition of his diplomatic missions.[9]

With what he hoped would be a distinguished career of public service beginning to take shape, buoyed by the financial backing of his marriage and his successful resurrection of the family's claims to an earldom, Strafford was desperate to rebuild the Wentworth name and rehabilitate it in the new metropolitan landscape of eighteenth-century society. His quest was initially successful. Through his ambassadorial duties, the earl gained a respectable political profile and his wife participated in the social and political routines of fashionable London. They failed, however, to secure long-term rights to membership of the metropolitan elite. In 1715, the Whigs attempted to have the earl impeached for his involvement in the unpopular Treaty of Utrecht, claiming that he had treacherously corresponded with the French enemies whilst acting on behalf of Queen Anne. Although he was never prosecuted, the attack was damning enough to force his withdrawal from London, ending the Straffords' attempt to infiltrate the ranks of the beau monde. Thomas Wentworth, proud Earl of Strafford, retired to Stainborough Hall (now Wentworth Castle), the family's new Yorkshire seat, until his death in 1739, returning to London occasionally to speak, or perhaps vent his frustration, in the House of Lords. There, in his later years, he was described by the sharp-tongued Lord Hervey as a 'loquacious, rich, illiterate, cold, tedious, constant harrangeur'.[10] Despite the unhappy ending, the Straffords' ambitious bid to join London society and their initial success is extremely revealing. The letters written in the early years of their marriage illuminate their shared determination to break into London's highest social ranks and disclose the strategies used to promote their status and, more particularly, the key role played by material goods in that mission.

For the Straffords, establishing a suitable marital home in London was indispensable to their intended metropolitan profile. The couple secured a residence in St James's Square, purchasing number five in November 1711. Developed in the 1670s and 1680s on freehold land belonging to the Earl of St Albans, St James's Square represented one of the most prestigious town addresses, with the majority of its residences occupied by members of the peerage throughout the eighteenth century.[11] Number five was itself sandwiched between properties owned and occupied by the Earl of Portland (soon to be elevated to a dukedom) and the Duke of Kent (Figure 12). No doubt the aspirational earl hoped that one day Strafford House would also be fit for a duke. With her husband posted abroad for his diplomatic duties, Anne, Countess of Strafford, was left to shoulder responsibility for furnishing their house and, with it, their claims to membership of London's beau monde.

FIGURE 12 *A View of St James's Square, London*, Thomas Bowles, *c*.1753.

Strafford House was typical of the terraced properties that surrounded the capital's West End squares, consisting of three main sto-
reys, an attic, and basement. Generally speaking, such town houses
were organized with grand reception rooms laid out on the ground and
first floors facing the street, ensuring those rooms (and their occupants)
might be easily admired by a passing public. Showy bedrooms, regarded
as an extension of space for entertaining rather than necessarily a place
for sleeping, also often formed part of first-floor or ground-floor suites.
More private and more modest bedrooms and closets (small withdraw-
ing rooms) for family and guests occupied the second floor. Servants'
rooms and other household offices were clustered in the attic or over
stables, with the kitchens buried in the basement or in rooms extending out to the back of the house. Though terraced, such properties were
still substantial. A property previously considered by the Earl of
Strafford boasted its own washhouse, a brewhouse, stabling for eleven
horses, as well as a servants' dining room; whilst an inventory for the

St James's Square house of the Duke of Ormonde registers the contents of fifty separate rooms.[12]

It took over a year for the Straffords to finish equipping their property, and the suite of the rooms on the first floor—described as the 'best' bedroom, drawing room, and dining room—was the primary focus of the newly minted countess's efforts. These rooms, built for entertaining, were to be the main vehicle for the Straffords' assault on London society. The countess took pains to reassure her husband that the 'best' rooms would remain closed until he joined her in the capital and that for the time being she merely 'design[ed] to see company below stairs', making use of the reception rooms on the ground floor.[13] A hierarchical distinction between the ground and first floors of the property, between the rooms that she would use whilst alone in London and those that they would use for entertaining society as a couple, was clearly delineated in the countess's selections for furnishing. Although she ordered an expensive new damask bed for the bedroom on the first floor, the countess opted for a second-hand green camlet bed—'clean'd tis as good as new'—for the lower bedchamber.[14] Similarly, she arranged for chairs for her downstairs apartment to be upholstered temporarily in the earl's old robes, to make them ready for her winter entertainments, but was determined to have them refurbished at a later stage before they were repositioned in the 'best dining room' above.[15]

Despite her emphasis on marital deference, the countess routinely used her presence in London and her direct observations of the fashionable world to justify her decorative choices to the earl, and to negotiate and demand their conformity to an apparently shared material culture. Indeed it was primarily the London-based countess, rather than the absent earl, who was entrusted with the major selections. She was quick to demonstrate to her husband that, regardless of her own untitled lineage, she was now adept at identifying an inappropriate choice. Writing in December 1712, for instance, she confidently scoffed at the mistakes she had witnessed being made by their less refined acquaintances:

> I wonder Mr Marshall can talk of his great living here, for they had a very indifferent Lodging in St James's Street & the house was kept the Nastiest I ever see a House…& she sat in the first room with the Cole fire and Tallow candles which I know was made a great jest on.[16]

According to the Countess of Strafford's measure, the Marshalls had failed to make the grade on a number of counts. A house in St James's Street put them alongside but, crucially, not within the most fashionable London locale of St James's Square. Moreover, their use of smoky and pungent tallow candles and a coal fire, rather than the more expensive wax candles and wood fuel, exposed their inability to maintain the material standards of London's elite, if not their ignorance of its conventions.

The devil really was in the detail. The ability to offset the darkness of the season's winter night with effective and expensive lighting equipment was essential to life within the beau monde, and the type of candle used was no frivolous matter. A distinction was routinely drawn between better-quality wax candles, made from beeswax or spermaceti (sperm whale oil), and cheap tallow candles, made from animal fat. Wax was far and away the more prestigious choice. 'Tallow candles', claimed one satirical guide to polite society, 'are at all times detestable and their existence is not even known in genteel life.'[17] The frugal and conservative spinster Gertrude Savile always noted in her diary when wax candles were used instead of tallow, specifically recording 'wax candles for the Countis' when honoured with a visit from the Countess of Cassells in the 1720s.[18] Sir Thomas Robinson was so impressed by the 130 wax candles shimmering in Sir Robert Walpole's dining room in the early 1730s that he stood back and counted them. Details of candles in account books for the royal court in the 1790s reveal explicit hierarchical distinctions, with some royal interior spaces always lit by wax, other rooms lit by wax or tallow depending on their daily use, and back rooms continuously lit with tallow. Different household servants were granted the ends of wax and tallow candles, according to their seniority, and account books for private properties also carefully note expenditure on wax.[19] Fortunes were displayed as candles burned. The Duke of Newcastle spent £25 every month on wax candles for his London home in the 1760s, no mean sum when the annual salary for a maid was approximately £3 per year. Newcastle's monthly expenditure on candles was comparable to the cost of provisioning his kitchen.[20] That, however, was small change compared to the £200 the Duchess of Montagu was rumoured to have spent on wax candles in a single night for an assembly in 1712, or the incredible £603 that the Duke of Bedford reputedly spent to illuminate his evening entertainments with over 1,000 wax candles.[21] The ability to subvert nature and turn night into day did not come cheap, but few risked using the much cheaper tallow.

The Countess of Strafford did not hesitate to correct her husband if she felt he was about to make an ill-informed decorative decision. In 1712, for instance, she reprimanded the earl with the curt rebuttal: 'the round sconces [wall-mounted candlesticks] you speak of for Chimneys are quite out of fashion for there is a sort they now make for Chimneys of a particular pattern which if you'll have I can give directions.'[22] Following her letter the countess quickly set about ordering the necessary lighting equipment. Selecting sconces and candlesticks made from expensive materials and incorporating the family crest on most objects, the countess did not shy away from flashy shows of rank and wealth, but her choices also extended beyond such blunt assertions of status. She closely observed the style favoured by figures associated with London's beau monde and then sought to lay claim to the same urban networks by replicating them. When commissioning new silver sconces, the countess turned first to the advice of her neighbour, the Countess of Portland. 'I see Lady Portland yesterday who told me Lord Portland has some Sconces now made the handsomest she ever see & she will borrow won of them for me to show Mr Shales [the Straffords' house-hold steward].'[23] The countess did not stop at a single source but extended her search still further. Updating her husband on her actions, she reported:

> Now the Queen has some new made which I see & they are very handsom they are looking glass in the middle & silver round about & the Seat for the Candle are Silver...I was last week to see the Duke of Marlboroughs house which is extremely fine, they have great Branches for the middle of the rooms in imitation of Plate in wood silver'd or Gilded over & they look very well, now if you have not won of Silver I should think won [*sic*] of them for the middle of our great dining room would doe very well for there must be won of some sort or other.[24]

It was not only during her hunt for sconces that the countess monitored the choices made by other metropolitan figures. When commissioning accompanying furnishings her letters are packed with similar comparisons. For example, when the Earl of Strafford sent her two japanned cabinets in 1712, she had frames made by 'the man who did them at Montagu House and at the Duke of Marlboroughs which are by much the neatest I ever see'.[25] The countess also bought matching tables 'done by the same man [for] he has don all for the Dutchess of Marlborough, the Dutchess of Montagu and now is doing for Lady Massam'.[26] And, when trying to convince her husband to commission a very handsome 'dish of plates and covers', she assured him that 'they are very much used, the Duke of Somerset has won, Lord Hallifax, the Duke of Kent, Lord Portland and a great many more just made'.[27]

As well as focusing on the finer points of fashion protocol, the countess's decision-making process reveals that it was a high-profile metropolitan group of nobles who set the standard the Straffords sought to meet. Significantly, the Straffords' chosen role models crossed political and court-related divisions. When examining material culture, historians have often strained to link stylistic change to political allegiance, fixing particular aesthetic preferences to particularly political agendas.[28] Without denying the potential for material display to convey politicized identities, it is striking that the Countess of Strafford's preferences more often transcended those divisions. The Marlboroughs, for example, were major political powerbrokers in the early eighteenth century. Formerly the court favourite, the Duchess of Marlborough was estranged from the monarch at the time of the Countess of Strafford's visit to peruse the Marlboroughs' lighting furniture. The duchess had left her prestigious court post as groom of the stole and was effectively presiding over an opposition court at Marlborough House. A staunch supporter of the Marlboroughs, Lord Halifax was similarly out of favour with the queen. Lady Masham (referred to as 'Massam' by the Countess of Strafford) had at this stage usurped the Duchess of Marlborough as the queen's confidante, and the Duchess of Somerset had replaced the Duchess of Marlborough as groom of the stole. In their political conduct, the Straffords backed courtiers, such as the Somersets, and opposed the Marlboroughs.[29] Indeed, the Countess of Strafford's letters record the political tensions felt between the opposing courtly and political groupings, detailing (with not a little pride) the 'spleen and mallis' with which she was met by the Duchess of Marlborough and her daughter, the Duchess of Montagu, at an inter-party social event. The countess willingly accepted invitations to assemblies hosted by the new court favourite Lady Masham, but never attended those held at Marlborough House.[30] Yet, though shunning their company, the countess was happy to include the Marlboroughs and their allies in her search for leaders of fashion.

The process of comparing, contrasting, and replicating high-end possessions within an identifiable urban cohort (as revealed by the Straffords' own quest to join fashionable circles) can be found reiterated in other manuscript collections. For example, when, in 1778, Frederick Robinson undertook to source English silver plate for his brother Thomas, 2nd Baron Grantham (an ambassador based in Madrid), he too looked around his titled acquaintances in London to check suitable examples. After very careful comparison his instinct was that few owned tureens finer than Thomas's current model (although Frederick was impressed by a £1,000 dinner service so fine that the owner had decided to extend his household and employ 'a burnisher to keep it clean').[31] When Lady Mary Coke advised on the resetting of jewels for the new Duchess of Buccleuch in 1767, she recorded in her diary that both the Duchess of Grafton's and Duchess of Portland's jewellery were sought out as models.[32] Lord Nunehum, meanwhile, commissioned Matthew Boulton to make him a pair of ormolu girandoles (wall-mounted gilded candlesticks) 'precisely the pattern of Lord Edgcumbe's'.[33]

Such name checking might read as snobbish boasting, but it also creates the impression of a commonality of styles and possessions and, with it, a shared identity forged through material goods. Notably, this shared material world appears to have stood apart in some key respects from the commercial marketplace. Designers are rarely mentioned. Merchants seldom feature. It was not so much where an object was made or purchased that was the primary preoccupation in these accounts, but who else possessed them. From this perspective, stylistic authority, as defined by the metropolitan elite themselves, rested with those at the top of the social ladder.

This combination of costly consumption and insider knowledge can be brought sharply into focus through the beau monde's penchant for one category of possessions in particular: diamond jewellery. With prices running into the thousands of pounds and single pieces costing more than the annual rent of a fully furnished London town house, diamonds were the ultimate in ostentation and a powerful marker of social prestige. However, as the next section explores, routinely remade, and readily transferred between family and acquaintances, this jewellery exhibited certain mercurial qualities that are central to understanding its significance to London's fashionable world. Through systems of inheritance, borrowing, and gift giving, diamonds moved repeatedly through different hands, and were worn on many different bodies. By recovering the systems of borrowing, transfer, and exchange inherent in the beau monde's lavish consumption of diamonds it is possible to capture some of the subtleties of a material culture which extended beyond individual material displays to involve shared associations and allegiances. In turn, such self-conscious display of social networks helped create and consolidate an exclusive group identity that was closed to the everyday consumer and which rendered fashion a social privilege and not just a stylish purchase.

A love of jewellery, and of diamond jewellery in particular, was widely deployed by satirists and critics as a characteristic motif of fashionable society, one that underscored its frivolity. '[H]er chief idea of happiness in marriage was the possession of jewels and the paraphernalia of a countess,' wrote Maria Edgeworth of a female protagonist in her didactic short story 'Ennui'.[34] Published as part of her *Tales from Fashionable Life* (1806), Edgeworth (who had formerly concentrated on moral stories for the schoolroom) turned her matronly attention to correcting deficiencies evident in the adult world and, particularly, 'the errours [*sic*] to which the higher classes of society are disposed'. Following the dissipated trail of an Earl of Glenthorn, who lost his moral and financial way in the London season and found redemption and clarity of purpose only after returning to his provincial duties at his family seat, 'Ennui' was advertised as an exploration of 'the causes, curses and cure' of high society.[35] In the context of the plot, the newly wed Countess of Glenthorn's enthusiastic amassing of jewellery, although only briefly featured, appears symptomatic of her vanity, and also of the moral weakness of her arranged, loveless marriage. So prodigious were her jewels that 'she scarcely knew them all', and when questioned about their origins she was unable to respond. For Edgeworth, as for other critical writers, the exterior magnificence associated with London's beau monde signified a lack of interior moral purpose. Like their diamonds, the fashionable world dazzled and sparkled. However, while the precious stones exuded wealth and vanity, they—like their owners—might be found, on closer inspection, to be colourless, cold, and empty within.

At the same time, there was a certain expectation amongst the public that members of the fashionable elite would appear bedecked with jewels, and indeed a certain disappointment if they were not. Whether in London during the season or on a duty visit to a regional powerbase, the ritualistic exhibition of family stones emerges as an integral part of patrician public displays. As we will see, after a new marriage had been made, the appearance of a bride at court adorned with her in-laws' gems was read as a formal marker of the match. When the new Lady Scarborough completed a tour of her husband's regional estate, the local gentry were suitably impressed by her bejewelled glamour which included 'diamonds all down her stays and a necklace that almost covered her neck', ear-rings reputed to have cost £120, and a diamond-encrusted coat of arms adorning her hair with 'a pelican as ye Crest & that [with] a very large diamond in its mouth'. In total, Lady Scarborough was draped with over £10,000 worth of diamonds, worn on one evening to a Lincoln assembly.[36] Lady Williams Wynn met with similar local approval when she appeared 'very brilliant—quite dazzling', ablaze 'with fine necklace, earrings, watch and chain all diamond, a stomacher with four bows all diamond', to a value of '£20,000 exclusive of her inestimable self'.[37] Rank was expected to carry brilliance (and brilliants) before it.

The attitudes towards jewelled display taken by those beyond the privileged circle of the beau monde do not, however, entirely represent the motivations of those who purchased them. In order to reveal these

agendas it is necessary to sketch out a broader context. Although diamonds emerge as the most highly prized gem of the period, such privi-
leging of these precious stones was, in fact, a recent development. It was
only in the late seventeenth and early eighteenth centuries that heavy
gold jewellery embedded with the richly coloured rubies and emeralds
favoured by Renaissance and early modern European elites was sup-
planted by jewellery dominated by the dazzling but colourless diamond. By 1755, one London tourist observed that 'the use of diamonds
is more received in England than that of other jewels: they are richer,
less variegated and less liable to imitation'.[38] The discovery of new diamond supplies and the opening of new mines in Brazil stimulated
trade, and the development of new cutting techniques maximized their
allure. The light-refracting qualities of the diamond made it the ideal
ornament for Georgian candle-lit social encounters, and the refine-
ment of the brilliant cut (introduced from the 1710s) purposefully
enhanced its sheen. Indeed, the expensive and highly skilled crafts-
manship required to transform the unpromising black stones extracted
from the mine into shimmering gems contributed to their magical
appeal and, of course, to their market cost. The precedence of the diamond over other gems in this period is made clear by the major changes
that took place in jewellery design. Rather than setting stones directly
into a heavy precious metal base, claw feet were created to hold the gem
proud above the setting, encouraging light to dance through all its facets. Previously, gems had been permanent ornaments to thick and
weighty silver or gold settings. Jewellery flaunted the expensive metal
as much as the jewels, encasing stones in a deep pillow of precious
metal. In the eighteenth century it was the gems, not the setting, that
commanded attention with delicate silver and gold settings used ever
more sparingly (Figure 13).

Despite their cultural significance and high value, extant pieces of
eighteenth-century English diamond jewellery are extremely rare, and

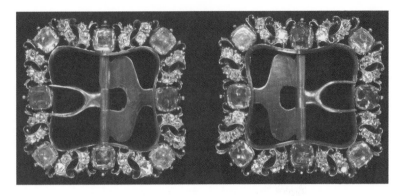

FIGURE 13 Brilliant-cut diamond and sapphire shoe buckles, *c.*1750. Although many buckles set with paste or cut steel survive from the period, diamond-set buckles such as these are rare. This pair exemplifies the eighteenth-century developments in jewellery design. The simple silver claw-foot setting allows light to refract through the gems.

their popularity suggested in images, texts, and paste replicas is not matched by the material record. Yet the comparative absence of contemporary examples is itself revealing. As a few surviving pieces disclose, diamond jewellery was intentionally and repeatedly reset. In contrast to the rigidity of early pieces, the simpler settings of eighteenth-century jewellery allowed gems to be quickly and easily released. Moreover, jewellery was often designed in a way that permitted it to be split up into separate parts, so that a brooch might be swiftly extracted from a necklace or a hair accessory from a stomacher (Figure 14).

Tellingly, the Churchill family records (for the estate of the dukes of Marlborough) include inventories of diamonds in which each gem rather than each piece of jewellery is listed. The inventories consist of a written description of each stone, often including its provenance, and a pencil sketch of its facets and appearance to permit, it would seem, the easier identification of the stones regardless of the form in which they were set. It was only the diamonds, rather than the accessories they created, which were expected to pass from generation to generation.

FIGURE 14 Large diamond spray bodice ornament. This single piece is made up of a number of different parts. Although it is estimated that the jewellery was made into this final shape in the mid-nineteenth century, it consists of pieces that date from earlier in the 1800s and from the 1700s. The different parts of this large piece could be dismantled and worn separately.

Very few business records for eighteenth-century jewellers survive. Trading in such valuable stock was a gamble and many jewellers went to the wall, ruined by unpaid bills, limited cash flow, the theft of their stock, or the loss of a shipment from the mines. Jeweller Dru Drury was one who recorded his bankruptcy, blaming his losses on miscreant

FIGURE 15 Trade card for Dru Drury & Son, Goldsmith, 1741. The son took over the business in 1748 and became bankrupt in 1778.

clients who refused to pay their bills (Figure 15). Writing in 1778, when deciding whether or not to re-establish his business yet again, he reminded himself, 'last year I lost more £16,000 the effect of which was O! terrible to relate, I was obliged to be a Bankrupt.' Miserable and broke, he filed away the reams of unanswered letters he had issued to clients begging them to make good on defaulted payments.[39] It would be another century until market stability allowed the trade to flourish to the extent that it colonized its own corner of London, Hatton Garden. In the eighteenth century, the risk-takers who comprised London's jewellers set up shop in Soho, scattered near The Strand, or in the east and City side of the metropolis around Cheapside. Newspaper advertisements and trade cards told of their desirable goods, but the fact that few trading names survived beyond a generation (at best) is yet further evidence of the perilous nature of the business.[40]

Against this background of instability, the existence of over thirty years of accounts for a jewellery business owned by the Webb family provides a rare insight into the diamond trade.[41] With the firm passing across generations, from father Peter to his son Arthur, the Webbs appear to have been one of the more established jewellers of the eighteenth century, running their operation from city premises in Throgmorton Street, just north of Cheapside. Although the financial records begin in the mid-1730s, there is evidence that the business had a longer history. One Mr Peter Webb, a jeweller of Throgmorton Street, is mentioned in an advertisement in *The Daily Courant* on 12 August 1718. Thereafter, jewellers named Webb, located at Throgmorton Street, appear routinely in newspaper announcements (including marriage and death announcements) and trade directories until the late 1770s.[42] Surviving household inventories suggest that business was buoyant for both Peter and Arthur. With all manner of genteel equipment incorporated amongst their possessions—including fishing rods kept in the garret, a well-stocked library, a fossil collection, and a full complement of modish and expensive scientific gadgetry such as a telescope, microscope, barometer, and hygrometer—the Webbs earned a comfortable and elegant city living.[43]

A number of high-ranking customers patronized the Webbs. Their surviving order books list sixty-two titled clients, including the Duchess of Portland; the countesses of Hertford, Yarmouth, and Neath; the earls of Rockingham, Grandison, and Arran; and Viscount Windsor. Big sums were at stake in their business transactions. In 1753, for example, Arthur Webb billed the Duchess of Portland £483 for one pair of single-drop diamond ear-rings, and Earl Spencer was charged £900 for one pair of shoe buckles in 1755. This figure was topped by Lord Tullamore, who was presented with a heart-stopping bill of £1,054 (one of the largest single charges evident in the accounts) for his order in 1737 for a diamond ring, two pairs of diamond ear-rings, and a diamond encrusted girdle buckle.[44] The Webbs' routine business was also supplemented by less grand clients. These customers usually eschewed diamonds in favour of the more affordable garnets or other semiprecious gems, such as one Miss Goddard who purchased two 'mocca bracelets with garnets' for £7 7s. in 1758. Nonetheless, sixty-two grandees represented a substantial proportion of the peerage based in London every season. Moreover, most of these clients were loyal. Lord Irwin, for instance, spent £245 on a pair of diamond ear-rings in 1737, returning in 1739 to purchase a diamond ring for £180. Viscount Windsor bought a whole range of goods between 1741 and 1756, from a diamond necklace that exceeded £400 after setting, to ear-rings, rings, and buckles.

Closer inspection of the orders left by Webb's titled clients reveals that a vast disposable income was not necessarily a primary precondition of achieving a bejewelled show. Although Webb was fortunate enough to persuade most of his clients to keep up with their bills, elite consumption of these luxuries was managed by running up lengthy accounts that were later paid off in small instalments in a system that effectively operated as interest-free credit. In addition, Webb's business accounts expose a significant system of part-exchange. Smaller items of jewellery were deposited with Webb to offset bills. Garnet bracelet, ruby rings, pearl necklaces, and ear-rings were all bartered by clients in part payment for larger diamond-set pieces. The Duchess of Portland, for example, met a bill for £1,472 (for items purchased in 1758) with a sequence of cash payments as well as depositing a pair of old ear-rings.[45]

The most striking feature of Webb's order books is the preponderance of resetting. Between 1735 and 1768, over a quarter of the orders placed with Webb by titled clients were for refashioning existing jewellery. Clients either requested that an item was entirely remade into a different piece—ear-rings into a necklace, for example—or asked for additional stones to be inserted into existing items to increase their show. Orders placed with Webb register the multitude of forms in which diamonds were set: from shoe buckles, knee buckles, coat and waistcoat buttons, to stomachers (which decorated a woman's bodice), rings, bracelets, necklaces, brooches, ear-rings, hairpins, tiaras, and crowns. They were sewn onto clothes, sunk into snuff boxes and patch boxes, and set into miniatures and sword hilts. Yet all of these forms were fleeting, as Webb's clients had items repeatedly and routinely remade. So it was then that buckles became necklaces, necklaces became hairpins, bracelets, or rings, and diamonds from rings were removed and reset into buckles.

Recovering the ways in which diamond jewellery was worn and used by consumers explains this pattern of rapid and repeated remaking. Personal accounts testify to the regular transfer of pieces between different figures. In particular, the public exchange of jewellery between family members registered crucial moments in family history and jewellery was used to mark out dynasties and lineage. For example, both Lady Mary Coke and Lady Mary Yorke separately noted that a match between 'Mr Grenville' (Richard Grenville, later 2nd Earl Temple) and Mary Elizabeth Nugent (eldest daughter and co-heiress of Viscount Clare) was confirmed once the groom's mother, Lady Temple, was seen to '[give] up all her jewels' to the young bride.[46] In 1773, a proposed match between Amelia D'Arcy, 9th Baroness Comys, and Francis Godolphin Osborne, Marquess of Carmarthen (heir to the dukedom of Leeds), came to the attention of acquaintances when the Duchess of Leeds presented Amelia with her diamond necklace.[47] Soon after the marriage, the new Lady Carmarthen was seen at court 'brilliant in [her] jewels', wearing not only the Duchess of Leeds's gems but also a diamond bracelet gifted by the queen.[48] Occasionally, the bequest and transfer of bejewelled luxuries were reported in the press. On 25 October 1731, for instance, *The Gentleman's Magazine* noted, '[t]he Dutchess Dowager of Marlborough gave a sword set with diamonds and a pair of diamond buckles of great value (presented to the late Duke of Marlborough by the present Emperor of Germany) to her Grandson the Earl of Sunderland'.[49]

Although the gift of diamonds was widely recognized as a proclamation of a marriage or a public confirmation of other family links, the jewellery in question was not necessarily inherited intact. Indeed, particularly with regard to marriages, it was more often the case that family sets were purposefully reset to mark the transition. Speculative applications made by eighteenth-century jewellers to families when a marriage was rumoured demonstrate the routine nature of this practice. Before his bankruptcy Dru Drury, for example, wrote to Lady Ramsden to promote his services in the 1760s,

> Madam, Permit me the favour of this application to your Ladyship which is to request your recommendation of me to Lord & Lady Sevile [*sic*] as a Goldsmith and Jeweller whose marriage I have seen mentioned in ye newspapers. Suffer me Mad^m [Madam] to mention that if I have the honour of any commands from them I will most assuredly execute them upon the lowest terms possible so as to engage their future favours.[50]

Intricate exchanges of diamond jewellery, and their subsequent reconfiguration, also took place after marriage. When the Countess of Strafford prepared for her first appearance at court after her wedding in 1711, she assiduously collected jewels from her entire family. The countess went to lengths to ensure that she was seen with the most jewels of anybody attending court. She carefully restrung diamonds lent by her mother-in-law and looped them around the edge of her dress. These were supplemented by large jewels that the earl sent over from The Hague, where they had been set in diamond rings and buckles for his own use. The countess combined her husband's stones with others already in her possession, breaking up existing items from her jewellery collection and commissioning new-set ear-rings and a necklace to accompany her jewelled dress. She reported her complicated actions back to her husband, picking through the various new forms into which his and other family items had been set:

> I put the best of them you sent and my ring, for the tops [of the earrings] and the top great ones for the Drops & then if you remember my own topps of earrings was good Brilliants and them I have set in single collets for the forepart of my necklace with the great diamond in the middle.[51]

Significantly, the jewellery did not remain in this form or in the possession of the Countess of Strafford for very long. A few months later, the earl requested the return of his diamonds so that he could have them reset once again as buckles and buttons for his formal suit to support his diplomatic duties. Later still, the jewels were again collected back in England, this time to adorn the court dress of the earl's unmarried sister, Lady Betty Wentworth, when she was presented to the queen. Remarkably, over a period of eighteen months, the Straffords' diamonds appeared in rings, ear-rings, a necklace, buttons, buckles, and other dress accessories; they were set and reset and shipped back and forth across the Channel, and worn by husband, wife, and sister.

These practices help to explain why such a significant proportion of the Webbs' business with their high-end clients involved adjusting and resetting rather than new commissions. Correspondence such as this also brings to light the shared consumption of the jewels amongst different family members, although we should not presume that shared consumption necessarily equated to shared ownership. When the Earl of Strafford shipped the largest diamonds to his wife, he insisted that the countess signed a declaration confirming that the diamonds were part of the Strafford family's property before he agreed to release them. Dutifully she swore, 'I promis at Death either before or after Ld Strafford to have back to him or his family the Diamond Earring he now gives me or to return them whenever he demands them.'[52] Carefully archived amongst family documents, this declaration is a pointed reminder that, although the countess was entrusted to have the jewels reset, and was encouraged to combine those diamonds with others, they were not her personal possessions. Although she wore the tokens of the family's wealth and status, she could not retain or bequeath them. The eventual fate of those jewels is unknown. But the contract signed by the countess implies that, should they have remained reset within other items of her jewellery when she died, the jewellery in question would have been broken up to release the gems. These would then have been returned to the estate (or estates) of which they formed a part.

This is precisely what happened at the death of another Strafford family member, the countess's wealthy grandmother Lady Rawstorne. After Lady Rawstorne's funeral, the Earl of Strafford was quick to break up her jewellery and attempt to redeem those items he regarded as the rightful inheritance of her granddaughter, his wife. The Countess of Strafford assisted with the complicated re-appropriation, picking through the family history of certain pieces and reminding her husband that a pearl necklace, for example, was most likely not hers but originally 'Mr Rawston's fathers for Lady Rawston always told me it came by her second husband & it was to return to his family and tho it is not expressly named in the will it might well be reconed [reckoned] amongst the jewels'.[53] She reprimanded her husband for his unseemly haste in claiming the gems, writing, 'I am very sorry you have brok up Lady Rawston's Diamonds till you are very sure wch belong'd to us'.[54]

Similarly subtle interpretations of ownership are revealed in other collections of personal papers. For example, the family histories of particular pieces of jewellery were carefully plotted by members of the Marlborough dynasty during a dispute between different generations in the 1720s. In 1725, relations had soured between the Duke of

Bridgewater and his daughter Anne, Duchess of Bedford (whose maternal grandmother was the indomitable Duchess of Marlborough). As the relationship broke down, the duke demanded the return of all the Bridgewater jewels from the Bedford estate. The Duchess of Bedford and her husband then turned to her grandmother, Sarah, Duchess of Marlborough, to intervene and defend particular items. The Bedfords argued that amongst the items the Duke of Bridgewater requested were diamonds that had originally belonged to the Duchess of Marlborough's daughter (the Duchess of Bedford's mother and Bridgewater's wife), and which had been left to the Duchess of Bedford in her will. The Bedfords asserted that these diamonds therefore formed part of the Bedford estate and should not be returned with the Bridgewater jewels. When listed in the original will, the diamonds had been set in shoe buckles, but were subsequently reset as pendants by the Bedfords. Writing to the Duchess of Marlborough about the matter in May 1725, the Duke of Bedford explained the jewels Bridgewater sent for 'were [the] same [that] were made of Buckles w[hi]ch were [the] late Countess of Bridgewater y[ou]r Grace Daughter their value under £200 wch makes his graces actions rather ye meaner. I am no less obliged to y[ou]r Grace for sending us the extract of her mothers will. The pendant she has at present.'[55] Following the advice of the Duchess of Marlborough, and armed with the paperwork to prove their case, the Bedfords kept the jewellery.[56] Regardless of the form they took, the contested diamonds were still presumed to be identifiable, and the Bedfords were adamant that the stones belonged to them.

Significantly, these systems of exchange were not confined to family networks. Borrowing items appears to have been commonplace within elite culture. In 1768, for example, Sarah Lady Cowper lent her diamond stomacher to Lady Spencer, 'which added to her own jewels made her very brilliant'.[57] An earlier member of the Cowper family, Mary Lady Cowper, lady of the bedchamber to Queen Anne, recalled how she had worn Madame Gouvernet's necklace to a court ball in 1716. Significantly, she claimed it was an obligation to acknowledge connection, rather than a desire for adornment, that underpinned this display: 'I accepted because…I was afraid of disobliging her, than to make myself fine,' she explained, 'for I don't care one Farthing for setting myself out.'[58]

As implied by Cowper, the display of a borrowed item broadcast the wearer's contacts. Contemporaries monitored the display of borrowed or gifted gems closely, reading and reporting them as signals of shifting alliances. For example, smoother intergenerational relations were suggested amongst a subsequent generation of the Bedfords, when it was reported that the Duchess of Bedford was to wear the dowager duchess's jewels at court—an act interpreted by observers as signalling the 'comfortable terms' between the generations.[59] When Lady Mary Coke saw an acquaintance bedecked with a vast array of jewels, she wrote back to friends in London to ascertain their origin. 'I was amazed at the increase of her diamonds', she reported, 'pray tell me if she appear'd at London with a very fine diamond necklace, tis certain she has not bought it herself.'[60] The diamond ear-rings worn by the courtier Lady Sundon in the early eighteenth century were widely reported as symbols of the favours she had received for advancing the interests of the low-church clergy, and were read as a signifier of her courtly authority. In the early eighteenth century, the Duchess of Marlborough strategically and publicly distributed items of diamond jewellery to her acquaintances in an act that was presumed to be politically expedient. The Countess of Strafford, watching London business closely, informed her husband that on leaving town the Duchess of Marlborough had 'given a great many of her dear friends Diamond rings', eventually giving away 'in jewells to the value of 6000£', with 'none of her Whigg Friends but she had given Jewels of considerable value'.[61] Such distribution of jewels appears to have provided a means of consolidating the

Whig network (the opposition political group led by the Marlboroughs) within the London elite at a time when it was at risk of breaking down following the Duchess of Marlborough's fall from favour at court. For those wearing her cast-off baubles, the display broadcast their high-profile contacts and also their advocacy of an opposition political cause. Diamonds, therefore, were repositories not just of wealth but of family history, interpersonal association, and exclusive contacts.[62] When the London jeweller reset the precious gems, familial, social, and political relationships were realigned and secured.

Showy, grandiose, and grotesquely expensive—these are the qualities routinely associated with fashionable goods. On this score, those participating in the new business of eighteenth-century metropolitan life certainly do not disappoint. Prestigious town houses demanded similarly prestigious furnishings, and their high-ranking occupants delighted in glittering adornment. Letters, household accounts, diaries, and bills affirm the staggering cost of maintaining a profile in fashionable London. In 1778, with tongue firmly in cheek, Frederick Robinson explained the rules of material show to his brother, Thomas, 2nd Baron Grantham: 'I not only partake of the amusements but of the extravagances of London, but I assure you it is out of economy and prudence that I have bought a vis a vis [town carriage] painted brown.'[63] Extravagance was, in his interpretation, a prudent necessity.

However, where critics berated pompous ostentation, fashionable insiders registered more complicated messages. Wealth was a precondition of impressive material show, but the payment strategies delineated in the Webbs' business accounts demonstrate that the consumption and display of high-end goods was far more than the index of flashy expenditure that commentators claimed. Satirists lambasted spendthrift peers who wasted their fortunes on fripperies. But Webb's clients, by staggering payments, dealing in part-exchange, and refashioning existing items, rarely needed the disposable income to match the market cost of the items they wore. Family members requested, tracked, and lent items of jewellery within the family group and family ownership overruled individual use. Moreover, movements of items between non-kin networks were read as maps of marriages promised, political allegiances made, and new relationships emerging. Kinship, social, and political relationships were made, remade, and proudly exhibited by metropolitan elite consumers, and astutely observed by members of their circle. In a similar vein, by echoing the styles favoured in Marlborough or Montagu House, the Countess of Strafford's displays in St James's Square appear to have been constructed, at least in part, with a view to trumpeting her connection to the high-profile members of London's society.

As such, for the beau monde, fashion was not achieved through modish trendsetting. The circulation of mass-produced goods did not fuel it, and the majority of the population could never attain it. Instead, it was an internal currency that underpinned social networks and alliances and informed group identity. While the *nouveaux riches* could certainly buy imported diamonds and attempt to outshine the beau monde, they could not purchase the connections and alliances that were interwoven with the gems when they were worn by the titled consumer. Fashion, in this regard, provided a corporate identity that bound a newly configured metropolitan elite, the beau monde, together. These material practices stigmatized interlopers and created a network of identifiable 'people of fashion'. Fashion was both a reformulation of rank and a fiercely defended expression of the beau monde's self-proclaimed superiority.

2

Life in the town
'All together and all distinct'

Oh! St James's is a lovely Place,
'Tis better than the City,
For there are Balls and Operas,
And ev'ry Thing that's Pretty.

(Henry Carey, 'The beau monde,
or the pleasures of St James's',
Poems on Several Occasions, 1729)

I Hate the Town and all its Ways,
Ridottos, Operas and Plays,
The Ball, the Ring, the Mall, the Court,
Wherever the Beau-Monde Resort.

(Henry Fielding,
Miscellania, 1743)

All the Modish World appear,
Fond of nothing else my dear,
Folks of Fashion eager seek,
Sixteen concerts in a week,

(James Hook,
The Musical Courtship, 1788)

In January 1765, Yorkshire landowner Mr Godfrey Bosville was staying in London for business and pleasure. With money, time, and inclination enough to participate in the capital's social world, Bosville

63

made regular sojourns from his Yorkshire home, Gunthwaite Hall, to London to sample all manner of urban pleasures: sipping coffee in the coffee houses, sauntering in the pleasure gardens, dancing at masquerades, and appraising actors and singers on the stage.[1] A prosperous country squire enjoying the metropolis, Bosville appears typical of the untitled yet urbane gentlemen who reputedly characterized the century's commercial society and its expansive middling sorts. He was an enthusiastic visitor to London, attending a whole range of new types of entertainments and forms of urban leisure. Yet, despite the diversity of new pleasures available, Bosville was left dissatisfied with his social adventures. As he bemoaned to his rural neighbour, John Spencer of Cannon Hall near Barnsley:

> We go here to Public places but though we do it is but a public life in appearance, for everybodys conversation is in a manner confined within the compass of a few particular acquaintance. The Nobility hold themselves uncontaminated with the Commons. You seldom see a Lord and private Gentleman together....An American that saw a Regiment of Footmen drawn up might think the officers and soldiers mighty sociable. Just so is the company [here], all together and all distinct.[2]

Bosville's disgruntled complaint about the limitations of his sociable interactions is arresting. The marked proliferation of commercial leisure resorts in eighteenth-century London, and in other contemporary towns, has been the subject of particular academic attention. Marketing high culture and art to all for the price of a ticket, these novel venues are said to have represented a move away from court patronage and elitist principles and towards the profit-making entrepreneur and the wider public. Moreover, at venues such as assembly rooms, pleasure gardens, and even art exhibitions, high society and more of society are believed to have 'mixed', bringing previously divided social groups into closer social contact.[3] In this regard, London's leisure grounds have not been investigated as spaces associated with the fashionable elite per se, but rather as innovative sites that catered to a far broader public.

It is notable, though, that despite the emphasis historians have placed on the contemporary ideal of sociable interaction at new leisure venues, we know comparatively little about how such sociability and social interaction was actually practised on the ground. As betrayed by the verbs and analogies historians have depended upon—'mixing', 'mingling', and, occasionally, 'rubbing shoulders'—our understanding of the encounters that may have taken place in commercial resorts is only loosely defined and vaguely suggested. Reliance on such murky constructions leaves key elements of the eighteenth-century social experience unresolved and lacking critical examination. Moreover, although these models of interaction depend on the presumption of elite involvement (for such sites would not offer much opportunity for 'mixing' if those at the top of the social scale did not participate), the ways in which London's beau monde responded to these ostensibly shared public places have gone relatively unexplored.

This chapter revisits London's famous leisure venues through the eyes of the beau monde, focusing particularly on the pleasure gardens of Vauxhall and Ranelagh, and London's West End theatres (which staged both plays and operas). In some respects, the theatres and pleasure gardens were very different commercial leisure spaces. Pleasure gardens have been categorized as the ultimate expression of eighteenth-century entrepreneurialism and an exemplar of the vibrant social 'mixing' stimulated by public sociability. In contrast, rather than operating on a free market principle, London's theatre world was controlled by royal patent and, unlike the 'open' pleasure garden, the enclosed and hierarchically organized auditoria visibly sorted the theatrical audience into differently priced sections.[4] Yet, the pleasure gardens and theatres also shared significant features. Many singers, actors, artists, and impresarios moved between the different resorts, which had aesthetic and cultural connections. Most importantly for the concerns of this study, the practices of fashionable sociability performed at each resort were marked by similarities. Whether in private boxes at the theatre or on the shared walks of a pleasure garden, the world of fashion harnessed urban sociability to consolidate and advertise their prestigious rank. In this regard, the social practices of London's beau monde were less about mingling and more about parading distinction.

Through this investigation it becomes clear that fashionable sociability effectively represented more a ritualized public performance than an idle and individualistic pursuit of pleasure. Returning to venues again and again, week after week, season after season, attendance at social venues was firmly embedded into London's leisure system and formed an integral part of the capital's social attractions. The beau monde's visibility had a market value that drew other spectators, but that visibility itself depended both upon predictable appearances by fashionable figures and also upon clear separation between fashionable society and the rest of the urban crowd. To this end, by purposefully parading with their equals, by repeating excursions religiously, by using specific spaces at certain resorts at particular times of day in particular ways, and by flaunting impenetrable circles of acquaintance, the manner in which the beau monde socialized in London actively promoted their group identity.

The public pleasure garden was an innovation that originated in eighteenth-century London.[5] Open to anyone for an affordably priced ticket, the enclosed and landscaped grounds of the most sophisticated pleasure gardens boasted promenades, sculptures, water features, illuminations, and painted transparencies, and offered al fresco evening entertainments in the summer months. Eventually such gardens were found not only in London. Other British and European cities created their own commercial competitors but, tellingly, from Paris to Bath, many gardens were named Vauxhall or Ranelagh in homage to London's most famous resorts.[6]

Vauxhall Gardens, formerly known as Spring Gardens and situated on the south side of the Thames, set the trend that many others followed. There is ample evidence that public gardens had existed on the site since the 1660s (and most likely earlier) when it was a comparatively seedy park frequented by Samuel Pepys.[7] However, it is the redesign and reopening of the gardens in the late 1720s, by the ambitious entrepreneur Jonathan Tyers, that marks the turning point scrutinized by historians (Figure 16). Carefully laid walks embellished with curiosities transformed the gardens into a space of theatrical illusion and fantasy. Musicians and singers were accommodated nightly in a central bandstand, a statue of Handel was erected in the heart of the garden, and supper boxes (where visitors could enjoy a little light refreshment) showcased work by the period's most illustrious artists.[8]

Ranelagh Gardens, Vauxhall's main metropolitan competitor, opened in 1742.[9] Planted on the north bank of the Thames and occupying a plot of similar size to Vauxhall, Ranelagh battled for a market share of

FIGURE 16 *A General Prospect of Vauxhall Gardens*, after Samuel Wale, *c.*1751, engraved for *The Universal Magazine*.

London pleasure seekers. While replicating some of Vauxhall's attractions, such as tree-lined promenades, live music and singing, fireworks displays, and masquerades, Ranelagh eschewed the more exotic installations of its rival and built a great Romanesque rotunda as its principal innovation, 'a vast amphitheatre, finely gilt, painted and illuminated into which everybody that love eating, drinking and staring is admitted' (Figure 17).[10]

For historians, much of the importance of the pleasure gardens lies in the fact that tickets not titles secured admission to their entertainments. Much has also been made of their affordability. At a shilling a go (comparable to cheap seats in the theatre), Vauxhall was theoretically accessible to those of modest means, and is usually portrayed as the more socially mixed resort. Ranelagh's higher cost of entry, at around two shillings, is seen as commensurate with its claims to being the more genteel destination, catering to a more affluent crowd. The fact that these venues lay partly or completely outdoors has also led to

FIGURE 17 *An inside view of the Rotunda in London*, 18th century.

the presumption that they were places where stifling codes of deference and decorum did not apply. Walks and surprising curiosities encouraged perambulation and chance encounters that seemed to command visitors to become part of a mobile, throbbing crowd. Cultural historians have thus emphasized the pleasure gardens' significance as stages for fluidity and social mixing.[11] Furthermore, the pleasure gardens were apparently places where social norms and identities were suspended, and where reality was blurred by artifice. Vauxhall's opening was marked by a boisterous masquerade, Ranelagh hosted masked *ridottos* (musical entertainments) as part of its regular series of diversions, and fancy-dressed guests were routinely depicted in engravings of both grounds. The gardens' dependence on whimsy also extended to showmanship and deception. Innovative mechanical trickery at Vauxhall (including simultaneously triggered lighting, *trompe l'œil* paintings, and artificial birdsong) was designed to confuse the visitor as to what was genuine and what was not. As historical geographer Miles Ogborn has argued, these illusory schemes not only generated new pleasures but also unique tensions. In the changeable world of the pleasure garden, the personages present were perhaps unknowable, complicit in a world of falsified appearances.[12] Here, if anywhere, it was believed that the prostitute could present herself as a peeress and the rake as a respectable man.

Contemporary satirists made much of the reputed diversity of the pleasure gardens' crowd. *A Trip to Vauxhall* (1737), for example, described the *mêlée* thus:

> The motley Croud we next with Care survey,
> The young, the Old, the Splen[e]tic and Gay:
> The fop emasculate, the rugged Brave,
> All jumbled here, as in the common Grave.
> Here sat a Group of 'Prentices and there,
> The awkard [sic] Daughters of a late Lord Mayor.[13]

The cast featured in *Ranelagh House: A Satire* (1747) was similarly assorted, extending from a debt-ridden nobleman to a highwayman, by way of a bluff sea captain, a smart-suited tailor, a haughty lawyer, a politician, a journalist, a prostitute, and a pickpocket.[14] Citing precisely such ready assertions of social variety, the pleasure garden has been characterized in almost exactly the same terms by historians. 'Eighteenth-century London', David Solkin writes, 'offered very few other places [than Vauxhall] where the different classes could mix more freely at such close quarters.'[15] These were the resorts, Paul Langford notes, 'not merely of high society but of pickpockets, rakes and whores'.[16] 'The mingling of classes at Vauxhall', suggested Dorothy Marshall in her earlier study of Georgian London, 'was characteristic of London as a whole.'[17] As places of unorthodox social promiscuity, the pleasure gardens might appear unlikely resorts for the people of fashion and the parade of social distinction. The fact that the gardens embraced a full social range, from aristocrat to apprentice, is presumed to be one of their greatest fascinations, but the manner in which the titled were incorporated, and the repercussions of that inclusion, have been left unaddressed.

Throughout the century, and contemporaneous with satirical jibes about their promiscuous diversity, the gardens were zealously promoted as venues to encounter the fashionable society and parade with royalty. Vauxhall was patronized by Frederick, Prince of Wales, and, through him, associated with the opposition political elite. Newspapers logged the prince's attendance. 'Their Royal Highnesses the Prince and Princess of Wales, with their Royal Highness the Duke, were last Saturday at the Spring Garden Vauxhall,' trumpeted *The Daily Post* on 21 June 1742.[18] On 23 May 1743, it was announced, '[t]heir Royal Highnesses the Prince and Princess of Wales, accompanied by several Persons of Distinction, [were] last Saturday evening at the Spring Gardens Vauxhall.'[19] Once Ranelagh opened, the prince's allegiance to Vauxhall wavered and he went to both. 'On Monday night their Royal Highnesses the Prince and Princess of Wales were at the Spring Gardens, Vauxhall,' reported *The Westminster Journal* or *New Weekly Miscellany* on 31 August 1745, and 'Last Tuesday Night their Royal Highnesses the Prince and Princess of Wales were at Ranelagh Gardens.'[20]

Alongside royal patrons, both Vauxhall and Ranelagh were also advertised as a more general rendezvous for the beau monde. The gardens' managers puffed the presence of 'the Quality', and newspapers judged the success of the gardens according to the level of elite attendance. In the 1750s, commentators noted with relish that Vauxhall was still 'mostly frequented by the Nobility and Gentry'.[21] At Ranelagh, titled patrons were to be found orchestrating special events at the gardens in the 1780s (such as the gala held by Boodle's club in 1789 to celebrate George III's return to good health). Journalists mapped the metropolitan society present at such events, listing leading figures by name: for instance, William Pitt, Lady Duncannon, the Duke and Duchess of Devonshire, and Lady Haggerston were all seen supping in 1780s Ranelagh.[22] Vauxhall, too, retained a lengthy association with named personnel. A 'Grand Rural Festival' to be held at the south bank site, patronized by the Princess of Wales, the Marchioness of Hertford, 'and many other high and very distinguished personages', was advertised in 1805.[23] In early June 1810, *The Morning Post* enthused about the brilliance of a Vauxhall night, '[t]he fine evening of Friday last... attracted a very numerous assemblage, a great proportion of whom were of the first rank and fashion.'[24]

Existing analyses of the pleasure gardens suggest the widespread reporting of elite attendance was a promotional strategy, commissioned by the gardens' managers to support the venues' claims to be respectable sites of entertainment.[25] In this regard, they are approached as well-placed puffs rather than accurate accounts.[26] These reports must certainly have functioned in some form of advertising capacity, but they can also be read as portraying London society as an identifiable set. By singling out and naming prominent individuals in this way, the newspapers presented them as an alluring spectacle, a newsworthy troupe prominent amidst an otherwise nondescript 'public' promenading in the grounds.

Significantly, an explicit linkage between exalted company and the public gardens, and an implicit suggestion that fashionable society was somehow knowable and identifiable, was not unique to press coverage and published rhetoric. The chance to catch a glimpse of the glitterati was demonstrably a major draw for other cohorts of the pleasure gardens' public. For example, when gentlewoman Dorothy Richardson left her Midlands home to see the sights of the capital in 1775, she included Vauxhall and Ranelagh in her hectic itinerary. Her subsequent descriptions of the gardens reveal that, for her, their pleasures depended almost entirely on the quality of those who frequented them. Although Vauxhall offered a more varied aesthetic experience, Richardson was disappointed by the class of visitor she found on the night of her visit. The gardens themselves were 'certainly pretty', she conceded, but the company 'too numerous and too blackguard' to be attractive. 'Curiosity tempted me once to Vauxhall but I shall scarce venture there again. The Gardens must formerly have made a fine appearance,' she mused, 'when they were the resort of the People of Fashion.'[27] In contrast, Ranelagh she found to be elegant. The company delighted her. Both 'numerous' and 'brilliant' were the other guests, Richardson noted in her journal with glee.[28] Not only did Richardson hope to share the gardens with a genteel crowd, she also expected the 'brilliant' company to be visible—a discrete company who would, and should, be seen.

It is precisely this process of distinction within the crowd that Rowlandson delineates in his famous sketch of Vauxhall (Figure 18). Highlighted in the centre foreground are two elegantly dressed women surrounded by a cluster of staring spectators. The women, it is widely

FIGURE 18 A view of Vauxhall Gardens, Thomas Rowlandson, *c*.1784, reprinted in Rudolph Ackermann, *Microcosm of London*, 1809.

73

agreed, are portrait sketches of Georgiana, Duchess of Devonshire, and her sister, Lady Duncannon. Amongst their oglers, Rowlandson apparently depicts Edward Topham, proprietor of *The World* (shown quizzing the women through a glass pressed to his eye), William Jackson of *The Morning Post* (peering out from behind a tree), and, beside him, James Perry, editor of *The Morning Chronicle* (in Highland dress).[29] In this image then—which is surely the century's most famous visual representation of Vauxhall's 'mixed' crowd—the distinctiveness of the fashionable company, and the role of the press and public in promoting that social differentiation, is explicitly realized (Figure 19).

The presence of fashionable figures at these venues can also, of course, be extracted from their own accounts. During a single week in May 1752,

FIGURE 19 Detail from a view of Vauxhall Gardens, Thomas Rowlandson, *c*.1784. The figures shown were reputedly the Duchess of Devonshire and Lady Duncannon (centre), Edward Topham, proprietor of *The World* (with the eyeglass, to the left), William Jackson of *The Morning Post* (behind the tree), and James Perry editor of *The Morning Chronicle* (in highland dress).

for example, the Marquess of Carnarvon went to the pleasure gardens on four evenings, once to Vauxhall and three times to Ranelagh.[30] In 1756, his father, Henry Brydges, 2nd Duke of Chandos, went to Ranelagh twice a week in May.[31] Later in the century, future Prime Minister William Pitt went regularly to both gardens. When, in 1781, a busy political week and long debates in the Commons meant he missed a trip to Vauxhall, he nonetheless managed to squeeze in a visit to Ranelagh.[32] In the 1790s, the Earl of Sheffield's daughter, Lady Maria Josepha Holroyd, never failed to visit the gardens on Wednesdays and Fridays throughout May, sandwiching Ranelagh excursions between two trips to the opera, two assemblies, two balls, and two concerts a week.[33] Such calendars of repeated visits are significant. Not least, these patterns have financial implications. Vauxhall's cheap entry has been key to existing historical interpretations of its social inclusivity. No doubt a single visit was comparatively affordable. What proportion of the pleasure gardens' public, though, could stretch to a twice- or even a thrice-weekly visit?

The regularity with which the metropolitan elite attended the gardens implies a widespread use of expensive and more exclusive subscription tickets. In 1738, subscriptions to Vauxhall cost twenty-five shillings, a substantial fee that undoubtedly narrowed the market.[34] Furthermore, the Marquess of Carnarvon routinely spent between five and eight shillings per night at Ranelagh, and spent that twice a week in May.[35] His monthly spend of over £3 per season just for attending the gardens (broadly equivalent to £400 today) required deep pockets. In addition, the admission fee was not the only financial cost of an evening at the pleasure gardens. For instance, and notwithstanding its lower admission charge, Vauxhall's famously overpriced refreshments may have quickly racked up the bill for the unwary, suggesting that further layers of financial division may have operated within the grounds distancing, for example, those who supped from those who did not.

Fashionable figures therefore spent more at the pleasure gardens, and attended them more frequently, than less exalted pleasure-seekers. More importantly, though, they also visited them for different reasons. The dramatic illuminations and exotic installations that thrilled provincial tourists were of only tangential interest to these *habitués*. Instead, it was company alone—and expressly and exclusively 'good' company—that drew the beau monde. In the 1760s, the Duchess of Sutherland, for example, delighted in the 'very genteel company' at Ranelagh, citing Lady Cardiff amongst those she encountered.[36] 'I think I never saw so much great company tighter,' mused Lady Mary Coke in 1767, 'I make use of that expression instead of good, for great and good are not always the same [but] there was ten Duchesses, countesses in plenty and I believe I may say hundreds of nobility.'[37] Fashionable society had no fear of encountering a disorderly social muddle. Indeed, so predictable was the crowd encountered that, in 1784, Lady Louisa Stuart met precisely the same titled troupe in the gardens as had been entertained at a private assembly at Bolton House some hours before.[38]

In a similar vein to the newspaper reports, titled commentators registered their companions and the privileged company by name. In 1765, Elizabeth Countess of Pembroke and her sister had set out to Vauxhall specifically to meet the Duke and Duchess of Bedford.[39] Lady Mary Coke was variously accompanied to the gardens by Lady Jane Scott, Lady Litchfield, Lady Dalkeith, and Lord March, and met other named nobles in the grounds. Amongst the 'sprinkling of good company' that Lady Amabel Yorke enjoyed at Ranelagh in the 1770s were Lady Buckley and Lady Carlisle, Lady Beauchamp and Lord and Lady Pelham, and the Honourable Frederick Robinson (Amabel's future brother-in-law) also promenaded with the Pelhams at Ranelagh.[40] Similarly well acquainted with the prestigious public, Lady Harriot Pitt, sister of politician William, ventured to Vauxhall with Lady St John and to Ranelagh with Lady Monson and Lord and Lady Clarendon.[41]

Rather than heading to the gardens to gaze upon a wider mob, it was the precise clustering of titled personnel present at the gardens that emerges as the principal preoccupation of the London society. Shows of acquaintance were noted and read as strategic displays of alliance and association. When Lady Mary Coke was spotted visiting Vauxhall regularly in the company of Miss Pelham and Charles Townshend in 1758, their public parades fuelled speculation about the possibility of a future marriage.[42] Indeed, finding company of similar rank was so vital that visits were cancelled if it was thought suitable companions might not be found. A late sitting of parliament kept titled men from their social engagements and ensured attendance at the gardens would be thin. In June 1781, Lady Harriot Pitt found 'a good Ranelagh' on a night when the Commons was up, but in May 1783 a late sitting at the house made her decide 'it will not be any means worthwhile to attend Ranelagh'.[43] Parties to Vauxhall were similarly disturbed: 'I cannot say ye Vauxhall party was as propitious...for ye House of Commons set late,' she reported dejectedly that same year.[44]

Mingling hardly mattered to the beau monde; if anything it was purposefully avoided. Whilst topographical perspectives show crisscrossed walks that seem designed to encourage spontaneous encounters, first-person descriptions hint at a more carefully choreographed use of the space. Opportunities for chance encounters appear to have been rare rather than the norm. At Vauxhall, for instance, instead of roaming the grounds at whim, the fashionable society more often remained sequestered for lengthy stretches in the supper boxes. When the Duchess of Devonshire was spotted at the gardens in the 1790s it was with a large party, noisily supping and facing the orchestra, 'french horns playing to them all the time'.[45] Oliver Goldsmith explored the divisive potential of supper box seating in his satirical, but wryly observant, novel, *The Citizen of the World*:

> Mr and Mrs Tibbs would sit in none but a genteel box [at Vauxhall]—a box where they might see and be seen—one, as they expressed it, in the very focus of public view; but such a box was not easy to be obtained for though we were perfectly convinced of our own gentility, and the gentility of our appearance, yet we found it a difficult matter to persuade the keepers of the boxes to be of our opinion; they chose to reserve genteel boxes for what they judged more genteel company.[46]

Goldsmith's aspirant couple found themselves sidelined and unable to jockey to the centre of the 'public view', but those boasting titled connections met with more success. Horace Walpole, for one, gives a ready account of supper box showmanship. Heading to Vauxhall in 1757 with Lady Caroline Petersham, a high-profile fashionable hostess, Walpole recorded the public impact of their exuberance and activity. 'The whole air of our party was sufficient... to take up the whole attention of the garden,' he declared, 'so much so, that from eleven o'clock till half an hour after one, we had the whole concourse round our booth.'[47] By eleven all other attractions, like the tin water mill and night time illuminations, would have long gone off, leaving the posturing of Petersham's set uncontested in their command of public attention.[48]

It is hard to find comparable accounts as lively as Wapole's tale, but a handful of brief references shed further light on broader systems of distinction and social separation. At Ranelagh in May 1767, for example, Lady Mary Coke remained an entire evening in seats in the rotunda previously occupied by Lady Litchfield and Lady Dalkeith ('Lady Litchfield and Lady Dalkeith gave us their places; where we stayed till we came away').[49] Of course, we cannot be sure of Lady Mary Coke's motivation. Inclement weather may have been as much the cause of her incarceration in the rotunda as anything else. But her passing reference to apparent place keeping, seat swapping, and the suggested immobility of her visit to the gardens is reminiscent of Lady Caroline Petersham's noisy commandeering of supper boxes at Vauxhall or, as we shall see, of the place holding and management of box seating that was standard practice in the more stratified London theatres.[50] In a similar fashion, society gossip about an affair between the Duke of Gloucester and Lady Waldegrave was given further credence when the pair was spotted sharing a Ranelagh box and then meandering about the rotunda.[51]

While the likes of Dorothy Richardson were impressed by the chance to view the *ton*, references to contact with less rarefied company are extremely rare in records written by the nobility, testifying to their determined social snobbery. Other Londoners and non-metropolitan interlopers may well have ventured into the same space at the pleasure gardens but they were shunned by the beau monde. A letter written by Lady Sarah Bunbury to Lady Susan O'Brien offers one exceptional acknowledgement of a broader public. In so doing, however, the parameters of social acquaintance and the restrictions on integration are laid bare. In the letter Lady Sarah Bunbury sets out an unexpected, and unwelcome, encounter with one Mrs Cary (possibly the wife of John Cary, a city merchant growing rich on the sale of modish globes and maps). 'I was vastly diverted with my *friendship* with Mrs Cary,' Bunbury began, underlining the word 'friendship' in her original account to hint at her satirical intent:

> You know she dined one day at the pay office. I saw her at Ranelagh one night this year & went up to make her a civil speech and that is <u>friendship</u>. As to her fashions, I am sorry to say they are but too true among the common run of people here, for such figures as one sees at public places are not to be described.[52]

Mrs Cary may have misinterpreted her brief encounter with a noble lady at a pleasure garden as a signal of greater acquaintance, but for Lady Sarah Bunbury the intercourse was incongruous. Meaningful association with the 'common run' was as ridiculous as the city fashions on display. Although there was clearly an exchange between the two women (for Bunbury deigned to offer a 'civil speech' to Mrs Cary), Lady Sarah Bunbury mocked the alleged promiscuity of public sociability, which in no way threatened or dissolved the reality of hierarchical distinctions. Once the *ton* had entered the grounds, it was very clearly the company rather than the culture that the beau monde revered, but specifically the company of those of comparable rank.

The enclosed and structured auditoria of the theatre and opera offered a very different social environment from the outdoor pleasure garden. Comparing these diverse venues allows for a more detailed investigation of the nature of fashionable sociability, but one that only adds to this picture of social segregation.

Often the first port of call for the visiting provincial tourist and urban resident alike, theatres were a long-established form of public entertainment. During the season, both theatres usually ran daily performances (excluding Sundays) with a varied repertoire ranging from Shakespearian productions to new comedies of manners. Starting at around seven p.m., an evening's schedule could run for up to five hours, with prologues and epilogues, sung performances, performed masquerades, and even additional multi-scene plays buffering the headline show. Principal performers were the masters of many characters, reprising old parts, trying out new ones, and taking on a sequence of different major roles during the course of a week to furnish a programme that changed every few nights during the season.[53]

Musical and operatic interludes were often showcased at the venues patented for plays. Major operas, though, were staged at the King's Theatre, Haymarket, every Tuesday and Saturday. Unpatented but licensed by the Lord Chamberlain, the Italian Opera, with its continental character, aristocratic patrons, and European stars, was the more prestigious form of theatre, its social cachet reflected in the generous salaries commanded by imported Italian and German performers.[54] Even the pockets of supporting staff were well lined. A specialist Italian tailor affiliated to the opera in 1741 was enticed with a life-changing stipend of £400 for the year.[55] With running costs, scenes, salaries, and costumes that far outweighed box office takings, the opera depended on a subscription system (whereby individuals 'owned' a box for a season) to establish start-up capital every autumn. Even then it routinely ran at a bankrupting loss. Yet, buoyed by bottomless aristocratic investment, the opera kept re-emerging from crippling debts until, by the end of the century, it was firmly established as a leading if not an especially lucrative part of London's world of entertainment.[56]

The experience of attending the theatre or the opera was certainly very different from that of strolling around the pleasure garden. Within a theatre's auditorium the structural hierarchy of boxes, pit, and the galleries imposed status-oriented divisions on the audience from the start. Unsurprisingly, for both theatre and opera, box tickets were the most expensive seats in the house. *The Man of Pleasure's Pocket Book* (1780) warned that the average cost of a single theatre box ticket was five shillings, a ticket for the pit cost three shillings and the cheaper gallery seats between one and two shillings per head, much the same price as they had been at the start of the century.[57] Boxes for opera performances were, theoretically at least, only available by seasonal subscription and, in 1780, a seasonal subscription cost a steep twenty guineas (420 shillings), and half a guinea secured a pit seat for a single performance. Even a gallery seat at the opera cost five shillings a time, or ten shillings a week for those keen to attend both performances.[58]

Although information about seat prices is easily located, precise data on audience demography, particularly for stage plays, has proved harder for historians to retrieve. Theatre box office takings survive but it is almost impossible to ascertain exactly who sat in each seat and who

FIGURE 20 An audience watching a play at Drury Lane Theatre, Thomas Rowlandson, 1785.

paid one shilling, two shillings, or more. Anecdotal references have therefore been used to flesh out the balance sheets, leading historians to conclude that stage play auditoria were packed with all ages, classes, and occupations.[59] The gentry and nobility inevitably occupied the boxes ringing the pit (Figure 20). The pit attracted a mix of peers, gentry, merchants, artists, and others of the middling sort. The galleries comprised the seating furthest away from the stage (with a seat in the lower level costing approximately 1s. 6d., and 1s. in the upper level) and housed the most humble spectators, including, it is suggested, apprentices, servants, and prostitutes.[60]

In contrast to the mixed crowd that hustled in to the playhouse, the opera at the King's Theatre was proudly aristocratic. Published and unpublished subscription lists provide more systematic data on the opera's audience than is available for the playhouse, and testify to the fact that most seats were filled with high-ranking personnel (Figure 21).[61] Carole Taylor's important analysis of the early eighteenth-century

FIGURE 21 Fan showing a plan of the boxes at the opera with a list of their subscribers, 1788.

audience identified 130 individuals who were long-term subscribers, 72 per cent of whom were titled with the remainder untitled relatives, MPs, or government officials.[62] By the closing decades of the century, popularity for the opera was at its peak, but even then it was predominantly the titled who populated the auditorium. Some well-heeled parvenus secured a space but, as Jennifer Hall Witt has demonstrated, a swelling audience from the 1780s did not change the social equilibrium. It was an increasing number of nobles rather than an increasing number of bourgeois professionals who made up the numbers.[63]

Due to its aristocratic credentials, musicologists and opera historians compare the King's Theatre to a private club, exclusive in its membership and tightly controlled. That it attracted a community of closely connected individuals is confirmed by William Weber's remarkable discovery that over three-quarters of the 350 subscribers to box seats at the opera in 1783 were individually named in Lady Mary Coke's diary for that year.[64] Moreover, a principal subscriber could 'claim' a box year after year until they chose to relinquish their rights, ensuring formality, longevity, and consistency in the seating arrangements season after season. Hall Witt has revealed the rigidity of this system, noting that 57 per cent of subscribers in 1797 were still in the same box five years later, and between 1804 and 1805 an incredible 88 per cent of principal subscribers retained their box.[65] Even without crunching the figures, a glance at the lists soon reveals continuities. The Duchess of Rutland, for example, retained her box for at least ten years, appearing in both the 1797 and 1807 lists in the same location. The Earl and Countess of Jersey were listed as box subscribers in the 1797 lists and appeared a decade later in the 1807 register, as did the Earl and Countess of Chesterfield, the Duke of Bedford, and many others besides.[66] Not only did the opera's audience return to their seats week after week, it seems probable that a significant number occupied them for a generation. Without question, the vast majority of those present at the opera were known to each other, with the minority outside that closely woven network rendered a glaring exception that proved the rule.

Despite these marked demographic distinctions, both the opera and the playhouse predominate in personal accounts of life in 'the town'. Engagement diaries kept by Elizabeth, Duchess of Grafton, in the 1790s reveal that of all London's public resorts it was the playhouse and opera that she most frequented. For the quarter century covered by her diaries, the duchess on average attended the opera five times more often and the play three times more often than she ventured to subscription concerts, subscription assemblies, or the pleasure gardens.[67] Others were committed to a similar regime. Viscount Barrington visited a playhouse on no less than seven of the fourteen evenings he spent in London in September 1777. In that month, the opera was not yet open but by November the imported divas and castrati had taken to the stage, and over four weeks the viscount went to the opera four times and the play twice.[68] Surviving accounts for the early eighteenth century suggest a comparable routine. James Brydges (later 1st Duke of Chandos) was a regular visitor to the plays in the 1690s and Henry Grey, 12th Earl of Kent (later Duke of Kent), averaged between four and six excursions to the opera and play during each month of the season in the same decade.[69]

As with repeated attendance to the pleasure gardens, routine visits to both the play and opera were pricey. The Duke of Kent's excursions were recorded in personal account books that catalogued his monthly expenses. Excluding the cost of transport home (usually one shilling for a hackney carriage), his 1690s theatre habit cost an average of twenty-five shillings per month. This was only 2 per cent of his overall monthly outlay and a snip in comparison to the broader expenses of maintaining a flashy London life, but such expenditure was beyond the reach of the vast majority. If we presume that the London season lasted an average of six months, then such attendance would cost approximately 150 shillings (over £7) per year. When Viscount Barrington made seven visits to the playhouse over a fortnight in 1777, his outlay would have reached at least twenty-one shillings, paying three shillings for a pit seat for each visit. He did not record where in the auditorium he chose to sit but if Barrington opted for a box seat then the cost would have rocketed to thirty-five shillings for those visits alone, meaning he probably spent in the region of seventy shillings (over £3) each month.

The opera was even more prohibitive in price. Hall Witt has noted that the average peer with £2,800 disposable income per annum would need to invest just over 1 per cent of that income to fund a box subscription (at twenty guineas per person per annum) for himself and his wife. Tellingly, a solicitor with a respectable pay of £140 per annum would need to spend the same percentage of his income for himself and his wife to visit the opera only twice during the season, and even then they would only be able to afford a seat in the pit.[70] For certain visitors of respectable means attending the opera was a possibility, and tourists' travel journals tell of the dazzling thrill of the one-off operatic treat. The cost of regular attendance, however, was in a different league. Even the cheaper playhouse rapidly became a luxury when repeat visits were made and box seats secured.

The cash investment demanded by these social routines reveals one important part of the story, but it is not the whole story. The widespread practice of lending tickets and sharing subscriptions meant that it was quite possible for a theatre seat to have been acquired free of any charge, or at a significant reduction on market price. Crucially, the social capital required to participate in such exchanges was a far rarer currency than ready money. Lady Mary Coke's diary, for example, is replete with routine references to the begging and borrowing of tickets that was rife amongst close acquaintances. In February 1767, she secured seats in the opera boxes of Lady Hertford, Lady Strafford, and the Duchess of Bedford as well as in a box she described as 'ours', and she was decidedly affronted when a request to Lady Howe for a seat in a box at the play did not meet with a successful response. 'I've wrote to L[ad]y Howe to try if I can persuade her to give me a place in her box at the Drury Lane playhouse tomorrow night. She sends me word she does not go & has no box. I think her answer rather short,' Coke recorded tartly, 'especially as she told me she always had a box.'[71]

Frantic negotiations to share subscriptions to opera boxes emerge as a seasonal theme in contemporary correspondence. Year after year, the Grey family debated how best to manage their box. In 1782, the question at hand was whether the recently married Mary, Lady Grantham (daughter of Jemima, Marchioness Grey), would be able to share a subscription with her sister. Lady Grantham's involvement required the permission of her husband, who not only agreed to her expenditure but was himself persuaded to share the cost of the subscription with his wife for a single seat. By 1793, Lady Grantham (now married for a decade) took control of the box subscriptions, sharing a ticket with her mother and also attempting to move to a different box for the season. She rejected the offer of a larger box previously used by Lady Hampden for fear that they would not have enough suitable joint subscribers. The Greys noted with admiration that Lady Hampden herself had moved to a lower (and therefore socially more prestigious) tier.[72] In 1805, Lady Grantham and her sister, Amabel, were once again distracted by their opera plans. Wanting to divide a single subscription between them they considered an offer by Lady Breadalbane to take over her subscription for a short part of the season whilst she remained in Scotland. Another option, that of subscribing to box number eleven, was quickly rejected for being 'a very bad box, not worth much or taking for a long period [as] the last box on the row'.[73] The sisters preferred box number twelve but feared it was too costly. A cheaper alternative was to follow up a newspaper advertisement from one subscriber but, on further enquiry, the sisters discovered the sale only entitled them to access every second week and in a box on the less prestigious second tier.[74]

Finding the right type of company for a shared subscription, and securing a box in the most desirable part of the auditorium, was sometimes vexing. In 1793, Lady Stafford teased her daughter, Charlotte, for 'being so nice in the choice of subscribers to our box when you cannot get of any sort', and forwarded a suggestion from her sister to try Lord Gower. 'I think it a good thought', she strongly affirmed.[75] A few years later, Lady Stafford's other daughter, Susan, rejected an offer to share a playhouse box with the Duchess of Devonshire on account of the duchess's open patronage of Charles James Fox's wife, Elizabeth Armistead. A former high-society courtesan and Fox's long-term mistress, Armistead was a surprising spouse for the colourful politician. Married in private in 1795, the scandalous union had been kept secret until the early 1800s. Lady Stafford vociferously condemned the duchess's open visiting of Mrs Fox, suggesting it transgressed social protocols and polite behaviour. 'This shameful conduct of the Dss. of Devon patronizing and countenancing vice and the vicious is most truly wicked,' she declared, '…how woefully has her Grace's conduct proved the fatal effects of a dissipated life….I am very sorry for her. She profess's Susan to belong to her play house box, to which Susan was not inclin'd though she long to belong to a box with pleasant unscandalized people & Ld Har[rowby] has too right a way of thinking to wish his wife to appear intimate with so blasted a character.'[76]

Such accounts vividly illustrate the importance ascribed to both location and to company.[77] The theatre and opera boxes most highly prized by the beau monde were those closest to the stage where the view of the performance was constrained but their view of the audience, and visibility to that audience, was maximized. Much earlier, in 1711, Sarah, Duchess of Marlborough, had favoured the majestic accommodation of the stage box at the theatre. Buttressing the players' boards, this box was perfectly placed for a public show of fashionable exclusivity. Her presence in a box that was primarily, but not exclusively, associated with royalty was also commented upon by others. Not infrequently, and particularly for benefit shows, additional seating was placed on the stage itself. Positioned behind and around the actors, the audience were both part of the set and part of the supporting cast. Here again, we find the indomitable Duchess of Marlborough spotted by Lady Pembroke who wrote the following day in confirmation of her visibility, 'I did se[e] you yesterday at the play but,' she noted in shared acknowledgement of the rigours of a fashionable life, 'I easily believe you were heartily tired and very hott the stage was so crowded.'[78]

In contrast, Gertrude Savile was a regular theatre-goer in the 1720s but, lacking the means or connections to subscribe to season tickets or secure box seats, she usually viewed the play from the galleries or pit, where she was less likely to be seen and felt herself comforted by a cloak of anonymity. Occasionally, family obligation demanded that she accompany more esteemed kin to the theatre to cement connections. On these trips Savile found the act of theatre-going to be primarily about the show of status, rather than the enjoyment of the entertainment. Attending the famous *Beggar's Opera* with Lady Castlemaine in March 1728, Savile was perturbed that her company, with a 'quality air', did not even take their seats at the theatre until the performance was nearly over. Moreover, a mistake by Lady Castlemaine's footman meant too few seats had been reserved for the party and Savile, as one of the lowest-ranking members of the group, was separated from her company, forced to wait until box-keepers were sure that other ticket-holders were not about to arrive, and was only shown to a seat in a cramped back corner of a different box over an hour later. From her uncomfortable vantage point, poor Savile lamented that she 'saw nobody I knew, nor any of fashion [*sic*]. The stage was crowded with sad folks; here were people of Quality, beside the Countiss I went with, but out of my sight.'[79]

Once a seat was secured—whether by a sole subscription, a shared subscription, a gift from a friend, or by purchasing a single ticket—the audience was not necessarily static. Men in particular were permitted to roam between sections of the auditorium. Their diaries routinely record the company seen and encountered within the audience, with very little mention of what happened on the stage. In his diaries from the 1690s and early 1700s, James Brydges, 1st Duke of Chandos, focused almost entirely on the company met. For example, on Monday 15 February 1697 he noted, 'went to ye playhouse in Covent Garden where I met Mr Knight, after which I went to ye other playhouse & there saw Sr Charles Barriston & Mr Mildmay. Before ye play was done I came hence home.' In a similar fashion, on 29 January 1700, he 'went to ye playhouse in Lincolns Inn fields & saw my Cozen Hussy and Coz [cousin] Roberts there I staid an act & then went to see Mr Gore.'[80] In

1756, Henry Fox wrote a brief note to his wife Caroline which betrayed the specific social purpose that informed his visit to the play, a visit undertaken so late in the evening the performance was practically over: 'I am just come from the play where I went about a quarter of an hour before it ended to see the Countess who looks & is very pert & well. She was with L[ad]y Hester Pitt whose husband has not shone of late.'[81] In the 1770s, Frederick Robinson used the opera as a key location to meet acquaintances and gather news for his brother, then ambassador to Madrid. The opera itself, he explained, 'is long & dull & the dances bad, but I always go as I am sure to meet all my acquaintance of all sorts there'.[82]

Both play and opera then were spaces used to cement interpersonal acquaintances and consolidate group networks. With social encounters so carefully managed, subtle associations and subdivisions were extrapolated by metropolitan elite observers from the social performances of their equals. For the beau monde, insider knowledge and regular attendance ensured that a range of prized information might be gleaned by monitoring subtle social movements in the theatre's auditorium. For example, public resorts served as a particularly important barometer of the marriage market. Jemima, Marchioness Grey's two daughters routinely swapped excited updates on the conquests and amours of the fashionable world using information drawn from their visits to the opera. '[T]hough the House was not full', wrote Lady Mary in 1775, 'there was a sprinkling of the beau monde',

[A]s to matches it is said Colonel Luttrell is to marry Miss Elwell Lady Ranelagh's daughter...Miss Duncombe you may remember was to have married two years ago has lately run off with a Mr Beauwater. Some say her friends disapproved the gentleman others they that they approved him but could not make the settlements till she was of age, which though it was only Christmas she thought too long to wait and chose a more expeditious method. She appeared last Tuesday in an upper box at the Opera pour se montre avec son mari [to show herself with her husband] I suppose for he was with her.[83]

Society knew a woman was to be wed once she had shared a box with her beau. The opera or play was as good as an altar for making and promoting a match.

Such was the social power of an appearance at the theatre that it was also deployed strategically to counter damaging rumours rather than merely showcase a connection. In 1778, when gossip mounted that Lady Derby was having an affair with the Duke of Dorset, her mother the Duchess of Argyll attempted to brazen out the scandal by accompanying her daughter to the opera and showing the world the family had nothing to hide. London society looked on with interest. As recorded by Lady Mary Coke: 'This day sen'night the Dutchess of Argyll came to the Opera with Lady Derby to the surprise & concern of everybody that wish'd her well, the Tuesday after she came again when their Majesties were there but sat in the front Boxes & Lady Derby opposite to the King & Queen, all this is talk'd of in the manner you may guess.'[84] The ever-watchful Jemima, Marchioness Grey, similarly made a disapproving note of Lady Derby's opera presence, engineered, it would seem, to challenge society's judgement on her conduct. Individually, such disjointed references might be easily overlooked as trivial snapshots of social frivolity.[85] The fact, though, that such instances were routinely found repeated by different correspondents in disparate collections testifies to both the insider knowledge that operated within this social world, and the perceived significance of these public performances.

The public displays enacted at the theatre could also be of a distinctly political hue. In the heat of party divisions in the 1710s, Anne, Countess of Strafford, interpreted and reported patterns of social attendance at the theatre and opera as potential signals of allegiances and shifts in political mood. In March 1712, she explained to her husband that the fallout of recent announcements of court and ministerial appointments reverberated in the auditorium of the opera: 'L[or]d Scarsdale is so Angry that he has noe place that he declares he will turn Whigg & as a mark of that he led the Duchess of Marlborough out of the Opera.'[86] And it was not only through a fleeting display of acquaintance that the play or opera could become a political arena. On another occasion in the same year, the Countess of Strafford recorded a 'play to day at Drury Lain for all the Whigg toasts'.[87] The Tory countess did not herself attend, for the playhouse was effectively draped in party colours. In 1711, Lady Hervey had warned her husband she might be engaged and away from home on his return to London after being 'mightily solicited for the Opera for the Benefit of Pilosta who has a great interest made against her because she came from Hanover and has so many Whig friends'.[88] Fearful that the benefit would be boycotted by the Tories, the Whiggish Lady Hervey claimed she felt obliged to attend.[89] As the work of Elaine Chalus and others has demonstrated, London's theatres, and indeed other social resorts, were retained in the political landscape of the metropolitan elite in the second half of the century.[90] The Duchess of Devonshire, for instance, recorded how the opera audience was politically divided during the furore over the 1784 Westminster election, and representatives of William Pitt (Tory) and Charles James Fox (Whig) hurled insults at each other across the auditorium. 'It was very full and I had several good political fights,' the duchess noted with relish.[91]

Unsurprisingly, the social and political information gleaned at the theatre was often closely intertwined. Writing to his father after a visit to the opera in 1769, Richard, Lord Temple, revealed just such a collision of social and political news:

> The political barometer is full. The D[uke] of Grafton exhibited last night almost as much love and tenderness to his future Bride in the exalted box of the Dutchess of Bedford as he manifested last year in the humble Pit to that Divinity Nancy Parsons...This marriage connects him I think very closely with the Bedfords whom he is to govern or who are to govern him. In that light, as unconnection was his only strength at St James's, connection may prove his weakness. The Butes may be alarmed.[92]

This was a display with a complicated back story. In 1767, a few years before this public appearance, the Duke of Grafton (then prime minister) had engineered a ministerial coalition with Bedford, breaking a vociferous opposition and incorporating the Bedford Whig faction into government. The eventual making of a marriage seemed to confirm that a longstanding political relationship had been forged. It was no coincidence that Grafton's intended, Elizabeth Wrottesley, was niece of the powerful 51-year-old matron Gertrude, Duchess of Bedford. With a divorce from his first wife in hand, Grafton had cast off his mistress, Nancy Parsons, and taken up a more respectable and politic match. Lady Mary Coke corroborated the presumed political underpinnings of the marriage. 'His Grace [the Duke of Grafton] I think intends to continue first minister, every step he takes seems to be with that view', she noted, 'tho' he might have other motives for his marriage, nobody I think doubts but that one of them was to secure the Duke of Bedford and his party to his interest.'[93]

The theatre, then, like the pleasure garden was used in a range of strategic ways by fashionable society. The theatre, with its commercial spirit, its home-grown talent, its mixed repertoire, and its reputation for social diversity, is read as a representation and expression of a broader polity and a national institution. The opera, with its continental character, imported stars, unprofitable programmes, and aristocratic hue, is cast as the opposing character, the 'other' of the theatre world but all the more glamorous for its exceptional status. The nobility, however, did not eschew one form of entertainment and restrict their attendance to another. Instead the titled world can be found to have routinely and consistently frequented both the opera and stage plays. Echoing the division between Ranelagh and Vauxhall, it is not surprising to find that the opera featured more regularly than plays in the social timetables of London's fashionable world, but this should not lead us to overlook the ongoing significance of the theatres royal. Both the opera house and playhouses are revealed to have proved viable and valuable arenas for the beau monde's own staged displays.

It is striking that investigating the theatre from the perspective of the fashionable elite sheds very little light on the rich cultural legacy for which the eighteenth-century playhouses and opera were renowned. David Garrick's ambitious entrepreneurialism and talent, for example, ensures he is one of the best-known figures from the eighteenth-century theatre world. Existing histories also illuminate the social and cultural acclaim and status awarded to the period's leading ladies, flagging the centrality of an artistic culture to London's fashionable world.[94] Yet this important supporting cast rarely features in the ordinary and routine reflections of the titled. This is not to suggest that such figures are entirely absent or ignored. David Garrick's friendship with the Earl and Countess Spencer is well recorded and there were certainly important patronage networks linking artists and aristocrats across the theatrical community. However, as represented in the elite's own records, the systems of sociability that structured the world of fashion placed such contacts at the periphery rather than at the centre of the social world. For them, the theatre functioned as an extra-parliamentary arena, as an extension of the patrician drawing room, as another manifestation of a members' club and as a showcase for the marriage market. The way in which the beau monde used such resorts demanded routine attendance and an understanding of networks woven from knowledge and practices built up over generations. In the hierarchically ordered auditoria, such public display permitted parades of social and political conflicts and alliances that were targeted at other privileged participants. At the same time, however, such displays also served as corporate shows of exclusivity aimed at a broader audience.

The nature and structure of fashionable society can only be appreciated in its proper dimensions if these disparate locations of pleasure gardens, theatres, and also more private entertainments are joined together. It was this mosaic of activities that defined the beau monde, rather than any of them by themselves. On 11 June 1765, Elizabeth Herbert, Countess of Pembroke, totted up her planned excursions in a letter to Lady Susan Stewart. In self-mocking acknowledgement of her comparative restraint she declared, on Saturday 'I went *only* to the Opera'. Expanding on the schedule that awaited her, the countess explained she was to 'meet the Bedfords at Vauxhall on Wednesday...On Friday I think it would be best to go to Ranelagh and walk in the gardens...and perhaps to Vauxhall on Saturday after the Opera'.[95] Such a pattern of busy sociability and time-tabled attendance at the same venues is typical of the social routine of those resident in London for the season. Certainly, the accounts this chapter draws upon are shadowy and defy easy interpretation. While references to social excursions were routinely made they were also typically brief, functional, and, to the modern reader, easily missed. George, 2nd Earl Spencer's hasty reminder that he was 'now to the concert in Hanover Square'—added midway through a letter to his mother written in April 1785—is characteristically succinct. In comparison, the Honourable Frederick Robinson's mention of a visit to Ranelagh pleasure garden in 1778—'at Ranelagh last night with Lord Pelham and Tom it was very full'—verges on the effusive for its reference of place, company, and atmosphere.

Such material poses particular challenges for the historian. Traces of social calendars have to be chiselled out and broad trends extrapolated from fractured references scattered throughout an individual's lifetime of letters. Yet the value of such reports lies precisely in their brevity. They are characteristically concise because, for fashionable society, excursions to public resorts were unremarkably routine, repeated week after week, season after season, year after year. Whereas an awe-struck tourist might transcribe lengthy accounts of trips to gardens, theatres, and exhibitions, filling page after page of a travel journal purchased specifically for the purpose, the regular visitor did not.

A remarkable series of memorandum books kept by the Duchess of Grafton allows us to penetrate a little further into what was a mundane and quotidian reality for fashionable figures. Logging her daily London excursions over a twenty-five-year period, they reveal a relentless round of sociability.[96] In 1789, the year of the first surviving diary, the duchess spent three and a half months in London. During this time barely a day passed without company. Each week she attended at least one concert, ventured to the opera twice, and went repeatedly to the theatre. Almost every day brought a different assembly or 'small party' hosted by an acquaintance.[97] With the exception of Sundays, which she devoted to church, and the occasional day spent at home 'a little unwell', the Duchess of Grafton sallied forth, routinely combining multiple public diversions with private entertainments in a single night. The ritualized nature as well as the sheer scale of her social life is striking. Opera nights were always Tuesdays or Saturdays, theatre or concert excursions were most often undertaken on Thursdays, and titled hostesses timetabled their assemblies to prevent a clash. Lady Horton held hers on a Wednesday whilst the Dowager Duchess of Chandos opened her doors every Tuesday (after the opera). The peeresses threw their parties every week, and the Duchess of Grafton dutifully attended.[98]

Few match the Duchess of Grafton's administrative efficiency, but many other personal diaries reveal similar social routines built on habitual excursions and an ordered schedule of social engagements (Figures 22 and 23). William, 2nd Viscount Barrington, for instance, kept a fourteen-year run of memorandum books from 1777 onwards. He struggled to apply himself to his record and over half the entries consist of one simple confession: 'forgot.'[99] Still, for those days when he was able to recall how his time had been spent, a packed rota of public and private engagements emerges, with weekly opera and theatre attendance appearing alongside daily dinner appointments and visits to his club. Earlier accounts reveal comparable patterns of repet-

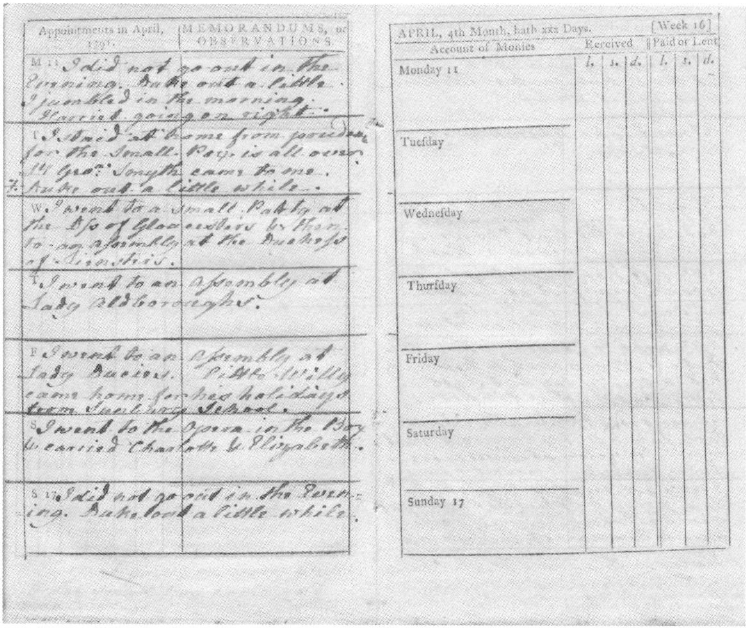

FIGURE 22 Page from Elizabeth, Duchess of Grafton's engagement diary, April 1791.

itive and timetabled sociability. Each May during the 1730s, Lord Egmont, for example, alternated visits to Vauxhall and Ranelagh in between weekly attendance at the opera and theatre and attended private parties at domestic residences almost every day of the week.[100] Needless to say, this varied, structured, and incessant routine demanded financial resources of a quite different order from those required for a twice-yearly trip to the pleasure gardens by one of London's middling visitors.

For those who observed, or believed they observed, fashionable society at play, this heady round of sociability was often taken as evidence of vacuous and pointless frivolity. For the beau monde, however, this lattice of events was the indispensable raw material from which they

FIGURE 23 Endpapers from the engagement diary of James Brydges, 3rd Duke of Chandos, 1786.

fashioned and re-fashioned personal connections and social networks. In this regard, the primary function of participating in these occasions was the rich, complex, and inward-looking articulation of group identity. At the same time, played out under the public gaze, such sociability allowed the beau monde to parade their distinction and exclusivity.[101] It was no surprise that Godfrey Bosville found London's public pleasure grounds riddled with division. The appearance of public togetherness disguised a reality wherein the titled lady dismissed the wife of a city merchant, and a wealthy Yorkshire gentleman rarely conversed with a lord.

3

The court and fashionable display
'Most tastefully spangled'

As you're settl'd among us, I know 'tis expected,
(and indeed I opine has too long been neglected),
That at Court you appear, as your person and fashion,
Will surprise and inflame all the Ladies with passion,
To court your acquaintance the Nobles will flock,
As they know you're deriv'd from a true ancient stock.
…
'Twas certainly right on this bustling day,
With hacks on the sides, thus to cram up the way;
They serve to embank us, a proper line to keep,
I wish they had rang'd but another row deep,
We shou'd then have stood longer, I ne'er could be tir'd,
Of hearing my carriage, and liv'ries admir'd.
With bustling and struggling, and jolting and clatter,
(A few vulgars run over, but that's no great matter).
…
[F]orward we mov'd amidst the Ladies and Lords,
A charming confusion; hoops, trimmings and swords,
As they mingled together delightfully tangled,
No doubt the whole floor was most tastefully spangled,
Lace, tissue and gauze, flowers, feathers and foil,
So pleasant a romp I hadn't had a great while.

(J. Moser, 'The Birth Day; or, a Squeeze
at St Jame's', *Adventures of Timothy Twigg*, 1794)

At least three times a year London's pickpockets rejoiced. The royal birthdays of the king, queen, and the heir apparent brought easy pickings for the efficient thief. As dense crowds surrounded the palace gates, pocket watches, money, bracelets, rings, handkerchiefs, gloves, ribbons, buttons, pomanders, patch boxes, and snuff boxes were stealthily separated from their owners. For days following the commemorations, pawnshops glistened with contraband booty and newspaper advertisements promised rewards for the safe return of precious lost property. Very occasionally an unlucky robber was hauled before the Old Bailey. Such was the misfortune of former sailor William Harvey, indicted in 1751 for stealing a silver watch from one Samuel Sunderland in a throng surrounding the Prince of Wales's Leicester House residence. Reported by a pawnbroker's servant and apprehended by constable Christopher Cammel, the court found him guilty and issued a sentence of seven years transportation. For hard-up William Harvey the metropolitan celebrations that marked the Prince's birthday brought an unhappy fate.[1]

Petty crime and urban pawnshops offer an unlikely backdrop to London's royal court and royal celebrations, and their perpetrators and proprietors lived a world apart from the privileged beau monde. Yet stories such as William Harvey's testify, indirectly but still evocatively, to the existence of lively crowds drawn to royal residences at moments of court ceremony. What enticed the numbers was not simply the hope of glimpsing majesty, for there was no guarantee that the monarch would make a public appearance. Nor was it necessarily a straightforward expression of loyalty, for not all subjects were willing to bow to the post-Glorious Revolution monarchy. Instead, a main draw was the glamorous parade of crested carriages, liveried footmen, and their noble employers resplendent in court dress.

The ceremony of going to court formed a staple component of metropolitan elite life, and the royal palaces comprised yet another venue in the many-centred map of urban resorts frequented by the beau monde. Significantly, much like other aspects of fashionable London life, attendance at major court events—such as royal birthdays or anniversary celebrations of successions and coronations—was a public act performed under the gaze of a wider audience. Law student and ambitious young politician George Canning, for example, squeezed into the crowds in 1794 to see the traffic heading to court, and was uncharitably amused by the sight of a robust matron with 'the most formidable head-dress and bust' prising herself from the wreckage of a carriage overturned in the mayhem.[2] For those unable to witness the spectacle in person, newspapers provided lengthy reports of the street-level show and its most striking participants.

Notably, one aspect of these parades was subject to particular journalistic attention: the ornate appearance of the clothing worn by those processing to court. From its first issue, *The Gentleman's Magazine*, for example, printed extensive sartorial reports. In a report from March 1731, it declared Lord Portmore to have been attired in the 'richest dress' of all the company present, but also admired the 'flower'd Muslin' worn by the queen.[3] The magazine retained the practice of cataloguing court clothing at the end of the century, publishing an account in January 1790 which described in meticulous detail the clothing of twenty-five titled men and women. The princess royal's 'particularly elegant' birthday gown with its riotously decorated petticoat was especially admired, and the magazine published a detailed description of the fabric: 'striped with wreaths of laurel embroidered on crape, intermixed with purple foil that appeared like a worm twisted round the wreath…the space between the stripes covered with small embroidery in gold and coloured foil.'[4] Embroidered, striped, embossed in gold, adorned with twisted foil, no detail of the dress was too small to escape the eye of the fashion-conscious journalist. *The Gentleman's Magazine* was far from singular in its obsession with court attire. *The Times* likewise addressed court clothing in comparable terms amidst its routine reporting, as did the *St James's Chronicle*, *Morning Herald*,

Telegraph, *Bath Chronicle*, and many other regional and national newspapers throughout the century.[5]

The pronounced interest in courtly wardrobes evident in print can also be found echoed in unpublished accounts incorporated in manuscript letters. Lady Frances Bathurst, for instance, sent notes to the Duchess of Marlborough describing dresses at the court of William III and Queen Mary in 1692.[6] In the 1710s, Thomas Wentworth, Earl of Strafford, received court dress reports from his wife Anne, Countess of Strafford, and his brother, Peter Wentworth.[7] One four-page letter received by Lady Anne Campbell in the 1730s was entirely devoted to the dresses seen at a birthday court, and itemized the attire of over forty-five different figures. In this account, Lady Deloraine's gown was declared the 'handsomest' whilst Lady Pembroke's choice of a 'dark green ground [with] yellow flowers' was panned for being 'as thick as a board and ye ugliest thing', and the writer was perplexed by Lady Cardigan's eccentric attire, 'with a sleeve of her own invention contrived to look as if her arms were pinion'd'. Of the men, Lord Holderness's 'brown coat with cuffs', offset with a scintillating waistcoat with 'gold stares upon something blue', met with approval. Overall, the conscientious writer concluded that there were, disappointingly, 'a vast number of old clothes', with the exception of Lord and Lady Shannon who were both dressed 'clean and new'.[8] Other reports included similar judgements on the style and 'newness' of the clothing worn. Lady Hertford regularly sent her correspondents details of court attire, noting in 1742, for example, the fine 'white satin' gown of Lady Caroline Lennox, 'embroidered with gold and colors [*sic*]' and Lady Brooke's 'pretty stuff of silver and colors upon yellow ground'.[9] Lord Egmont noted in his diary each occasion when he and his family wore new clothes to the courts of George II and Frederick, Prince of Wales, and also recorded the clothes worn by others.[10] In the 1770s, Molly Hood included descriptions of court clothing in letters to her friend Hester Pitt, Lady Chatham, and Lady Mary Yorke sent her sister, mother, and other correspondents lengthy accounts of dresses seen at the court of George III and Queen Charlotte.[11] Monarchs came and went but a fascination with who wore what to court lingered.

What, though, did this preoccupation with court attendance, and particularly with the fashions displayed at court, signify? As the following discussion explores, this contemporary interest in the company attending royal events and the appearance of that company brings into focus the nature of the beau monde's relationship to the court. What constituted 'the court' in the eighteenth century can, of course, be variously interpreted and defined. In this analysis, the court is approached as a venue and a physical location of fashionable display, rather than as an arm of state authority. Certainly this definition only offers one view of the operation of the royal institution and of its relationship to the eighteenth-century nobility. It tells us little about the administrative infrastructure of the court, the experience of servitude and office-holding or of broader contemporary ideals of kingship.[12] However, it is the pattern and significance of court attendance and the widespread publicity such attendance generated which is the focus here. The act of 'going to court' rested on longstanding customs. On the one hand, it aligned the beau monde to a prestige system rooted in lineage, heritage, crown, and constitution. Yet, it also functioned as another form of metropolitan sociability. In addition, the widespread reports that circulated detailing the costumes worn to court reveal that court attendance operated as a moment of specific and conspicuous fashionable display. It was a type of display, though, that had a particular political and not just a sartorial significance. The dresses worn to court were minutely scrutinized because they often broadcast political positions, and were used to communicate loyalty and also opposition to the crown. In this way, both court attendance and court dress became a vehicle for the political agendas of London's beau monde.

✦

The loss of Whitehall Palace to fire in 1698 left the eighteenth-century royal court without a majestic address.[13] A warren of lodgings, offices, public rooms, and recreation spaces (including four tennis courts, a cockpit, and a tiltyard for jousting), and housing crown, courtiers, an army of servants, and all the machinery of state, the mega-palace of Whitehall had occupied a twenty-three-acre campus in the heart of the capital. Initially designed by Henry VIII as a chivalric fantasy adorned with turrets, battlements, and heraldic beasts, it is believed that Whitehall as it stood in the 1690s was the largest palace in Europe: an internationally recognized symbol of state power.[14] After the palace's accidental destruction, the residences and rituals of the eighteenth-century court were split between multiple satellite buildings: Kensington Palace, St James's Palace, and the Queen's House (later Buckingham Palace) in London; as well as Windsor Castle and the Tudor pile of Hampton Court, which were both a day's ride away. All were modest in comparison to the centrally located Whitehall—only Hampton Court came close to its scale—and none of the London palaces was large enough to retain full retinues for all members of the royal family and to host the ceremonies of court. In consequence, rather than consisting of a single ghetto marked out by a turreted boundary wall, 'the court' in the eighteenth century consisted of a constellation of smaller residences dispersed across a wider metropolitan map.

The lack of a grand palace after 1698 was long cited by historians as material testament of the court's dwindling role in Britain's constitution and culture. Whereas European monarchs promoted their power through ostentatious powerhouses, such as Versailles and the Royal Palace of Madrid, Britain's monarchs had to make do with low-key living that echoed the restrictions placed on their prerogative after the Glorious Revolution. To a significant degree, the traditional 'whig' conception of the century as a moment of emerging political and cultural modernity has rested on a picture of royal constraint.

In this context, the court was perceived as a dreary irrelevance to the period's more exciting history of political and commercial development. An independent parliament, it was asserted, was able to mature precisely because there was no autocratic monarch to stifle its growth. In addition, the abject failure of the royal court to provide adequate entertainment or patronage of the arts was presumed to have been a boon to the burgeoning commercial sector that was strengthening beyond the palace walls. Whereas the Tudor and early Stuart kings cultivated courtly magnificence through spectacular masques and fêtes, their successors allegedly succeeded only in presiding over what G. M. Trevelyan famously damned as 'occasions of proverbial dullness'. Even the nobility were said to have been seduced by the brighter lights of London's leisure industry, preferring the temptations of Ranelagh to the tedium of the royal house.[15]

More recently, the assumption that the court necessarily declined has come to be questioned and substantially revised. As historian Linda Colley has argued, rather than being forever against the ropes, the Georgian monarchy came to play a key role in the configuration of a newly British national identity in the late eighteenth century. Ideas of monarchy and reverence for George III, with his 'British' values of prudence and domestic virtue, formed the basis of a powerful popular culture of royalism and loyalty that contributed to the imagining and identity of a single nation.[16] Even the reputedly lacklustre courts of George I and George II have been reassessed. Caricatured for their foreignness and preference for private retirement, the first two Georges had long borne the brunt of responsibility for the court's apparent obscurity. Historian Hannah Smith, however, has demonstrated that their combined half-century reign warrants more subtle appraisal.[17] Enjoying greater popularity than has usually been credited to them, the Hanoverian monarchs and their courts were less a neglected backwater and more the location of a politically expedient Protestant and enlightened model of kingship. It was a model that relied less on the veneration of divine right and awesome spectacle (attributed in the contemporary imagination to the Catholic tyranny of former reigns and neighbouring countries), and more on ideals of modesty, patriotism, and the humanity of the king. As Smith makes clear, a shift in the nature of monarchical power does not necessarily equate to an outright 'decline'. Furthermore, Smith brings to the fore the variety of ways in which the Georgian court continued to operate as a venue of social and political activity, even as the constitutional role of the court in the state and the high political role of the monarch and the principal members of his household waned. As a resort of formal and informal sociability, the royal court can be regarded as one of London's numerous extraparliamentary spheres of political activity, and home to the type of 'social politics' now widely identified with the coffee house, theatre, private residence, and other venues. Consequently, rather than approaching the court as an anachronistic institution in abeyance, its personnel and culture are recognized as forming one part of a newly plural social and political landscape.

The court's altered location can also be interpreted as representing a change in its nature rather than just a symptom of its decline. In particular, the scattering of the court across multiple sites integrated the court more substantially into the London landscape. As a result, the general metropolitan population was now likely to encounter something of the court in a variety of different places, and a sense of assimilation was potentially enhanced by the fact that the royal household occupied buildings that were comparatively open to the public gaze. St James's Palace, Kensington Palace, and the Queen's House were each surrounded by public parks that were open to all (Figure 24). The Leicester House and Carlton House properties of successive princes of Wales started out as little more than ordinary (though substantial) residences nestled against other properties within fairly densely populated

FIGURE 24 View of St James's Park, anon., 18th century. The royal palace of St James's can be seen to the left of the park.

streets. Bringing the court out from behind Whitehall's high walls was not necessarily to its detriment.

Moreover, the court's new physical structure changed the practice of monarchy and the nature of court culture in significant ways. Ceremony and residence, for instance, were increasingly divided, with drawing rooms and balls routinely held at St James's and domestic lodging for the royal family and their attendants provided at Kensington, Windsor, or the Queen's House.[18] In addition, various strands of the state were separated, with parliament housed in accommodation that was distinct from the home of the royal court.[19] Furthermore, the royal family itself was often spread between properties, and the existence of at least two key courts—one presided over by the monarch and the other by his heir—became a distinguishing feature of the century. Critically, this decentralized court did not always act as a single unit. The existence of separate households for the monarch and heir proved particularly divisive, and the periodic dissociation of the heir apparent from the main

107

royal court provided the disaffected political elite of the day with their own royal centre and court culture, placing the reversionary interest (the heir to the throne) in opposition to the crown. As we will see, a fractured, and often fractious, court landscape had significant implications for the nature and meaning of court attendance, for the interpretation of courtly displays, and for the relationship between the monarchy and London's beau monde.

Despite the limited accommodation provided by the eighteenth-century palaces and the new conditions of monarchical rule, court attendance remained an indispensable part of elite London life and a powerful framework for social behaviour.[20] Presentations at court were the traditional markers of alterations in social identity, undertaken on reaching adulthood, on marriage, on promotion through the peerage, or on entrance into a court or other official state position. The anecdotal evidence provided by contemporary letters reveals that the rigmarole of being presented, as well as subsequent routine participation in court events, was customary for the metropolitan beau monde.[21] For example, following the birth of her child, Mary Robinson, Lady Grantham, acknowledged that attendance at court was a necessary part of her re-entrance into London society. 'I believe I must make my appearance [at court next Thursday]', she wrote to her mother, 'as I shall be known to be out in the World by being at Lady Mary Forbes on Wednesday.'[22] When her sister, Lady Mary, entered fashionable society in 1774, her first appearance at court marked the beginning of her involvement in the whirl of metropolitan life. 'I do not know whether Mama informed you,' she wrote to her sister in 1774, 'we made our appearance at Court last Thursday sevennight, and since then we have seen all that is to be seen.'[23] The same engagement diaries that betrayed tireless commitment to commercial leisure also illustrate frequent visits to the court. James Harris (later 1st Earl of Malmesbury) attended a court drawing room every week when he was in London in 1770.[24] In 1778, the

Honourable Frederick Robinson restricted himself to attending a *levée* and drawing room once a fortnight.[25] The diaries of James Brydges, 3rd Duke of Chandos, indicate a substantial court presence, with the duke routinely attending court up to four times a week in 1786.[26]

But what did 'going to court' involve? The motivations behind the highest levels of attendance certainly varied. For some, a formal court post or ministerial position made daily participation obligatory, but it is clear that the seasonal calendar of ceremonies attracted more than just those in service. The precise timetable of entertainments and ceremonies associated with the court differed according to the politics and personality of each sovereign. During the winter parliamentary season, though, the schedule usually consisted of Sunday church services, *levées*, drawing rooms, and the celebration of royal birthdays or other key dates such as coronation days and twelfth night. *Levées* tended to be held for important ministers and high-ranking noblemen, allowing powerbrokers to foregather with the monarch in comparative seclusion. Drawing rooms were larger affairs. They were attended by women as well as men, and were the location of formal presentations to the monarch.[27] The size, scale, and timing of drawing rooms varied considerably from reign to reign. Newspapers advertised court gatherings, keeping the titled up to date with the changing routines. In 1717, for example, it was reported that a 'with-drawing room is order'd to be kept at court every Monday, Wednesday and Friday night during the winter'.[28] In 1722, the Prince of Wales held two drawing rooms each week at Leicester House and, not to be outdone, his father George I hosted twice-weekly meetings at St James's.[29] In addition to the monarch's and the heir to the throne's drawing rooms, similar congregations were routinely held by other members of the royal family. Queen Charlotte, for instance, held her drawing rooms on Thursday evenings in the 1790s, before the king's ministerial *levée* on Fridays.[30] It is impossible to be certain how many attended every meeting, and it seems unlikely that even the most deferential peer attended each and every event. However, with royal drawing rooms routinely scheduled more often than, say, the opera, they formed a major component of the beau monde's metropolitan routine and potentially crowded the schedules of loyal participants with palace engagements.

Although attendance at drawing rooms was commonplace, annual royal birthdays were the largest and most prestigious events associated with metropolitan royal ceremony in the 1700s. For the monarch, a birthday celebration usually commenced with a church service in the morning. Later an ode in their praise, penned by the poet laureate and set to music by the crown's master of music, was performed for royal approbation. A special drawing room was held in the late morning or early afternoon after which the royal family retreated for dinner. As night fell, society and royalty came together again for a court ball that was the grand finale of the day.[31] No raucous assembly, this principally involved a rota of decorous minuets, with each couple dancing in strict order of precedence and choreographing their routine in an intimate space under the scrutiny of the company present (Figure 25).[32] Although the birthday of the monarch was the pre-eminent anniversary in the court calendar, anniversary celebrations were routinely held for many other members of the royal family too. The consort was similarly honoured, as was the heir apparent and, usually, their siblings. In consequence, attending birthday courts could be a comparatively regular undertaking. As Jemima, Marchioness Grey, complained in the last week of November 1752, 'this week has been so full of birthdays that one has nothing to do but go to court'.[33]

Access to the court for these scheduled events was apparently policed by informal criteria. Few written protocols were produced or survive. In theory, the court was relatively permeable, for formal dress alone granted passage to the most public spaces of the London palaces (such as courtyards and entry rooms) on any day of the week. It is clear that

Engraved for the Lady's Magazine.

A View of the BALL at S.t James's, on the King's Birth Day June 4, 1782.

FIGURE 25 *A View of the Ball at St James's, on the King's Birth Day June 4, 1782.* Only a handful of interior court scenes were produced in the eighteenth century. This engraving, published in *The Lady's Magazine*, emphasizes the intimacy and crowding of a court ball.

the nobility sallied forth confident that the privileges of rank bought a right of entry. It is equally apparent, however, that this was not just a club for the peerage. The provincial gentry hankered to show themselves at court and curtsey to the crown. Most went at least once in their lifetime, enthusiastically asserting their apparent right to witness drawing rooms and balls on birthdays, marriages, and coronations.[34] Knighthoods and garters were clearly not obligatory, for city merchants and professionals also navigated their way through the maze and told of their participation at events within the palace walls. Dudley Ryder, for example, the son of a linen draper, would seem to have had few courtly qualifications except his ardent support for the Hanoverian crown (which was so consuming that Ryder dreamt he personally vanquished the Stuart pretender). Nonetheless, his diary reveals his attendance at five drawing rooms over two years, few in comparison to the routine participation logged in elite records but significant all the same.[35] For Josiah Wedgwood, the court's corridors represented a fertile ground for new commissions. 'Pray put on the best suit of Cloaths you ever had in your life and take the first opportunity of going to court', Josiah urged his brother John, who was then representing the business in London.[36]

Although securing entrance to court buildings was not in itself a challenge, gaining access to the epicentre of the court's ceremonial spaces was beset with greater obstacles. To attend a particular ceremony, such as a weekly drawing room, court-goers had to pass through an enfilade of spaces and rooms that acted as a powerful filter and check on their credentials.[37] With admirable gumption, Dudley Ryder's preferred technique was to feign membership of a noble entourage and shuffle in behind a group, rather than risk rejection by trying to negotiate entrance on the back of his own curriculum vitae.[38] Access to one event, though, did not automatically confer access to all, and birthday courts appear to have been the most restricted.[39] These were most often held at St James's, where the gates to the royal palace were the first barrier. Here public crowds gathered to watch the grandees pass in their finery. On occasion the pressure at the gates and in the yard was alarming. In 1729, newspapers reported that one young woman was wounded in the arm by a guard's bayonet as he tried to clear a path through the crush to allow her to clamber into a waiting sedan chair after attending a drawing room.[40] A report by the *St James's Chronicle* in 1762 claimed one unorthodox drawing room hopeful was swiftly expelled from the yard: 'On Sunday a young gentleman scarce twenty, dressed in a shabby suit of cloathes, bag wig, white silk stockings, silverlaced hat with broad Point D'Espaigne [Spanish lace], brass hilt sword and a large oaken stick in his hand and a long black beard attempted to get into the Drawing Room but was turned back by one of the Marshalmen; he made strong opposition and with great difficulty was got out of the courtyard.' Whether it was the stick, the beard, the shabby suit, or his demeanour, the man never made it beyond the first checkpoint.[41]

Court attendees left liveried servants and chairmen to wait in the yard, and proceeded on foot to a staircase in order to 'ascend' to the presence of the monarch. At the top of the staircase they entered the guard chamber. From here, attendees passed through the presence chamber and then the privy chamber until finally reaching the 'with-drawing room' where the monarch presided over the meeting. It should be noted that the event of a drawing room, whether for a birthday or not, involved multiple spaces, and continuous movement in and out of these rooms was common. At each stage, and most particularly at the final room where the company moved into the monarch's presence, high-ranking courtiers acted as watchful gatekeepers, ejecting those without rank or connection enough to progress.

Although courts and palaces suggest spaciousness and architectural grandeur, the interiors used for these formal events were in fact remarkably compact. Even at St James's Palace, the largest of the central London palaces, the available space was limited. Lively complaints of overcrowding litter the letters of the fashionable society. In the 1780s, Lady Louisa Stuart described the 'frightful scene' of a court drawing room with 'people crying and fainting and going into screaming fits'. Such was the squeeze that Lady MacCartney had been lost to 'violent hysterics' on her return home and Lady Mary Montagu, Lady Sydney, Lady Elizabeth Yorke, Mrs Adair, and Miss Chaplin were all seen 'fainting away'.[42] Lavinia, Lady Spencer, found the crush of court similarly hard to endure. 'Oh! Oh! Oh! My hips! My feet! My head!', she exclaimed in a letter to her husband after attending court in 1792, 'I am just returned from Court which was fuller than a birthday and lasted an eternity and Lady Ely nearly squeezed me flat against Mrs Ellis.'[43] Mary, Lady Grantham found 'heap and disorder' at court in the 1790s, and in the early 1800s Lady Sarah Spencer likened the drawing room crowd to a pack of cards.[44] The hyperbole should not be read too literally, for the court was not always packed to its capacity. Nonetheless, such commentary draws our attention to the comparative intimacy of the court experience. The cavernous interior of Ranelagh's rotunda was far superior to the accommodation on offer at court, and the major

FIGURE 26 English court dress, c.1740–5. The dress is made from scarlet ribbed silk and decorated with silver thread embroidery.

FIGURE 27 English court dress, c.1740–5. The white silk dress is embroidered with coloured and silver thread.

assembly rooms at towns such as Bath, Newcastle, and York were considerably more commodious than the rooms used for a birthday ball.

Wearing appropriate dress was an essential passport for access, and the clothing demanded by court events followed specific protocols.[45] Women wore expensively embroidered gowns (mantuas) with extraordinarily wide hoops, and head-dresses with long lace lappets hanging from the crown. Both were rarely seen outside the court in the second half of the century, and by 1800 such styles were an arcane relic of a former age (Figures 26 and 27). Men's court clothing between 1680 and 1800 kept more abreast with modish trends in male fashion, with the three-piece suit (consisting of a coat with tails, a waistcoat, and knee breeches) a commonplace style worn in many different contexts. The expensive fabrics and heavy embroidery used for men's court suits and the addition of fine silk stockings, however, would only have been worn to the most formal occasions elsewhere, such as in a box at the opera or at a private ball. The additional accoutrements worn by a man at court, namely a hat, bag wig (where the hair at the back of the wig was drawn together in a black silk bag), and formal sword, would typically only be displayed together at court events (Figure 28).

This increasingly anachronistic and distinctive livery was dearly bought. Personal bills and household accounts reveal the staggering expense that could be incurred to equip a person for regular attendance at court. Anne, Countess of Strafford, confessed to a £100 price tag for her court dress purchased in 1711.[46] The Duchess of Hamilton's dress, purchased in 1752, cost almost as much as her husband's brand new and luxuriously fitted sedan chair.[47] In 1767, Lady Mary Coke spent £70 on silk alone and, in 1790, the Duke of Bedford's brown striped silk suit embroidered in silver, spangles, and brilliant-cut diamonds was reported to have cost in excess of £500.[48] No wonder Lady Louisa Stuart calculated that 'fifteen or sixteen hundred a year would not do very much for two people who must live in London and appear in fine clothes at St James's twice a week'.[49]

Such expenditure poured money into London's luxury trades, providing a massive financial injection to the metropolitan economy every season. The creation of a single court suit for a man or gown for a woman involved many different industries. Silk weavers in Spitalfields, for instance, produced the many yards of fine cloth. Tailors and mantua makers made up the garments, sending pieces to embroiderers who then added the rich detailing around suit cuffs and pockets, and worked up the abundant decoration which adorned a woman's man-

FIGURE 28 English male court dress, with plum-coloured velvet coat and ivory satin waistcoat. *c.*1800. By 1800, the standing collar and ornate embroidery seen here (and obligatory for men's court clothing) were significantly out of line with the more sober styles favoured in male fashionable dress.

tua gown. Jewellery was reset or bought new, and buttons, sprigs, spangles, and all types of fringes and trimmings were selected from multiple sources. Expensive lace was an essential component of women's headdresses, and lace ruffles were a uniform feature of both male and female attire. Shoes, stockings, and buckles all had their makers and the construction of court clothing drew on networks of subcon-

117

tracted labourers, artisans, and craftsmen. Such was the fiscal significance of these moments of court magnificence to the capital's economic
infrastructure that anxious trades routinely petitioned the court when
lengthy periods of royal mourning threatened their business by limiting
the amount of new clothing and adornment that could be worn. On the
day of a royal birthday, those tradesmen who had contributed to the
creation of court finery illuminated their shops and houses to publicize
their contributions, and even opened their premises to spectators prior
to the event to show the luxury wares in the making.[50]

Given their complexity, commissioning outfits for the seasonal run
of royal birthdays demanded time as well as money. The Countess of
Stafford, for one, worried over the details of her court dress for a full
four months, insisting that her husband purchased velvet for the dress
from Holland while she scoured London for appropriate trimmings,
keen to secure 'a gold trimming which everybody will allow to be the
finest they ever see', onto which she would later string the entire complement of the Strafford gems.[51] In the 1750s, David Garrick and his
wife often acted as proxy shoppers for the Duke of Devonshire, and
they were empowered by him to seek out fabric for his court suit over
ten weeks before the king's birthday celebrations were to commence.
Sending samples of various combinations of velvets and embroidered
panels for his approbation, the Garricks did most of the legwork before
the duke even got to town.[52] When the Earl and Countess of Sutherland
decided to make the long journey from Highland Scotland to London
in order to present themselves at the first court held by George III after
his marriage to Princess Charlotte of Mecklenburg-Strelitz in 1761, their
London-based acquaintances, the Erskines, warned against appearing
in the London court without allowing sufficient time to prepare. With
only two months remaining before the Sutherlands were due in the
capital, Lady Erskine stressed the urgency of finalizing their court
wardrobe. 'I beg you would send me any commissions by the first post

which you have to give about cloaths,' she wrote in a flustered letter to the countess, '[e]very mortal is making up fine cloaths for the wedding and the silks are already risen considerably in their price.'[53] Lord Erskine added his voice to hers, writing directly to the Earl of Sutherland with the reprimand that unless swift attention was given to clothing 'Lady Sutherland may as well walk amongst the Rocks at Dunrobin [the Sutherland's Scottish seat]...for none would know her,' and she would only be remembered as the 'woman whose Robes and dress so ill fitted her person'.[54]

Once a dress had been purchased, close acquaintances were given early previews and personal viewings of the investment. Lady Anne Connelly delighted her aunt, Ann Donelan, by visiting her in court dress and jewels in 1733, and Lady Jane Coke discovered that Lady Betty Germaine's house was 'where great numbers came to show themselves' before court events in the 1750s.[55] Such reports suggest these pre-court viewings were carefully stage-managed. To be invited to such a show acted as a mark of favour to certain family members and acquaintances. Private viewings of court dress, however, also offered the opportunity for a select audience to glean specific and highly detailed information about the clothing worn, information that could then be circulated through the letters and news networks of the company present.

Displaying court dress in this manner becomes more meaningful when the value attached to court clothing is considered. Notably, purchasing and wearing expensive court dress was not just a means of displaying wealth. It was understood to have a political function too. In particular, investing in new clothes for a court event was widely interpreted as a sign of respect of the monarch. For example, during Queen Anne's reign, Lady Scarborough wrote to the Duchess of Marlborough about court dress. Rumour had reached Lady Scarborough that the duchess was to appear in new clothes at court. 'I take this opportunity to tell you deare Lady Dutchess [that] I am very glad to heare you talk of being drest on ye birthday', Lady Scarborough explained, 'and wish you may make many for ye same purpose, and if you have use of such cloathes this yeare, I verily believe you may have so for many to come.'[56] Here, then, intelligence that the Duchess of Marlborough was making new clothes for court was taken as a hopeful signal of her ongoing allegiance to Anne's court and, moreover, of her favour in those circles—although that position was soon to change. In 1712, the ambitious Earl and Countess of Strafford were desperate to curry favour with Queen Anne. The countess recorded that the 'new sute of clothes' she and her husband took time to prepare was specifically intended to 'make a compliment' to the queen.[57] Bedecked with diamonds, gold trimming, and the finest velvet and lace her husband could source, the countess's compliment was well received. 'Twas allowed I had the most jewels of anybody there,' she wrote proudly to her husband after the event, and 'the Queen told me I was very fine'.[58] Marked with the queen's personal approbation there was no doubting the countess's sartorial statement had been a success. Pleased with his wife's achievement, the earl promptly reimbursed her for the cost of her dress, reassuring her that the bill would be paid by their steward and not deducted from her personal pin money. Her individual performance represented a familial success and so the family estate bore the expense.

Such was the symbolic importance of court clothes that even if the owner was unable to attend court they still let it be known that they had invested in new attire. The Duchess of Marlborough, for instance, advised Lady Cowper to inform the court that she had made clothes for a court birthday even though Lord Cowper's illness prevented her from attending in person.[59] When, in 1733, the Earl of Egmont was unable to attend the queen's birthday court he nonetheless sent word to court that he had new clothes made for the event. His assiduousness was rewarded with a formal acknowledgement by the queen's first minister,

Sir Robert Walpole, who, the earl noted, also appeared to take it well 'that my brother Parker who very rarely of late years went to Court, was this day there in a very fine embroider'd suit'.[60] Ensuring that a newly purchased gown was seen by family and friends also helped broadcast the fact that the owner had invested in a statement of respect for the crown.

Court dress could operate as an expression of other political positions too. In certain contexts, for instance, purchasing court finery was used strategically as a means to disguise political intent. In 1716, the Earl of Bristol had found his lengthy absences from London were generating rumours about his political sympathies. In an effort to quash the gossip he wrote to his wife, then in London, instructing her to wear a new and especially costly dress to court as a public statement of continued allegiance to the monarch, finessing his commands with verse. 'Since your finery is come from France,' he explained, 'you cannot with good grace stay in Town and not appear on the Birth night, which I desire you woud do to shew them,'

> Our loyalty is still the same,
> Whither it wins or lose the game,
> True as the diall to the sun,
> Altho it be not shind upon.[61]

While Bristol was keen to make a show of loyalty, it transpired that hearsay about his position was far from groundless. One year later, the earl made public his move to political opposition and never again attended court. However, until he was quite ready to act, he used court dress to cloak his manoeuvring and buy more time.

Further political uses of court dress are evident in attempts made by political factions to boycott or undermine shows of loyalty to the crown. For example, when the relationship between the Marlboroughs and the queen soured in late 1712, those who aligned themselves to the Marlboroughs' opposition politics attempted to skew reports of court attendance to make it appear that the court and its supporters were losing ground. They claimed that no new clothes were to be seen at court and that attendance was poor. With newspapers publishing similar accounts, those who supported the crown and government endeavoured to set the record straight. One such correspondent was Peter Wentworth. Explaining the situation in a letter to his brother, the Earl of Strafford, he detailed the competing reports of sartorial show that were coming from the court:

> The Whigs are pleased to give out that there was but very odd figures at Court of the Birthday…they gave out before that there wou'd be very little company, and 'twas said the Queen wou'd not come out, but there was as much fine cloaths as ever.[62]

The Countess of Strafford also wrote to clarify press reports and expose the Whigs' attempts to boycott court events, noting that 'none of the Whigg Ladys now ever goes to Court because the Queen shall not have a full Drawing room & they give out that nobody goes near her'. Despite the political wrangling, she reassured her husband that court events remained 'fine'.[63] In this context, the issue of whether or not new and splendid clothes were worn to court became of paramount importance. In the midst of Whig attempts to boycott the court, the queen's ambassadors sent expensive and luxurious clothing from their postings abroad for their wives and female acquaintances to wear. No doubt hoping for such a gown herself, the Countess of Strafford archly reported that 'Lord Bullinbrock has given his Lady for today the finest manto and petecoat that could be had in France & Sir J Hammond has sent the Duchess of Grafton a very fine won'.[64]

It was not only with splendid new dresses that the Tories attempted to denigrate the opposition Whig attack. Taking their campaign still further, the Tories orchestrated their own press reports. These claimed that the Marlborough opposition was so extreme and unconstitutional that they were effectively setting up a court of their own. Significantly,

Tory reports claimed that those who were to attend the 'Marlborough court' had commissioned new clothes to honour the Marlboroughs and snub the queen. Once again, Peter Wentworth worked through the swirling and contradictory accounts to shed light on the mood at court for his brother's benefit:

> Twas talkt of as if the Duke of M[arlborough]—intended to make a ball that night at his house, . . . but that morning there was paper cry'd about the Street as representing it a design to sett up for themselves, [and] that there was several people that had made cloath for that day that had not for the birthday . . . they put off their Ball but sent to all the Ladies they had invited there woud be no dancing but that the Dutchess wou'd be at home, and shou'd be glad to see any of them that wou'd come.[65]

Although they denied the rumours, the Marlboroughs would not have been the first to engineer an opposition 'court' that encouraged the wearing of new clothes to undermine rather than honour the monarch. As Robert Bucholz notes, the opposition Whigs attempted to generate an alternative ceremonial calendar in 1703 that challenged the celebrations of the Tory-dominated court. For example, in November of that year the Whig Kit Kat Club determined to commemorate the birthday of the previous monarch William III (rather than that of Queen Anne). The Whig nobles gathered at the club to toast the former king, and made it known that they were wearing new clothes to celebrate the event, an honour traditionally bestowed on the current monarch alone.[66]

Later in the century the existence of an adult heir apparent allowed for the creation of an alternative royal court around which political opposition could rally. In the 1730s, the relationship between the Prince of Wales and George II was fragile and disintegrating. Those attending the court used court birthdays and appearances at court to register their opposition or affiliation to different factions of the royal household. In 1734, for example, Lord Egmont noted that he had new clothes made for the Prince of Wales's birthday when, previously, he only recorded ordering new clothing for the birthdays of the king and queen.

While he ensured his family appeared at the king's court dressed in new clothes, Egmont himself became irregular in his attendance. As early as April 1733, he noted that the king had looked 'cool' because he 'did not go often enough to Court', and the queen's vicious rebuke to Egmont's wife, recorded in 1736—'tis so long since I have seen you I thought you were dead'—testifies to the uncertain ground on which they stood.[67] Although his diary does not state his intentions explicitly, the fact that Egmont eventually commissioned clothes to honour the Prince of Wales's birthday certainly appears loaded. If it was not so much a direct insult against the official court, it may nonetheless have been an attempt to garner favour from the heir apparent when such recognition from the current monarch was less forthcoming.

Others certainly avoided wearing any new clothes to the court of the errant Prince of Wales. Mary Delany, for example, recorded her desire to appear 'humbly drest' at the prince's court, whilst opposition politicians such as the Duke of Portland were reported to have been dressed 'very fine' in the presence of the prince.[68] By 1742, tensions had eased, but the Prince of Wales nonetheless retained a separate residence at Leicester House in Leicester Square. Arriving in London in November of that year, Lady Hertford wore the same new clothing to both courts to demonstrate her arrival in the capital and loyalty to the crown. She noted that the court that was held at Leicester House involved a 'great crowd but there were very few new clothes' amongst those in attendance. By contrast, at St James's—and although the king and queen were not flaunting new clothing—the nobles attending their court were spectacularly attired.[69]

Comparable attention to court clothing can also be identified in the second half of the century. In 1767, Lady Mary Coke was certain that royal court favourites and fellow Scottish nobles the Duchess of Hamilton and Lady Susan Stewart were conspiring against her. Coke was convinced that Hamilton and Stewart had informed their royal patrons and other acquaintances that the new and 'fine' dress Coke wore to court for Queen Charlotte's birthday was 'old', and were thus trying to damage her reputation at court. Lady Mary Coke was reassured by the king's brother, the Duke of York, that the king had indeed 'taken great notice of [her] Clothes', but the duke also confirmed her fears that it had '[been] said before that [she] had an old Gown'.[70] Lady Mary Coke was herself quick to note when old clothes were seen at court. 'I'm sorry to tell you,' she wrote to her sister in 1773, that 'Lord Cathcart shew'd the antiquity of his Cloaths by the cut of the sleeve; twas of an unreasonable size', a *faux pas* lessened by the fact that his wife wore 'a very slight green and white lutestring' which Lady Mary Coke believed to be new even if it was not particularly showy.[71]

Whilst the proportion of 'new' clothes to 'old' was an enduring pre-occupation, material statements of loyalty or opposition were also worked into court clothing through the manipulation (or blatant disregard) of certain sartorial regulations commanded by the royals. In the 1770s, for example, Queen Charlotte made clear her dislike for the yard-long ostrich feathers and towering head-dresses favoured by fashionable society. 'For two or three years no one ventured to wear them at Court,' Lady Louisa Stuart claimed, 'except some daring spirits either too supreme in fashion to respect any other kind of pre-eminence or else connected with the Opposition and glad to set her Majesty at defiance.'[72]

Fraught political tensions resurfaced at court and were similarly mediated through court displays in the closing decades of the century, when the political elite responded to the fluctuating relationship between George III and his dissolute son the Prince of Wales. In the early 1780s, the king and his heir apparent continued to appear together at court events. However, contemporaries watched the court closely for signs of discontent, and a host of conflicting reports about the finery seen at court soon hinted at the mounting tensions. 'One hears of many different reports,' noted Jemima, Marchioness Grey, of the queen's birthday ball in February 1781,

> it is wonder'd *why* some were invited and *why* others were not invited. It is said to have been very handsome and it is said the contrary. There were about twenty couples consisting chiefly of the Families of Ministers and of Persons belonging to the Court...but then some with such Pretensions being left out and some without any such taken in, [which] always makes a wonderment. The Maids of Honour were not asked and are very many of them angry (some of them you know are thought not to be in great favour).[73]

During George III's lengthy period of illness between 1788 and 1789, Whig politicians flaunted their support for the Prince of Wales and his campaign to become Regent while the king was incapacitated. On the king's recovery, however, overt displays of loyalty were demanded from all to celebrate his health. As *The Times* noted in June 1789, 'even the forlorn, melancholy, disappointed Members of The Party' presented themselves at court to celebrate the king's recovery, and 'dressed up their countenance so as to give the appearance, however they might be destitute of the spirit, of loyalty' (Figure 29).[74] 'Loyalty is a most expensive virtue at present,' Lady Louisa Stuart declared.[75] Nevertheless, the most extreme Whigs still found ways to accessorize their sartorial displays with messages of opposition, while ostensibly bowing to the authority of the crown. In late April, a formal service of thanksgiving was held at St Paul's Cathedral to commemorate the king's return to health. Brooke's club, the St James's haunt of the Whig party, hosted its own gala to 'toast' the king. Newspapers, however, wryly reported that the dress required would be court dress in full embroidery but rendered in 'blue and buff'—colours routinely adopted by the Whig party, and echoing the uniform of the American revolutionary army.[76]

Celebrations and political displays continued elsewhere too. On 30 May 1789, men who supported the king attended a gala held by the French ambassador dressed in the Windsor uniform (a blue hunting

RESTORATION DRESSES.

FIGURE 29 *Restoration Dresses*, anon., 1789. This caricature satirizes the sartorial displays of women celebrating the king's recovery. In particular, it highlights the fact that even those women associated with the political opposition (and the Prince of Wales's campaign for a regency) were eventually required to broadcast their support for the king. The women depicted here are believed to include Lady Archer, the Duchess of Devonshire, and other members of the Prince of Wales's set. A woman in ostentatious court dress is shown second from the right, with 'The King Restored' emblazoned in a ribbon in her hair.

suit commissioned by George III to be worn by himself and male courtiers at Windsor Castle), while their wives wore their most recently purchased court dress. It was noted in the papers, however, that 'those Noblemen distinguished in the opposite Party . . . did not wear any uniform', and the women associated with the opposition camp, including high-profile Whig hostesses such as the Duchess of Devonshire, shunned court-inspired clothing and attended the gala in other more fashionable gowns.[77] At a ball held by the Duchess of Gordon to celebrate the king's recovery, Lady Carlisle, Lady Caroline Howard, and

Lady Villiers nevertheless took the opportunity to advertise their support for the Prince of Wales, flaunting his feathers and *Ich Dien* motto on their caps.[78] In 1792, a further attempt by the Whigs to orchestrate a collective display of political opposition at a court birthday was thwarted by the vigilance of customs officers. Contravening late eighteenth-century court protocols stipulating that English silks should be used for court dress, the Whig party had commissioned their clothing in France as a snub to the crown. However, all did not go to plan, and the imported suits were seized at Dover. In a report weighted in support of the government, *The Times* smugly noted it to be 'astonishing the Nobility will suffer the anxiety and run the hazard of disappointment when it is an acknowledged fact that the best dresses which appeared at court were entirely of English manufacture'.[79]

The Times was often quick to applaud the clothing worn by figures associated with the government and lambaste the stylistic choices of the opposition, a stance that betrayed the politics of the paper itself. It is important to recognize that partisan agendas routinely informed the way in which court display was subsequently reported, as well as shaping the actual act of dressing for court. In the 1790s, *The Morning Chronicle*, for instance, often carried reports spun to support the opposition. Under the proprietorship of Richard Brinsley Sheridan, the paper was the mouthpiece for the Foxite Whigs who repeatedly boycotted court events. On 20 January 1795, the newspaper ridiculed the whole tradition of scrutinizing and reporting the clothing worn to court birthdays. Denouncing sartorial reports as 'unintelligible gibberish', the newspaper's editor sniffed that details of the clothing worn to court could hardly be considered news:

> It eternally consists of a satin or velvet train, and an embroidered petticoat, which glitter with half a dozen ornaments of tassels and fringe, flowers and foil, gold and silver through so many insipid columns. The etiquette of Court demanding the obsolete hoop in the Ladies dress,

and the standing collar in the Gentleman's, there is no scope for the exercise of either fancy or taste; the whole variety of description consists in the colour of the body and train … whether the embroidery is in bouquets of roses, or branches of wheat-ear, all of which is extremely useful to the Court milliners, and interesting to no human creature beside.[80]

The paper, however, mischievously juxtaposed its strongly worded critique of court birthday reports with news of another birthday celebration, that of Charles James Fox, leader of the Whigs.[81] By carrying a front-page promotion of Fox's anniversary and dismissing the need to cover court splendour, the newspaper made its political affiliation clear.

Far from being sidelined from fashionable society, the royal court was socially, culturally, and politically significant to the beau monde. Court excursions remained a routine part of metropolitan elite life and formed an additional strand to the systematic displays of distinction enacted elsewhere during the London season. Moreover, the enthusiastic circulation of information and press reportage concerning the court defy any attempt to portray this as a closed and separate world. For the beau monde, the court was always part of a bigger picture. At the same time, the court also provided the setting for a range of functions that the other metropolitan institutions and contexts explored in this book could never wholly replace. Throughout this period, relationships and rules of engagement were being defined between fashionable society and a newly constitutional monarchy. The parameters for these uneasy negotiations were unresolved and often unspoken. In theory, the fashionable elite could have asserted its constitutional authority by shunning the court entirely; but such an extreme statement of opposition was something that few were ready to consider, let alone attempt. Indeed, rather than posing a threat, the beau monde doubtless relied on both monarchy and court to fix a seal of legitimacy on their own claims to status and prestige.

In consequence, the court became an arena for more nuanced jostling, in which politicized relationships could be defined and redefined rather than demolished, and in which the authority of the crown could be challenged rather than attacked head-on. It was the tentative and wary nature of this environment that gave court clothing such power and relevance. Through sartorial statements that were both direct and somehow indirect, critiques of the sovereign, and the political agendas that these usually involved, could be advanced or deflected. By selecting foreign-made fabrics, by wearing old instead of new (or new instead of old), or even by loading a dress with trimmings better suited for another garment, the clothing worn to court became a versatile instrument of intervention. Of course, political machinations may not always have been the concern of the wearer. While some figures, such as the Earl of Bristol, recorded their intentions in their personal papers, not all those who dressed for court leave us with confessions of political intrigue. Nor is it my intention to imply that the aesthetics of personal choice and changing fashion preferences had no role in the sartorial system surrounding court show. Long-running correspondence describing shopping practices, the fingering of trimmings and distribution of samples, the careful consideration of fabrics, and the use of proxy-shoppers to advise on the final formulation of court clothing, all testify to the multiplicity of agendas involved. As with every other area of the beau monde's activities, the political, social, and cultural were seamlessly blended, each informing the others.

4

Politics and fashionable life
'All the chatter chitter I heard'

Party rage has of late years very much crept into conversation. There is nothing so bad for the face as party zeal. It gives an ill-natured cast to the eye, and a disagreeable sourness to the look; besides that it makes the lines too strong, and flushes them worse than brandy...And indeed I never knew a party woman keep her beauty for a twelvemonth.

(*The Spectator*, 1711)

'Politicks, politicks and more politicks, that's all one hears in these parts at present'

(Lady Sarah Spencer, London, to the Honourable Robert Spencer, 1810)

When the Countess of Strafford moved into St James's Square, the first letter she sent to her husband from their new metropolitan base was filled with pride. 'I can now tell my Dearest Life and Soul that much to my Sattisfaction I am now settled in our house.' 'I am extremely Pleas'd with the work'd Bed', she continued merrily, 'for now 'tis Clean'd 'tis as good as new & looks very Gentell.' Having updated her husband about the status of their accommodation the tenor of her letter swiftly changed, and the countess immediately moved on to report that both the queen and Lord Oxford were 'very ill of the gout, tho' I find,' she added conspiratorially, 'the Whigs will have it that neither of them are ill but for reasons of State & for the same reason the Parliament is Adjourn'd'.[1] Significantly, this initial letter marked the countess's inauguration as a political commentator. For the Countess of Strafford, setting up home in St James's Square involved not only mastering the beau monde's 'fashion' systems and its social infrastructure but also brought participation in its political culture.

The deep incorporation of political concerns within the culture of the beau monde is illustrated by the subsequent content of the countess's letter. Claiming to be unsure of her ability adequately to interpret political news, the countess explained, 'you bid me send you all the Chatter Chitter I heard so like any obedient Wife I'll obey your Commands tho at the Same time I show myself a Fool in sending you that for news what you know before but nevertheless to obey your commands I'll begin again.' And begin again she did, rattling off a barrage of detailed information in quick succession:

> Count Gallas is leaving this Court very soon with the Greatest Disgrace in the world 'tis said he is wholy wrapt up in the Whigg interest & so by consequence opos'd the pease [peace] with the utmost rigour, if so I am so very angry at him I could ring his neck off, tho I keep all these violent inclinations to my self. L[or]d Harley is very soon to Marry the Duke of Newcastle's Daughter, Mrs Kingdom tis generally said to be married to Lord Conway but tis not yet own'd. Sister Wentworth gave a ball before she left Windsor, a Lady told me yesterday that she was making a Visit to the Dutchess of Shrewsbury & Sister W[entworth] came in and the Dutchess entertain'd her with no other discourse but commending of me & how glad she was that you were marr[i]ed...I am told the Dutchess of Marlborough intends to sett up an Assembly to out do the Dutchess of Shrewsbury.[2]

These few sentences were crammed with information that provided the absent earl with valuable insights into the political climate of the metropolis. The countess's commentary is so dense that unpacking its political content requires far more text than she expended. To begin with, in her fleeting mention of Lord Oxford's and the queen's battle with gout, the countess intimated that their ill health had become a topic of partisan dispute. Opposition politicians alleged that the reported indisposition of the monarch and her most influential minister, Robert Harley, Earl of Oxford, was simply a strategy to buy Harley time to shore up the position of his Tory-dominated government.[3] It was certainly the case that at this date Harley was judiciously bolstering his powerbase after a bill outlining details of a proposed peace treaty with France (to end the costly European War of the Spanish Succession) had recently met with fierce opposition in the House of Lords, and scraped through by only one vote. Harley spent the following months persuading Anne to dismiss from court service any lords who had blocked the proposals, and to create a dozen new peers who would wave through future peace bills.[4] Given the Straffords' loyalty to both court and government, the countess cast no aspersions on the official claims that Harley and the queen were suffering with gout. However, she was clearly wise to the fact that political business and not just personal health was possibly influencing the delay. John Wenceslaus, Count Gallas—a man the countess mentioned in her letter with murderous contempt—was also implicated in the same political disputes over the peace treaty's progress. As the Austrian envoy to the court of Queen Anne, Gallas had been instructed to encourage England's continued engagement in the war, because Austria feared for its position in a Europe where French hegemony was unchecked. In consequence, the count sided with those opposition Whig peers who challenged proposals for peace. Such details of London-based political skirmishes were of critical significance to the Earl of Strafford, based in The Hague and beginning complex European peace negotiations across multiple powers that eventually resulted in the Treaty of Utrecht (1713).

The additional information the countess provided, though masquerading as social comment, was also infused with subtle political significance. The proposed marriage of Lord Harley to Henrietta

Cavendish united the offspring of two key political allies. The groom was the eldest son of Robert Harley, Earl of Oxford. The bride was the only surviving child of the recently deceased Duke of Newcastle, one of Oxford's most dependable Tory affiliates. The Duchess of Marlborough and Duchess of Shrewsbury, moreover, were the female representatives of the major and opposing political factions. The latter was Adelaide Roffeni, wife of Charles Talbot, Duke of Shrewsbury, then lord chamberlain and one of Harley's key allies. Italian-born, the vivacious Adelaide struck an exotic note in London, attracting attention, and not a little censure, for her exuberant manner. The Duchess of Marlborough cattily claimed that at court the lord chamberlain's wife acted with unconventional animation, 'entertaining everyone aloud [and] thrusting out her disagreeable breasts with such strange motions'.[5] Even the respectful Countess of Strafford soon decided that Shrewsbury could be 'ridiculous in her talk'.[6] However, along with her husband, the Duchess of Shrewsbury hosted a sequence of widely publicized assemblies and balls to rally the governing political interest at times when Queen Anne was unable to host court events due to periodic ill health.[7] The Duchess of Shrewsbury's reported commendation of the Earl and Countess of Strafford probably carried political rather than just social weight, recognizing the Straffords' affiliation to a factional nexus that was loyal to government and court. Meanwhile, the Duchess of Marlborough, recently dismissed from Anne's court, was reputedly ambitious to create something of an opposition court for disaffected Whigs at the newly built Marlborough House.[8] As the Countess of Strafford notes, this act was regarded as a public challenge to the Duchess of Shrewsbury and her pro-court assemblies. Social rivalry was recognized as a form of political rivalry, with competing forums established for competing factions.

The Countess of Strafford's swiftly dispensed 'chatter chitter' therefore suggests the range of ways in which political identities, politicized displays, and political power were an integrated part of her new London life. In her letter, the social, the personal, and the political are inextricably connected. Assemblies, visits, balls, and marriages signalled hardening divisions, new connections, and the bolstering of established factional alliances. Absences and periods of ill health triggered rumours of political ploys and backroom manoeuvres. Not least, women as well as men are portrayed as significant and unremarkable political agents, consolidating and endorsing networks, facilitating factional gatherings, representing oppositional groups, and disseminating political news.

This chapter explores this politicization of metropolitan elite society to recover the close-knit relationship between the social and political culture of London's beau monde. Rather than attempting to trace particular political careers, it uses anecdotal commentary such as that penned by the Countess of Strafford to recover the everyday ways in which politics was practised. As earlier chapters have already indicated, politics, broadly conceived, bubbled close to the surface of the lifestyles and preoccupations of London's beau monde in many different contexts. From Sarah, Duchess of Marlborough's distribution of diamond jewellery to her 'Whigg friends', and Lord Scarsdale's decision to escort the same grand lady out of the opera to signal his affiliation to the Whigs in the 1710s, to the Duke of Grafton's posturing at the theatre with the politically powerful Bedford clan in the 1760s, and the use of court dress to broadcast partisan positions, all manner of ostensibly social performances enacted within the context of the London season were interpreted through the prism of politics.

Such marked intersections of social and political concerns within the culture of the beau monde are not, of course, surprising. We now have a far more subtle understanding of eighteenth-century political culture that looks beyond parliamentary debates and ministerial histories to extra-parliamentary arenas and to the political influence exercised by the disenfranchised. Such approaches have significantly altered how historians characterize 'political' history for the eight-eenth century, stimulating investigations into popular politics and recovering non-elite political agents whose activities and power were previously hidden from view. More particularly for this study, how-ever, it has also reframed our understanding of how politics func-tioned for those whose political power is taken for granted—the titled elite.[9]

This chapter aims to understand how a political culture operated within the context of the beau monde, and begins with a brief overview of eighteenth-century elite political culture as it is now understood. The experiences of the previously mentioned Straffords form a key resource but will also be juxtaposed with those of their St James's Square neighbours John and Elizabeth Hervey, Earl and Countess of Bristol. The Straffords and the Herveys pursued divergent political paths and aligned themselves with opposing political factions. Their contemporaneous experiences are therefore particularly valuable, illu-minating how an ostensibly shared political culture of the beau monde was inflected (for their generation at least) by partisan preoccupations and factional identities.

A concluding section takes a broader look at the relationship between the social and political culture of the beau monde over the course of the century, drawing together threads from other manuscript collec-tions to develop a more general picture of the integration of political priorities within London life. It is only possible to suggest this wider picture in rough strokes and my interpretation of the available mate-rial is significantly indebted to pioneering research by other scholars. Tracking the political activities and concerns of the metropolitan elite in this manner illustrates the centrality of politics to the cultural iden-tity of London's beau monde, and suggests how the structure of the beau monde itself supported the political functions of the London sea-son. It also demonstrates, from yet another perspective, the remarkable power of the interpersonal connections and exclusive networks that structured the beau monde.

In order to understand what politics meant to the beau monde, it is necessary to appreciate the nature of parliament as it existed after 1689 and before 1832, and also to look beyond parliament to less formal political arenas. Throughout the 1700s, parliament effectively remained an upper-class enclave. Voting rights and access to parliament itself were primarily defined by property ownership, which was regarded as a necessary asset that defended a man against corrupting influences and encouraged him to act independently. In this way the parliament—representing propertied interests with a material stake in the nation—would act as a check on the court. Though condemned in nineteenth-century critiques and by later historians as corrupt and oligarchic, to its eighteenth-century occupants parliament was a 'democratic' institution suited to a 'modern' government.

For men of the English peerage, a seat in the House of Lords was an incontrovertible hereditary right. Whether fit for such office or not, an English noble lord could not be prevented from taking a place at Westminster.[10] The power of the Lords was substantial. Cabinets were controlled by peers well into the nineteenth century and, perhaps most significantly, the personal, familial, and patronage influence of members of the upper chamber ensured the lords enjoyed considerable and resilient power by proxy in the Commons.[11] Described by the Earl of Chatham as 'a parcel of younger brothers', the House of Commons was packed with members who boasted direct blood lines to the peerage.[12] In 1760–1, Lord Hardwicke could count no fewer than four sons and two nephews in the Commons, and one son-in-law beside him in the upper chamber.[13] Moreover, the proportion of younger sons and heirs who made up the Commons increased as the century progressed. Such was the scale and legacy of noble influence that it was only in 1885 that MPs from commercial and manufacturing backgrounds finally outnumbered those from landed families.[14] Nor was it through kinship networks alone that the Lords exerted influence in the lower house. Their claims to extensive acreage and property also endowed them with sizeable and direct control over numerous parliamentary seats. The majority of land was held by the titled minority, and with land came places to fill in Westminster.[15]

The exclusively aristocratic nature of the eighteenth-century parliament has ensured that historians interested in the political actions and culture of the non-elite have had to move well beyond Westminster. Few would now argue that the broader political history of the period was only, or even primarily, concerned with what took place within the Commons and Lords. For the disenfranchised majority, popular political culture involved diverse actions in a wide variety of ways and places, from riots to theatre productions and from consumer choices to civic celebrations. Yet, inevitably, the political perspective and culture of the elite was rather different. Given that parliament was effectively their property, it remained at the centre of their activities. The male members of the beau monde described here enjoyed privileged and usually inherited access to the corridors of power. For most, a future seat in the Lords was a certainty, and family influence ensured that a provisional seat in the Commons for an heir, prior to his succession to the Lords, was par for the course. Men who were promoted to the peerage in their lifetime (such as the Straffords' neighbour the Earl of Bristol) had usually long sat in the Commons, as had their ancestors before them, and their title was granted in recognition of established parliamentary service. Of course, access to a seat in Westminster did not necessarily mean that the incumbent was politically active. It was quite possible for young heirs to be elected to the Commons in absentia whilst cruising Europe on a grand tour. Moreover, many a bucolic lord preferred rural pleasures and local paternalistic duties to national political business, and refused to be prised from his country seat to vote in the Lords. Nonetheless, the sense of proprietorship and of a personal 'right' to participate in parliament underpinned the meaning of politics for the eighteenth-century elite in a way that it did not for the majority of the population.

That said, however, elite political culture was not delimited to the parliamentary institution they dominated. Parliament's official accommodation was, in fact, severely constrained. The House of Lords and House of Commons gathered in rooms that had once been part of a warren-like medieval court abandoned by the monarchy since 1512. Unlike the iconic Victorian Gothic building that stands by the Thames today (built after the original complex was destroyed by fire in 1834), the old Palace of Westminster had no purpose-built parliamentary accommodation. As a result, the eighteenth-century Commons were squeezed into a deconsecrated chapel, St Stephens, which at fifty-seven feet long and around thirty-two feet wide accommodated approximately half the MPs who officially made up the House. The House of Lords met in similar confinement, convening in what was known as the Queen's Chamber, a former medieval hall.[16] Such cramped spaces were far from conducive to the increased business and extended sittings wrought by post-1689 constitutional change, and politicians routinely decamped to coffee houses, chop houses, clubs, and taverns for meetings, seats, and sustenance (Figure 30).

Spill-over sites surrounding Westminster were not the only extra-parliamentary politicized spaces frequented by the beau monde. The busy round of assemblies, visits, balls, and other social excursions pursued by both men and women has also been increasingly recognized as a valuable system of 'social politics', or 'political sociability', that operated as an integrated and essential part of London's political culture.[17] As will be seen, the timetabled and predictable nature

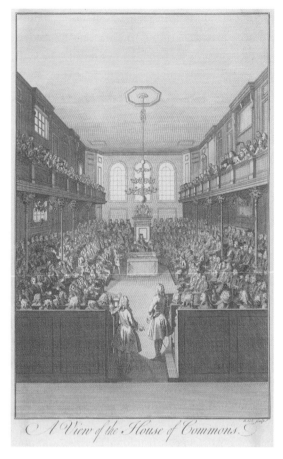

FIGURE 30 *A View of the House of Commons*, 18th century.

of fashionable sociability outlined in the previous chapter was in many ways ideally suited (and at times specifically tailored) to the need to obtain and share politicized information and broadcast political activities.

While this urban topography is important, the diversified and explicitly sociable nature of eighteenth-century political culture should not be seen simply as the result of the lack of formal parliamentary space combined with a convenient availability of extra-parliamentary resorts. It was also, and more fundamentally, an expression of how the metropolitan elite expected and understood politics to operate in the period. Although history has tended to focus on dramatic legislation, in fact local concerns not major or abstracted national agendas formed the bedrock of the political business passed in parliament in the 1700s.[18] Politics therefore operated primarily on a local and personal level. The importance of web-like patronage networks within eighteenth-century political life lay at the heart of what later reformers characterized as 'corrupt' within the 'unreformed' eighteenth-century political system. More recent histories, however, have looked again at how political patronage functioned in the period, arguing that it should not be dismissed as 'a vast morass of corruption' but interrogated as an active 'expression of how individuals within [a] hierarchical society related to one another; not on the basis of mutual equality but on the basis of mutual dependence'.[19] The prevalence of patronage ensured that eighteenth-century politics was 'influenced-based', and such influence could be wielded in all manner of forms. The purchase of a horse or an invitation to visit had the potential to act as a precursor to direct political negotiation.[20]

An appreciation of the social nature of eighteenth-century politics has also significantly altered historians' understanding of who participated in that political culture. Far from being the preserve of a few parliamentary men, eighteenth-century politics is now recognized as the ordinary business of many patrician women. As Elaine Chalus and Judith Lewis have demonstrated, titled women's political activities were wide-ranging, encompassing direct canvassing on behalf of candidates in elections, the facilitation of patronage requests, and the management of social forums to establish or cement political connections. '[S]ociety', explains Chalus, 'became an extra parliamentary stage upon which small and large political dramas could be enacted.' It was also a stage upon which women could play

leading roles. Social politics 'was a fact of eighteenth-century political life'.[21]

This revised understanding of contemporary politics provides a framework from which to approach the political culture of London's beau
monde. With the royal court no longer the sole executor of political authority, and parliament confirmed as a permanent feature of the political landscape, politics after 1689 impinged on many aspects of fashionable society.
Following the rhythm of the political season, sociability in the metropolis
burgeoned whilst parliament was sitting. Members of the beau monde
participated in an urban political culture where visits, assemblies, and
excursions could be undertaken within the confines of distinct political
communities. Political intrigue and metropolitan life were inseparable.
Political networks and responsibilities were knitted into personal, familial,
and social connections, and politicized displays were enacted alongside
and within other performances of urban status and social prestige.

Installed at 5 St James's Square, the Straffords found themselves neighbours to Lord and Lady Hervey at number 6.[22] From 1694 until 1703,
'handsome horseman' John Hervey (1665–1751) had served as MP for
Bury St Edmunds, a position held by his father, Sir Thomas Hervey,
before him.[23] After his first wife died in 1695, he married the 19-year-old
Elizabeth Felton, daughter and co-heiress of another Suffolk MP.
Elizabeth brought substantial wealth, further local political clout, and
ultimately seventeen children, to Hervey's Ickworth estate. Elevated to
the peerage as Baron Hervey in 1703, Hervey left the Commons for the
Lords (Figures 31 and 32).

The Herveys had occupied their home for ten years when the Straffords
joined the St James's Square community in 1711. Nonetheless, the two
couples had much in common. Lord Hervey was only eight years
Strafford's junior and, in 1714, secured another peerage promotion, lift-

FIGURE 31 *The Right Hono[ura]ble The Lady Hervey*, John Simon, after Michael Dahl, 1695–1714.

ing him from Baron Hervey of Ickworth to 1st Earl of Bristol. Both men were over forty when they received their titles. As first earls, the fate of a new noble line of distinguished descendants rested on the shoulders of each, and both were backed by wealthy wives. The two couples also endured similar separations. The Earl of Strafford's diplomatic duties brought long-term absences from London that were not demanded of his neighbour, but Hervey's love of the turf meant he was often in Newmarket tending to his stable or watching his stud of thoroughbreds compete. Consequently, Lady Hervey, like the Countess of Strafford, was

143

FIGURE 32 *John, Lord Hervey, Lord Privy Seal in the Reign of King George 2d*, Jean-Baptiste van Loo, *c.*1740–1.

routinely in town unaccompanied by her spouse, and moments of estrangement generated a mass of correspondence covering the same years as letters sent by the Countess of Strafford to the earl.[24]

However, although the Herveys and the Straffords shared the same side of St James's Square they stood resolutely on opposite sides of the political track. Whereas the Straffords regarded themselves as loyal Tories, the Herveys were unshakeable Whigs. Hervey was an ardent supporter of the 1688 revolution and, subsequently, of the Hanoverian succession.[25] Whilst the Straffords repeatedly espoused their dislike and disapproval of the Duke and Duchess of Marlborough, Hervey sided with the Marlboroughs following their split with Queen Anne and her ministry. Indeed, the Duke of Marlborough dined at Lord Hervey's St James's Square house with other high-ranking Whig politicians the day after the queen had dismissed him from his military command.[26] When the Earl of Strafford was hammering out details for the Treaty of Utrecht, Hervey was actively opposing the peace in London. In this way, comparing the experiences of the Straffords and Herveys is especially revealing. Of similar rank, similar means, similar ambition, similar circumstances, with similar manuscript records of their experiences, yet representing different political interests, the nature of the beau monde's ordinary political culture is brought vividly to light.

From the outset, the Herveys' routine correspondence bears witness to the defining role of politics within their London life. In the first year of their marriage, a doting Elizabeth sent parcels of cheesecake from the St James's Square kitchen to Westminster to sustain her husband—her 'dear life'—during his days of parliamentary business. Enclosed with the rations was a cajoling note urging him to 'eat for her sake who is with the greatest height of affection my dear yours for ever'.[27] He, in turn, composed love poetry whilst listening to debates and enclosed newspapers and snippets of political information in notes addressed to his 'ever new delight'.[28] Whenever Hervey left town to watch one of his prize horses race, his wife wrote to him every day to keep him abreast of political developments. Like the Countess of Strafford, Lady Hervey took it upon herself to seek out and then forward on to her absent husband what she designated as current 'news' (or 'publick news'), an eighteenth-century term that implied information of political import. Her efforts did not go unrecognized. 'I thank my pretty industrious bee for all...news she gather for me', read a sweet-toned note of gratitude sent by Lord Hervey in 1702.[29] As

Elaine Chalus has discussed, the dissemination of 'news' in corre-spondence can be seen to have two interlinked purposes. It functioned as a powerful way of fostering a sense of community and inclusivity (by representing shared gossip that bound a group together). At the same time, news carried political value precisely because a family's opportunities and prospects might hinge on early knowledge of new developments and a rapid response to changing political tides.[30]

Both the Countess of Strafford and Lady Hervey were careful to ensure that their 'news' was as accurate as possible, corroborating or correcting details as necessary in subsequent missives. A flustered Countess of Strafford, for instance, found herself forced to retract a statement presented as verifiable 'news' in an earlier letter, lamenting that shifting tides of information meant that 'one writes one post to contradict the next'.[31] The more experienced Lady Hervey specified when she felt there was 'no news to depend on' or reassured her hus-band about the veracity of previous reports by stating clearly that 'all the news I wrote you in my last is true'.[32] Distinguishing between stra-tegic partisan reports, intended to obfuscate or otherwise skew the flow of information around town, and accurate news that reflected London's political temperature posed a particular challenge. For this reason, the Countess of Strafford routinely added caveats that certain information might only be 'Whigg news' designed to facilitate a specific political end, and singled out moments when the Whigs appeared to be gener-ating partisan reports with a view to unsettling the Tory-led peace process.[33]

Such was the importance of accuracy that the Countess of Strafford and Lady Hervey applied a common sliding scale of information that ranged from 'news' at one end (comprising information that was relia-bly confirmed) to 'scandal' at the other (which amounted to unreliable and possibly scurrilous hearsay). Between the two extremes lay 'town talk' and 'chatter chitter' or 'chit chat'. 'Town talk' suggested unconfirmed but potentially significant information. 'Chit chat' was deployed to designate information they feared either might be regarded as frivolous by the recipient, or which was potentially less reliable even than 'town talk' but not as dubious as 'scandal' (such as a rumour gleaned from a single visit rather than discussed at a number of locations).[34]

The scrupulous care taken by the Countess of Strafford and Lady Hervey to convey and categorize news with exactitude testifies to its importance. However, it is not simply the emphasis placed on political information in their letters that is significant. It is how and where the women received the news in the first place that is especially suggestive. Both women exploited their social connections and fully expected that routine social excursions would generate information of political merit. Following these women's quest for 'news', mapping the places they frequented and people they sought out to obtain it brings into sharper focus the indispensable role of metropolitan sociability to the political culture of London's beau monde.

Lady Hervey's acquisition of news extended across a range of social forms including: daytime visits to acquaintances at their homes (and receiving visits at hers); sociable suppers and dinners in the early afternoon or evening; regular theatre excursions; gaming parties; attendance at 'circles' (her description of assemblies) sometimes late into the night; appearances at court; and also occasional, irregular outings such as visits to fairs. On 25 April 1696, only a few years after their marriage, she reassured her new husband that she had on purpose visited Lady Manchester to 'see what [she] coud pick up for the day'.[35] The wife of an eminent Whig lord, Charles Montagu, Earl of Manchester (later, from 1719, Duke of Manchester), Lady Manchester was regarded by Lady Hervey as a key contact for news—'a great newsmonger'—and she routinely wrote to Manchester requesting written updates on days when she was unable to visit her ladyship in person.[36] As it happened, Lady Hervey's visit on 25 April 1696 proved fruitful. On the back of that single social call, she gleaned details of the movements of the navy, learned the date that parliament would adjourn, heard about the rumoured deaths of Lord Derwentwater and Lord Powis (significant Catholic courtiers who had remained loyal to the exiled James II), obtained information about the king's plans to 'besiege Dunkirk and Calais', and was given information about a grand entertainment planned at Portland House to welcome the Venetian ambassador. All this she dutifully relayed in a letter to her lord.[37]

It is clear that Lady Hervey routinely undertook visits to social contacts with the prime intention of obtaining political news. In May 1702, she reported discontentedly that a whole day had been spent in visits 'where I did not hear any thing but chit chat'.[38] Suggestively, she kept an open letter with her throughout the day, enabling her to add information as it was obtained. 'I am now going to my Lady Albermarle where I hope to meet with some news before I conclude this,' she wrote conversationally to her husband on one occasion. At first it seemed as though nothing of political interest would emerge from that outing: 'I am much disappointed having mett with no news here as I expected', she ended her letter before signing off. At the last moment, however, worthwhile news stirred and Lady Hervey added a hasty postscript: 'Lord Marlborough goes tomorrow, they say, if he is well enough', and explained the note was written 'from my Lady Albermarle's closet (where she has shut me to conclude this)'.[39] Taking an open letter with her on a visit to the Duchess of Grafton in March 1707 enabled Lady Hervey to add a separate account of the queen's speech that was given to her by the Duchess of Grafton's husband, Sir Thomas Hanmer, before signing off the missive to her husband.[40] In April 1709, she finished a letter during a visit to the Duchess of Marlborough where she heard the Treason Bill (which coordinated the treatment of treason across the newly unified England and Scotland) had passed in the Commons by twenty-three votes.[41] Another visit to the Duchess of

Grafton, this time in April 1713, allowed Lady Hervey to extend her letter to include recent news from a Commons debate and vote.[42] She also carried unfinished letters with her on routine outings to public social resorts. When attending a play in 1713, she reassured her husband that, 'if I can meet with anything before I come home, you shall hear from me again'.[43] Likewise, on 6 April 1716, Lady Hervey explained that she was taking her open letter with her, and should she hear any more news there then he would 'have it in a postscript after the Play'.[44]

Moreover, on closer examination, the pattern of sociability revealed by Lady Hervey's letters appears to be highly strategic. Throughout the 1710s (the decade when the Straffords were also resident in St James's Square) her epistolary accounts of routine urban activities testify to her integration in a factional web of politically significant personnel. By way of a sample, letters written between 1710 and 1712 reveal fortnightly, weekly, or even daily visits, dinners, and other forms of social encounters—such as theatre excursions, court attendance, and private assemblies—with a network of twenty-five titled women, the vast majority of whom were married to leading Whig politicians and courtiers. Most markedly, the Duchess of Marlborough and her daughters (all of whom were married to Whig peers who occupied offices of state) sat at the centre of that network, receiving regular visits from Lady Hervey, who also accompanied them to public social events. In these years she also attended the opera and dined with Lady Betty Germaine, former lady in waiting to Queen Anne and, from 1706, wife of Sir John Germaine (a Dutch army office who was reputedly the illegitimate half-brother of William III). By the 1710s, Sir John Germaine was an aspiring Whig politician and, unsurprisingly given his own status and his wife's court and family connections, had secured a seat as the MP for Morpeth in 1713. Another important social contact for Lady Hervey in these years was Lady Wharton who held regular assemblies for her acquaintances. Her husband Thomas Wharton, 5th Baron Wharton, was one of the 'Whig Junto' who (along with the likes of the Duke of Marlborough and the Earl of Sunderland) formed the collective leadership of the Whigs during the reigns of William III and Queen Anne. Also featured regularly in Lady Hervey's visits, dinners, and other social excursions was Lady Portland, wife of Henry Bentinck, 2nd Earl of Portland (shortly afterwards Duke of Portland), yet another key Whig figure, whose father had been a trusted adviser to William III.

While her female networks provided her with access to women who were sources of up-to-date news given their proximity to influential men, it is important to note that Lady Hervey's socializing was not limited to women. She recorded the Duke of Marlborough's presence at one of her own assemblies in April 1712 and, although usually attending the theatre or assemblies in the company of women, such sociability routinely brought her into conversation and contact with eminent Whig men.[45] What is clear from her letters is that Lady Hervey used these connections very specifically, as conduits to political information and by extension to political power and influence. She tapped both men and women for specific details of the progress of debates and the outcomes of parliamentary votes, for information about international affairs, and for insight into the shifts of personnel at court. Moreover, these agendas were both accepted and shared by her acquaintances. Such details, of course, were not simply valued as up-to-the-minute political news. They also had the potential to flag opportunities for personal advancement and familial power. Although Lord Hervey proved an ambivalent politician in the long term, much preferring the thrill of the racecourse to the thrust of the Westminster debate, the Herveys nonetheless sought parliamentary seats and court posts for their sons, and Lady Hervey pursued a lengthy campaign to secure a position as lady of the bedchamber for herself. In this regard, Lady Hervey's socio-political networking had overlapping aims, involving both short-term access to information and also long-term strategies for extending her family's position and power.

The factional nature of Lady Hervey's social networks is all the more evident when compared to the Countess of Strafford's practices. Although the countess's letters reveal that she followed a broadly similar pattern of sociability—involving visits, dinners, assemblies, and theatre visits—her main social contact was with a very different set of nobles. Detailing the first social calls she had made since moving into St James's Square in 1711, the Countess of Strafford reported to her husband:

> I have this day been to Lady North and Gr[e]y, and made her all the fine speeches I could think of & have promised to carry her to the opera wch she seem'd very pleas'd with...[at court] the Queen took a good deal of Notis of me & the Dutchess of Somerset is most extremely Civill to me [and] ingag'd me to dine with her & Lady Scarborough invited me to dinner but I was ingag'd before...Lady Bathurst and that family makes the greatest court in the world to me, Lord Berkeley has been twice to see me but I was not at hom[e] but I have been to see his daughters.[46]

The countess's immediate and respectful courting of Lady North and Grey highlights the importance the Straffords attached to her as a contact. Lady North and Grey's husband, William North (who held the titles of 6th Baron North and 2nd Baron Grey), was a high-church Tory and a powerful speaker in the House of Lords who routinely opposed any policies or initiatives introduced by the Duke of Marlborough. Notably at this time, the queen's leading minister lord treasurer Lord Harley focused on cultivating support not only amongst hard-line Tories such as Lord North and Grey but also amongst wavering and renegade Whigs such as the Duke of Somerset. Somerset's wife, noted by the Countess of Strafford as being particularly gracious at court, had recently replaced the Duchess of Marlborough as groom of the stole. Therefore, by ingratiating herself with Lady North and Grey and the Duchess of Somerset, the Countess of Strafford was singling out the wives of some of the most powerful governing grandees. The attention shown by Lady Bathurst was also surely welcome to the Straffords. Her husband Allen, Baron Bathurst, had been a Tory MP for Cirencester until he was raised to the peerage as part of Queen Anne's twelve new creations that parachuted reliable Tory gentlemen into the House of Lords as strategic support for Harley's government.

In the weeks that followed her initial overtures, the countess carefully cultivated her acquaintance with these and other women. Five days after meeting her at court, the countess was entertained at the Duchess of Somerset's grace and favour apartment. Encouraged and introduced by the duchess, she then made a formal visit to Queen Anne's newest confidante, Lady Masham, who readily avowed her friendship to both the countess and the absent earl. Having successfully introduced herself to Masham, that same evening the countess ventured to the Duchess of Shrewsbury's assembly, a regular *soirée* set up (it would seem) to provide a gathering point for Harley's Tory supporters.[47] Two days later, the countess accompanied Lady North and Grey to the opera, proudly reporting to her husband after the event that 'she seem'd mightily pleasd at my carr[y]ing of her'.[48] Shortly after that, the Duchess of Somerset visited the countess at St James's Square; 'she staid with me a great while and was very free and obliging', the countess explained with satisfaction. The connection seemed to be further secured when, the next day, the Duchess of Somerset's three daughters followed their mother's lead and paid a visit to the countess.[49]

Within a fortnight, the Countess of Strafford had exploited a range of a social forms—including visiting, attending the opera, and attending an assembly—to cultivate significant relationships with women who exercised political influence through their status as wives of prominent ministers or, in the case of Lady Masham, as court favourites. The success of her endeavour was marked by the fact that by December (only a

month after her initial overtures to Lady North and Grey and others)
the countess was delightedly receiving visits from these politically connected women as a group and not just as individuals. In a very clear
show of power on 11 December 1711, the countess was thrilled that
'Lady Oxford, [her daughter] Lady Betty Harley and Mrs Masham cam
hither together to night.'[50] By May 1712, the countess was acting as an
additional chaperone for Lady Betty, daughter of Lord Harley (lord
treasurer). 'The Ld Tresurer [*sic*] wont let Lady Betty goe to any Public
places with anybody but Lady Oxford except myself', she reported
proudly to her husband, 'Lady Oxford told me her L[or]d said if I wou'd
doe her the favour to let her goe with me he should be very glad.'[51]
There was no firmer statement of affiliation than acting as entrusted
escort to the lord treasurer's unmarried daughter.

Although her overtures appear to have been successful, the Countess
of Strafford's web of connections seems modest in comparison to Lady
Hervey's more expansive network. Excluding visits to immediate family, only between ten and twelve titled women are routinely mentioned
in the Countess of Strafford's letters as paying and receiving visits,
hosting the countess at assemblies and dinners, or accompanying her
to the court, theatre, and opera. Lady Hervey was juggling twice as
many established contacts. However, even though the countess's social
circle was relatively small, the Straffords were measured and strategic
in their identification and cultivation of key contacts. With only a few
exceptions, the countess courted the wives of critical Tory powerbrokers whose fortunes were ascending in light of ruptures between Queen
Anne and her former Whig ministers. As we have seen, Lady Hervey's
social circle, on the other hand, rotated around eminent Whigs and
opposition politicians.

The factional nature of the Countess of Strafford's and Lady Hervey's
social practices are clearly illuminated when placed side by side, but
this should not lead us to presume that they occupied metropolitan

worlds that were divorced from each other. Political partisanship was certainly important in shaping their networks, but their social contacts were not defined by faction alone. Lady Hervey, for instance, records the receipt of an invitation from the vibrant Duchess of Shrewsbury—the Duchess of Marlborough's rival—to join her for dinner and for cards. Similarly, the Countess of Scarborough invited the Countess of Strafford to dine with her on one occasion, despite the fact that the Earl of Scarborough was a close associate of the Marlboroughs (and therefore part of a political faction the Straffords treated with suspicion). Of course, these invitations may themselves have been politically strategic. Moreover, it is noteworthy that neither Lady Hervey nor the Countess of Strafford actually records *accepting* the invitations, only the receipt of them.[52] Nonetheless, such contacts point to the possibility of cross-party interaction. Similarly suggestive is the Countess of Strafford's passing mention of an unexpected encounter with the Whig Duchesses of Marlborough and Montagu. The tension between the women was palpable, with the countess claiming, with not a little pride, that both peeresses 'looked upon me with the most Spleen and mallis I ever see'. Notably the sneering encounter occurred 'in a visit'. The countess does not record to whom she was making the visit, but whosoever it was clearly welcomed visitors from various political camps. Significantly, although the Countess of Strafford made much of distancing herself from the Marlboroughs' politics it is important to recall that she had been quick and keen to seek them out as leaders of fashion. While factional divisions might loom large, then, in the management and nature of everyday social interactions such coteries were nevertheless incorporated under the broader umbrella of the beau monde.

The Countess of Strafford and Lady Hervey's ordinary correspondence to their out-of-town husbands is therefore compelling. Their purposeful, sustained engagement with the political currents of the metropolis in many ways corroborates the broader picture developed in recent scholarship on women's deep integration in contemporary political culture and in the politicized activities of their class.[53] 'Politics', as experienced by the Whig Herveys and the Tory Straffords, involved not just the formal institutions of court and parliament but also the web of social connections and interactions that made up the beau monde. The similarities between the forms of politicized sociability practised by the Countess of Strafford and Lady Hervey present them as comparable actors in a shared urban culture, even though their personal political preferences positioned them on opposite sides of a factional divide.

The chance survival of sets of letters written by near neighbours of comparable status and circumstances, covering the same years and the same society, but composed from different political perspectives, represents a rare archival treasure. From a different perspective, though, the scope and content of the Hervey and Strafford papers are unsurprising and commonplace. As other historians have noted, many eighteenth-century archives boast similar material. During the course of research for this book almost every collection of manuscripts, every bundle of letters, and every page of correspondence consulted has contained, to a greater or lesser extent, some reference or anecdote that could be construed as broadly 'political' in its intent. From this perspective, the politicized urban culture in which the Straffords and Herveys moved appears not to have been unique to their era, to a particular political moment, or to those individuals. It was, instead, typical of the very ordinary business of seasonal metropolitan society. The plethora of such anecdotal material reveals that the full expression and social dimensions of metropolitan elite political culture were long hiding in plain sight. Transcripts of parliamentary debates and a politician's 'official' papers might convey the period's political history in its most formal details. However, it is in the personal pocket book, in private correspondence, and from first-person comments on the routines of metropolitan society that the everyday business of politics is brought into view.

Moving away from the tense political climate encountered by the Straffords and Herveys in the 1710s and looking to the second half of the century, this final section provides a more general picture of how politics functioned in the context of fashionable life. The nature of the sources means that the information is inevitably subjective and does not lend itself to easy chronological or thematic comparison. Nor does it readily lead to comprehensive conclusions. Yet the broader portrait of political culture sketched by these accounts is still valuable, suggesting some marked continuities that reveal how the political agendas and social structures of the beau monde were bound together in the post-1689 metropolis.

The first striking feature of later eighteenth-century correspondence is an ongoing preoccupation with 'news'. In the 1740s, for instance, Jemima, Marchioness Grey reported in letters to her husband how visits to Lord and Lady Hardwicke at Grosvenor Square, and dinners at the same residence, furnished her with specific details of parliamentary machinations and news of the ill health of William Pitt (father of William Pitt the younger).[54] The 1750s saw her writing to her aunt from Richmond, a town whose 'nearness to London makes it the best News-mongering place that can be had in these curious and critical times'. 'We have all the Truths and all the Lies almost as fresh here as in the Capital,' she noted, 'and between the two we have totally different accounts every day of what is passing in the *Great World* in town.'[55] In the 1760s, Lady Anne Robinson wrote a teasing note to her brother Thomas Robinson, 2nd Baron Grantham, claiming herself unfit to convey any metropolitan news. 'You will perhaps begin to think I have forgot my promise of writing you all the news I hear but indeed what is said one day is so flatly contradicted the next that I should despair of ever writing if I waited till I could send nothing but truth.' 'I don't insist upon your believing all that I say,' she continued, 'but will send you my yesterdays intelligence.' The 'publick' news she conveyed included notes on who had been well received at a court *levée*, movements of personnel out of town, and the hopes of particular individuals for new offices and places.[56] 'I write all the news that I am hearing,' Lavinia, Lady Spencer, promised her husband in 1783, outlining her efforts and apologizing if she was unable to garner any new information.[57] 'I am now just going to the Opera where if I heard any more news I will write it to you but I shall send this letter now for fear I should return too late for the post,' she explained in one letter of that same year.[58] 'I went out in search of news, [but] found none,' she confessed in another.[59]

A similar information hierarchy to that found in the Hervey and Strafford accounts is also suggested in some later letters. Lady Harriot Eliot for one used 'chit chat' in a comparable way to its early eighteenth-century configuration, to delineate 'news' of a questionable status. 'I don't think that much occurs to me to day either in ye way of chit chat or anything better,' she confessed in 1783 within a letter to her brother, future Prime Minister William Pitt. 'Ye chit chat world', she noted a few years later, 'are entirely occupied with the Prince of Wales and Mrs Fitzherbert.'[60] Lavinia, Lady Spencer, carefully flagged news that could be relied upon and that which should be disregarded. 'In a bit of a letter I wrote to you last night was all the news that is new however I saw the D[uches]s of Devon[shire] at Ly Spencer who told me the Duke of Portland was exceeding pleased with everything that's going on...and she says Ld North has declared he will take no place.' 'Everything else that is said to be known,' she warned, 'is false and founded upon speculations and conjecture.'[61] Moreover, women's strategic use of social excursions to secure prescient political information appears to have been well recognized. Such was the connection that in 1771 *The Lady's Magazine* implied that ministers' wives were disguising newsgathering excursions as shopping trips, combining their search for court silks at Spitalfields with a quest for insight into the political and voting sentiments of the city residents. 'Several court ladies', the magazine asserted, 'have been lately to the city under the pretence of buying silks &c &c to gain intelligence of the disposition of the citizens. Amongst the rest Lord Talbot's daughter, Lady Cecil Rice, went on Tuesday last a shopping for news.'[62]

While these brief anecdotes reinforce existing analyses of women's close involvement and significant role in contemporary political culture, it is important to note that it was not only women who distributed news in this way, nor was it only men who received it. The Countess of Strafford regularly directed her husband to the additional details supplied by her father and brother-in-law, often acknowledging that they were better placed than she to relay specific information directly from parliament. Countess Spencer received regular political updates from a range of male correspondents in the 1760s, such as William Hamilton and various extended members of the Cavendish family, all of whom acknowledged their responsibility to send the latest information directly to her. Thomas Robinson, Baron Grantham, not only received news from his sister, he also received regular bulletins from twenty different London-based male letter writers when he was on diplomatic duties in Madrid.[63] One such correspondent was his younger brother, Frederick, who dutifully recorded the social encounters he had pursued in his quest for 'news'. A letter of 26 March 1779 revealed his presence at a private dinner, a private assembly, a ball, and the opera. He offered up all that he had heard, starting with articles of 'scandal' (with the proviso that Thomas paid no more credit to them than he 'would to the Morning Post') and continuing to the political 'intelligence' (that, again, Thomas was to treat with caution unless Frederick 'gave it as certain').[64]

Although the qualitative value of 'news' gathered at various social venues is hard to measure over time with any precision, in broad terms

FIGURE 33 *Politics*, Robert Pollard and John Wells, 1791.

the schedules and urban routines of those who participated in the London season in the late eighteenth century reveal the continued centrality of sociability to the political culture of the beau monde (Figure 33). So indivisible was the presumed relationship between social and political agendas that a ball hosted in 1764 by the usually reclusive Lord Cardigan perplexed society. 'I have been up all night at a magnificent ball at Lord Cardigan's', wrote one of the Countess Spencer's correspondents, 'it was a very handsome fete but people are curious to know *why* it was given as it is the first entertainment that has been known in that house.'[65] When William Pitt became prime minister, both his mother and sister routinely impressed on him the importance of maintaining social as well as political appearances. Unmarried himself, his sister, Lady Harriet Eliot, took on the role of hostess. Writing to her mother in 1786, Eliot explained how imminent childbirth was preventing her from fulfilling all social obligations, but that 'as soon as I am forth coming we are to give ye world some parties which I think will have some good effect'.[66] Pitt, it appears, concurred with his female relatives, acceding on more than one occasion that a timely ball might have its own political merits.

As intimated by the earlier Strafford and Hervey material, the metropolitan socio-political system associated with the season and the beau monde involved multiple sites and varied types of social encounter. Visiting networks, combined with other forms of domestic sociability, are repeatedly revealed as providing ballast to London's political infrastructure. In 1767, for example, Lady Mary Coke recorded a visit she received from Mr Erskine and Sir Gilbert Elliot during which they 'talk'd politics'. Coke noted with satisfaction that her visitors 'agreed with me that Mr Townshend having differ'd with Lord Chatham was very unlucky, & had been detrimental to the publick affairs'. She furnished them with the news that 'Lady Rockingham [had] invited Mr Townshend to supp with her & that she had done the same by Mr Conway when he was supposed to be cool toward the ministers.' 'A fine lady w[oul]d always have influence', Coke noted tellingly, '& [therefore] I wish'd [ministers] wou'd not accept of her invitations.'[67] On another occasion, an evening's excursions took Lady Mary Coke first to dinner at the Duke of Richmond's, then to a concert attended by the Duke of York (who had, himself, come from the theatre), and then on to Lady Temple's for cards. At her final engagement, Coke scrutinized the behaviour of eminent politicians. 'The Opposition heads', she noted, 'seem'd very busy. Lord Weymouth and George Grenville were in a whisper a long time together. Lord Suffolk by his gayety one must think has quite forgot his Lady tho' I believe she can't have been dead above a few months, but his Lordship is so great a politition [sic] he cou'd not give the usual time to sorrow.'[68] In his memoirs, Thomas Robinson, Baron Grantham, similarly acknowledged the centrality of sociability at private residences to the political culture of his era. Recalling October 1761, he remembered how 'the Earl of Granville used in general to set at home & receive such visitors as his high matron

& lively conversation attracted at all hours of the day'. 'People of all ranks & parties were fond of seeing him,' Grantham noted, '& he one day told Lord Winchelsea, my father & myself that by staying at home he saw the Ministers that were out as well as those that were in & that he had very lately been visit by Mr Pitt & Lord Temple, Lord Bute and my Lord Egremont. The two former had just resigned their employments & ye latter were both secretaries of state.'[69]

Contemporary awareness of the protocols that structured sociability was finely tuned. The sudden cessation of visits, marked absences from dinners or assemblies, and more subtle signs such as frosty acknowledgements between individuals were closely monitored lest they suggested a cooling of socio-political acquaintance. For example, in 1765 George Grenville regarded the Duchess of Bedford's failure to visit Lady Bute as a signal of increased tension between the Bute and Bedford factions. Following mob attacks on Bedford House, the duchess remained at home receiving a stream of well-wishers whose visits in conspicuous equipages doubled as public displays of support. Lady Bute's carriage, however, never once drew up to the door.[70] In the 1740s, Lady Hertford found that her husband's political position and actions had pronounced ramifications on her social reception. Following the resignation of Robert Walpole in January 1742, the Earl of Hertford had been asked by the king to give up his office as a commander of the Guards in favour of the Duke of Argyll, a major figure who had been instrumental in Walpole's demise. Although Argyll was initially offered the post and for a time accepted, a few months later he had resigned and the office returned once more to Hertford. Shortly after, Lady Hertford encountered Argyll's family en masse at an assembly, where they made no small show of their discontent. 'At night I went to the Duchess of Norfolk's where there was as assembly, and the first object that struck my eyes was the Duchess of Argyle [sic] and her daughters,' she explained. 'Her Grace did not, or would not, see me. I made a curtsey to Lady Caroline who returned it, but my Lady Stafford and the two other sisters chose to look as if they did not know me, though when I was talking to somebody else I saw Lady Mary making remarks upon me and laughing with another lady whose back was toward me.' It was to prove a trying assembly for Lady Hertford as the Argylls continued to make their dissatisfaction clear:

> Presently, after the Duke of Argyle came in and I rose from my seat to make him a curtsey but he tossed his head the other way and passed by me with two or three of the most stately strides I ever beheld. Yet I had command enough upon my countenance to forbear laughing, though I had like to have lost my gravity when I saw my Lord Bathurst who followed him in (and whom I was intimately acquainted with) durst not venture to look upon for fear (as I suppose) of offending his Grace; though all my crime was being my Lord Hertford's wife a crime which (as the Duchess of Marlborough said upon another occasion) I could neither help nor repent of. When I was going away, I was to pass through a small, narrow rooms in the right hand of which the Duke of Argyle's four daughters, my Lord Hertford's sisters and two or three people whom I did not know were sitting all in a row. I curtsied as civilly to them as I could in passing by, but not one of them moved from their chairs.[71]

It was not only at private events such as visits and assemblies that politics informed sociability. London's burgeoning commercial resorts were also clearly harnessed for socio-political interaction and information exchange. As has already been noted, the value of the theatre and opera as potential locations for the gathering of 'news' can be found flagged in a number of different accounts. From Lady Hervey's promise of carrying her unfinished letter to the theatre in the 1710s to Lady Spencer's similar intention with regard to the opera in the 1780s, London's major auditoria offered more than staged entertainment. For James Harris, the opera proved as good a place as any to exploit encounters with high-ranking politicians in order to express and exchange political sentiments. Indeed, his personal papers vividly illuminate the informal and highly flexible nature of the socio-political systems that operated in the metropolis.

Significantly, Harris kept two sets of parallel memorandum books when in London during the 1770s. In small pocket diaries he recorded a minimal tally of his daily routine.[72] Alongside these diaries, Harris also wrote an informal log on separate sheaves of loose papers variously titled 'Conversations in London' (1770), 'Memorandums in London' (1775), and 'Stories and Facts in London' (1776-7).[73] These scraps contained brief conversations and information deemed to be of political importance but garnered during ostensibly sociable encounters.

Read side by side, Harris's two systems of record keeping illustrate how even the most ordinary social excursion had hidden political potential. With regard to the opera, for example, a diary entry in Harris's pocketbook for 7 March 1776 simply logs his attendance ('at ye opera').[74] Amidst his informal notes on 'Memorandums in London', however, an entry dated 7 March 1776 reads: 'I met Lord Temple at the opera—I exprest my satisfaction on ye speech he had made in ye Lords house in favour of our measures against America—he talked much on the subject—said they were always his sentiments.'[75] A diary entry for February 1777 places Harris at an assembly at Mrs Pitt's ('assembly Mrs Pitt').[76] His separate notes on 'Stories and Facts in London', though, reveal that while there he 'saw Lord Templeton', who took the opportunity to share some forceful political views:

> He [Ld Templeton] told me that David Hume not long before his death should fortell the total diffusion of the colonies from Great Britins [sic], the loss of the east indies and all its territories, and annihilation of the national debt & ye first suppression of the democratic power amongst us in consequence of many patriots who would make their last dying speeches for treason at tyburn. That we should then pass a kind of aristocratical term compos'd of the king the nobility & a few of the most opulent & powerful commoners. He added that he did not expect to see this during his own time but did not appear much to disapprove the project.[77]

Clearly kept as personal notes not intended for a wider readership, Harris's small pocketbook diaries detail only the barest bones of a metropolitan schedule stripped of all context or description, whilst the additional notes he compiled under separate headings amount to a few hundred words of hastily scribbled, half-formed sentences. Yet it is precisely these features that make them so evocative and valuable. The titles Harris gave to his personal accounts are themselves compelling. He underscores that these are '*London* conversations', '*London* memorandum', '*London* stories and facts' and, specifically, '*London* diaries'. In this way, his metropolitan routines are singled out as something specific, meaningful, and distinct. The exchanges happening during the course of the season were, for Harris, worthy of a separate account. Moreover, working like footnotes to his diary, the primarily political nature of his 'notes to self' expose in plainer view what is so often buried deep in personal accounts or left unrecorded. At the opera, at court, at assemblies, at salons, through visits and dinners, Harris obtained—sometimes through accident and sometimes through design—information that he valued for its political potential.

The evidence presented here reveals a political culture that was embedded in the daily routines of the beau monde. The concentrated nature of elite society in London during the season, combined with the timetabled and predictable form of much of that society's sociability, made all manner of socio-political encounters possible. Indeed, it is the very ordinariness of the intersection between social and political activities and intent that emerges most clearly from such personal records. Few seem to have questioned the way in which politics spilled into metropolitan networks and into sociable excursions. These accounts suggest that these interconnections were flexible, functional, and taken largely for granted by metropolitan participants.

It is important to recognize that this predominantly inward-looking pattern of political information exchange should not be regarded as the sum of what 'politics' meant within London or within eighteenth-century Britain more broadly. The anecdotal and metropolitan nature of the material cited here certainly has the potential to accentuate the insularity of elite political culture. In addition, manuscript letters and diaries are in their very nature personal artefacts and not necessarily the place where lengthy political strategies were outlined and ideological positions expounded. Moreover, very different political cultures and very different sets of political practices are likely to have operated in the context of regional authority at the level of the parliamentary seat. There, as other studies have shown, outward-facing and direct engagement with the electorate (even if a limited electorate), and also with a non-voting public, was essential for the maintenance of political power. Perhaps the common thread of these different political realms was their community-based and local nature. The London community in which the elite operated during the season, however, was of a different, more exclusive, and more explicitly parliamentary-oriented nature.

Although this study can only offer a partial view of contemporary politics, the model that it provides of London's beau monde and its political culture has a number of arresting features. The principal urban spaces that the beau monde frequented—from commercial leisure resorts to private homes, from the streets of Westminster to the interior rooms of court and parliament—ensured that high-ranking peers, key political figures, aspiring politicians, their extended families, acquaintances, and intermediaries were likely to be encountered in a range of predictable places and contexts. This created an exclusive political culture limited to those who enjoyed access to such circles. At the same time, its informal and sociable nature ensured that all those who boasted a passport to London's fashionable ranks, women as well as men, were able to participate in its interior political systems. Indeed, the commonality of the political experiences of different participants is especially striking. James Harris's record of political conversations and the places in which they occurred does not seem so very far removed from the

Countess of Strafford or Lady Hervey's use of social networks and venues to generate political knowledge and 'news'. Divided not only by gender but by half a century, their experiences suggest a social world of robust continuity. The material assembled here makes no claim to complete coverage of the period. Yet the ways in which fashionable society practised politics, and the language they used to describe it, were remarkably enduring. These patterns of continuities are themselves suggestive of the nature of London's beau monde. Specific political affiliation created partisan divisions within metropolitan elite society but they did not necessarily imply major social or cultural ruptures. Instead both opposition and loyalty were successfully accommodated within the broader collective culture of the fashionable elite. Arguably, London's beau monde was highly politicized precisely because such a range of political identities could be expressed within its ranks.

If anything, it appears that a broader principled conviction existed that politics in general rather than party in particular was the core business of the beau monde. Indeed, the very act of participating in fashionable society could be said to have effectively constituted a political performance. After all, the season itself was built on a parliamentary timetable, and the bringing together of a concentrated coterie of elite personnel in the capital was deemed an essential component of a balanced system of governance. Even at those times when attendance at the opera and theatre did not furnish fresh political insight, when visits provided only gossip but no 'news', and when interactions at an assembly failed to expose any changes in political allegiances or ambition, the simple presence of the elite in London and participation in that social world was a political statement. Highly visible to the public, the beau monde's seasonal activities in London represented the importance of the parliamentary timetable, and the responsibility now taken by the governing elite to function as a cohesive body that would check the power of monarchy and court.

5

Beauties

'So pow'rful her charms'[1]

> Thus Kitty, beautiful and young,
> And wild as colt untamd,
> Bespoke the fair from when she sprung,
> ...Inflamed with rage at sad restraint,
> Which wise mamma ordarin'd,
> And sorely vex'd to play the saint,
> Whilst wit and beauty reign'd.
>
> (Matthew Prior, *The Female Phaeton:*
> *Upon Lady Kitty Hyde's First Appearing in Publick*, 1718)

Several ladies of quality, offended that so many persons of inferior rank should be admitted into all public places with them have determined upon having an assembly by subscription...at the head of this scheme are the three noted beauties, the Duchess of Devonshire, Lady Derby and the Marchioness of Granby.

> (*Morning Post and Daily Advertiser*, London, 24 June 1776)

There was more Company at the Ball than I had ever seen...[Lord Polwarth] might have had the more superlative happiness of setting down to Maco, [with] the two beauty Duchesses of Devonshire & Rutland...the Duchesses seem to be full as eager at it as any body, which considering their beauty & rank one cannot help being sorry for.

> (Manuscript letter from Lady Mary Yorke to Amabel, Lady Polwarth,
> 15 March 1780)

In October 1776, the *Morning Post* published a 'Scale of Bon Ton' that graded twelve fashionable women according to their beauty, figure, elegance, wit, sense, grace, expression, sensibility, and principles. Listed by rank, the Duchess of Devonshire and the Duchess of Gordon topped the chart. They were followed by the Countesses of Derby, Jersey, Barrymore, and Sefton; Ladies Harriet Foley, Anna Maria Stanhope, and Melbourne; and Mrs Damer (daughter of Lady Ailesbury), Mrs Crewe (later Lady Crewe), and Mrs Bouverie (later Lady Robert Spencer).[2] A month earlier, the *London Chronicle* had carried its own 'Scale of Beauties' which compared the 'person', 'expression', 'complexion', and 'grace' of seven women. The Duchess of Devonshire, Lady Derby, and Mrs Crewe were once again singled out, alongside Ladies Sarah Lennox, Townshend, Ligonier, and Carpenter.[3] These women, though, were not the only recognized beauties of the age. From Matthew Prior's celebration of the Duchess of Queensbury as 'Kitty beautiful and young' in his poem of 1718 to a letter written by Lady Mary Yorke that styled the Duchesses of Rutland and Devonshire simply as the 'two beauty duchesses', beauty appears as a distinguishing trait of women of 'the ton'.[4] Subsequent biographers and historians, particularly those writing in the first decades of the twentieth century, have been quick to reproduce these descriptions, seemingly dazzled by their subjects' charm. Horace Bleackley's 1907 history of Elizabeth, Duchess of Hamilton, for example, was published as *The Story of a Beautiful Duchess*. John Fyvie offered a collective study of the *Wits, Beaux and Beauties of the Georgian Era* (1909), and both Frances Calvert and A. M. Broadly stressed the avowed 'beauty' of their subjects with, respectively, *An Irish Beauty of the Regency* (1911) and *The Beautiful Lady Craven* (1914).[5]

However, simply acknowledging and reiterating that these figures were 'beautiful' tells us little about them. The biographical recitation of the claim that beauty was amongst their main claims to fame has arguably done little for the history of these women, merely confirming stereotypes of their superficiality and frivolity. For many feminists, beauty remains the final frontier of female oppression in modern society. 'No woman escapes beauty,' writes Francette Pacteau, 'unavoidably from her earliest years, beauty will be either attributed or denied her. If she does not have it, she may hope to gain it, if she possesses it, she will certainly lose it.'[6] Naomi Wolf has strongly argued that 'the ideology of beauty is the last one remaining of the old feminine ideologies that still has the power to control women'.[7] What then should we make of the repeated contemporary assertion that certain women of the beau monde were 'great beauties'? Does the representation of elite women in these terms suggest their fundamental cultural subjugation? For all these women's evident political involvement and social authority, does the persistent allusion to fashionable women's beauty in fact attest to the ideological limits imposed on their power and position?

This chapter explores the commonplace attribution of 'beauty' to women of the beau monde to establish what the accolade meant when applied to the titled ladies of fashionable London. Through this investigation, it becomes apparent that 'beauty' was not so much a subjective celebration of women's physical allure but was rather intended as a more objective acknowledgement of their social status and public profile. When associated with women of rank, the values presumed by contemporaries to comprise their beauty were closely tied to ideas of behaviour, manners, and other qualities that were perceived to make these women fit and proper holders of their social station. In this regard, 'beauty' becomes a less surprising attribute for fashionable elite women, for on one level it functioned as another statement of their social prestige. To be a 'beauty' was, in certain forms of commentary, synonymous with being a female member of the beau monde. A fashionable woman could not, by definition, be anything but 'beautiful'. Yet, the link to social status was not wholly straightforward. Like 'fashion', although 'beauty' can be found to have been a regular adjunct to noble title ('beautiful duchesses' in particular are commonplace), it was also perceived as encompassing qualities that extended beyond inherited rank alone. This created certain discursive tensions, for although the social position of a 'beauty' might be elevated, commentators warned that it might not be wholly secure.

Attempts to define the beautiful are age old. Retained as a central problematic of Western philosophical thought, questions about how beauty was expressed and experienced have been variously addressed in moral philosophies, theology, natural science, aesthetic discourse, and literature. A history of ideas about beauty has long been approached as one of philosophical complexity, demanding studied familiarity with tracts penned by male thinkers from Plato to Aquinas and Nietzsche to Marx. In such works, beauty is variously approached as a supreme expression of cosmological symmetry, of divine intervention in the natural world, a profound form of human secular sensibility, and even as a fiction used to shore up capitalist power.[8] Yet amidst this broad literature, eighteenth-century philosophies and theories about beauty have been singled out as representing a specific moment of change.[9]

During this period, a broad range of contemporary tracts, from poetry to artists' manuals, espoused the traits presumed to compose the beautiful. Some eighteenth-century writers restricted their discussion to standards of artistic style. Others pondered the appearance of the ideally beautiful woman. Alongside those who argued over which features or elements did or did not make up the beauty ideal were commentators and theorists who asserted with equal vigour that beauty could take on many different forms and, indeed, that part of its appeal lay in its originality. Like a phoenix, the beautiful woman was deemed matchless and unique. As one early eighteenth-century writer lamented, 'how uncertain Beauty is thy State, ten thousand ways defin'd, thou ist the Fantom Creature of each mind'.[10] The diversity of contexts in which 'beauty' was analysed and debated means that it is not possible to chart a single or neat trajectory of change in the eighteenth-century ideas that surround it. There are, however, a number of identifiable shifts and broad patterns in the way in which beauty was described and debated that help nuance our understanding of the concept. To begin with, and as demonstrated by Robert Jones, there was a substantial shift in what might be termed the 'beauty paradigm' that became particularly pronounced from the mid-century onwards. Rather than regarding beauty as an abstract or metaphysical construction, commentators increasingly defined it as a human quality primarily attributed to women.[11]

In terms of the female form, eighteenth-century commentators approached the nature of beauty in a wide range of ways. Unsurprisingly, descriptions of women's attractiveness were often articulated in terms drawn from a varied and changeable artistic climate. For instance, the 1733 poem *Beauty and Proportion* noted that female beauty often 'lies in symmetry of parts', with 'roman nose', 'high-turn'd forehead and well-set eyes', a language that echoed a contemporary preoccupation with ordered classicism.[12] In contrast, artist William Hogarth's famous mid-century treatise on beauty argued that a more disorderedly style was truly beautiful, with curved lines and uneven structures providing a greater delight to the eye than regularity. The notion that 'the greatest part of the effects of beauty results from the symmetry of parts' had 'no foundation', he claimed. Instead, 'when the head of a fine woman is turn'd a little to one side, which takes off from the exact similarity of the two halves of the face, and somewhat reclining, so varying still more from the straight and parallel lines of a formal front face, it is always look'd upon as most pleasing'.[13] Consequently, for Hogarth, an 'irregularity' of features—either created by nature or constructed 'by a lock of hair falling across the temples' to break the 'regularity of the oval'—was essential to the tribute of 'beauty'.[14] Hogarth went further still and moved beyond the face to promote a curvaceous female form, celebrating,

> the elegant degree of plumpness peculiar to the skin of the softer sex, that occasions these delicate dimplings in all their other joints, and... presents to the eye all the varieties in the whole figure of the body, with gentler and few parts more sweetly connected together, and with such fine simplicity as will always give the fine turn of the female frame...the preference over men.[15]

For some commentators, physical beauty consisted of a multitude of small details. *The Ladies Magazine* of 1772, for instance, argued that beauty required an 'oval face', 'skin transparent', 'firm [and] vermillioned' cheeks, 'moderately large' eyes, and a small bosom as 'too much bosom disfigures and appears rather vulgar'.[16] At the end of the century round-ness was back in vogue. The 1795 *Dictionary of Love* set out 'perfect beauty' in a daunting list of twenty-eight specific points, of which the first was youth. Also demanded of the 'beauty' was a 'well-rounded head', 'cheeks wide but not plump with red and white, finely blended', a 'white, round, firm and soft' arm and a 'white and charming' bosom with 'breasts equal in roundness, whiteness and firmness', an 'even and well rounded knee', 'sweet breath', and 'an agreeable voice'.[17]

A range of artificial aids were available that claimed to help women replicate such ideals. In fact, the basic products, colour schemes, and application of make-up changed relatively little over the course of the century. Beauty patches, and ornate containers for their storage, often appear in representations and records of eighteenth-century women. Their use peaked between the 1690s and early 1700s. Ostensibly designed to cover smallpox scars, beauty patches were also presumed to form part of a subtle sign system. The position of a patch was said to betray a wealth of meanings, from political persuasion (depending whether the patch was worn on the left or right side of the face), to temperament and marital status (a single patch to the side of the upper lip would be the favoured style for the single but flirtatious young woman). Applying make up required time and skill. The skin would first be softened with beeswax or lard, and then whitened with lead-based ceruse paint. The cheeks were rouged with henna or carmine made from cochineal, a red dye extracted from crushed beetles, and a glazed effect was achieved by painting a layer of egg white over the decorated skin. By the end of the century, the development of a pearl-based powder was a more practical alternative that achieved less sticky but equally luminous results. Inside the mouth, porcelain plates were often inserted to disguise black and rotten teeth, and cork 'plumpers' puffed out sunken cheeks.[18] Women's use of cosmetics was also about more than the manipulation of physical appearance. The ornate, expensive, and often gilded items of eighteenth-century 'toilette' furni-ture—including matching table, mirrors, pots, and brushes—were regarded as essential accoutrements and provide vivid testimony to the value placed on this aspect of a fashionable woman's routine.[19] Demanding wealth, time, space, and the aid of servants and know-ledgeable assistants, beauty routines were powerful forms of (and sites for) status display (Figure 34).

Whilst often reflecting status, the use of products to counterfeit or exaggerate attributes was also a source of considerable anxiety for many commentators. In the early years of the century, criticisms of artificial beauty were particularly vicious. Many tracts thundered that beauty was only ever granted by nature, and that the use of cosmetics was a path to the moral decay of the individual and even the nation. In this context, cosmetics were variously cited as yet another symptom of the curses brought with foreign imports, evidence of the perils of urban living and the debilitating effect of 'luxury'.[20] More importantly, though, the fact that these materials might be purchased and used by all and sundry was

FIGURE 34 *Six Stages of Mending a Face dedicated with respect to the Rt Hon Lady Archer*, Thomas Rowlandson, 1792. In this vicious portrait, Rowlandson depicts a fashionable hostess, the fifty-one-year old Lady Archer, at six different stages of her toilet from undress to a 'youthful' beauty created by artifice.

often viewed as a threat to rank and status. From this perspective, cosmetics enabled an 'unnatural' mimicry of exclusivity by those lower down the social scale who were 'naturally' unworthy of such an accolade. The prostitute might daub her face, mask her depravity, and present herself as a virtuous lady. In 1755, *The World* warned titled women away from paint, arguing that such practices placed them too close to 'inferiors' and also made emulation too easy. After listing the various methods of 'face-painting' increasingly employed (it was argued) by women of different ranks, *The World* called for the protection of the natural order:

> Let us follow nature, our honest and faithful guide; and be upon our guard against the flattering delusions of art. Nature may be helped and

improved, but will not be forced or changed. All attempts in direct opposition to her are attended with ridicule…The woman to whom nature has denied beauty, in vain endeavours to make it by art.[21]

Although at times the site of anxiety, therefore, physical beauty was highly prized by elite society, and was widely discussed and evaluated within their correspondence. Moreover, to these insiders, beauty could itself become a commodity that might bring advantage within London's marriage market. These letters frequently overlap descriptions of beauty with those of rank, but the importance of physical attractiveness is nonetheless clear. For instance, commenting on Frances Anne Greville, Lady Sarah Bunbury wrote in 1766 that,

> Miss Greville is vastly improved and is prettier than ever; she and her mother go to Munich next spring Mr Greville is Envoy there…I hope she will be married though for once she goes abroad, nobody knows how long she may stay, and if her beauty goes off her money won't get her married.[22]

Here, 'beauty' is depicted as a short-term commodity that could be traded against other valuable qualities, such as wealth and title. Although a 'Miss', Frances Anne Greville was not without aristocratic connections and credentials. Her parents, diplomat Fulke Greville and poet Frances Macartney, enjoyed close friendships with Henry Fox, his wife Lady Caroline Lennox, Lady Spencer (mother of Georgiana, Duchess of Devonshire), and others in that Whig elite set. Yet, dynastically removed from the highest peaks of the peerage, Frances's marriage prospects were comparatively precarious. In Lady Sarah Bunbury's definition, Frances Anne Greville's 'beauty' related to a more overtly physical prettiness, which counterbalanced her ambiguous social status. Her physical 'prettiness' conveyed a status of its own, ensuring that she would at least appear to be of 'rank' even if the external image did not match up to the reality of her heritage. This arithmetic could also work both ways. When commenting on the proposed match between Miss Sackville, the Duke of Dorset's granddaughter, and Sir Francis Molyneux (a baronet and courtier holding the post of Black Rod), Lady Mary Coke feared the match might not meet the proposed bride's 'expectations', given that 'great birth and great beauty might certainly have found something more advantageous'.[23]

As this begins to suggest, physical beauty stirred another element of risk and unpredictability into the world of the beau monde. Attractiveness of face or form was not decided by antiquity of title or depth of pocket, but could work its influence upon both. More worryingly still, a pleasing appearance could be possessed by someone on the margins of this elite, or even outside it altogether—with or without the use of paint and plumpers.

It is in this context that we should consider a moment in early 1753 when two grand carriages, escorted by liveried coachmen, left the bustle of London and rumbled northwards on separate roads out of the metropolis. Closely followed by entourages hauling a rich bounty of clothes, linen, and jewels, they steadily progressed through the provinces. En route, crowds mobbed the conspicuous caravans in an effort to glimpse their cargo. Causing the frenzy were two women, each leaving London to visit their new husbands' country seats and thereby entering patrician life. Born Elizabeth and Maria Gunning and married to wealthy, titled bachelors soon after their inaugural London season, the Countess of Coventry and Duchess of Hamilton seemed unable to escape the bubble of publicity in which they moved. Describing the 'great racket' the Duchess of Hamilton provoked in the north, Jemima, Marchioness Grey told Catherine Talbot how 'people of the best fashion in the place hired Windows at the Inns to see her get out of the coach', and 'ladies who had been dancing all Night at the Assembly' were 'at the Inn at five o'clock in the morning not to miss her going out'. 'As to the mob below stairs', the Marchioness continued, 'they were so thick that the Servants were obliged to make way by force & pull the Duchess from the Coach to the House.'[24]

The successful elevation of the Gunning sisters into the peerage, and into the world of fashion, captured contemporary imagination. However, it was not only their remarkable social climb that intrigued commentators and observers. Instead, their fame also rested on their reputation as 'incomparable beauties'. 'As you talk of our beauties I shall tell you a new story of the Gunnings, who make more noise than any of their predecessors since the days of Helen', wrote Horace Walpole to Horace Mann in 1752, continuing:

> They went the other day to Hampton Court. As they were going into the Beauty Room another company arrived. The housekeeper said, 'this way ladies; here are the beauties'. The Gunnings flew into a passion and asked her what she meant, they came to see the palace and not to be shown as a sight themselves.[25]

After arriving in London in 1752, the Gunning sisters had been catapulted into public acclaim, fêted in poems, memorialized in engravings and miniatures, reported by the press, and endlessly discussed in contemporary gossip (Figure 35). Reputedly from impoverished gentry stock, Maria and Elizabeth Gunning had little conventional currency to trade in the London marriage market, and few of the assets required to secure membership of the fashionable world. Their immediate fame and ultimate social success was instead portrayed as the result of their beauty alone. 'The two Miss Gunnings,' explained Horace Walpole, are 'two Irish girls of no fortune who are declared the handsomest women alive. I think there being two so handsome and both such perfect figures is their chief excellence, for singly I have seen much handsomer women than either; however they cant walk in the park or go to Vauxhall but such mobs follow them that they are generally driven away.'[26] Such was the celebrity generated by their physical allure that the gates of fashionable society opened to receive them. Two gilded

FIGURE 35 White enamel plaques of Elizabeth and Maria Gunning, John Brookes, *c*.1752. These transfer-printed portraits were engraved after pastel portraits by Francis Cotes. This technique allowed for quick, and comparatively cheap, reproduction of portrait miniatures.

bachelors, the Duke of Hamilton and the Earl of Coventry, moved swiftly to claim the sisters as beautiful brides. Indeed, Hamilton reputedly lost a fortune on the gaming table when, dazzled by the sight of Elizabeth, he failed to pay attention to his cards. After their marriages, the Gunnings—now known as Elizabeth, Duchess of Hamilton, and Maria, Countess of Coventry—continued to excite attention. Their court presentations were reported to have generated an unseemly and un-courtly crush when the nobility crowded the drawing room and clambered on furniture to witness the moment the women were formally acknowledged by the crown. In 1755, a number of years after her marriage, Lady Coventry still found herself the object of, on this occasion unwanted, attention at a masquerade. Repeating a story heard second-hand, Mary Delany reported that Coventry was approached and scrutinized at the entertainment by a masked woman who, after careful consideration, declared she had 'heard a great deal of [Lady Coventry's] beauty', and pronounced 'it far surpasses all I have heard'. According to the tale, Lady Coventry exclaimed in response, 'What! Did you never see me before?', as though not to know her and be familiar with her 'beauty' was a surprise and even an insult.[27]

Much of the commentary detailing the Gunnings' social trajectory—whether in manuscript letters describing their appearance or in the multitude of published poems that praised their beauty—verged on hyperbole, with their apparent 'rags to riches' story generating its own mythology and mystique. Contemporary descriptions of their effect on society were not, however, straightforwardly celebratory; sharp and critical undercurrents were never far from the surface. Walpole's description of the Gunnings' unwarrantedly haughty reaction at Hampton Court, and Delany's report of Lady Coventry's similar conceit at a masquerade, portray the women in a dubious light. The ambiguous tone of such commentary accurately reflects the fact that the Gunnings' celebrity and social success had an unsettling and disruptive quality. Pursued by 'mobs' in public places, and triggering similarly rabble-like behaviour even amongst the 'people of fashion' themselves, disorder seemed to trail in these women's wake; and their beauty was the cause of this mayhem.[28]

The drama that surrounded the Gunnings was thus tinged with disapproval and ridicule, and carried the deeper misgiving that beauty was their only qualification to membership of fashionable society. That this chance possession had somehow been transformed into a different form of status baffled and alarmed the fashionable world. After their marriages, commentators still dwelled on their physical beauty but coupled that preoccupation with an emphasis on the Gunnings' lack of breeding and inability to master the manners and mores of the fashionable world. 'Poor Lady Coventry', Horace Walpole scoffed, 'besides being very silly, ignorant of the world, breeding, speaking no

French . . . she had that perpetual drawback upon her beauty, her lord, who is sillier in a wise way, as ignorant, ill-bred and speaking very little French himself—just enough to show how ill-bred he is.'[29] Vulgarity unworthy of noble rank, such commentary implied, lay beneath the Gunnings' beautiful veneer. As this infers, Walpole also made little effort to disguise his disdain for the Duke of Hamilton's and Earl of Coventry's actions. In his view, Hamilton's loss of sense at the gaming table and hasty, impassioned decision to wed Elizabeth Gunning 'damaged his fortune and person', and Coventry—a 'lord of the remains of a patriot breed'—dishonoured 'his credit' by marrying Maria. The key concern, as Robert Jones has highlighted, was that these aristocrats had somehow been unmanned by the Gunnings' beauty and, moreover, had been driven to act against the interests of their patrician heritage and status.[30] By marrying the women, rather than taking them as mistresses, Hamilton and Coventry sullied their own titles but, significantly, they also rewarded mere physical beauty with verifiable rank.

In the longer term, the personal experiences and cultural representation of the two 'beautiful' Miss Gunnings followed very different trajectories. Maria, Countess of Coventry, died in 1760 only a few years after her marriage, allegedly poisoned by her lead-based white make-up. That beauty should be her downfall as well as the source of her elevation figured as a form of divine retribution that became part of the Gunnings' story, resurrected by early twentieth-century biographers. To contemporaries, the fact that Maria should have been so keen to maintain her physical allure merely confirmed suspicions that she lacked any other credentials to support her position. In contrast, Maria's sister, Elizabeth, enjoyed a smoother transition into fashionable society. Key to Elizabeth's subsequent career was the death of the Duke of Hamilton in 1758, six years after their whirlwind marriage. Mother to three children, including an heir (James Douglas Hamilton, 7th Duke of Hamilton) and a spare (Douglas Douglas-Hamilton, later 8th Duke of Hamilton), the demise of her husband left the 24-year-old Elizabeth as the effective head of a substantial ducal estate. Until her son came of age, the duchess was invested with the authority to control the family's associated political and economic interests. Therefore, whatever the limitations of her background, there was no disputing Elizabeth's subsequent status. Her credentials were further bolstered with a second marriage to Jack Campbell, heir to the 3rd Duke of Argyll, and a place at court as a lady of the bedchamber to Queen Charlotte from 1761. In stark contrast to images and descriptions of Maria, which emphasized her vanity and social vulgarity, the widowed Elizabeth was portrayed in contemporary portraiture and popular narratives as a sober peeress, bearing all the armorial insignia associated with her rank (Figure 36). Her absorption was complete.

Biographers of the Gunnings have often been swept up in the romantic drama of their lives. It is perhaps tempting to cite their famed 'beauty' as symptomatic of the potential inclusivity of the beau monde, or at least of its ill-defined grounds for membership. After all, both enjoyed titanic celebrity, but brought little except their physical attractiveness to barter their way into London's fashionable world and aristocratic families. It is more likely, though, that the intertwined celebrity and notoriety they achieved attests to the exceptional nature of their experiences. Fashionable individuals might, from time to time, be inconveniently felled by love or lust, but the beau monde as a whole was determined to minimize such vulnerabilities, and one of its key strategies lay in placing the accolade of beauty beyond common reach. It is, therefore, highly significant that the period saw a fundamental redefinition of beauty itself. Within elite ideals of femininity, physical sex appeal and exterior attributes were downplayed, and a range of social qualifications were brought to the fore, among them: grace, morality, virtue, manners, and politeness. This interpretation of beauty as 'social beauty' is critical to understanding why and how the accolade

FIGURE 36 Elizabeth Gunning, Duchess of Hamilton and Duchess of Argyll,
Sir Joshua Reynolds, c.1760.

was so readily attributed to women of the beau monde, and what their
beauty was taken to signify. By these means, beauty could be aligned
to rank, and a vast hinterland of complex cultural codes could be mar-
shalled to reveal the pretty parvenu as an interloper.

Conflating beauty and rank made it a simple matter to present women
of established social status as London's leading beauties. Routinely

known as the 'beauty Duchess', Georgiana, Duchess of Devonshire, was perhaps the most famous of them all. Significantly, the meaning of her beauty quite clearly extended beyond physical allure. Politician George Selwyn, for example, referred to the 'peculiar fascination of her manners', citing these as the heart of the duchess's attraction.[31] Nathaniel Wraxall, a contemporary memoirist, offered a more elaborate homage: 'The personal charms of the Duchess of Devonshire constituted her smallest pretension to universal admiration,' he explained, 'nor did her beauty consist...in the regularity of features and faultless formation of limbs and shape, it lay in the amenity and graces of her deportment, in her irresistible manners, and the seduction of her society.'[32] For Fanny Burney, it was the duchess's personality that made her a beauty. 'I now saw the Duchess far more easy and lively in her spirits, and consequently far more lovely in her person...Vivacity is so much her characteristic, that her style of beauty requires it indispensably; the beauty, indeed, dies away without it.'[33] Few claimed, then, that an aesthetic charm or physical perfection lay at the heart of the Duchess of Devonshire's beauty. Instead, the categories used by contemporaries to define her brand of beauty prioritized terms and values associated with her social manner and her demeanour.

It is from this perspective that we should revisit those extraordinary 'scales of beauty' with which this chapter began. What is so striking about them is the relatively limited weight they place on physical attributes. The previously quoted *London Chronicle* for September 1776 evaluated its trawl of seven beau monde women on the basis of 'person', 'expression', 'complexion', and 'grace'. Twenty points could be allocated for each.[34] Reprinted in at least five other newspapers, this particular 'scale' was widely circulated, but it was not the only one of its ilk. A month later, the *Morning Post*'s 'Scale of Bon Ton' expanded these categories to: 'beauty', 'figure', 'elegance', 'wit', 'sense', 'grace', 'expression', 'sensibility', and 'principles'. As with the *London Chronicle*'s coverage, the Duchess of Devonshire and Lady Derby were awarded the palm once again, alongside other prominent women including the Duchess of Gordon, the Countess of Jersey, Lady Melbourne, and Anne Seymour Damer.[35] *The Man of Pleasure's Pocket Book* (1780) simplified the criteria in its 'Scale of Beauty', grading women according to only three characteristics: 'beauty', 'grace', and 'elegance'; with Lady Derby, Lady Sarah Bunbury, and the Duchess of Devonshire featuring most highly. The latter triumphed at the top of the table, doubling the scores allocated to any other titled woman. The *Pocket Book* allocated forty-six points out of a potential fifty to the duchess for 'grace', and forty-five for 'elegance', whereas Lady Augusta Campbell achieved a more modest twenty-three and twenty-one, just above Lady Jersey's twenty-two and nineteen for the same criteria.[36]

In the 1790s—and in spite of the fact that nearly two decades separate some of these charts—the Duchess of Devonshire was still reigning supreme. Both the *Gazeteer and New Daily Advertiser* and *Woodfall's Register* printed a 'Scale of Modern Beauty' in their news for June 1793.[37] Breaking beauty down into nine sub-categories of 'form', 'elegance', 'grace', 'fortune', 'complexion', 'countenance', 'softness', 'expression', and 'loveliness', these newspapers singled out nineteen women, with twenty points representing 'perfection' in each category. Top marks were allocated to the Duchess of Devonshire for 'countenance', and to Lady Ann Lambton and Princess Mary for 'loveliness'. Poor Lady Stormont was allocated a shameful five points for her 'loveliness' in *Woodfall's Register*, but the *Gazetteer's* reprint of the same table scored her at fifteen, revealing *Woodfall's* single-figure assessment to be a printing error rather than a particularly cruel evaluation.

Although created and consumed beyond the beau monde itself, these scales offer compelling evidence. Their emphasis on criteria such as grace, elegance, and manners illuminates how the broader beauty ideal was presumed to relate to specific characteristics involving something more than mere looks. Notably, however, the characterizations of contemporary beauty exchanged between women themselves share many of the same features. Lady Caroline Lennox, for example, deployed almost identical terms to the published tables when describing her sister Lady Sarah Bunbury's beauty as residing in a 'vastly engaging manner' which transformed her 'ordinary face and figure' into 'an overwhelmingly attractive one'.[38] The interrelationship of beauty with perceptions of rank is also evident in another description of contemporary femininity penned by Lady Sarah Bunbury herself. In a letter, she used the yardstick of 'beauty' in reference to women she had met in Paris:

> There are very few handsome women at Paris…the P[rince]ss of Monaco is reckoned a great beauty, there, here she would only be a very pretty woman; her face is round and flat, her countenance is meek and sweet, her complection [*sic*] very fine, and her figure the most perfect made of any woman in the world, I believe she is the only lady who don't wear rouge, for all the rest daube themselves so horribly that it's shocking. Madam[e] D'Egmont is the next beauty; she has a pretty Chinese face, is very affected and fashionable, and so is made a beauty.[39]

Her implication is that although the Princess of Monaco's figure might be 'the most perfect made of any woman in the world', her simplicity and naivety relegated her to the status of 'very pretty'. In Bunbury's eyes, though, it was Madame D'Egmont's studied fashionability, rather than her 'pretty Chinese face', that made her a 'beauty'.

Nor were such judgements restricted to the final few decades of the century. In 1742, Mrs Delany had made a similar analysis in her description of the Duchess of Queensbury. 'The Duchess of Queensbury was remarkably fine', Mrs Delany noted, 'she had put on all her best airs and certainly showed she still had a right to be called beautiful.'[40] Tracing these associations back to the 1730s, a poem dedicated to the 'beautiful Molly Lepel' (Lady Hervey) aligned Lepel's 'beauty' to her 'pleasing' nature. 'That face, that form, that dignity, that ease', the poem exulted, 'these powers of pleasing, with that will to please'.[41] Lord Chesterfield characterized the same Lady Hervey in comparable terms in his letters to his son, describing her as a woman with 'easy good-breeding politeness'.[42] For Lady Mary Wortley Montagu, it was the deportment and 'unaffected' gentility of Lady Charlotte Campbell that constituted the latter's claim to beauty. 'What a beautiful woman she was,' Montagu recalled, 'I have seen the whole opera House turn to look at [her arm and hand] on the front of the box. The last time I ever met Lady Charlotte was walking with her brother in Kensington Gardens. She walked so well! Not mincing like some women, nor striding like others, but with a perfect use of her limbs, unaffected and graceful.'[43] The interconnected nature of elements such as grace and elegance with the concept of beauty is reinforced by Samuel Johnson's dictionary definitions of the terms. 'Beauty' he specified as a 'particular grace'. 'Grace', he decided, comprised 'a dignity, ease and elegance of manner', and 'elegance' a 'beauty of propriety'.[44]

By aligning overall beauty to such constituent features, contemporary definitions implied that 'true' beauty rested not in God-given physical allure but in actions and performances that were in the control of the individual. In theory, there was presumably nothing to prevent any woman mastering a style of beauty granted through 'grace' and 'ease'. Yet the clear implication of these descriptions was a crisp correlation of beauty with social rank. Rather than the product of life-long tutelage and cultural familiarity, terms such as 'good-breeding', 'unaffected', 'best airs', and 'dignity' were routinely deployed in eighteenth-century contexts as the natural birthright of the elite. The published scales effectively reinforced those associations in their elevation and celebration of titled women as model 'beauties'. Although the precise constellation of women they promoted changed from table to table, some names were repeated again and again. This is most striking in the case of the

Duchess of Devonshire, who appears in all of the scales cited above. A number of other women, such as Lady Derby, Lady Sarah Bunbury (née Lennox), Lady Ligonier, the Countess of Jersey, and the Countess of Barrymore, were featured in at least two separate tables, and often in three. In this way, the 'beauty scales' acknowledged the cultural visibility of a select group of women, flagging their exclusivity and status and not simply their physical allure. These 'beauties', of course, so often designated by the same press as 'leaders of fashion' and 'heads of society', were the female faces of London's beau monde.

It is important to acknowledge, though, that the categorization of prominent women in these published scales was not necessarily straightforwardly celebratory, and that these lists resist straightforward interpretation. Notably, a number of them created specific, if subtle, juxtapositions which suggest they could also be read as more than a representation of the power and public profile of fashionable society's leading ladies. Two of the scales in particular had pronounced political overtones. The *Morning Post*'s 'Scale of Bon Ton' (from October 1776) is especially striking for restricting the field to women associated with the Whig opposition. Without exception, each 'Bon Ton' beauty was renowned for her factional allegiance. The Duchesses of Devonshire and Gordon, Lady Melbourne, Mrs Damer, Mrs Crewe, and Mrs Bouverie were well-known hostesses for the Whig opposition and canvassers for its candidates, noted especially for their involvement in Charles James Fox's 1784 Westminster election campaign. The other women in the list were all associated by marriage or other family connections to leading Whig figures.[45]

Moreover, a range of other subjects and complexities are either obviously apparent or at least discernible within these pages. For instance, the 'Scale of Modern Beauty' for June 1793, published in the *Gazetteer* and *Woodfall's Register*, offered a companion section entitled 'Modern Talents', which scored twenty-two men according to criteria such as 'genius', 'learning', and 'taste'. The list included a number of political 'talents', such as Charles James Fox, Edmund Burke, Richard Brinsley Sheridan, and William Pitt, and also compared the merits of leading politicians to those of literary 'talents' such as Samuel Richardson. Furthermore, included at the end of the list of 'modern beauties' was Richardson's most famous though decidedly fictional heroine, Pamela. Other lists contained still more varied combinations.[46] The seven 'British beauties' singled out by the *London Chronicle* in September 1776 were printed alongside five untitled 'Irish beauties'.[47] The *Man of Pleasure's Pocket Book* grouped all its titled 'beauties' at the top of the scale, but underneath it included comparative scores for famous courtesans including Elizabeth Armistead, Kitty Fisher, Nancy Parsons, Gertrude Mahon, and Grace Elliot.[48]

Therefore, although in broad terms each list foregrounded a constellation of elite women—and, more specifically, women associated with the fashionable world—their scores and identity as 'beauties' were often positioned in a discursive relationship with some other group. Precisely how these juxtapositions should be read awaits a different study. Perhaps, though, they offer a reminder that different constructions of 'beauty' and social power coexisted in an uneasy dialogue. By comparing elite women to courtesans, the *Man of Pleasure's Pocket Book* might possibly imply that the 'beauty' acknowledged to reside within women of rank was not so dissimilar to that learned by women of ill repute. Perhaps the public fame of 'beauty' brought unpredictable consequences and unwanted comparisons. By comparing 'beautiful' women to 'talented' men was the *Gazetteer* calling both to some form of public account? Whatever the intention, such comparisons point to the potentially unstable and temporary nature of the status enjoyed by a beau monde 'beauty'.

Within the eighteenth-century beau monde, 'beauty' was recorded as the very real attribute of a number of fashionable women. To recognize the prevalence of this tribute within fashionable society is not to suggest that only female members of the beau monde were deemed 'beautiful'. Throughout the century the form and location of ideal 'beauty' was the subject of ongoing and heated debate. Different commentators maintained that 'beauty' could be displayed in different ways and through different media. For some, it was the structure of classical male statues or the pleasures of a natural landscape that were the exemplars of the 'beautiful'. Yet the linkage between 'beauty' and the female form was also particularly pronounced. Significantly, we need to read these references to 'beauty' in their socio-cultural context, as signifiers that are rich with information about the priorities and values of the age, rather than as descriptions of an unchanging physical appeal. From this perspective, the accolade of 'beauty' tells us as much about the construction and protection of social status and social identity as it does about aesthetic or physical norms.

As this chapter has demonstrated, for the women of the beau monde 'beauty' was not just determined by aesthetic ideals nor was it simply the celebration (or eroticization) of classless physical allure by male observers. Instead, notions of fashionable 'beauty' were often linked to other aspects such as 'character', 'breeding', and 'air'. Crucially, such overt emphasis on good breeding and manners demonstrates that the style of 'beauty' enjoyed by women of the beau monde appears to have been understood primarily in terms of qualities that related directly to social status. Unlike physical beauty, a charming character was not necessarily a quality that occurred naturally. The display of 'breeding' was a key aspect of a fashionable education imbibed from nursery to presentation at court, and the display of 'good breeding' was an essential prerequisite for membership of London's beau monde. The

Duchess of Devonshire's 'irresistible manners', 'grace', and 'elegance' were regarded by contemporaries as qualities that confirmed her status as a high-profile fashionable hostess. Many 'beauties' of the beau monde were particularly prominent members of the fashionable world. Elizabeth (Gunning), Duchess of Hamilton and Argyll, held a position in Queen Charlotte's court and was an important patron for aspiring members of fashionable London. The Duchess of Queensbury was also a prominent figure, retaining her status and responsibilities as a hostess even after her abrupt exile from the court of George II in the 1720s. The prominence of these 'beauties' is central to understanding the accolade conferred upon them. The position obtained by many fashionable 'beauties'—for instance, the Duchess of Devonshire's remarkable influence as political hostess and patroness—demanded certain essential skills. A 'pleasing air' was crucial to engendering the 'seductive society' that smoothed the social entertainments central to the structure and networks of the beau monde. It is therefore not surprising that related attributes such as 'grace', 'elegance', and 'manners' were celebrated under the umbrella accolade of 'beauty'. Significantly, these were attributes that could be retained, and even advanced, with age. Within the beau monde, celebrations of beauty extended beyond the sexualized authority of the youthful maid.

It is striking that many features of 'beauty', such as 'grace', 'charms', 'pleasingness', and 'air', were also common tropes of politeness. The seductions and soothing charm of female company were central to the concept of politeness, and to models of polite society. Of course, 'politeness' was a much broader social construction rather than the sole preserve of the beau monde. Crucially, however, while the beau monde's idealization of 'beauty' incorporated many elements of 'politeness', other qualities were also included to supercharge the specific beauty of women of the beau monde and to distinguish them from the rest of polite society. This strategic use of other qualities is most vividly expressed in the repeated and explicit association between 'beauty' and 'rank'. This linkage provided a powerful means of protecting the accolade from the claims of middling sorts who deemed themselves 'polite'. In addition, given that 'beauty' was integral to much wider discourses incorporating art, taste, style, and aesthetics, the term was endowed with a flexible edge that could be manipulated according to the context or purpose of the accolade. As with the case of the Gunnings, or in Sarah Bunbury's description of Frances Greville, the application of the term 'beauty' in recognition of social place could still intersect with its use as a reference to physical form. Within the eighteenth-century beau monde, it was often position and not just powder or paint that comprised the charms of a 'beauty'. That power, however, existed in an uneasy dialogue with other manifestations of beauty. In this regard, the position of fashionable women in London society was elevated but not impregnable.

6

Exile and fraud

A changeable world

[The fashionable world's] population is more fluctuating and uncertain than that of any people upon the face of the earth. There are among them certain tribes or families, distinguished by different descendible titles, who claim a sort of prescriptive right to the name of fashionables. In them the federable appellation continues hereditary ... [yet] their body is mutable in the extreme. There is a perpetual reciprocation of numbers between them and the society in which they reside. The gossip of every day announces that some have migrated from the region of Fashion, and that others have made their appearance within it for the first time. The causes which produce these variations, and the reasons upon which they are founded, are in some instances too mysterious, and in others too frivolous, to become subjects of recital. In general it may be affirmed, that though persons become fashionable with the concurrence of their will, they cease to be such against it.... the greater part of those who retire have been superseded and resign their places, only because they cannot any longer retain them.

(Theophilus Christian Esq [John Owen], *The Fashionable World Displayed*, 1804)

In *The Fashionable World Displayed*, first published in 1804, John Owen—former gentleman's tutor and curate—returned once again to a problem that had vexed commentators for the past century: precisely how was membership of the world of fashion conferred and defined? Writing under the pseudonym Theophilius Christian Esquire, according to Owen it was a world that could only be mapped in the broadest terms because its population was continually changing. Those with 'descendible titles', he asserted, enjoyed a 'prescriptive right' to membership. Yet, at the same time (and despite the apparent certainty of status brought by hereditary 'quality'), the fashionable population was in a constant state of flux, routinely drawing in new members and ejecting others already established in its ranks.[1]

The mercurial nature of fashionable society was a recurring motif of contemporary commentary, and there does appear to have been some reality behind the rhetoric. Throughout this book, life in London's beau monde has been revealed as involving various inter-related social, cultural, and political performances. These demanded extensive resources and different forms of investment, which effectively distinguished the fashionable population and comprised an urban system of prestige. Equally, though, those same elite experiences imply that participation in the beau monde and the successful display of fashionable status required constant maintenance. Frenetic sociability, the close attention paid to the display of networks and allegiances (whether broadcast through material possessions, social performances, or political connections), and the energy expended not simply to obtain entrance to a metropolitan elite but also to retain membership season after season, all suggest that access was neither secure nor taken for granted.

This chapter rounds out this book's investigation of the culture and society of London's beau monde by exploring its theoretically fluid boundaries, and approaching the experience and perception of membership from alternative, and in many ways atypical perspectives. It looks initially at the basis on which access to fashionable society might be revoked, drawing on case studies of individuals exiled from fashionable society in the second half of the century. Tracking the experiences of former members who were either temporarily or permanently excluded from the beau monde is particularly revealing, illuminating fundamental codes of behaviour to which the fashionable elite were expected to adhere. The main examples considered here all involved titled women who suffered social disgrace on account of their perceived sexual misconduct. Given that licentiousness and adultery were routinely caricatured in critical attacks as distinguishing features of life in the fast-paced society of fashion, the fact that exile was imposed in response to sexual conduct is perhaps surprising. That these are the most readily available narratives of exile, however, is itself important, suggesting that (women's) sexual behaviour was one of the most tightly policed areas of fashionable London life.

A final section explores fashionable society as a terrain vulnerable to exploitation by impostors. Some of the century's most famous fictions, from Daniel Defoe's *Roxana* (1724) to Frances Burney's *Evelina* (1778), explored the space created at fashionable society's fluid boundaries for opportunistic interlopers.[2] Scenes of pretence, mistaken identity, and masquerade feature repeatedly in various guises in these novels. Lesser-known contemporary pamphlet stories, such as *A View of the Beau Monde: Or, the Memoirs of a Celebrated Coquetilla, A Real History* (1731), mined similar themes.[3] In *Coquetilla*, the title's protagonist followed a comparable path to Defoe's Roxana, using artifice to seduce male patrons and feigning rank and a 'fashionable' air in ways that allowed her to infiltrate the beau monde and circulate amongst its membership (albeit never for very long).

Although a popular trope of contemporary fiction, factual instances of successful masquerade or impersonation are nonetheless rare. Two such cases are explored here, the stories of Alexander Day (in the 1720s) and James Hobart (in the 1790s) who both captured public attention for their audacious posturing as 'men of fashion'.[4] Whether or not they fooled the beau monde is highly questionable, for those that they duped were not fashionable society themselves but tradesmen and servants who supplied and serviced the elite world. Both Day and Hobart adopted 'fashionable' personas with the particular intent of defrauding purveyors of luxury goods. In this sense, though, they were interlopers who exploited widely held assumptions about the nature of fashionable status. Day and Hobart's histories are visible because both were eventually caught and tried for theft and fraud. The details that came to light in court, and the witness testimonies summoned in order to convict these two miscreants, illuminate the ways in which a fashionable status was judged and interpreted by those outside the beau monde's exclusive ranks. Together, then, the case studies outlined in this chapter illustrate how certain individuals tested the rules and regulations of life in the beau monde, either by breaking specific codes of conduct or by attempting to ape and fake the criteria required by the world of fashion.

While the strategies pursued by London's beau monde imply that fashionable status was hard won, the grounds on which that same status might be jeopardized or lost are harder to ascertain. Subtle shifts in the personal connections that made up the beau monde were certainly carefully monitored. As has been shown, it was possible for an individual to be welcomed at one assembly or to participate fully in one visiting network but be shunned by a separate social cohort. Partisan politics also impinged on the ways in which the beau monde was subdivided into broadly competing (if still overlapping) constituencies. Rapidly changing codes and signals were also used to differentiate between degrees of membership, enabling the fashionable elite to single out particular acquaintances and distance themselves from others. All such strategies suggest a level of mobility and fluidity within the beau monde, albeit still contained within its parameters.

On what basis, though, did individuals find themselves removed from the ranks of fashion altogether? Fleeting comments buried in personal letters imply that one routine cause of retirement was, quite simply, inadequate finance. The Duchess of Kimbolton, for example, remained at Kimbolton Castle in Cambridgeshire for at least one season in the 1790s 'for lack of rhino [money]', and many archives are peppered with letters warning family members to retrench their London expenses lest they bankrupt the estate.[5] Personality may also have played its part. The highly personal diary of Gertrude Savile, for instance, can be read as a poignant narrative of thwarted ambition.[6] She routinely evokes the 'Beau Mond' as an aspirational society she felt 'unfit' to join. Yet Savile's melancholic temperament, disabling shyness, and substantial bouts of depression prevented her attempting even modest engagement with the busy sociability that defined life in the fashionable world. Consequently, Savile tells us something about the desire for inclusion, but offers little insight into how behaviour was managed once access to the beau monde had been achieved or on what grounds membership might be revoked.

Perhaps more significant is the impact of political fortunes on an individual's and a family's longevity within London society. Here, the experiences of the Earl and Countess of Strafford are a case in point. Despite their preliminary success in mastering the networks and machinery of fashion, their endeavours were eventually undermined by Strafford's politics. After an attempted impeachment for his involvement in the Treaty of Utrecht, Strafford found himself excommunicated from formal London politics and threw in his lot with the Jacobites instead. Barred from the Hanoverian court, discontented, and with no hope of re-entering government, Strafford retired in the 1720s to his Yorkshire estates. Tainted by his father's Jacobitism, there was little chance for his son, William, to recoup the lost ground once he inherited the earldom in 1739. When the second earl died without an heir, the title passed to a cousin who also died without issue and so the earldom became extinct. The fate of the family silver is symptomatic of the

Straffords' short-lived splendour and comparatively rapid decline. Despite having been so carefully commissioned and overseen by the countess as one of her first marital responsibilities in the 1710s, the silver was locked in a bank vault in the mid-nineteenth century, where it remained unneeded, unused, and apparently forgotten, until rediscovered over a century later.[7] In near mint condition today, the silverware tells its own story, illustrating not only the Straffords' original pretensions but also their effective expulsion from the ranks of the beau monde within a single generation.

Penury, personality, and politics therefore caused many ambitions to unravel. These were not, however, the only considerations that could ensure either temporary or permanent ejection from the fashionable world. The most notorious instances of exile all centred around the sexual behaviour of titled women. This is placed in sharp relief by the near contemporary experiences of one group of women in particular—Lady Sarah Bunbury; Elizabeth, Countess of Derby; Lady Susan Fox Strangeways; and Georgiana, Duchess of Devonshire. All four breached accepted codes and were subject to varying degrees of exile according to their perceived social crime.

Lady Sarah Bunbury was a court favourite and society 'beauty' banished from London's fashionable world at the age of 25 following an adulterous affair. Born Lady Sarah Lennox in 1745, on entering London society she was widely spoken of as a possible match for the Prince of Wales, the future George III—although it proved to be as chief bridesmaid rather than bride that she eventually attended the royal wedding. In 1762, she broke a secret engagement to the Marquess of Lothian to marry Thomas Charles Bunbury, a Whig MP for Suffolk. Reputedly more attentive to his first love of horses than to his elegant young wife, the marriage was not a success. By the summer of 1768, gossip circulated that Lady Sarah was pregnant with an illegitimate child. 'The town is rather ill natured upon her subject', noted Lady Mary Coke, at first challenging the rumours. 'I don't believe a word of the report & think it a lucky circumstance for her that this pregnancy happens at a time when she has no particular lovers.'[8] Six months later, however, the 'town talk' was confirmed when Lady Sarah Bunbury left her husband and absconded with Lord William Gordon, son of the 3rd Duke of Gordon and father of her unborn child.

Once again, Lady Mary Coke picked up the news from friends and acquaintances, hearing of the scandal first at a court drawing room:

> Went to Princess Amelia's Drawing room, which was very numerous. L[ad]y Charlotte Finch told me there was a bad piece of news, & she fear'd it was true that Lady Sarah Bunbury was gone away with Lord William Gordon, that she had desired Lady Louisa Conolly [her sister] to take care of the Child she lately lay in of which 'tis supposed Ld William is father to & had left a letter for her husband, Sir Charles Bunbury & for Lady Holland [her eldest sister]. Tho' I never thought Lady Sarah to be a Lady of the best conduct, I was much concern'd She had thrown off all regard to decency...Lady Sarah Bunbury's story was all over the drawing room.[9]

It was not only at court that Sarah's story was discussed. After leaving the drawing room, Lady Mary Coke joined a dinner hosted by Lady Anne Conolly. There, Coke shared what she had learned. 'I told her the Story of L[ad]y Sarah, but she did not seem surprised,' Coke observed, 'L[ad]y Anne Conolly had only heard it as a report & hoped it had not been true but Col Howe...confirm'd it.' Having exchanged confidences over supper, Lady Mary Coke travelled on to an assembly at Northumberland House, where the same scandalous news reverberated around the company. She continued her log of the gossip: 'At a little before eight o'clock I went to Northumberland House, where there was a terrible crowd of Company...Lord Pelham told us Lady Louisa Conolly [Sarah's sister] had...brought back L[ad]y Sarah Bunbury but why, no mortal can tell, as she declares she will return to Ld William Gordon who, she says, is the father to the child.'[10]

With news travelling so fast, there seemed little that Lady Sarah could do to avert a scandal. At first, she left disapproving London and fled with Gordon to Scotland. Their co-habitation, though, was short-lived, and by 1770 Sarah committed herself to the protection of her family.[11] There was no question at that stage of her returning with dignity to the capital, and so she was provided with a small cottage on the family estate of Goodwood. Rural retreat, it would seem, was deemed an appropriate penance for her sins. Shocked when it first appeared that Lady Sarah was prepared to throw in her lot with Gordon, Lady Mary Coke for one felt that the very least she could do was to 'retire from the world and live decently'. 'So wild a declaration & so void of shame or principles I have seldom heard from a Lady whose birth & education must have instructed her with sentiments far different to those she seems to have adopted,' Coke solemnly pronounced.[12]

Lady Sarah's retreat to the country was no brief interlude. Instead, it marked the beginning of a lengthy social exile that lasted for twelve years. During this time she resided at the cottage, a small and sparsely furnished home reflecting her reduced status. With just a drawing room and dining room below, and two main bedrooms and a dressing room above, the property was more hermitage than home in comparison to the substantial properties to which Lady Sarah would have been accustomed.[13] The company she was permitted was as restricted as the accommodation. Close family were her only approved visitors and when her brother, the duke, entertained other guests at the estate, his sister was expected to keep out of sight, cloistered in her quiet corner of the grounds.[14] As Sarah herself acknowledged, from the age of 25 until her late thirties, she lived a 'solitary life', sorrowfully 'confined' to her home by her 'situation'.[15]

Her banishment from society was long and lonely. Over her period of exile, though, subtle changes in her circumstances led to gradual shifts in the nature of her isolation. The first and most significant alteration was divorce. For some members of the elite at this time divorce was proving to be a useful, if controversial, measure deployed to help resolve scandals by making it possible for adulterous parties to remarry. The Duke and Duchess of Grafton, for instance, endured an acrimonious separation in 1764, but their eventual divorce in 1769 freed both to marry again. Once the marriage was formally dissolved on 23 March 1769, the duchess wasted no time and wed her lover John Fitzpatrick, 2nd Earl of Upper Ossory, three days later. The Duke of Grafton was not quite so swift but was nonetheless engaged by May to Elizabeth Wrottesley, and married in June. For the Duchess of Grafton, and indeed for some other titled women, divorce provided a means of reinvention and an opportunity to obtain a degree of re-acceptance within fashionable society under a new married name. For Lady Sarah Bunbury there was to be no quick second marriage. Although her estranged husband initiated divorce proceedings in 1769, the procedure was not completed for a further five years, too late for a judicious engagement to Gordon. During this time, following the original scandal and before her formal divorce, Sarah's exile was at its most constrained, restricted almost entirely to her penitent's cottage. However, once the marriage was annulled in 1774 she reverted to her maiden name of Lennox. After a decent interval of years had passed, there is some evidence to suggest that she ventured beyond the estate perimeter, at first to Bath and eventually, though still rarely, to London where she went at least once to the pleasure gardens.

Whilst such excursions suggest a marginal relaxation in the nature of her exile, they did not mark the end of Lady Sarah's exclusion from the fashionable world. Her visits to the pleasure gardens are recorded only in family correspondence and not, as far as I have been able to establish, in either the unpublished letters or in published accounts, such as newspapers. As her biographer Stella Tillyard notes, given their reputation for 'openness' both the pleasure gardens and Bath were more fluid social environments that existed at the edges of fashionable society.[16] Other resorts regarded as the beau monde's inner sanctum—for instance, the opera, private assemblies, and the court—remained off limits to the disgraced Lady Sarah Lennox. The continued limitations imposed on her movements are therefore more pronounced than the partial expansion of her social horizons. By Sarah's own account, significant relationships with former acquaintances had been permanently severed. For instance, in November 1778 she noted in a letter, 'you ask me about Ly Bellamont; I *hear* she is near London now, but I know nothing of her from herself. *My Lord* [the Duke of Richmond] is *too virtuous* to permit her to acknowledge me as a relation, *et je m'en console*.'[17]

It was only from 1781, over a decade after her affair with Lord William Gordon, that Lady Sarah Lennox was able to re-enter some of her former circles and take more substantial steps back into London society. Notably, it was marriage that bought her new freedom and signalled an end to her exile. In the late 1770s, once the more constricting terms of her seclusion had begun to loosen, Sarah became acquainted with George Napier, the impoverished younger son of an aristocrat, an army officer and, when they first met, a married man. Following the death of his wife in 1781, Napier turned his attention to Lady Sarah, and the couple wed at Goodwood later that year. Her family and closest friends at first disapproved of the union, regarding it as an indecorous act that would undermine the penance she had already paid. '[T]here was a certain propriety in your retreat,' counselled her childhood friend Lady Susan O'Brien, 'and a dignity annex'd to the idea of *one great passion*, tho' unfortunately placed, that gratified y[ou]r friends and silenced y[ou]r enemies. I have so often heard you praised and admired for not marrying again...I grieve that you sh[oul]d change a plan, the only one in the world that perhaps c[oul]d thoroughly reinstate you in the good opinion and esteem of everybody.'[18] Despite such warnings, Lady

Sarah went ahead with the match and her married name, Lady Sarah Napier, provided a new mantle under which she could venture back into the metropolitan world. As she outlined herself in the following letter, her altered circumstances meant that progressively more of London's fashionable resorts were open to her:

> By the bye *I* have been at the Play...I have never yet been to an Opera but I have to several assemblies, where I went on purpose to show that it was not my husband's wish that I should shut myself up, but on the contrary his most earnest desire for me to return the civilities I have met with from so many people of character...The very kind reception I met with from all my old acquaintance (the Dss of Bedford excepted) has fully answered our purpose in going, for now I have the satisfaction of proving that it is not the rage of being in public that guides me, as I decline most occasions of appearing when it is in my power, not from necessity but choice, prudence and a degree of indifference.[19]

The cause and circumstances of Lady Sarah's prolonged exile and its gradual cessation are illuminating. There is evidence that she engaged in a series of extra-marital affairs before her adulterous relationship with Lord William Gordon in 1768.[20] It was not, therefore, necessarily the simple fact of adultery that triggered her expulsion. Instead, in this instance, the breach of fashionable society's codes rested on her pregnancy, which made her adultery far more public than might otherwise have been the case. The now public nature of the affair was then compounded by what observers regarded as Lady Sarah's rash and unseemly decision to abandon her marriage and abscond with her lover. Even before her attempted elopement, society's rules appear to have demanded some form of modest retreat and immediate removal from London. Lady Sarah's initial resistance to swift social retirement further scandalized society and worried her protectors. As a result, when she finally acceded, her cloistered exile was made to endure for over a decade—the severity of the sentence of confinement reflecting the perceived gravity of her social crime. For at least three years, and possibly more, her quarantine was near total, and in truth she never regained her former status. For instance, one of the most powerful hostesses of her time, the Duchess of Bedford, refused to welcome the newly wed Lady Sarah Napier at all. Writing to her friend, Lady Susan O'Brien (who, as will be seen, had herself experienced enforced social exile), Lady Sarah ruefully acknowledged, 'you and I shall never go again all bonneted up and hooded up in publick, and giggle and laugh at the ridiculous people we see, but I won't promise but that we shall laugh at them at home and have the more comfort, as by that means we shall not run the risk of being abused as we have been, but enjoy our fun in a quiet way.'[21]

In the same years that Lady Sarah Napier was taking tentative steps back into London society, another woman found herself exiled for a similar crime and subject to a similarly restricted fate. In the 1770s, the young Countess of Derby appeared poised to reap all the power and prestige that was on offer within London's beau monde. Born in 1753 as Lady Betty (Elizabeth) Hamilton, the daughter of the 'beautiful' Elizabeth Gunning and the Duke of Hamilton, she was widely esteemed as 'one of the finest women of the age'.[22] By the end of Lady Betty's first London season, her name was being linked as the likely future spouse of many a high-ranking young nobleman. In the event, it was Edward Smith Stanley, Lord Strange (also styled Lord Stanley by contemporaries), later the Earl of Derby, who ultimately secured Lady Betty as his wife.

Educated at Eton and Cambridge, Lord Stanley ran a typical course for a young male heir. Elected as an MP for Lancashire on a family ticket in 1774, he later graduated from the Commons to the Lords after inheriting the earldom from his grandfather in 1776. Although he was never a particularly enthusiastic or industrious politician, Lord Stanley was loosely integrated into Charles James Fox's Whig opposition, supporting their political cause in the Lords and their social pleasures beyond parliament. On paper, Lord Stanley was quite a catch. Vastly wealthy, he was no less than the twelfth earl in continuous succession, and his property portfolio gave him great influence. A keen horse breeder and racer, as the Earl of Derby he established the famous racing fixtures of the Epsom Oaks and Derby Stakes, often jockeying his own thoroughbreds to victory. With a reputation for boisterous fast living, extravagant dress, and a flair for the theatrical, Stanley was certainly no dullard.[23] Caricaturists, however, singled out his short, squat physique and prematurely receding hairline as Stanley's most distinguishing features, and Lady Betty was reputedly a reluctant bride persuaded into the role by her ambitious mother.

Their wedding in June 1774 was marked by a magnificent inauguration. Throwing a French-inspired *fête champêtre* for 300 fancy-dressed 'persons of distinction', Stanley spent £5,000 on choreographed entertainment. Acrobatic troupes danced and dangled from the trees, and London's most famous opera stars burst into song in the grounds before the company witnessed the grand finale—a mock wedding ceremony presided over by dancing nymphs and a sombre druid, with Lady Betty presented at an altar dressed, rather prophetically, as 'Iphigenia preparing for sacrifice'.[24]

At first the marriage proceeded well enough, and the efficient Lady Stanley bore her husband two daughters and the necessary heir within a few years (Figure 37). In 1776 Stanley had inherited the earldom and, now promoted to the rank of countess, his wife continued to thrive in the beau monde, with her parties, social presence, and pre-eminence in London's society receiving extensive press coverage. Regularly co-hosting dinners and parading in public with the Duchess of Devonshire, the Countess of Derby was widely acclaimed as a leader of the fashionable world in the 1770s.[25] Her status at the pinnacle of London's beau monde was, however, dashed by an extra-marital affair.

In 1778, rumours had begun to circulate associating Lady Derby with Frederick Sackville, Duke of Dorset. By May of that year, cryptic

FIGURE 37 *Edward Smith Stanley, Twelfth Earl of Derby, with His First Wife* (Lady Elizabeth Hamilton) *and Their son* (Edward Smith Stanley), Angelica Kaufmann, *c.*1775–7.

comments about the duke's affair with the Countess of Derby were appearing in the London press. Frederick Robinson, second son of 1st Baron Grantham, picked through the gossip for his brother's benefit, decoding the clues that publicized the scandal. 'The Morning Post is the vehicle of scandalous intelligence. It has been employ'd in applying passages of Shakespear[e] to particular people and situations,' Robinson reported. Printing two quotes attributed to *Richard III*, 'Stanley look to your wife' and 'Dorset is fled to Richmond', the newspaper issued a snickering reference to the scandal enveloping the Derbys' marriage.[26] By restricting itself to Shakespearian quotes, and making no explicit mention of living individuals, the *Morning Post* avoided printing libel, but its targets were clear. The scandal soon escalated. By August 1778, the countess had left Stanley and retreated to the country. Newspapers continued their insinuations, noting her disappearance from London society. Once again, Frederick Robinson passed the latest gossip on to his brother. 'The newspapers will have perhaps inform'd you that L[ad]y Darby is retired...that L[or]d Darby is suing for divorce and that the Duke of Dorset will marry her. All the former part is I fear true,' he explained, 'the last Article is reported confidently but his relations do not allow it.'[27]

The question of whether or not the Duke of Dorset and the Countess of Derby would eventually marry was a critical one that stood to determine the countess's social fate. In many ways, her situation replicated Lady Sarah Bunbury's earlier transgression. It was not the alleged adultery that was the sum of the countess's social crime or the reason for her retreat from London to the country. Rather it was her perceived 'desertion' of her husband that tipped the balance and represented the real violation of society's norms. The moment she left the earl, the Countess of Derby effectively shed the social authority and fashionable status she had accrued as his wife. On these grounds, her removal from London society seemed certain. It is striking, however, that whilst remarriage was rumoured, her social expulsion was not absolute. Indeed, many of the Countess of Derby's former acquaintance were cautious about cutting her completely lest she returned to society as Duchess of Dorset the following year. '[I]t is imagined the Duke of Dorset will marry Lady Derby, who is now in the country keeping quiet and out of the way. There is a sort of party in town of who is to visit her and who is not,' noted a sympathetic Lady Sarah Bunbury, 'which makes great squabbles as if the curse and blessing of the poor woman depended upon a few tickets more or less.'[28] Although rather less compassionate, Jemima, Marchioness Grey, similarly suggested that the countess might yet weather the storm of scandal that threatened to engulf her. 'I much suspect that Lady Derby's cause is to be Brasen'd out & carried off with a high hand more than any have yet ventured at.' Reading the public signs that suggested the countess's exile was not yet complete, the marchioness explained to her daughter that 'most of her fine Friends have they say visited her, you heard how the Dss of B[edfor]d talk'd about her, & 'tis asserted that the D[uke] of D[orset] told the K[ing] of his Intention to marry her. The Imprudence of that would be amazing but 'tis certain that he appears more & more degagé than usual. Placed himself in the Front of the Drawing Room on Thursday last & industriously bowed & talked to the Ladies & anybody he could get at.'[29]

With her status unresolved, the Countess of Derby remained in the country. Meanwhile, the earl resolutely ignored her and continued with his usual routine, shuttling between his estates and the London season. After nearly a year had passed, he eventually made the pronouncement that decided the countess's fate: he had no intention of divorcing his estranged wife but nor did he wish for a reconciliation. No divorce meant no chance of remarriage, and the lingering possibility that the countess might re-enter society elevated to duchess was dashed. Significantly, the countess's experience of social exclusion rapidly changed in response to her husband's damning decree. She left her rural retreat and moved abroad: rural solitude transformed into foreign exile.[30]

While the countess toured Europe and lived quietly in Switzerland, her family launched a series of fruitless attempts to convince Derby to rethink his position and countenance a reunion with his wife.[31] Her mother, Elizabeth Hamilton (née Gunning), Duchess of Hamilton and Argyll, made every effort to defend the countess and prevent her total exclusion from the fashionable world. At the duchess's behest, the countess made brief visits to England in 1780, and tentative forays into London's beau monde. Writing to Lady Gower in February of that year, Lady Mary Coke recorded the effect of her public appearances. 'This day sen'night the Dutchess of Argyll came to the Opera with Lady Derby to the surprise & concern of everybody that wish'd her well, the Tuesday after she came again when their Majesties were there but sat in the front Boxes & Lady Derby opposite to the King & Queen, all this is talk'd of in the manner you may guess.'[32] Jemima, Marchioness Grey, also spotted the countess at London's public resorts. 'L[a]dy Derby has appeared lately at the Opera & the Pantheon with Lady Carlisle, looking very gay & as she used to do; at the Pantheon last week, we were told that on their entrance, the two beauty Duchesses [the Duchesses of Devonshire and Rutland] & L[a]dy Melbourne happened to be walking together, & immediately their three heads were seen in close conference after some time, the D[uche]ss of Rutland sat down, & the others went & spoke to L[a]dy C[arlisle] & her companion, but soon left them & joined the D[uche]ss of Rutland, who behaved I think very properly on the occasion.'[33] Although the countess secured brief acknowledgement by Lady Melbourne and the Duchess of Devonshire, the Duchess of Rutland's refusal to greet her was telling. Over two years after her affair with Dorset, fashionable society was still not ready to readmit Lady Derby into its ranks.

For the next few years, the countess spent the majority of her time on the continent while the family continued to press Lord Derby to reconsider. In a letter to a friend, Lady Derby later acknowledged the necessity of such attempts, as well as the unhappy situation in which she was left by their failure. 'I have now run the gauntlet for two years. For the sake of my children I have often written to Lord D. and the last was a very strong letter at the instigation and begging of a friend towards our reunion. I own it contained more than I felt,' she acceded.

'Thus I am situated,' the countess continued, 'without further settlement, and in exactly the same predicament I stood in two years before.
Mama continues to hope to bring us together...I fully feel the unpleasant way in many respects in which I must remain in this situation.'[34]
The countess remained abroad until 1783, making no further effort to
re-establish herself in London society. Then, however, five years after
her affair with Dorset, the Countess of Derby's circumstances changed
in a way that facilitated her partial reintegration into the fashionable
world.

The main trigger for her return appears to have been a growing
public response to the behaviour of her estranged spouse. Since 1781,
caricaturists had been entertaining themselves at Lord Derby's expense.
The nobleman had developed a very public attachment to the actress
Elizabeth Farren, attending every one of her performances. Farren,
however, judiciously played hard to get. Chaperoned by her mother,
she refused to entertain Derby with any private audiences. The earl's
desperate and comical pursuit of the actress and her feigned *froideur*
was a gift to satirists, sparking print after print (Figures 38 and 39).
Notably, it was in this climate of growing ridicule targeted at the earl,
that the countess made a quiet return to London. From January 1783,
newspapers began to report Lady Derby's occasional appearance at
metropolitan events. Seen first partially hidden in an 'upper box' at the
theatre, stories soon circulated that she was to make an 'official' return
to London by attending court.[35] On 18 January, both the *Morning
Herald* and the *Public Advertiser* claimed that the countess was preparing her dress for the queen's birthday ball.[36] From March, newspapers
reported that Lady Derby was now firmly established at her brother's
house, and regularly ventured to public concerts at Hanover Street,
masquerades at the Pantheon, and to Vauxhall and Ranelagh.[37] A
year later, she was re-integrated into society to the extent that she
joined her former friend, Georgiana, Duchess of Devonshire, and other

FIGURE 38 *Derby Diligence*, John Raphael Smith, after Henry William Bunbury, 1781. A squat Lord Derby is shown in hot pursuit of Elizabeth Farren's carriage.

female canvassers to support Charles James Fox in the Westminster election.[38]

Like the experiences of Lady Sarah Bunbury, the nature of Lady Derby's exile can be mapped through a series of stages. The initial ambiguity in her social position attests to the overriding power of noble rank. The possibility that the disgraced countess might return as a duchess muddied the rules of expulsion. However, once the earl made it clear he would not facilitate a divorce, the countess's banishment was made far more explicit and, in response, she immediately retired abroad. The initial failure of her family's efforts to help the countess 'brazen it out' and

FIGURE 39 *The Platonic Lovers*, William Dent, 1784. This crudely-drawn caricature shows the Earl of Derby sharing a box with Elizabeth Farren and her mother, who acts as chaperone but ignores the intimacy of the lovers. Farren is wearing a narrow belt inscribed 'Cestus' to suggest a chastity girdle. Derby's features are depicted on the head to the left of the image, adorned with a cuckold's horns (one of which is inscribed 'Dorset').

escort her to London's public resorts underscores fashionable society's powerful arbitration of its interior social networks. Despite the considerable social authority wielded by her mother, the acquiescence of other personnel was critical in determining the countess's social position.

For as long as she was visited and 'talked of' by hostesses such as the Duchess of Bedford, the countess was able to retain some degree of social credit. However, once those same individuals refused to acknowledge their acquaintance, her exclusion from society became more concrete. It is striking that her eventual return to London occurred under the cover of public attention focused on the maligned earl. Apparently, once a husband forfeited his right to social regard then credit could be partially restored to a disgraced wife.

A brief examination of two further contemporary experiences further clarifies how social exile was managed and codified within the fashionable world. In 1764, Lady Sarah Bunbury's close friend and confidante Lady Susan Fox Strangeways also became a victim of society's systems of exclusion. Rather than an adulterous affair, Lady Susan's indecorous act was that of a clandestine marriage. Born in 1743, the daughter of Lord and Lady Ilchester, the niece of Henry Fox, Lord Holland, and cousin to Charles James Fox, she was (like Lady Sarah Bunbury) of high-ranking and well-connected lineage, ideally suited to success in London's beau monde. In 1764, however, to the surprise and disapproval of society at large, she eloped with a leading man from the London stage, William O'Brien. Many were shocked that the relationship had been able to develop at all. The idea that a mere player had been able to ingratiate himself into the affections of a peer's daughter was incomprehensible. Countess Spencer received details of the affair from correspondents charged with sending her London news. 'Lady Susan Strangeways was married last Saturday,' explained one writer. '[I]t is a very extraordinary match, not so extraordinary tho for her to be the first Earl's daughter that has made the kind of choice she had after seeing him when in company with her best Friends & yet it is very amusing that she could ever get so very particularly acquainted with him…it seems they knew of her admiration 3 years ago, but hoped it was over, till a fortnight ago when they were told of a meeting they had

had & it is said upon that Ld [Ilchester] won her word that she wd never more speak to him & consent to go into the Country.'[39] 'The town talks of nothing else', reported Lord Villiers, 'all her family and friends are in the utmost concern and vexation'.[40] It was not only Lady Susan's reputation at stake. Her family's failure to stop the association, and their mistaken reliance on 'her promise to give up all thoughts of it',[41] also met with disapproval. Notably, whereas Lady Sarah Bunbury was corralled into a rural retreat, Lady Susan O'Brien and her new husband suffered a more extreme form of banishment from London's fashionable world. At the behest of her family, the disgraced couple were sent to live abroad, in far-away New York.[42]

After a lengthy stint in North America, moving from New York to Philadelphia and Quebec, the O'Briens eventually decided to try their luck again in London, returning in 1771. There they at first hoped to be able to use Lady Susan's family connections to ease their path back to acceptance, to assist O'Brien in his new career in law, and to climb their way into the ranks of the fashionable world. Such help, however, was not forthcoming. As Susan O'Brien's journal entries relating to her London experiences reveal, the couple found all doors, even those on the periphery of the fashionable world, firmly closed. Writing in 1771, she confessed her hope that her near relation Lady Holland would 'introduce me again into her society & among my former friends'. It was, she claimed, 'in [Lady Holland's] power to have placed me again in an agreeable situation in society'. Unfortunately, she found 'Lady Holland was not much dispos'd', and lamented 'she did not wish me to be again in the World'.[43] Following a number of years of frustrated metropolitan social exclusion, the O'Briens retreated to Kent and regretfully accepted their fate.[44]

Although Lady Susan O'Brien failed to orchestrate any degree of re-acceptance into London's fashionable world, another woman fared better. In the early 1790s, Georgiana, Duchess of Devonshire, faced social disgrace following her affair with Charles Grey. Pregnant with Grey's child, the duchess had committed perhaps the gravest misdemeanour. Illegitimate progeny not only threatened personal reputations but also the future of titles, the security of estates, and the perceived purity of the family tree. Such a transgression, as Lady Sarah Bunbury had discovered, was redressed with absolute exile. For the Duchess of Devonshire, though, the repercussions were dramatically reduced because, in stark contrast to Lady Derby and Lady Susan Bunbury, she retained the protection of her husband. To be sure, some form of exile was unavoidable. The duke arranged for his wife to travel abroad in order to hide the pregnancy and birth from public view, and for two years she lived out her foreign seclusion. The duchess's absence was noted in the press, but no hints were made about the cause of such retirement. Travel for health rather than for penance was the official explanation for the temporary loss of such a celebrity. Once the baby was born and her sentence was completed, the duchess returned to London.

The duke formally acknowledged his wife's arrival in England with a widely reported gift of a town carriage, surely a strategic choice given that a carriage was the ultimate expression of urban sociability and public status. Her mother counselled the errant but rehabilitated duchess, warning her to act with modesty and restraint. 'I am sure I need not warn you to observe the strictest sobriety and moderation in your dress,' read a stern letter. 'Let it be simple and noble but pray do not let it be singular and how glad I should be if you could tell me you had quite done with rouge. The credit such a conduct would be to your character would far outweigh the trivial and really false idea of your looking more shewy.'[45] By and large, the Duchess of Devonshire's re-entrance into society appears to have been relatively smooth. However, and notwithstanding the strength of her own fashionable brand and the public show of unity orchestrated by her husband, there is evidence that the Duchess of Devonshire never quite regained her former social prestige. The constant public presence that marked her out in the late 1770s and 1780s was replaced by a more muted approach both to her political responsibilities and social activities.[46]

Although such well-recorded instances of expulsion are comparatively rare, the unhappy histories of Lady Sarah Bunbury, Lady Susan O'Brien, the Countess of Derby, and the Duchess of Devonshire reveals some of the means by which membership of fashionable society was internally managed by the beau monde as a group. Even the most vivacious leaders of fashion were not immune to exclusion when their conduct was deemed to have breached society's unwritten codes. In each case, the nature and length of the social exile they endured varied. Yet their exclusion always necessitated a temporary or permanent departure from the crucible of the beau monde: London itself.

For all the titillating details that surround these scandals, their overriding concern appears to be with the threats female behaviour posed to structures of social position, property, and inheritance. It is striking, if predictable, that titled men were judged by different standards. No strategic retreat was required of Charles Grey following his relationship with the Duchess of Devonshire. Lord William Gordon was not exposed to calumny on account of his liaison with Lady Sarah Bunbury, and the Duke of Devonshire famously housed his illegitimate offspring in the nursery of Devonshire house, to be cared for alongside the legitimate children born by his wife. And while Lord Derby succeeded in making himself appear thoroughly foolish, his freedom of movement and association was not seriously imperilled. While it took two to transgress, it was through the punishment of women that the beau monde's delicate mechanisms—thrown temporarily into dangerous confusion by scandal—were returned to their usual rhythm. The combination of female sexual misbehaviour with publicity and notoriety was also especially toxic to the beau monde. In Lady Sarah Bunbury's case, her public behaviour—and particularly her abandonment of her husband and co-habitation with her lover—

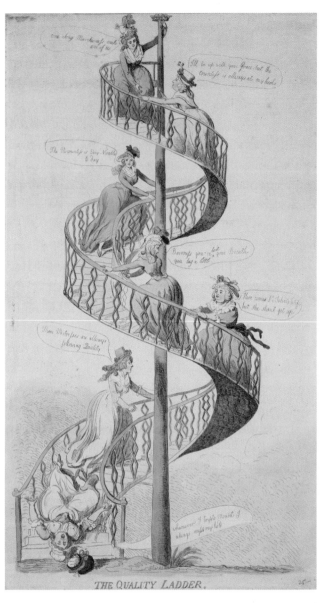

FIGURE 40 *The Quality Ladder*, Isaac Cruikshank, 1793. Cruikshank's 'ladder' satirizes the significance of title. A duchess stands at the pinnacle, with a marchioness, countess, viscountess, baroness, and 'Sir John's wife' climbing up the ladder beneath her. At the bottom, an untitled mistress, who has fallen from the ladder, exclaims 'whenever I try's to mount I always miss my hold'.

216

compounded her social and sexual crime. Whereas the Duchess of Devonshire hid her pregnancy from public view, Lady Sarah Bunbury's flight from her marriage and initial refusal to conform to society's need for retirement threw fuel on the fire. It was as much the publicity surrounding the Countess of Derby's affair with the Duke of Dorset as the fact of the affair itself that appears to have made their personal sexual relationship into an unacceptable social scandal. With thinly veiled innuendo and gossip circulating in the press, the countess's position in London society looked increasingly untenable. Retreat from London society was certainly one strategic way to manage burgeoning publicity, for removal from London amounted to removal from the public stage.

It is not simply the rationale for ostracizing these women that is revealing, but also the way in which the metropolitan elite mobilized itself to receive or rebuff those who had transgressed. An impoverished visiting list, a snub at the opera, the failure to receive an invitation to an assembly may seem inconsequential or the stuff of playground politics. Yet, once social connections were severed so too was access to London's fashionable world, its power and its influence. Once again, then, the corporate identity of the beau monde can therefore be found to rest in complex and communally policed interpersonal relationships. Internal systems of visiting and acknowledging, spurning and 'cutting', were highly effective managerial mechanisms that drew the majority together, while dealing savagely with those who challenged its norms (Figure 40).

The thicket of interpersonal connections that made social life so uncomfortable for Lady Sarah Bunbury and the Countess of Derby also led to other unintended consequences. Occasionally it smoothed the way for the daring and knowledgeable impostor. The world of fashion was, of course, somewhat impermeable in reality, its resilience suggested by the fact that no stories of fakery or masquerade can actually be retrieved from records penned by the elite themselves. For those outsiders who were duped by fraudulent 'men of fashion', however, a conman's boasts of personal acquaintance with named insiders often proved one of the most persuasive elements of their performance. The following section focuses on two high-profile cases of fraud, which offer suggestive counter-narratives to those of exile. Whereas the latter exposes how membership could be achieved and then revoked, illuminating how access was managed from within the beau monde, stories of criminal interlopers say much about how the beau monde was perceived by outsiders in general.

In late autumn 1722, one Marmaduke Davenport Esquire, reputedly a 'man of quality and fortune', embarked on a remarkable London shopping spree.[47] After taking a set of finely furnished rooms in Queen's Square, Davenport called Ralph Greathead, a London stable-keeper and horse-dealer. Accompanied to the stables by 'Lewis', a liveried footman, Davenport explained to Mr Greathead that he had left his own coach, horses, and coachman at his country seat in the north of England. He then agreed terms to hire a handsome town carriage, a pair of horses, and a 'lusty' coachman to drive the set. With both temporary coachman and salaried footman handsomely attired in matching liveries, and with resplendent coach and horses now in hand, Davenport soon had the necessary equipment to cut a dash about town.

With no prior knowledge of this new client, Ralph Greathead took care to establish that Marmaduke Davenport was all that he seemed—a necessary endeavour given that, in true gentlemanly fashion, no money would change hands until the chaise and horses were later returned. A day or so into the agreed period of hire, the conscientious stable owner discreetly tracked down the coachman and enquired where

Davenport had taken his expensive equipage. The coachman offered the perfect reassurance. Having driven the carriage on repeated visits to the Duke of Montagu's house, to Hanover Square, and to the houses of 'other persons of rank', as well as to coffee houses and the usual places of fashionable resort, Davenport, it appeared, was following the expected course for a 'man of rank and fashion'. Well satisfied with the details, Mr Greathead left the coachman to continue with his work, confident that his equipment was in credit-worthy hands.

Thereafter, Davenport busily visited all manner of London tradesmen with a view to acquiring various fine articles necessary for new suits, for the complete establishment of a permanent London residence, and for other items associated with his supposed imminent wedding to a wealthy heiress. Excited by the prospect of lucrative commissions, London's purveyors of luxury goods readily responded to Davenport's requests. One Mr Gravestock, for example, first encountered Davenport when the gentleman pulled up at his shop with his impressive carriage and placed a substantial order for gold lace. Gravestock swiftly fulfilled the order, allowing Davenport to take the goods on credit, and he later called on Davenport in his luxurious lodgings in Queen's Square. There he saw designs for liveries that Davenport claimed were to be 'as rich as the Duke of Newcastle's' and 'gayer than any nobleman in town', and for which he hoped Gravestock would provide silver lace and silver knots. After lengthy discussions, Davenport suggested that he should return the next day with samples, at which point Davenport's steward would settle his bill. Mr Scrimshaw (a linen draper), Mr Kendrick (a tea dealer), and Mr Hinchliffe (a silk mercer), were also convinced by the smooth-talking Davenport. They, in turn, dutifully attended Davenport at his own lodgings, where they provided samples and fulfilled initial orders of goods worth in the region of fifty pounds each, all hopeful that more profitable commissions would soon follow from the same client. In this way, Davenport collected armfuls of rich brocade, cambric, podesay and lace, and packets of expensive tea. However, when these merchants later returned to the Queen's Square rooms to receive payment and obtain details of the next promised order, Marmaduke Davenport (and the goods left in trust) had vanished.

Davenport's cover was eventually blown when a goldsmith, Mr Markham, recognized that a tiny silver collar for a pet squirrel that was in Davenport's possession had recently been made by his shop for a different client. With his suspicions raised, Markham tried to establish the veracity of Davenport's claims about his background and his assertion that he was soon to marry. In the course of his enquiries, it soon became apparent that Davenport was not what he seemed, but was in fact 'one of the greatest Bites and Sharpers of the Town' and a 'notorious cheat', one Alexander Day, alias David Alexander, alias Dodd, alias Finch Esquire (with 'more alias's thereto than we well find room for', as the *London Journal* later noted).[48]

Eventually arrested on suspicion of a different crime, but subsequently charged with theft and fraud, Alexander Day was brought before the Old Bailey in April 1723. There, tradesman after tradesman testified against the artful thief. Day offered a poor defence. Sticking to his story that he was indeed in possession of a sizeable country estate, he claimed he had designed 'honestly to pay for all the goods', and would have done so 'had they not disappointed him'. However, 'not proving any thing of it, nor giving any Account of himself, nor willing one Witness to his Reputation', the jury had little truck with his tale and were swift to pronounce Day guilty on all counts. Fined £200, required to stand in the pillory (once at Covent Garden and once at Ludgate Hill), imprisoned for two years, and also obliged to raise a security on his release to ensure good behaviour for a further two years, Day received a comprehensive sentence. Both London and national newspapers picked up on Day's story and issued gleeful reports about his public humiliation in the pillory.[49] Unable to raise a security to cover his bail or find supporters to testify to his character, Day's two-year term became a life sentence, and he languished in Newgate until his death in 1729.[50]

Some decades later, James Molesworth Hobart was accused of practising a similar fraud.[51] Indeed, Hobart's career as an impostor made Alexander Day's deception in the 1720s look rather amateurish in comparison. Unlike Day, who chose the ambiguous title of 'Esquire', which placed him in the vague territory between a wealthy untitled gentleman and the younger son of a peer, Hobart had no qualms about adopting more ambitiously aristocratic guises. In London in 1791, for example, he used the alias of 'Lord Massey' (also spelled as 'Massy') to fleece Bond Street goldsmiths Willerton and Green of over £700-worth of diamond jewellery in a swift but profitable deception that became one of his most famous escapades.

This particular fraud began in a similar vein to Alexander Day's *modus operandi*, as Hobart first set about acquiring a set of well-furnished London rooms. Selecting an apartment in 36 St James's Place on 15 March 1791, close to the fashionable heart of 'the town', 'Lord Massey' acquired a convincing stage for his masquerade. Next he selected his supporting cast. On the morning of 16 March, the 'Lord' took into his service an out-of-work French valet, one Joseph Lecree, who had advertised his services in the newspaper. At midday, the landlady saw both the lord and his French valet at the rooms, receiving a delivery of trunks containing, she presumed, Lord Massey's clothing and possessions sent from the country. Massey himself did not stay long. With his valet otherwise occupied he asked the landlady's own maid to call him a coach to take him to an appointment at the Duke of Argyll's. The maid obliged and Massey left the property bound instead for the jewellers.

Calling at Willerton and Green's Bond Street premises, a poised and elegantly attired Hobart asked to see some fine necklaces. Mr Green first showed him some necklaces of the 'common sort' that they kept on site, but 'Lord Massey' smoothly explained he wanted something far finer as an important present for a lady. He trusted that he would not be disappointed, mentioning that the goldsmiths had been personally recommended to him by Lord Salisbury, one of their long established clients. Providing Green with his card, which confirmed both his title and his London address, 'Massey' agreed that the goldsmith would visit him by appointment later that afternoon with some examples of his best pieces.

Green attended 36 St James's Square at the pre-arranged time, 4 p.m. on 16 March, taking with him a range of gems for Massey's perusal. Admitted by Lecree, the French valet, Green found his client at the apartment and together they looked over various quality gems. Their discussion was briefly interrupted by a visit from Dr Hunter—apothecary to the likes of the Duke and Duchess of Devonshire and other members of London's fashionable set—who had a private meeting with Lord Massey and apparently issued him with some kind of prescription. Once Dr Hunter had departed, Lord Massey picked out a pair of diamond ear-rings, a necklace, and a watch and chain to the value of £760. Massey offered to pay in full for the purchase. Reaching into a bureau he produced a cheque made out to 'Lord Massey or bearer' for £1,400 by Charles, Earl of Tankerville, against his account at Coutts bank, and offered this as 'cash' payment. Such drafts were a common form of financial transaction in the eighteenth century, particularly for large purchases. Theoretically, on acceptance Mr Green would have become the new 'bearer' and would have been able to turn the cheque into cash at Coutts. Pleased with the opportunity for a prompt settlement, but lacking the means to return the difference between the bill for the jewellery and the cheque that Massey proffered, Mr Green left the gems with his client, took the large cheque as a retainer and went back to his house to write a draft for the £700 due as change. Anxious to complete the transaction, he then hastened back to 36 St James's Place with the draft. On his return, however, Massey's valet informed Green that his lordship had left to keep another appointment. After waiting for thirty minutes, Green decided that Massey had most likely departed for dinner and elected to return the next day to conclude his business.

The next morning, Green's first stop was at Coutts to cash the cheque. There, however, he was devastated to discover that the document was a forgery, a fact quickly revealed by the clerk who explained that the Earl of Tankerville (the signatory on the cheque who had, therefore, purportedly issued the money to Lord Massey) kept no account with that bank. Realizing he had been hoodwinked, Green double-checked this detail with none other than Lord Tankerville himself, before hastening back to 36 St James's Place. There he found the hired (and by now rather confused) valet still in post but, unsurprisingly, no sign of 'Lord Massey'. It later came to light that, on the same day, James Hobart also presented himself at a Holborn watchmaker's, this time as the 'Duke of Manchester'. Following a similar strategy to that which he adopted to dupe Mr Green, Hobart ordered two expensive watches and requested that they be sent to his lodgings later that day. The watchmaker, though, proved harder to fool than Green. A few enquiries by way of due diligence revealed that the real Duke of Manchester was in fact out of town, and so the suspicious watchmaker sent two Bow Street Runners to Hobart's lodgings, but Hobart outmanoeuvred them.

Like Alexander Day, James Hobart's mimicry of elite male gentility and attempted deception of London tradesmen had multiple layers and depended on a variety of different accoutrements. In many ways, the success of the fraud he executed on the goldsmith hinged on both speed and slickness. Hobart approached the landlady for the lodging rooms the day before the crime and only feigned moving in at noon of the day upon which he then visited the jeweller. By hiring an out-of-work French valet before he entered the rooms, Hobart gave the impression of boasting his own staff. Whereas Day's footman was an accomplice posing in the role (alongside an unsuspecting coachman who was hired with the carriage), Hobart exploited London's teeming market of unemployed servants to pick up an authentic and experienced prop on the day of the crime. The valet, of course, believed Hobart was 'Lord Massey', and had no reason to doubt his credentials. Hobart's timings appear to have been critical. By requesting that the goldsmith visit his lodgings at 4 p.m., Hobart made it difficult for Green to test the authenticity of the cheque that afternoon. In court, Green later explained that it was too late for him to visit Coutts by the time the transaction had been completed, and so he was forced to wait until the next day. The fact that 'Lord Massey' then left the premises in the late afternoon, before Green returned, also appeared to elicit little alarm. Both valet and goldsmith presumed that afternoon visiting followed by dinner would be the norm for a man of his rank.

Hobart's nonchalant name-dropping was also convincing. When later defending his apparent naivety, Green argued that the fraudulent client's assertion that Lord Salisbury had personally recommended the jewellers was particularly persuasive. Indeed, in the event that Green had entertained any suspicions about Massey, showing concern at that stage would have risked potentially frustrating not only an apparently well-heeled new client, but also an existing and reliable one. Hobart's presentation of a card carrying both name and address provided further reassurance, and by encouraging Green to visit him at his private residence Hobart completed his act. There, Green witnessed him in appropriately fine surroundings, attended by a valet and even visited by London's doctor to the *ton*—although quite how Hobart managed to orchestrate this timely visit never came to light. With so much evidence pointing to Hobart's apparent credibility as 'Lord Massey', there were few grounds on which Green was able to question or challenge the authenticity of the cheque which Hobart offered as payment.

In adopting aristocratic titles, Hobart played for high stakes: the two names he borrowed had living incumbents. The Massy barons were members of the Irish peerage, and the holder of the title in 1791 was the 30-year-old bachelor Hugh, 3rd Baron Massy, who had only succeeded his father a year before. With Hobart approximately the right age (he is presumed to have been in his mid-twenties when the fraud took place), and claiming to be looking for jewellery as a pricey gift for a woman, he was a believable fit for the young heir. According to contemporary newspaper notices, the real Lord Massy appears to have been resident in London and Bath in 1791, giving further credence to Hobart's imposture.[52] By aiming higher still and posing as a duke, Hobart took even greater risks, as revealed by his near exposure by the Holborn watchmaker. Again, though, it seems possible that Hobart's selection was a careful one, the existing holder of the title being the unmarried 20-year-old William Montagu, 5th Duke of Manchester, who had succeeded to the dukedom following the death of his father in 1788.

It was not only in the metropolis that Hobart practised his dark arts. A few months after his fraudulent activity in London he appeared in Newmarket as 'the counterfeit Duke of Ormond'. On 7 October 1791, a Newmarket banker, Mr Hammond, was visited by Hobart who presented himself as 'a very genteel, well-made man', about 25 years old, rather dashingly dressed in a 'dark snuff-coloured great coat', under which he sported 'a new blue straight coat', with 'fashionable yellow buttons, six on each sleeve' and a 'dimity waistcoat'. The whole ensemble was finished off with 'blue ribb'd stockings' and 'new boots'. So equipped, 'with every exterior of a gentleman', he asked Mr Hammond to cash a cheque for £200 made out to the 'Duke of Ormond'.[53] When the banker noted the name on the cheque, Hobart reputedly declared with impressive hauteur, 'I am the Duke of Ormond.' Awed, the banker duly presented Hobart with his money. Hammond, however, had begun to feel suspicious and decided to follow the 'duke'. However, on seeing Hobart call at the Newmarket residence of the Duke of Queensbury (then in town for the races) and leave his card, and call next at the house of Mr Vernon (a famous Newmarket horse breeder who had a longstanding racing partnership with the Duke of Queensbury), the banker confessed that he could not summon the nerve to question him. 'I several times was inclined to call out, Stop Him, but supposing still he might be the Duke my resolution failed me,' he later lamented.[54] Hammond's hesitation cost him dear, because a few hours later Hobart had already left town. The next day, Hammond eventually established, to his chagrin, that 'upon inquiry that the only securities he had for his 200*l* were a false title and a forged draught'.[55]

Following the deception, Hammond published a description of Hobart and of the crime. London newspapers picked up the story but many were unable to hide their incredulity that the banker had been so duped because, on this occasion, Hobart had chosen a non-existent title. Although there was a living Earl of Ormonde in 1791, there was no duke. James Butler, 2nd Duke of Ormond (impeached for treason after he colluded in the 1715 Jacobite rebellion), had died in 1745, married but childless. The title had then passed *de jure* to his younger brother, Charles, but when he too died without issue in 1758 it became extinct. London papers lambasted Hammond for his basic mistake. 'It is a curious circumstance that a Banker should be defrauded of 200*l* by a man styling himself Duke of Ormond when no such title exists,' crowed the *Morning Chronicle*. 'A banker's clerk in London would be ashamed of such a fraud being committed upon him,' the paper confidently claimed.[56]

Tellingly, although he had some near misses, Hobart was never caught in the act as an impostor. He was first brought to trial for shooting a constable and a constable's son who were pursuing Hobart after he eloped with an innkeeper's daughter.[57] It was on this charge of 'malicious killing' that he found himself behind bars. An eloquent and clever defence meant that Hobart escaped a sentence.[58]

By then, though, his past had caught up with him, and Hobart was transferred to the Old Bailey to be tried for his impersonation of Lord Massy, and his defrauding of the goldsmiths Willerton and Green. Hobart was found guilty of the crime and sentenced to the gallows. Reported as being a man 'of very decent appearance' even when he was led to the scaffold, Hobart was hanged outside Newgate gaol on 13 February 1793.

The frauds enacted by Hobart and Day offer more than narrative drama. Their acts reveal the difficulties that tradesmen and bankers such as Green and Hammond faced when trying to establish the identity of new clients. Both these skilled impostors successfully played on contemporary perceptions of elite male gentility, and the content and orchestration of their fraudulent schemes hint at some of the criteria outsiders believed underpinned membership of 'fashionable' society. Both frauds rested primarily on the successful performance of external signals of status, a nonchalant air, and a sense of entitlement. Yet Day and Hobart also exploited other presumptions to shore up their deception. Most notably, some suggestion of access to well-known and named figures was critical to their success. It was, for instance, the fact that Day appeared to visit the Duke of Montagu and 'other persons of rank' that reassured the stable owner that his carriage was in trustworthy hands. Hobart's name-dropping at the jewellers fulfilled a similar function. In Newmarket, a timely knock by Hobart on the Duke of Queensbury's door confirmed to the banker that Hobart was a duke himself.

Naturally, the denizens of fashionable society would not have been taken in for a second. Their world was built on face-to-face familiarity; membership was the antithesis of anonymity. Denied this level of confident human connoisseurship, bankers and merchants fell back on less reliable forms of evidence that inevitably highlighted their outsider status. Observing the presentation of a calling card from across a street was not the same as witnessing the furrowed brow of the grandee to whom it was then delivered. Surfaces—whether of a front door, a gentleman's suit, or a servant's livery—became, in the absence of anything more conclusive, all important. Perhaps this helps to explain why for the general public, then and since, 'surface' has appeared to be what the beau monde was all about.

London's little coterie

While dull historians only sing of wars,
Of hood-wink's treaties hatching keen-ey'd jars;
Of wily statesmen splitting hairs asunder,
Of hills and orators who belch and thunder;
Of grinding taxes, and of tott'ring thrones,
Of him who eats up states and picks the bones:
Say shall the brightest glories of our ages,
Who best adorn the cut and grace the page,
Who on top of fashion's Ida dwell,
And gold in showers produce to either Bell;
O say shall these, who just so bright have shone,
Escape remembrance when they quit the Ton?

(Lady Anne Hamilton, *Epics of the Ton*, 1807)

In 1925, crowds of onlookers gathered on the pavement surrounding Devonshire House, as they had done since the mansion's eighteenth-century heyday. The attraction this time, though, was not its famous occupants, their politics, or their parties. Instead, it was the demolition ball that was parked up and preparing to take a first strike. Recently sold by the Duke of Devonshire to developers, in minutes the imposing town house was rendered to rubble. In the coming year, a sleek new apartment block, designed for modern living and a new type of resident, had been built over its dust.

Many other town houses, proudly erected and occupied by ambitious eighteenth-century nobles as their family base for the season, met the same fate in the first three decades of the twentieth century. Lansdowne House in Berkeley Square, designed by Robert Adam and purchased by William, 2nd Earl of Shelburne, in 1765, was half demolished in the 1930s to make way for a new road through the West End. The other half was rebuilt and remodelled as the Lansdowne Club, a private members' club adorned with modish art deco detail, while the original dining room used by Lord Shelburne was saved and later found a new use as an incongruous board room within the steel-clad Lloyd's of London building. In 1937, Kingston House (built in the 1750s for Elizabeth Chudleigh, Duchess of Kingston) was sacrificed for the development of prestigious flats, and the following year Norfolk House in St James's Square was razed and replaced with an office building that served as the London headquarters for Allied forces during the Second World War.

The destruction of the private palaces that had, long ago, housed the beau monde was symbolic. In the early 1900s, the remaining vestiges of the economic, social, and political conditions that had combined in 1688 to create the infrastructure of the season and underpin the beau monde's urban prestige finally unravelled. Many of the social and political functions of the season had substantially changed in the 1800s, but ongoing elite authority over Victorian 'Society' and the continued stronghold of the aristocracy in parliament ensured that metropolitan residences remained an essential part of a noble family's broader estate. By the end of the First World War, however, the landscape was very different. New income tax levels and, particularly, death duties (inheritance tax) placed unprecedented financial pressure on aristocratic estates. The Second Reform Act (1867) and the introduction of universal male suffrage (1918) also finally undercut age-old titled power in parliament. In such a changed climate, astute nobles like the Duke of

Devonshire recognized the huge cash value that could be released from the sale of their prime London real estate—property that no longer served a significant social, cultural, or political purpose.

As developers began to take over the town houses, biographers stepped in to recover the lives of their occupants. Between 1917 and 1935, a raft of celebratory memoirs sketched a nostalgic picture of the glamorous Georgian ghosts of the West End. Their priorities, the fairytale version suggested, were about hedonistic pleasure rather than fiercely defended political power; their fast-living sociability was a way for the super rich to pass the time rather than a means of broadcasting exclusivity; and their renowned 'beauty' was merely a genetic chance and confirmation of their ineffable charm rather than a codification of privilege and prestige. In this vision, the serious business of the beau monde, its political motivations, its power and its socio-cultural agendas were downplayed in favour of a picture of unfettered hedonism. Eighteenth-century fashionable life came to be remembered as one long party.

'What are they, who are they and what constitutes them people of fashion?'[1] This deceptively straightforward question, posed by Lord Chesterfield to readers of *The World* in 1755, lies at the heart of this book. The simplicity of Lord Chesterfield's query belies both the complexity and the importance of the answer. To study the beau monde is to recover a history of the high profile, the privileged, and the metropolitan. As such it is, by definition, a history of an atypical minority. Yet, born of the political, cultural, and social conditions of post-Glorious Revolution Britain, it was a minority that boasted disproportionate power and influence.

As historians have long asserted, a raft of new conditions was evident in 1700s Britain, from political affairs to a commercial culture centred around novel and accessible consumer products, and rooted in a newly urbanized society. Such dramatic and far-reaching developments had the potential to undercut existing structures of power and status in a range of ways. Indeed, much attention has been paid to the significant opportunities these changes presented to emerging social groups, especially a broadly 'middle' or 'commercial' class. However, as historian Judith Lewis observes of the late eighteenth century, 'the continued pre-eminence of the aristocracy is, in many ways, the elephant in the living room of the trumpeting middle class'.[2] The beau monde— its nature, membership, and associated practices—illuminates one of the ways in which an already established elite responded to and assimilated change while at the same time defending its dominant position.

Of all the criteria that underpinned a fashionable status, noble rank was among the most pervasive. On paper, commentators repeatedly asserted that 'fashion' was an indefinable quality that stood apart from established concepts of status. In practice, however, hereditary privileges and patrician lineage continued to matter. The vast majority of those listed in newspapers, drawn in caricatures, recorded in letters, and remembered in posterity as fashion's leaders were also members of Britain's comparatively small peerage.

This evident relationship between a fashionable status and rank is so far removed from our modern conception of what fashion means that it is difficult to recover the more subtle nuances of this contemporary construction. It is certainly not my intention to argue that the beau monde was 'just' a nobility in disguise or that 'fashion' was indistinguishable from, or interchangeable with, aristocratic title. Rather, in the eighteenth century, 'fashion' functioned as an additional system of prestige, one that overlaid an existing and more traditional hierarchical order.

Given the pre-eminence of titled personnel within London's fashionable world, it might be argued that the beau monde represented an *ancien régime* of limited innovation. It is certainly true that, in certain regards, the political and social elite of the mid- to late 1600s did not look so dramatically different from the beau monde of the 1700s. The names that recur in eighteenth-century fashionable registers—such as Cavendish, Churchill, Harley, Hervey, and Montagu—were all prominent members of the peerage a generation or more before the term 'beau monde' was coined. Indeed, a fair case could be made for tracing the beau monde's history back to the 1660s and the restoration of the monarchy, if not earlier. What must be recognized, however, is that cultural conditions in which such an elite operated changed markedly as the seventeenth century drew to a close. The political culture that evolved after 1688 was key to the beau monde's subsequent nature and function. In particular, the establishment of, and emphasis on, the London season brought fundamental alterations to the routines and responsibilities inherent in elite life. The level of investment made by titled personnel in metropolitan life in the 1700s (in terms of time, money, property, and culture) was unprecedented. Although pleasure seeking was unquestionably a major attraction of metropolitan life, it was politics, and the elite's unshakeable belief in their right to govern, that made the season's siren call so compelling.

As we have seen, in this new landscape, a fashionable status was accrued through a demanding array of public performances in a round of interconnected urban spaces, ranging from the court to the pleasure garden. Within the boundaries of this metropolitan map, prestige was determined through material displays, shows of acquaintance and sociability, insider knowledge, conduct, and reputation. Indeed, the critical importance of public display, manifested through material possessions as well as through social visibility at theatres, pleasure gardens, and other public resorts, is arguably one of the beau monde's most distinguishing features.

Cultural arenas such as these have long been foregrounded in histories of eighteenth-century Britain. Revisiting them, however, from the perspective of the metropolitan beau monde allows us to approach them in a fresh light. Public sociability and ostensibly 'open' commercial leisure venues were of great importance to the maintenance and display of a fashionable identity. Often cited by historians as evidence of the newly inclusive character of public life, these metropolitan leisure grounds have been the subject of a vast literature. The beau monde, though, can be found to have used such venues as contexts for the performance of social separation and distinction. Far from encouraging a widespread 'mixing' of society, such commercial venues supported a system of fashionable differentiation. Members of the beau monde used pleasure resorts in a particular way, laid claim to a particular space, and behaved in a particular manner that successfully distinguished them from the rest of the public present. Similarly, though exploiting a vibrant commercial culture and emphasizing the importance of material consumption and display, the beau monde's material culture was not easily purchased by a parvenu or interloper. By using possessions, such as diamond jewellery or court dress, to build and broadcast group connections, 'fashion' even in its most material sense involved something more than modishness.

An overriding emphasis on cultural qualifications offered considerable opportunities to certain cohorts within the beau monde, arguably most significantly to women who were able to establish themselves as leaders of fashion in their own right. Within much contemporary imagery, indomitable duchesses and countesses were portrayed as doyennes of the fashionable world. This image is reinforced by women's personal recollections and experiences, which detail their roles as its patronesses, powerbrokers and gatekeepers. Some caveats, though, need to be added to this picture of the beau monde as a site of expansive female authority. It is striking, for example, that for all women's involvement and participation, it was arguably men's interests, careers, and authority that formed the main focus of fashionable life. The central objective of female networking and intelligence gathering was, by and large, to protect and promote male kin. In this regard, the social and political activities of women such as Lady Hervey and the Countess of Strafford, while providing them with legitimate access to, and authority within, the beau monde, were largely framed by the personal and familial ambitions of their husbands. The extent to which ladies might act independently of their lords is notoriously difficult to measure and warrants further scrutiny. Nonetheless, the boundaries to female power within the beau monde are perhaps rather tellingly demonstrated by the comparative ease with which they were exiled from its ranks. In cases of adultery, for instance, it was the woman rather than the man of fashion who bore the brunt of the beau monde's censure.

Political objectives, broadly defined, can be found at the heart of much of fashionable life, from the day-to-day exchange of political and parliamentary information to the advertisement of political alliances and positions through interpersonal networks and personal accoutrements. Many such political activities and expressions were new to the age, created by and within the period's burgeoning urban and commercial culture. High political machinations spilled out of Westminster and into the opera boxes, dinners, assemblies, visits, and even the wardrobes of London's beau monde. At the same time, though, traditional institutions and practices were of continued significance. The royal court, for instance, remained an integral feature of the fashionable world. However, although many of the protocols of court attendance were immured in tradition, the beau monde's practice of attending court, of broadcasting complex political positions through that attendance, and the subsequent reporting and monitoring of those same appearances in a range of media, were innovative developments.

Recognizing that politics underpinned the beau monde's configuration helps us to make sense of many of its features. The emphasis placed on public display, for instance, was rooted not so much in the parade of individual ostentation (although ostentation still played its part) but in the consolidation of a group identity. This, in turn, derived from a conviction that the ruling elite should make its London presence visible in order to check the monarchy and provide a significant counterbalance within Britain's constitution. However, the beau monde also framed itself in relationship to a wider urban public. The prominence of public venues within fashionable social routines highlights the necessity of acknowledgement from a wider audience. As E. P. Thompson originally noted, visibility and theatrical gestures were a formidable feature of eighteenth-century elite culture, politics, and power.[3] For Thompson, such theatricality was an essential element of patrician power in provincial and rural settings. The beau monde demonstrates how the same principles played out in the metropolis—an environment where such strategies were perhaps all the more necessary given the city's greater anonymity and social variety.

As well as projecting politicized agendas outwards, politics also played a significant role in shaping the networks and alliances of individuals who comprised the beau monde. Notably a range of different political identities and factional affiliations appear to have been easily accommodated under the shared auspices of fashionable society. Histories of late eighteenth-century politics have often equated the 'world of fashion' solely with a single political coterie: the fast-living, extravagant, and high-profile Whig elite, who used public display and ostentation to trumpet their political opposition. Led in parliament by Charles James Fox, and in London's society and public more generally by Georgiana, Duchess of Devonshire, this Whig clique dominates current conceptions of who fashionable people were and what fashionable life involved.[4] Such notorious celebrities were unquestionably amongst the beau monde's most visible members, but equating fashionable society solely with a specific form of political opposition is problematically reductive. This book has demonstrated how, in many different contexts, the beau monde provided a framework for the consolidation and expression of different factional identities. In the early decades of the century, as in its closing decades, London's 'world of fashion' encompassed those who identified themselves as 'Tory' as well as those who identified themselves as 'Whig'. Of course, such political labels were not in themselves fixed, and changed considerably in their meaning over the course of the century. What is important to note here, however, is that the beau monde allowed for, and arguably even facilitated, the articulation of different ideological positions under its auspices. To be sure, such differences could only be accommodated up to a certain point. It is striking, though not surprising, that Jacobitism (support for the exiled Stuart crown) was not tolerated within the beau monde. Political opposition had to be expressed within the boundaries of the new political culture that was created after 1688, which was after all the very culture that created the beau monde. In the century's earlier decades, then, we find figures such as the Herveys who deemed themselves to be 'Whig' and those such as the Straffords who deemed themselves 'Tory' occupying a shared London landscape, pursuing many of the same social activities, meeting in many of the same arenas, yet using those shared contexts to articulate different factional political positions. It is possible that what was regarded as a permissible degree of opposition became more flexible as the century progressed, and it seems reasonable to suggest that there was greater scope for more public displays of opposition once the real threat of Jacobite uprisings subsided. One of the most striking features of the form of opposition politics played out by the Foxite Whigs was its aggressively and flamboyantly public nature. Their brand of political opposition was far more overt than the subtle factional disputes that had been encompassed within earlier generations of the beau monde.

The particular form of collective authority suggested by the beau monde was, of course, far from timeless. According to historian and sociologist Leonore Davidoff, the 'fashionable society' of the eighteenth century was transformed into a new 'Society' over the course of the opening decades of the 1800s.[5] Distinguishing the former from the latter, she suggests, was a fresh separation of the political and social functions of the metropolitan elite. Whereas within the eighteenth-century beau monde political and social activities were often indistinguishable and always interchangeable, nineteenth-century London 'Society' was more explicitly social. After the 1832 Reform Act, parliamentary activity became more professionalized and codified, and less easily transferred to public social arenas. As a result, by the mid-1800s, although a small number of high-ranking Victorian hostesses continued to preside over political *soirées*, these were perceived as distinct, more exclusive (and even arcane) arenas of sociability removed from the main social business of the season.[6]

Participation in the season became more formal and regimented as the nineteenth century progressed. A proliferation of etiquette manuals offered guidance through its complicated rules and codes of conduct.[7] Incredibly precise instructions outlining the protocols of court presentations were published, as were directories of Society's members, complete with addresses to facilitate diligent management of visiting schedules. More than anything else, a carefully controlled and contained marriage market became the principal *raison d'être* of the season, and a young woman's 'coming out' was scrupulously managed. If the eighteenth century was an age of 'people of fashion' then the nineteenth century, and especially the second half of the nineteenth century, was the heyday of the 'debutante'. Moreover, rather than purposefully parading status in public and commercial arenas, and using commercial leisure resorts as strategic social centres, nineteenth-century 'Society' operated from private locations that were more easily managed. Sociability shifted from the pleasure gardens and assembly rooms that had burgeoned in the 1700s to private drawing rooms.

This change is evident in the Victorian fate of London's 'public' social resorts. Theatres and operas were certainly still frequented but, by the mid-1800s, they were attended in a different way. The bustling and noisy socializing that had marked out the Georgian theatre audience was replaced by the practice of 'quiet listening' and a new type of formal, reserved, and codified social behaviour.[8] One of London's landmark subscription venues, The Pantheon on Oxford Street, which had hosted balls and concerts (and for a time operas) since 1772, ceased being a place of public entertainment from 1814. It was redesigned in the 1830s as a covered market. From the 1860s, it housed a wine merchant's showroom and today the site is occupied by a department store. Ranelagh's famous rotunda was demolished around 1803. The gardens were redesigned and lingered on, but by the 1880s they were home to a new social attraction, the football club, serving as Fulham's first ground. Vauxhall Gardens, in contrast, went through a series of reinventions, hosting exotic attractions from balloonists and circus troupes to a celebratory re-enactment of the Battle of Waterloo with 1,000 soldiers. The gardens stuttered through bankruptcy and new management before closing for the final time in 1859.[9] The ostensibly informal, seemingly 'open' and frenetic sociability that characterized the eighteenth-century town (at least in its appearance) was thus replaced by new entertainments, new codes of social behaviour, more restrained etiquette, and more regimented excursions. Moreover, the 'Society' that dominated nineteenth-century London enjoyed closer connections to country life than had been possible for its eighteenth-century fashionable predecessors. Creating fast links between the capital and the provinces, railways made weekend returns to the country house straightforward, especially for those nobles who pressed for railways to be routed close to their estates. As a result, the country house party offered a new type of social experience for those engaged in the London season.[10]

As well as being more formal and centred around different modes of sociability, nineteenth-century 'Society' is also regarded by historians as growing considerably larger than its eighteenth-century predecessor. The development of complex social codes has sometimes been attributed to a desire to retain the exclusivity of London's fashionable world, and erect impossible obstacles to thwart unwanted incursions. This might suggest then that 'Society' was set to contract, and early 1800s commentary in particular points to a preoccupation with the growing exclusivity of the 'people of fashion'. In her study of early nineteenth-century etiquette manuals, however, Marjorie Morgan gives a more nuanced analysis, arguing that these codes were required precisely because 'Society' was swelling. The larger the institution, the more extensive its management needed to be in order to defend its status and systems.[11] An expansion of the peerage through new creations and the greater survival of their offspring accounted in part for a marked increase in the elite population. In addition, the control exerted by 'Society' over the patrician marriage market effectively made some degree of participation inescapable for most titled families. Furthermore, statistical and anecdotal evidence indicates that a significant number of wealthy but untitled newcomers successfully infiltrated 'Society's' barricaded ranks in the second half of the nineteenth century.[12] As Morgan notes, the complex codes that surrounded 'Society' were not simply about keeping the unworthy out, but also managing the integration and assimilation of newcomers according to regulations and terms that were controlled and approved by the titled elite.[13]

The registers of membership, lists of court presentations, etiquette manuals, and instruction sheets that make nineteenth-century 'Society' comparatively easy to identify and quantify do not exist for its eighteenth-century predecessor. Indeed, the difficulty of subjecting the beau monde to any confident empirical analysis makes its history unavoidably shadowy and open to interpretation. Its opaque nature, though, is arguably one of its most significant features. Not only was the murkiness of the beau monde's membership criteria a source of contemporary fascination, it arguably contributed to fashionable society's striking resilience. It might reasonably be suggested that the lack of clarity about precisely how membership was obtained made the hope of access a viable proposition for a broad social catchment. Satirists' constant haranguing of misguided aspirants who rendered themselves ridiculous in their foolhardy mimicry of 'fashion' mocked such aspirations. Yet in so doing they also reinforced an image of potential inclusivity. On closer inspection, however, it was social, cultural, and political exclusivity that underpinned the beau monde. The eighteenth-century 'beau monde' was, therefore, a rebranded rather than a remade social order, with elite privilege flourishing under the rubric of 'fashion'.

USES AND MEANINGS OF 'BEAU MONDE': A SUPPLEMENTARY ESSAY

The people of rank and distinction...are properly called the people of fashion; because, in truth, they settle the fashion. Instead of subjecting themselves to the laws, they take measure of their own appetites and passions, and then make laws to fit them.

(*Universal Magazine*, September 1777)

There is among the more elevated classes of society, a certain set of persons who are pleased exclusively to call themselves *the fine world*....This *certain set* conceives of society as resolving itself into two distinct classes; the *fine world* and the *people*; to which last class they turn over all who do not belong to their little *coterie*, however high their rank or fortune or merit. Celebrity, in their estimation, is not bestowed by birth or talents, but by being connected with *them*. They have laws, immunities, privileges and almost a language of their own; they form a kind of distinct *cast*, and with a sort of *esprit du corps* detach themselves from others, even in general society...their confines are jealously guarded and their privileges are incommunicable.

(Hannah More, *Strictures on the Modern System of Female Education*, 1799)

The urban culture explored in this book was described by eighteenth-century writers in obscure terms that are now largely obsolete. The phrase 'beau monde' ceased to be used regularly in colloquial English from the mid-nineteenth century. Throughout the 1700s, however, routine reference to the beau monde was a commonplace of commentary across varied media, from plays and poems, to novels, essays, newspapers, periodicals, and ballads. In addition, an extensive attendant glossary of distinctive words and phrases were regularly cited in conjunction with 'beau monde', including: 'world of fashion', 'people of fashion', 'ton', 'bon ton', 'haut ton', 'haute monde', 'fine world', 'great world', and 'the town'. Of these, only 'fashion' and 'town' remain familiar to us today (albeit stripped of their eighteenth-century inflections and nuances). To understand the contemporary significance of the 'world of fashion', then, it is necessary to retrieve the use and meanings of this eighteenth-century language.

This essay surveys some of that linguistic context, exploring its cluttered and often contradictory field of reference to illustrate, as far as possible, a broad range of contemporary occurrences and meanings. Whilst such a semantic approach cannot hope to be exhaustive, the following analysis of the various uses of 'beau monde' aims to be as expansive as possible. Essentially an exercise in the historicized translation of words whose meanings have been lost across the centuries, this method of recreating contemporary written contexts is necessarily formulaic. Tracking the first use, repeated use, and disputed use of anachronistic phrases does not represent the most dramatic form of historical detection nor does it generate the ingredients for a gripping narrative exposition. Nonetheless, given the stereotypes and clichés that have come to surround the reputedly hedonistic 'fashionable society' of the eighteenth century, it is all the more imperative to start from the beginning, and give due attention to the complex ways in which contemporaries used 'beau monde' as a point of reference. With this in mind, the following survey first offers an overview of the occurrence of 'beau monde' in various printed contexts from its first use in the 1690s through to the early 1800s. The second, shorter section, then turns to more colloquial uses found in letters and diaries. Its purpose is to give a broader conceptual and methodological context to the definition and interpretation of 'beau monde' that has been applied in this book, which draws purposefully on some of the narrower and more explicitly hierarchical applications of the term.

The usual recourse for the historian resurrecting anachronistic words is to seek refuge in a contemporary dictionary. Unfortunately, although eighteenth-century dictionaries abounded, not all tackled these nebulous phrases.[1] The most famous lexicographer of the age, Samuel Johnson, eschewed the colloquial, spurned the Frenchified, and left 'beau monde' firmly out of his English language collation in 1755.[2] His omission did not go unnoticed. The satirical journal *The World* advised Mr Johnson to 'publish an appendix to his great work containing those polite, though perhaps not strictly grammatical words and phrases, commonly used and sometimes understood by the beau monde'.[3] Dictionaries that did register 'beau monde' as an English term most often translated it simply as 'people of fashion' or the 'world of fashion'. Such concise definitions are not, on their own, especially revealing. Accompanying explanations of 'fashion', however, are more useful. In particular, these demonstrate that 'fashion' was widely understood to denote a position in the social hierarchy (rather than just implying a modishness achieved through consumption and taste), though precisely where in the hierarchy fashion lay was disputed. For *A New Universal Dictionary* (1759), 'fashion' represented 'a rank superior to the vulgar'. Despite ignoring the term 'beau monde', Samuel Johnson tackled 'fashion' as a concept in his dictionary of 1755 and pronounced that 'men of fashion' were 'above the vulgar but below the nobility'.[4] *The Royal English Dictionary* (1762) took a more explicitly elevated view, suggesting 'men of fashion implies men of rank, state or dignity', an interpretation shared in 1800 by *Barclays Universal Dictionary*, which added that 'fashionable' also denoted 'high rank'.[5] Webster's *American Dictionary* followed suit with a similar emphasis on high rank, although more broadly defined, listing 'fashion' as 'genteel life or good breeding' and 'genteel company'.[6] This marked lack of agreement as to precisely where in a social hierarchy 'fashion' might be found is highly significant. The uncertainty as to which social ranks might or might not be encompassed by the 'world of fashion' meant, as we will see, that it could be invoked in reference to a wide variety of social contexts depending on the agenda of the author.

Plays and novels of the late seventeenth century represent some of the earliest printed uses of 'beau monde'. One such application can be found in a short travelogue, *Letters* (1696), written by the influential female author and playwright Delarivier Manley. *Letters* recounts a journey from London to Exeter during which Manley introduces her travelling companion, an overdressed baronet's son who was obsessed with his appearance and social station. During the journey the young man regales Manley with a story of an unhappy love affair. He described the object of his affections as a 'gentilely bred' beauty who had 'seen the *Beaux Monde*, made the Tour of all the places of Gallantry, shin'd in the Drawing Room, languish'd in the Boxes, adorn'd in the Park, in a word, was all a man of my circumstances could desire'.[7] The use of 'beaux monde' in this context is only fleeting, but for the ambitious baronet's son the young woman's association with the 'world of fashion' was one marker of her suitability as a marriage prospect. It was a world associated with sociability and public display (and being seen at the court, the theatre, opera, and urban parks). The young man, however, discovered to his surprise that the beauty was not all that she seemed. Despite her genteel and fashionable demeanour she engaged in an indiscreet love affair, passing him over for a married man. Even within its earliest applications, then, the 'beau monde' was problematically associated with personal display. Commentators worried about the difficulty of distinguishing between surface appearance and interior worth. Did all those who appeared to be 'people of fashion' have the manners or morals to match their projected status?

Contemporary to Manley's *Letters* were some of the most famous Restoration comedies within which 'beau monde' was a staple point of reference. Notably, in this context, it was principally a comedic device representing the social world occupied by the ubiquitous 'fop'. For example, Colley Cibber's comedy of manners *Love's Last Shift* (1696) included the scene-stealing character Sir Novelty Fashion. Although Sir Novelty obsequiously flatters and flirts with his female acquaintances, he is primarily concerned with his own appearance and his slavish observance of modish clothing and other fashionable trends. During the play, one character teasingly commends Sir Novelty Fashion for being 'a true original, the very Pink of Fashion'. 'Oh! Such an Air!', she continues, 'so becoming a Negligence! Upon my soul, Sir Novelty, you'll be the Envy of the Beau Monde!'[8]

It is in such momentary references that the commonplace use of 'beau monde' emerges on the late seventeenth-century stage. Its association with the social milieu of the fop is significant. Usually titled 'Sir' (such as 'Sir Fopling Flutter' in

George Etherege's earlier *The Man of Mode*, or 'Sir John Roverhead' in Mary Pix's *The Beau Defeated*, 1700), foppish characters were portrayed as members of the lesser gentry, rather than members of the peerage who would be styled lord.[9] It is difficult to determine from the texts alone whether these fops should be taken as representative of the beau monde as a whole, or were intended to ridicule key traits associated with that world. The fop's admiration of the 'world of fashion' is made very apparent, but his inclusion in such circles is usually left unresolved. Nonetheless, one of the central structural conceits of Restoration comedy was an emphasis on recognizable London settings and social types that allowed the audience to relate the drama to their own experiences.[10] These were not plays of fantasy worlds and distant locations, but sharp-tongued takes on the audience's immediate environs. The use of 'beau monde' as a routine point of reference in these plays thus testifies to a contemporary metropolitan familiarity with the concept by the 1690s.

The stage continued to provide a forum for airing ideas about fashionable society as the century progressed, and the beau monde was staple fodder for the popular comedies of manners that dominated the later eighteenth-century theatre. Indeed, it is arguable that fashionable society was the principal focus of many of the most famous plays by Samuel Foote, Richard Brinsley Sheridan, Hannah Cowley, David Garrick, and others.[11] The actual occurrence of the terminology— 'beau monde', 'ton', or 'fashion'—in the main body of such plays is sparse. In Sheridan's *The Rivals* (1775) and *A Trip to Scarborough* (1777), the terms 'beau monde' and 'ton' appeared only once in each.[12] Even Garrick's short, two-act *Bon Ton: Or High Life Above Stairs* (1775) only makes direct use of the phrase 'bon ton' on a single occasion, in the play's closing lines.[13] There, the resolutely unfashionable Sir John Trotley addresses the audience. Declaring himself 'a knight errant [rescuing] distress'd damsels from these monsters, foreign vices, and *Bon Ton* as they call it', he then called on the spectators: 'I trust that every English hand and heart here will assist me in so desperate an undertaking.'[14] However, as Gillian Russell has recently argued, the fact that fashion and fashionable society only received brief mention in such plays should not be taken as evidence of their marginality. Instead, these plays can be said to have taken the discourse of fashion, and the society of the beau monde, as their central target but revealed that society through characters and costumes, rather than elaborate linguistic descriptions.[15]

The invocation of 'beau monde' as a commonplace contemporary conceit extended far beyond this theatrical context. Throughout the 1700s, there was a barrage of sarcastic and satirical applications in many different print media. Verse satires found plenty in a fashionable way of life to cover pages and pages of humorous poetry. Henry Carey's 1729 poem *The Beau Monde: Or the Pleasures of St James's*, for instance, expounded on its subject's reputation for fast urban living.[16] Running to sixteen verses, the poem exposed the excesses and falsities of London's 'beau monde' from a variety of perspectives. In particular, sparkling exterior accessories were portrayed as a thin veneer masking a lack of interior worth:

> And there's your Beaux, with powder'd Cloaths,
> Bedaub'd from head to Shin;
> Their pocket-holes adorn'd with Gold,
> But not a souse within.
> And there's your pretty Gentlemen,
> All dress'd in silk and satin,
> That get a spice of ev'ry Thing,
> Excepting sense and latin.[17]

Many other poets mined this seam of outward display and inner vacuity. The beau monde's alleged frivolity provided enough material to cover no fewer than seventeen pages and twenty-nine verses in the anonymous 1748 poetic satire *The Important Triflers*. Addressed to 'the beau monde in general', the poem followed the daily routine of the world of fashion from morning until night, from court to park to pleasure garden. The sole purpose of such restless movement, the poem asserted, was a pointless pursuit of gossip and 'fresh matter for chatter'. The 'important triflers' who made up the fashionable world traded in rumour, recounted hearsay, and poured scorn on the society that surrounded them: 'now and then, cheek by jowl, we meet in a Cro[w]d, court'sey, scrape, wind and nod and talk *nothing* aloud.'[18] *A Sketch of the Beau Monde* (1764) also worried about the apparently aimless nature of a fashionable life, imagining a future in which every court vacancy and government and church post was filled with men of fashion until gambling and vanity was the sole preoccupation of the state.[19] Early 1800s poems continued to find the concept of the beau monde worthy of satire. Both *The Ton*, 'dedicated to the gossips', and *Haut Ton* took the world of fashion as their central theme.[20] 'What's Fashion? What's Bon Ton?', the latter asked in its opening stanza, 'the whim, the rage',

> The acted mummery of pleasure's stage.
> And what is pleasure? Tis a shadowy beam,
> The airy essence of a waking dream,
> A phantom which we follow to the grave,
> For which all hardships we can boldly brave,
> Disease, misfortune, loss of wealth and fame,
> Such fascination's in this mighty name.
> This *je n'sais quoi* which binds our wit and will,
> Shines like the glow-worm and deludes us still;
> …Such, such is Fashion, call it what you will;
> Go waking dreamers—take of it your fill.[21]

Sitting largely outside the literary canon, such rhetorical drollery has received little critical analysis within eighteenth-century English literary or historical studies. The survival of many examples and editions of these multi-verse poems would imply they were widely published throughout the century, yet it is difficult to establish precisely how such commentary should be interpreted, who composed much of it, or how it was read and received in its own age. The information provided by the texts alone is scant. With the exception of Henry Cary's *The Beau Monde or the Pleasures of St James's*, the majority of these poems were published anonymously and have not yet been attributed to known authors.[22] However, even though additional contextual information might be lacking, it is important to note that such poems share some interesting features. In particular, each portrays the beau monde as a hazily defined, or undefined, social collectivity: a stereotype that was used without reference to any named individual. Yet under that broad and vague stereotype, each poet foregrounded different anxieties and found different points for attack.

For Carey's *The Beau Monde*, for instance, one of the principal objects of ridicule was the 'green nobility' of the city, obsessed with mimicking the manners and pleasures of the 'fashion' in St James's. From this perspective, then, 'fashion' was portrayed as a problematic temptation damaging new money. In contrast, the anonymous *Sketch of the Beau Monde* (1762) regarded fashionable life as a more specific curse, corrupting the nobility, debasing genteel lineage, and diluting the prestige of the peerage. It was not simply that fashion was variously interpreted as a threat to an ambitious bourgeoisie or an established elite. Rather, the plethora of poems and ballads dealing with the topic used the man or woman of fashion as a scapegoat for all manner of perceived social problems, from the decline of religion to the instability of marriage, from the pernicious effects of luxurious consumption to the falsities of polite social practices, from women's neglect of their domestic responsibilities to men's gambling and political corruption. In this way, the 'beau monde' was often presented and used as an abstracted social type, within which any number of contemporary anxieties could be accommodated. Although stock words, phrases, and illustrative stories were routinely deployed, the purpose of such commentary varied from context to context, writer to writer, publication to publication, and, almost certainly, from decade to decade if not year to year. Arguably, it was precisely because the 'beau monde' was such a recognizable rhetorical stereotype that it operated as a powerful, and elastic, portmanteau term in critical commentary.

The combination of curiosity and concern surrounding the 'beau monde' is vividly revealed by a wider survey of literary representations. One category that has been singled out as central to the eighteenth century's remarkable media culture is the periodical and magazine miscellany. Key, here, are the establishment of *The Tatler* periodical in 1709 by Richard Steele, and its famous successor, *The Spectator*, in 1711 (launched by Steele in collaboration with Joseph Addison). Costing a penny for an issue, and appearing up to six times a week, these novel newssheets were composed as short, stand-alone essays. Rather than thumping moralistic tracts, the periodical essay was more cajoling and teasing. Written as ironic exposés of everything from the avaricious city slicker, the rustic squire, the vain debutante, the negligent wife, the unkempt bachelor, and the rakish libertine, they nudged the reader towards a path of decency and restraint. These early periodicals were rapidly followed by a multitude of competitors. By 1800, over 250 different journals had been launched, targeting a wide variety of readers, from women to gentlemen connoisseurs, urbanites to farmers, the peerage to professionals; and focusing on everything from art to politics, and trade to erotica.

It comes as no revelation to find that such periodicals routinely turned their attention to the world of fashion. Given their mission for cultural improvement, *The Tatler* and *The Spectator* spearheaded discussions about the pros and cons of fashionable society.[23] Guiding their readers to seek a rational middle course, the perceived whims and excesses of the beau monde were frequently addressed by Addison and Steele. 'Fashion,' in particular, was routinely singled out as a stimulant to immorality, and the writers castigated vanity, snobbery, and self-interest as symptomatic of the contemporary fashionable world.[24] In one essay, the beau monde was presented as the arbiter of 'senseless' social excess. 'I was reflecting this morning upon the spirit and humour of Publick Diversions five and twenty years ago and those of the present time,' began the commentary published in one issue, 'and lamented to myself that though in those days they neglected their morality, they kept up their good sense but that the *Beau Monde* at present is only grown more childish not more innocent than the former.'[25]

Although comparatively less well thumbed by historians, a number of mid-century publications continued to apply the chatty essay formula perfected in *The Spectator*, along with some of its targets. *The World*, for example, very purposefully homed in on the frivolities of London's beau monde. The first editorial essay outlined the publication's brief as being 'to ridicule, with novelty and good-humour, the fashions, follies, vices, and absurdities of that part of the human species which calls itself "The World"'.[26] Written largely by playwright Edward Moore, and supplemented with substantial contributions by other writers (notably a number of them aristocrats, such as Lords Lyttleton, Bath, and Chesterfield), *The World* was published weekly from 1753 to 1756. Broadly speaking, it often portrayed the beau monde in comparable terms to how it was perceived in the poem *The Sketch of the Beau Monde*, namely as a threat to the strength of the titled elite. In an essay from October 1754, the writer wondered,

has not a man of the first rank and fortune a greater opportunity, in proportion to that fortune, to acquire knowledge, than a man in middling circumstances? Most certainly he has; and I make no doubt but that persons of the first quality would be persons of the first understanding, if it was not for one very material obstacle, I mean *fashion*. There are no two characters so entirely incompatible as a man of sense and a man of fashion. A man of fashion must devote his whole time to the fashionable pleasures among the first of these may be reckoned gaming, in the pursuit of which we cannot allow him less than a third part of the twenty-four hours; and the other sixteen (allowing for a little sleep) are to be spent in amusements, perhaps less vicious, but not more profitable.[27]

Rival periodicals were packed with comparable preoccupations. In November 1754, *The Connoisseur* took 'into consideration what is generally understood by Ladies of Quality' (meaning ladies of rank). 'These', the magazine asserted, 'may be more properly called Ladies of Fashion; for in the modish acceptance of the phrase not so much regard is had to their birth or station, or even their coronet, as to their way of life ... [a] perpetual round of visiting, gaming, dressing and intriguing.'[28] Life was apparently so hectic in the fashionable set that, in 1755, *The Connoisseur* recommended a new almanack should be produced specifically for the use of people of fashion. The common calendar, the magazine acknowledged, 'can be of no use whatever to the polite world, who are as widely separated in their manner of living from the common herd of people as the inhabitant of Antipodes'. 'Red letters days' in the new fashionable almanack 'will distinguish those days on which the ladies of the first fashion keep their routs and visiting days', while 'that season of the year commonly called Lent, which implies a time of fasting [would be accorded] its real signification in the *beau monde* as a yearly festival and [mentioned] under the denomination of *the carnival*'.[29] An almost identical proposition was published in a rival periodical, the *Adventurer*, which recommended that a specific system of news reporting should be produced to cater to the demands of London's beau monde. Focused on 'relating what immediately passes in the fashionable world', such a press, the periodical recommended, would 'give up to brother journalists the dreams of politicians, the disputes of empires, and the fluctuations of commerce' and deal only with 'that more important business which claims every one's attention that is the happiness of living within the circle of politeness'.[30]

Such was the currency of concerns about fashionable life that they proved an attractive topic for the period's most innovative and long-lasting literary form—the novel. Indeed, the perplexing nature of the beau monde's key characteristics and membership famously formed the central premiss in one of the most successful stories of the century, Frances Burney's *Evelina* (1778). Narrating a tale of a naive country virgin surprised, and often near seduced by a thrilling London society, the beau monde in Burney's best-selling account was both desirable and dangerous, a high society defined by regulations that the unworldly heroine of the title found hard to fathom but to which she felt obliged to attempt to conform. A comedy of manners enfolds as Evelina's lack of familiarity with metropolitan culture means she mistakes rakes for gentlemen, interlopers for aristocrats, and greenly apes prostitutes rather than peeresses. From this perspective, the beau monde is portrayed as an urban society from which, thanks to her rural upbringing, Evelina had been entirely estranged. It is a world occupied by undesirable characters and influences, such as her Frenchified grandmother, Madame Duval, and Sir Clement Willoughby, a pushy and vulgar baronet of dubious merit. Through her 'entrance into the world', however, Evelina also encounters highly attractive characters, most particularly the eligible and elegant peer Lord Orville. In many ways, although the likes of Madame Duval and Sir Clement Willoughby declare themselves *au fait* with fashion, it is the modest and genteel Orville who Burney positioned as the ideal and truly fashionable man. In this regard, *Evelina* was not a straightforward critique of the beau monde in its entirety, for the most ridiculed characters were those lurking at the edges of the world of fashion rather than those securely positioned at its centre.[31] A further example of this perspective on the beau monde is offered by an unlikely hero, a dog named Pompey, in Francis Coventry's only novel, *The History of Pompey the Little; or the Life and Adventures of a Lap-Dog* (1751). In this account, it is aspirants to the world of fashion who receive the greatest vilification. From Pompey's unique position as an ultra-fashionable pet, the feisty pup acts as the story's narrator, sharing caustic confidences about an imagined *beau monde* with the reader, including figures such as the coxcomb Count Tag who, despite having 'no patent to shew his nobility', had successfully established 'a large acquaintance among people of fashion, who admitted him for the sake of laughing at him', until he was 'elevated to a conspicuous station of ridicule'.[32]

What emerges from even the most cursory survey of the period's varied print culture is, first and foremost, the familiarity of 'beau monde' as a concept, and the significance of fashionable society as a long-running concern for a range of commentators. To be sure, the diversity of ways in which 'beau monde' was deployed as a rhetorical point of reference can be bewildering. Within poems, periodicals, novels, and stage plays, 'beau monde' emerges as a moving target—not just a reference to a metropolitan cohort of nobles but also to aspirational upstarts, new money, imported luxuries, falsified manners, political corruption, and much more besides. There was, though, one especially marked shift in the eighteenth-century application of 'beau monde' that stands out in this varied frame of reference. From around the 1760s it is possible to identify a growing emphasis on named individuals and contemporary events when the 'beau monde' was invoked—a new form of 'people watching' and naming of 'celebrities' that ran alongside the broad-brush descriptions outlined above.

One such vehicle was the *Town and Country Magazine*'s incredibly successful 'tête-à-tête' series. Running for over thirty years from the 1760s, the magazine's stories exposed the 'gallantry' prevalent amongst the 'Bon Ton'. Each month, the magazine published 'head-to-head' portraits of a couple reputedly involved in an illicit liaison, alongside a titillating article that detailed their personal histories and the progress of their assignation. Although the identities of the individuals were theoretically obscured—each being given a thinly veiled pseudonym—ample information was included to allow the informed reader to establish which real, and typically aristocratic, personalities were under attack.[33] Nor was the *Town and Country Magazine* alone in this respect. In the 1780s, *The Fashionable*

Magazine routinely listed specific 'places of fashionable resort', from the public pleasure garden to private routs, and reported on the comings and goings of named fashionable figures, this time without satire or rebuke.[34] A similar use of 'beau monde' can be found in the early 1800s magazine *Le Beau Monde*, which focused almost entirely on the consumption choices of the 'world of fashion', disseminating information about the clothing and accoutrements associated with named celebrities.[35]

At the same time, certain plays were widely received by contemporaries as purposeful characterizations of well-known individuals. Sheridan's *The School for Scandal* offers the most famous example. As soon as the play was staged, it was said that Sheridan's central character, Lady Teazle, was based upon one of the prominent social and political hostesses in London's fashionable world: Georgiana, Duchess of Devonshire. Scholars have since cast significant doubt on the attribution, arguing that Lady Teazle was an unsophisticated country girl who had married up into the lesser gentry, whereas the Duchess of Devonshire was of more firmly blue-blooded stock.[36] Yet, regardless of whether or not Sheridan actually intended Lady Teazle to mirror the Duchess of Devonshire, what is most important is that the audience and critics (and, it seems, the duchess herself) believed that she did. Little work has yet been done on whether other plays contained similar personalized associations, but contemporary references suggest that this is highly likely. According to the Earl of Ossory, for example, theatregoers presumed the actress's characterization of Bélise in a 1774 production of Moliere's *Les Femmes savantes* purposefully mocked the indomitable but ageing Duchess of Bedford. 'I assure you the resemblance is perfect, it is the joke of all the town,' he snickered to Thomas Robinson.[37] Newspaper reports also hint at the possibility of similar connections elsewhere. How significant was it, for instance, that actress Frances Abington was widely reported to have worn a dress formerly owned by the Duchess of Rutland to play Beatrice for a reprisal of Shakespeare's *Much Ado About Nothing* in 1785, or that the Prince of Wales's birthday suit was adopted (or copied) by Lee Lewis for the role of 'Lord Spangle' in Hannah Cowley's play *Which is the Man* in 1782?[38] At the same time, caricaturists delighted in sketching known individuals (a habit especially true of work by Gillray and later by Cruickshank). Again, the Duchess of Devonshire was one of the most recognizable figures in eighteenth-century caricature, but she was far from alone. All manner of delinquent dukes and duchesses, royal figures, political powerbrokers, and well-known peers were parodied in the print shop window. With such fashionable figures being featured in newspapers, periodicals, theatre productions, and cheap caricatures, it seems all the more likely that their names enjoyed considerable popular currency.

A wave of novels from the 1770s similarly cast the beau monde as a community of metropolitan celebrities. Promoted as drawn from life, they were read as *romans-à-clef* of London's high society. One of the first, *The Sylph* (1778), was written by none other than the Duchess of Devonshire herself.[39] Published anonymously, the novel was believed to represent a thinly veiled study of her immediate circle. Yet this was no self-congratulatory story of her celebrity firepower, for the authoress was as ready to lambaste fashionable failings as the caricaturists and novelists who stood at one remove from that world. Despite its critical tone, the book was acknowledged to be the work of an insider. *The Gentleman's Magazine* declared that the female author 'showed too great a knowledge of the *ton* and of the worst though perhaps the highest part of that world', ensuring that her identity was swiftly laid bare.[40]

Hereafter, publishers clamoured to turn out the next high-society drama. Although a poem rather than novel, Lady Anne Hamilton's work *Epics of the Ton* (1807) berated thirty-nine leaders of the 'ton', twenty-two women and seventeen men. Criticizing the 'D of R', the 'D of M', the ' D of B', and the 'D of D' in her 'Lady's Book' of ton, Hamilton revealed her targets by their initials and it took the reader little effort to establish these were attacks on the Duchess of Rutland, the Duchess of Manchester, the Duchess of Bedford, and the Duchess of Devonshire respectively. Similarly in her 'Men's Book', Hamilton aimed fire at the 'D of P' (the Duke of Portland), the 'D of B' (the Duke of Bedford), and the 'E of C' (the Earl of Carlisle) amongst others.[41] Other publications retained a semblance of fiction, realizing that no small part of their commercial appeal rested in the game such novels offered to the reader of guessing the 'true' identity of characters sketched within their pages. Notably, many, like *The Sylph* and *Epics of the Ton*, were written by titled authors or at least publicized as penned by a 'lady of fashion'. 'People of ton', noted Lady Charlotte Bury in 1818, 'have taken to writing novels: it is an excellent amusement for them, and also for the public.'[42] Lady Caroline Lamb's partly autobiographical *Glenarvon* (1816) caused a storm of controversy due to its warts-and-all portrayal of her scandalous affair with the duplicitous Lord Byron. Titled society, critics, and other readers alike debated the likely origins of each character. Lady Holland fumed at the portrait that was allegedly drawn of herself, 'where every ridicule, folly and infirmity (my not being able from malady to move much) is portrayed'. Others, she noted, had not escaped unscathed:

> Few of her characters are portraits, but the *amplissage* and traits are exact. *Lady Morganet* is a twofold being—the D[uche]ss of Devonshire and her mother; *Lady Augusta* is Lady Jersey and Lady Collier; *Sophia* [is] Lady Granville...*Lady Mandeville* is Lady Oxford; *Buchanan* is Sir Godfrey Webster. *Glenarvon* and *Vivian* are of course Lord Byrone. Lady Webster is sketched and some others slightly. Lady Melbourne is represented as bigoted and vulgar.[43]

Marianne Spencer Hudson's novel *Almacks': A Novel* (1826), and Lady Charlotte Bury's *The Exclusives* (1830), later followed in the same mould.[44] Lest any reader missed the true identities of the individuals disguised within their pages, handy

keys soon followed that matched fiction to fact and revealed the origins of the
main protagonists. These explained, for instance, that 'Lady Tilney', the 'Duchess
of Hermanston', and 'Princess Leisengen' in *The Exclusives* were meant for the
Almacks' patronesses Lady Jersey, Princess Esterhazy and Princess Lieven, while
'Frank Ombre' was reputed to be Lord Francis Russell, and 'Spencer Newcombe'
the Honourable Spencer Perceval.[45] There was little suggestion in the pages of
these so-called 'silver fork' sagas that the concept of a beau monde was rhetorical
or representative of a broader set of critiques. Instead, the linkage to a 'real' world
of contemporary individuals was so pronounced that the fiction was both mar-
keted and consumed as an entertaining refraction of social fact.

This apparent shift towards associating the beau monde with sets of named
individuals is compelling. Given that a particularly marked relationship between
the 'world of fashion' and different forms of *romans-à-clef* is much in evidence in
the later decades of the century, it is tempting to read all such literature as part
of the heightened political critique of elite culture that is a well-recognized feature of the period. As historian Anna Clark, and others, have noted, the 1760s and
1770s witnessed a wave of scandal literature and *causes célèbres* that were forerun-
ners to radical attacks on the political infrastructure that emerged in a climate of
European revolution and English political reform from the 1780s and 1790s. To
be sure, certain representations of the beau monde, most notably the *Town and
Country Magazine*'s exposés, appear to fit readily in that mould. Others, though,
require further explanation. Most notably, the fact that the Duchess of Devonshire
penned what was interpreted as a *roman-à-clef*, and that popular characters in
plays were translated by the audience as being 'taken from life', perhaps points to
a broader, and also more subtle, cultural shift or movement. More work remains
to be done to understand this context. We know little, for instance, about how
such literary portrayals of the world of fashion were consumed. Who read them?
Who produced them and for what purpose? Such representations, however, are
especially important for this study. They suggest that the 'world of fashion' was
widely understood as real and not just rhetorical—a social community and not
just a concept—one occupied by known and named individuals. Moreover, when
named in such a manner, the beau monde's social configuration comes much
more sharply into focus. While dictionaries disagreed about precisely where
above the 'vulgar' fashion could be found, its known celebrities were, most often,
distinguished by title and social eminence. Peers packed out the registers of fashionable figures when such registers appeared in print.

Notably this interpretation of the beau monde as a high-ranking, as well as an
exclusive, society was one that was shared by the elite themselves. For instance,
one of the earliest uses of 'beau monde' I have identified in private correspondence dates from 1705 in a letter from Lord Raby (later Earl of Strafford) to
Brigadier-General Cadogan: 'news I have not a word to send you from hence, and
intriguing in this court is dull in action...besides you know none of our beau
monde here.'[46] For Raby, 'beau monde' appears to be an unremarkable turn of

phrase invoked to capture the courtly circles in which he then moved. Indeed, such off-hand usage was typical of certain types of contemporary manuscript letters and writing. In 1724, for example, Lady Mary Wortley Montagu described herself as 'one of the beau monde' hunting in Richmond Park with royalty.[47] Comparable uses continued throughout the century, from Lady Mary Yorke's mention in a letter to her sister of 'a sprinkling of the beau monde' present at the opera in 1775,[48] to Frederick Robinson's record of his attendance at an assembly given 'to the ton' in 1779.[49] In the 1780s, the Countess of Bute described the Duchess of Rutland as living in 'the bon ton company', and Lady Susan O'Brien noted that 'the beau monde goes on much as usual'; in the early 1800s, Thomas Creevey declared an ageing Lady Salisbury to have been 'the head and ornament and patroness of the beau monde of London for the last forty years'.[50] Notorious aristocrats from the late eighteenth century, such as Georgiana, Duchess of Devonshire, are arguably the best-known titled representatives of eighteenth-century London's fashionable set. However, they were but a few of the many dukes, duchess, earls, countesses, viscounts, lords, and ladies who were regularly portrayed (and indeed presented themselves) as dominating London's fashionable society throughout the 1700s.

Indeed, an implicit link between 'fashion' and an elevated position in the social hierarchy pervades many manuscript uses of this key terminology. In a 1741 description of the company enjoying a private London ball, Horace Walpole, for instance, signalled that high social rank was one of the principal determinants for membership of the 'world of fashion'. 'There were none but people of the first fashion', he began, before adding, 'except Mr Kent and Mr Cibber, Mr Swiny and the Parsons family',

> Kent came as governess to Lady Charlotte Boyle, Cibber and Swiny have long had their freedom given to them at this end of town, and the Parsons took out theirs at Paris. There were a hundred and ninety-seven people, yet no confusion... The dancers were the two Lady Lennoxs (Lady Emily Queen of the Ball, and appeared in great majesty from behind a vast bouquet), Lady Lucy Manners, Lady Ankram, Lady Lucy Clinton, Ladies Harriot and Anne Wentworth, Charlotte Farmor and Camilla Bennett; Miss Pelham (Lord! How ugly she is!) Miss Walpole, Churchill, Parsons, Pulteney, Mary Townshend, Newton and Brown. The men, Lord John Sackville, Lords Ancram, Holderness, Ashburnham, Howard, Hartington and Castlehaven, Mr Colebrooke, Poulett, Churchill, two Townshends, Parsons, Vernon, Carteret, Colonel Maguire and a Sir William Boothby... the ball ended at four.[51]

Walpole's register includes a number of subtle but arresting hierarchical suppositions about the 'fashion' status of those present. His conviction that Kent, Cibber, Swiny, and the Parsons family were exceptions to the general rule that 'none but people of the first fashion' were present at the ball is especially revealing. 'Mr

Kent' was the great Palladian architect William Kent, whose career was blossoming under the patronage of Richard Boyle, 3rd Earl of Burlington. 'Mr Cibber' was Colley Cibber, one of the most famous actors of his generation, a successful playwright and poet laureate. 'Mr Swiny' is presumed to be Owen MacSwinny, a dramatist, and 'the Parsons family' a reference to the son and daughters of Humphrey Parsons, a brewer who spent much time in France, but who was also Lord Mayor of London in 1730 and 1740. Although acknowledging the 'freedom given to them at this end of town', it is striking that Walpole implies that their inclusion was unusual. He declared that each of these exceptional individuals boasted an 'alloy' that made them acceptable to the beau monde—an additional qualification or patron that bought uncommon passage into fashion's serried ranks.

With those exceptions, the remainder of the society that Walpole mentions as being present was markedly aristocratic. Leaving aside the second tier Parsons children, the majority of the young dancers who took to the floor boasted titled credentials. Even those styled 'Miss' and 'Mr' were not far removed from the peerage. 'Miss Pulteney', for instance, was the daughter of William Pultney, politician and soon to be Earl of Bath, 'Miss Brown' was the daughter of Sir Robert Brown and 'Miss Mary Townshend', and the additional 'two Townshends' were the offspring of the 2nd Viscount Townshend. In Walpole's account then, 'first fashion' appears to be synonymous with high social rank.

Few references drew this line quite so explicitly, but a close affiliation between fashion, the beau monde, and the peerage is implicit in many commentaries.[52] For the dukes of Devonshire, family and fashion were welded together. 'What grieves me the most is the string of visitors you seem to have', wrote Lady Harriet Cavendish (the Duke of Devonshire's daughter) to her elder sister Georgiana. 'You always say "I am interrupted by"—and then a string of fashionables so interwoven into family connections that it is hopeless to escape from them.'[53] Such patterns are particularly clear in the complex negotiations surrounding elite marriages. According to the disapproving Mary Delany, 'an air of…"the bon ton"' was the additional gloss that rendered a titled and wealthy lord highly eligible in the marriage market; and, by her reckoning this was a qualification specific to the titled gent.[54] Others surveying the marriage market similarly linked rank to fashion. When the Duke of Buccleuch fixed his marital hopes on the pretty Lady Betty Montagu in 1767, his mother, Lady Dalkeith, confessed to being 'so very desirous of his marriage that provided he had made a choice of a lady of fashion she shou'd have been very well pleased'.[55] Making a similar connection, Lavinia, Countess Spencer, used 'fashion' to signal her approval of her niece, Lady Georgiana. Writing to the young girl's grandmother, she reported, 'I can't tell you how much she fulfilled my ideas of a girl of fashion and sense.'[56] In the early 1800s, fashion remained a byword for nobility. In 1818, for example, Lady Williams Wynn described a wedding 'attended by a first-rate list of fashionables', and noted the presence of lords Denbigh, Uxbridge, Stanhope, and Cholmondley on the guest list.

This is not to suggest that everyone possessing a title presented themselves as a part of London's 'beau monde', or that the relationship between fashion and title was unconditional. Lady Charlotte Bury routinely wondered whether she was 'in' or 'out' of London's most glittering ranks. 'I often say to myself in society, "*Ou trouverai-je ma place?*"—total retirement, secondary intellect [and] secondary rank do not suit me', she wrote in her diary, 'yet the world, and the first circles, and the wittiest and prettiest, suit me not either. This is not affectation, 'tis a melancholy truth.'[57] In the eyes of some who boasted a place in the peerage, the metropolitan lifestyle associated with 'people of fashion' was viewed with lack of interest, if not outright disdain. Hester Pitt, Lady Chatham (the wife of the leading politician William Pitt the elder), routinely professed her preference for a country rather than an urban existence. Although inevitably caught up in a powerful political network, she spent as much time as possible at the family's semi-rural villa in Hayes, Middlesex, rather than in the capital. Such was her avowed distaste for the busyness of London life that a rare trip to Ranelagh sparked comment by her sister-in-law, Elizabeth Grenville, who teased Hester for 'taking a trip into the great world in a very unexpected manner'.[58]

Nor was Hester Pitt alone in creating a self-conscious distance from the fashionable world. In 1720, Henrietta Howard, Countess of Suffolk, received a letter from her friend, one Mrs Bradshaw, who airily declared, 'as to what amusements the beau monde find in the park or anywhere else I am an entire stranger...I have a sovereign contempt for the beau monde and all their works.'[59] Frances Boscawen, wife of Admiral Boscawen, repeatedly peppered her letters with assertions that she disdained overindulgence in the metropolitan scene. She wrote in 1747 to her husband who was then sailing the high seas, 'I have been to one play...and one Opera which I heartily repented of...nor have I been anywhere, but to sit with some infirms of my acquaintance...you know I live little in the beau monde.'[60] Of course, the motivations for seemingly self-enforced exclusion are not always easy to trace with any certainty. In her declarations of social restraint and disavowal of the beau monde, Frances Boscawen may have been making a virtue of the less palatable fact that access had been denied.

'Beau monde' thus appears as a portmanteau term in the eighteenth century, deployed in media stretching from the 1690s Restoration play to the 1830s silver fork novel. The intention of this study is not to suggest that the term 'beau monde' was deployed with a single meaning across this stretch of time. Any application of 'beau monde' as a descriptive term can only be partially representative of the full scope of uses, and the full range of its functions awaits a different study. In taking as its focus the social, cultural, and political experiences of individuals participating in the London season, this book concentrates on one small fraction of this broad field.

The very fact that 'beau monde', and associated terms including 'ton' and 'fashion', appear in such a diverse range of locations and across such a broad chronology frustrates any easy translation of this obsolete language. At the same time, however, the sheer prevalence of the terminology testifies to the contemporary power and resonance of these concepts. It is, of course, striking that the vast majority of printed commentary ranged in tone from the gently condemnatory to the ferociously censorious. With a few notable exceptions, such as *Le Beau Monde* magazine, the concept of a 'beau monde'—a 'world of fashion' that seemingly operated outside any known rules—appears to have been intensely angst-provoking. Regardless of whether the author was warning the aspirant to give the fashionable set a wide berth, or condemning the titled for allowing 'fashion' to dilute their own credentials, the existence of a 'beau monde' was typically portrayed as a problem. The creation of colloquial and ultimately short-lived eighteenth-century terms (such as beau monde and a whole range of attendant words and phrases including ton, bon ton, haut ton, and fashion) testifies to an intense contemporary preoccupation with the new ways in which social status and elite power were interpreted and projected in the metropolis. With traditional markers of privilege undercut or recast in the developing framework of the eighteenth-century 'season', fresh categories were deployed to explain elite predominance and to make sense of urban manifestations of distinction.

ENDNOTES

Introduction

1 Bedfordshire and Luton Records and Archives Service (hereafter BRO), Wrest Park papers (hereafter WPP), L30/11/122/118, 4 January 1777, Jemima, Marchioness Grey, St James's Square, to her daughter Amabel Grantham (née Grey), Lady Polwarth, 4 January 1777.

2 The *Oxford English Dictionary* defines 'beau monde' as 'fashionable world' or 'society' and gives a date range of 1712 to 1823 for colloquial use. My research indicates a longer chronology spanning the 1690s to the 1840s. Despite its French origins, 'beau monde' is commonly found in eighteenth-century English writings and, as a reflection of its currency within contemporary English, the phrase is not italicized in this text.

3 Theophilus Christian Esq (pseud. for John Owen), *The Fashionable World Displayed* (1804), iii.

4 For example, *le donner le ton*—to set the tone; *de bon ton*—in good taste.

5 *The World*, 151, 20 November 1755, 51.

6 *The Man of Pleasure's Pocket-Book or the Bon Vivant's Vade Mecum, for the year 1780, being the Universal Companion in every Line of Taste Gallantry and Haut Ton* (1780).

7 Joseph Roach, *It* (Chicago: University of Michigan Press, 2007).

8 For an accessible, narrative account of the events of 1688–9 see Edward Vallance, *The Glorious Revolution: 1688 and Britain's Fight for Liberty* (London: Abacus, 2006).

9 Until the 1960s, 1688 was regarded as a domestic revolution and the moment when a distinctive parliamentary monarchy was established. This so-called 'Whig' interpretation had been outlined in the nineteenth century by Lord Macauley in his *The History of England* and famously revived in the early twentieth century by George Macaulay Trevelyan, *The English Revolution 1688–1689* (London: Taylor and Francis, 1938). Such a confident narrative of progress was subsequently questioned by historians who disputed whether the events of 1688 could be seen as truly 'revolutionary' and change making. For a review of these debates see William Arthur Speck, *Reluctant Revolutionaries: Englishmen and the Revolution of 1688* (Oxford: Oxford University Press, 1988). For more recent studies exploring the Revolution as a Dutch invasion, see Jonathan I. Israel, 'The Dutch Role in the Glorious Revolution', in Jonathan I. Israel (ed.), *The Anglo-Dutch Moment: Essays on the Glorious Revolution and*

its Global Impact (Cambridge: Cambridge University Press, 1991), 105–62 and, for a more narrative exploration, see Lisa Jardine, *Going Dutch: How England Plundered Holland's Glory* (London: Harper Press, 2008). For a thorough historiographical survey and for a reinstatement of an interpretation of 1688 as a moment of change, see Julian Hoppit, *A Land of Liberty? England 1689–1727* (Oxford: Oxford University Press, 2002). For 1688 as a 'modern' revolution, see Tim Harris, *Revolution: The Great Crisis of the British Monarchy 1685–1720* (London: Penguin, 2007) and Steven Pincus, *1688: The First Modern Revolution* (New Haven: Yale University Press, 2009).

10 John Brewer coined the influential phrase 'fiscal-military state' to describe the new financial infrastructure and its importance to the systems of governance that developed after 1688, see John Brewer, *The Sinews of Power: War, Money and the English State 1788–1783* (New York: Routledge, 1989). This concept has since been widely adopted not just by historians working on eighteenth-century Britain but also by those working on Europe and extra-European state development. For an overview of recent applications, see Christopher Storrs, 'Introduction: The Fiscal-Military State in the Long Eighteenth Century', in Christopher Storrs (ed.), *The Fiscal-Military State in Eighteenth-Century Europe: Essays in Honour of P. G. M. Dickinson* (Farnham: Ashgate, 2009).

11 Hoppit, *Land of Liberty?*, 26; Frank O'Gorman, *The Long Eighteenth Century: British Political and Social History 1688–1832* (London: Bloomsbury Academic, 1997), 36; Peter Jupp, *The Governing of Britain 1688–1848: The Executive, Parliament and the People* (London: Routledge, 2006), 19–22.

12 The period parliament sat varied from year to year. It met, for example, for a full twelve months in 1705 and 1795, but only from January to late May in 1700, 1737, and 1770. Most often, though, the parliamentary session ran from November to June. Details of the length and timing of every parliamentary session between 1610 and 1800 have been collated by Paul Langford. See Paul Langford, *Public Life and Propertied Englishmen, 1689–1798* (Oxford: Oxford University Press, 1991), 141–2.

13 On the changes in London's cultural landscape, see John Brewer, *Pleasures of the Imagination: English Culture in the Eighteenth Century* (London: Harper Collins, 2000). Importantly, eighteenth-century London, and Britain more generally, has been regarded as the location of a major 'consumer revolution'. In an early study of the phenomenon, Neil McKendrick suggested this 'revolution' was marked not only by an explosion of new goods but also by a middle-class aspirational emulation of elite conspicuous consumption which underpinned a culture of social mobility and modernity. See Neil McKendrick, John Brewer, and John H. Plumb (eds), *The Birth of a Consumer Society: The Commercialization of Eighteenth-Century England* (London: Europa, 1982). McKendrick's terminology of 'revolution' and focus on emulation has since been disputed, and replaced with a more nuanced and varied model

of consumer culture. See, especially, John Brewer and Roy Porter (eds), *Consumption and the World of Goods: Consumption and Culture in the Seventeenth and Eighteenth Centuries* (London: Routledge, 1994); Ann Bermingham and John Brewer (eds), *The Consumption of Culture 1600–1800: Object, Image and Text* (London: Routledge, 1995); Woodruff D. Smith, *Consumption and the Making of Respectability 1600–1800* (London: Routledge, 2002); Maxine Berg, *Luxury and Pleasure in Eighteenth-Century Britain* (Oxford: Oxford University Press, 2005); John Styles and Amanda Vickery (eds), *Gender, Taste and Material Culture in Britain and North America 1700–1830* (London: Yale University Press, 2007). For European comparisons see James van Horn Melton, *The Rise of the Public in Enlightenment Europe* (Cambridge: Cambridge University Press, 2001) and Timothy C. W. Blanning, *The Culture of Power and the Power of Culture: Old Regime Europe 1660–1789* (Oxford: Oxford University Press, 2003). On colonial America, see David S. Shields, *Civil Tongues and Polite Letters in British America* (Chapel Hill, NC: University of North Carolina Press, 1997).

14 Castle Howard, Carlisle MS J8/1/94, 6 February (no year, *c.*1730–5); Ruth Larsen, 'Dynastic Domesticity: The Role of Elite Women in the Yorkshire Country House 1685–1858' (unpublished Ph.D. thesis, University of York, 2003), 90.

15 University of Nottingham, Hallward Library, Newcastle papers, Ne C 2690, 7 November 1776 General Mostyn to the Duke of Newcastle; Rachel Stewart, *The Town House in Georgian London* (London: Yale University Press, Paul Mellon Centre, 2009), 32.

16 The growing importance of London as a political centre for the landed elite had the knock-on effect of increasing gentry authority in the provinces and the delegation of regional affairs and administration to a local elite. See Philip Jenkins, *The Making of a Ruling Class: The Glamorgan Gentry 1640–1790* (Cambridge: Cambridge University Press, 2002); Langford, *Public Life*, chapter 6 'Rural Duties', 367–436.

17 The allure of the early modern metropolis is discussed in Felicity Heal, *Hospitality in Early Modern England* (Oxford: Oxford University Press, 1990). Kevin Sharpe and Malcolm Smuts highlight the role played by Whitehall Palace in drawing the elite to the capital, see Kevin Sharpe, *Remapping Early Modern England: The Culture of Seventeenth-Century Politics* (Cambridge: Cambridge University Press, 2000), 201–5; R. Malcolm Smuts, *Court Culture and the Origins of a Royalist Tradition in Early Stuart England* (Philadelphia: University of Pennsylvania Press, 1999), i. 53–8. For aristocratic residential developments in early seventeenth-century London, see John Summerson, *Georgian London* (London: Pimlico, first published 1962; revised edn, 1991), chapters 2 and 3; Lawrence Stone, 'The Residential Development of the West End of London in the Seventeenth Century', in Barbara C. Malament (ed.), *After the Reformation: Essays in Honor of J. H. Hexter* (Manchester: Manchester University

Press, 1980), 167–214; Mark Girouard, *Life in the English Country House: A Social and Architectural History* (London: Yale University Press, first published 1978; new edn, 1994), 5–6.

18 In 1596, for example, Elizabeth I issued a proclamation ordering that all London-based gentry and nobility not in attendance to the court or pursuing legal business should return to their country properties. In 1632 a survey was completed of all gentry and nobility who contravened royal proclamations by being resident in London. See Stone, 'Residential development', 175; John T. Cliffe, *The World of the Country House in Seventeenth-Century England* (London: Yale University Press, 1999), 93; James F. Larkin and Paul L. Hughes (eds), *Stuart Royal Proclamations* (Oxford: Oxford University Press, 1973) and *Tudor Royal Proclamations: The Later Tudors (1588–1603)*, vol. iii (London: Yale University Press, 1969).

19 Edward Anthony Wrigley, 'A Simple Model of London's Importance in Changing English Society and Economy, 1650–1750', *Past and Present*, 37 (July 1967), 44–70.

20 BRO, WPP, L30/14/333/101, Frederick Robinson, Whitehall, London to Thomas Robinson, 2nd Baron Grantham, Madrid, 9 June 1778.

21 BRO, WPP, L30/14/333/96, Frederick Robinson to Thomas Robinson, 19 May 1778.

22 BRO, WPP, L30/14/333/152, Frederick Robinson to Thomas Robinson, 15 December 1778.

23 *The World*, 151, 20 November 1755, 51.

24 *The Man of Pleasure's Pocket Book or the Bon Vivant's Vade Mecum for the year 1780* (London, 1780), 146.

25 Hon. John Ward to Helen D'Arcy Stuart [1810], in Samuel Henry Romilly (ed.), *Letters to 'Ivy' from the First Earl of Dudley* (London: Longmans, Green, 1905), 89.

26 For Grosvenor Square, see Peter J. Atkins, 'The Spatial Configuration of Class Solidarity in London's West End 1792–1939', *Urban History*, 17 (1990), 40. For Hanover Square and St James's Square, see George F. E. Rudé, *Hanoverian London: 1714–1808* (London: Sutton Publishing, 2003), 42; Francis H. W. Sheppard (ed.), *Survey of London, Volumes 29 and 30: St James's Westminster part 1*, 78–81 and *Survey of London, Volumes 29 and 30: St James's Westminster part 2* (London: English Heritage, 1960), 143–55.

27 Leonard D. Schwarz, 'Social Class and Social Geography: The Middle Classes in London at the End of the Eighteenth Century', *Social History*, 7 (1982), 167–85.

28 Summerson, *Georgian London*, 73–86.

29 Atkins, 'Spatial Configuration', 56. Atkins also notes 'the residential segregation of the *beau monde* was a major factor in their reproduction, and the furtherance of their influence', see Atkins, 'Spatial Configuration', 36. Langford similarly flags the growing concentration of elite power in London,

noting that by the mid-1700s the majority of peers (and MPs) owned or rented a London property, particularly one that was near to Westminster, and that over the course of the century politicians were increasingly expected to do their political business from a London property. Langford, *Public Life*, 194.

30 The Strand houses of Bedford House, Norfolk House, and Salisbury House, for example, were all dismantled between 1674 and 1718 as their owners sought modern replacements on plots of lands away from the Thames.

31 Edwin Beresford Chancellor, *The Private Palaces of London Past and Present* (London: Keegan, Paul and Co., 1908); Christopher Simon Sykes, *Private Palaces: Life in the Great London Houses* (London: Chatto and Windus, 1985), 98–101.

32 Sykes, *Private Palaces*, 201–3; Amanda Vickery, *Behind Closed Doors: At Home in Georgian England* (London: Yale University Press, 2009), 153.

33 Summerson, *Georgian London*, 84. A similar point is made by George Rudé who notes, 'there were few, in fact, even among the wealthiest of London's aristocrats, who would have entertained the notion of investing such great sums in their town houses as those spent in building, extending or rebuilding their country seats'. See Rudé, *Hanoverian London*, 46.

34 This skew towards the country seat within architectural history has been addressed by Rachel Stewart, *The Town House in Georgian London* (London: Yale University Press, 2009).

35 George E. Mingay, *English Landed Society in the Eighteenth Century* (London: Routledge, 1963), 158.

36 BL, Newcastle papers, Add. MS 33159, Duke of Newcastle's housekeeping and personal expenses 1764–6. The modern equivalence has been calculated using the Economic History Association's 'Measuring Worth' tool (<http://www.measuringworth.com>). Given that human labour was comparatively cheap in the 1700s, both the Duke of Bedford's servants' wages and the Newcastle House grocery bill have been treated as commodities and calculated against the Retail Price Index, whereby £1 in 1760 is equivalent to £118 in 2010 (the latest date available for calculation).

37 BL, Althorp Papers, MS 78031, Valuation of contents of Spencer House and Wimbledon (1834).

38 Laura Battle 'Defining Moment: An Aristocrat's Residence Gives Way to Modern Life, 1925', *Financial Times*, 21 August 2010.

39 For Norfolk House see, Girouard, *Life in the English Country House*, 193–8; Michael Snodin and John Styles (eds), *Design and the Decorative Arts: Britain 1500–1800* (London: V&A Publications, 2001), 250–1; Arthur Oswald, 'Norfolk House, St James's Square: The Town House of the Duke of Norfolk', *Country Life* (25 December 1937), 604–60; Hannah Greig, 'The Beau Monde and Fashionable Life in Eighteenth-Century London, *c.*1688–1800' (unpublished Ph.D. thesis, Royal Holloway University of London, 2003), 89–90.

40 Musicologist William Weber gives a useful working definition of the beau monde as 'a milieu significantly larger, more diversified and less intimate than that of a court, but at the same time one much smaller and more distinct than the upper classes of the metropolis such as developed...in the second half of the nineteenth century'. 'This was', he continues, 'a public most of whose members knew most of one another by engaging in a closely linked set of social, cultural and political contexts...that could be fairly easily identified in terms of individuals and families.' See William Weber, 'Musical Culture and the Capital City: The Epoch of the Beau Monde in London, 1700–1870', in Susan Wollenberg and Simon McVeigh (eds), *Concert Life in Eighteenth-Century Britain* (Aldershot: Ashgate, 2004), 77. One of the most widely cited uses is J. Jean Hecht's passing referencing to the terminology. 'The cultural tone of eighteenth-century England', Hecht writes, 'was set by an elite composed of the highest nobility, the wealthiest gentry and their satellites. Variously styled the Ton, the Great, the Polite, the Beau Monde, the World of Fashion, or simply the World, this small group constituted the fount of norms and values.' See J. J. Hecht, *The Domestic Servant Class in Eighteenth-Century England* (London: Routledge and Kegan Paul, 1956), 200. For subsequent applications of Hecht's discussion, see J. C. D. Clark, *English Society 1688–1832: Ideology, Social Structure and Political Practice During the Ancien Regime* (Cambridge: Cambridge University Press, 1985; rev. edn, 2000), 225, and Gerald Newman, *The Rise of English Nationalism: A Cultural History 1740–1830* (Basingstoke: Macmillan, 1997), 41–2.

41 Diary entry for September 1721, in Alan Saville (ed.), *Secret Comment: The Diaries of Gertrude Savile, 1721–1757* (Kingsbridge: Kingsbridge History Society, 1997), 2.

42 Diary entry for 6 November 1727 in Saville (ed.), *Secret Comment*, 75.

43 Diary entry for October 1721 in Saville (ed.), *Secret Comment*, 12.

44 *The World by Adam FitzAdam*, 20 November 1755, no. 151, 51.

45 Savile's insistence on the 'Beau-Mond' as a sector of society she could not enter is of key significance. On the one hand, it is important to acknowledge that concepts such as 'beau monde', 'world of fashion', and 'people of fashion' were unquestionably used as rhetorical devices by different commentators for different ends. Therefore, like other terms routinely deployed by contemporaries and historians to delineate social groups and social status—including 'middle class' or 'middling sorts', 'plebeian', 'the poor', and, indeed, 'the elite'—these phrases were not consistent descriptions of an empirical reality but flexible conceits often applied in highly politicized ways. On the other hand, however, many commentators followed Savile's conceptual interpretation and used 'beau monde' to describe a visible community, citing the world of fashion in reference to named individuals. Indeed, 'beau monde' was deployed much more readily in this descriptive sense than was perhaps true of other contemporaneous social categories such as 'middling sorts'. Newspaper accounts listed

the 'beau monde' present in a theatre's audience or announced the arrival and movements of 'people of fashion' in London and other major cities. Even satirical and critical attacks on the excesses of the 'world of fashion' routinely lambasted individuals, naming and shaming ringleaders. See appendix for further examples of this type of use and interpretation of 'beau monde'.

46 *Bell's Weekly Messenger*, London. Issues from May 1796 to 29 June 1800.

47 125 'fashionable' names were listed between those dates. Of the 68 per cent representing royalty and peers, 48 per cent (sixty individuals) were peers, their wives, or heirs.

48 Miss Ballen (heiress to Mrs Lennox Mortimer, widow of a West India planter), Michael Leoni, and William Garrow were included in the 'Fashionables' list for *Bell's Weekly Messenger*, 1 May 1796; Sir James Hoare featured as a 'Fashionable' in *Bell's Weekly Messenger*, 21 May 1797.

49 Gillian Russell, *Women, Sociability and Theatre in Georgian London* (Cambridge: Cambridge University Press, 2007).

50 The predominance of title within the 'world of fashion' can be found expressed in a wide range of contexts. For instance, in 1780, a 'Scale of Bon Ton' published by *The Morning Post* included two duchesses, four countesses, three ladies, and only three 'Mrs' (though all three were the daughters of the younger sons of peers). A more substantial register was compiled by Lady Anne Hamilton in her anonymous poem *Epics of the Ton*. Published as an exposé of fashionable life by a fashionable insider, Hamilton lambasted thirty-nine leaders of the 'ton'. Revealing her targets by their initials, the prevalence of peers was easy to spot. Criticizing the 'D of R', the 'D of M', the ' D of B', and the 'D of D' in her 'Lady's Book' of ton, it took the reader little effort to establish these were attacks on the Duchess of Rutland, the Duchess of Manchester, the Duchess of Bedford, and the Duchess of Devonshire respectively. Similarly in her 'Men's Book', Hamilton aimed fire at the 'D of P' (the Duke of Portland), the 'D of B' (the Duke of Bedford), and the 'E of C' (the Earl of Carlisle) amongst others. Of course, such later eighteenth-century registers need to be handled with care. Often skewed with political intent, such commentary responded to many agendas, not least the critique of aristocratic culture that abounded in the decades before and immediately after the French Revolution. That said, the linkage between fashion, the beau monde, and titled rank also drew on a tradition that long pre-dated these attacks, and such connections were widely made by the elite themselves. A fuller exploration of these contexts and their chronology is given in the appendix. Broadly speaking, however, although notorious aristocrats from the late eighteenth century, such as the glamorous Georgiana, Duchess of Devonshire, are arguably the best known titled representatives of eighteenth-century London's fashionable set, they were but a few of the many dukes, duchess, earls, countesses, viscounts, lords, and ladies who were regularly portrayed (and indeed presented themselves) as dominating

NOTES TO PAGE 19

London's fashionable society throughout the 1700s. Moreover, my point in this analysis is not to deny the possibility that non-titled figures might associate themselves with the world of fashion, but rather more simply that given that the *majority* of the beau monde's membership were quite clearly titled, it is that particular cohort which forms the subject of this book.

51 John Cannon, *Aristocratic Century: The Peerage of Eighteenth-Century England* (Cambridge: Cambridge University Press, 1984), 10. The ranks of the British peerage consist of duke, marquess, earl, viscount, and baron (with duke the most senior hereditary rank). Peers' wives were styled respectively as duchess, marchioness, countess, viscountess, and baroness. Under certain circumstances a woman might inherit and carry a peerage title in her own right, but more often she was only granted a courtesy title in accordance to her husband's rank. All sons of a duke were styled lord, all daughters were styled lady and the eldest son of a duke often carried a lower-ranking peerage title in his own right (such as earl). The elder sons of marquesses, earls, viscounts, and barons were all styled lord. All younger sons and daughters, however, were technically commoners in the British peerage, which was not the case in Europe (where all offspring carried their own rank) and made the British nobility far smaller than continental counterparts. For comparisons to the much larger 'aristocracy' of European societies, see Cannon, *Aristocratic Century*, 2–3, 9; Jonathan Dewald, *The European Nobility, 1400–1800* (Cambridge; Cambridge University Press, 1996).

52 Contemporary calculations of the size of the fashionable world varied considerably. In 1791, the *Bon Ton Magazine* claimed the fashionable world included a fairly substantial 'one thousand macaronies and twelve hundred women of superlative taste'. *The Bon Ton Magazine*, 1/4 (June 1797), 137. The early nineteenth-century satirical *Book of Fashion: Being a Digest of the Axioms of the Celebrated Joseph Brummell* asserted that there were a maximum of 'fifty-one persons of *Ton* in this kingdom', see *Book of Fashion* (1832), 12–13. Whatever the precise number, the size of the beau monde was in many ways limited and self-defining. Most agreed it needed to be large enough to be visible and dominate London sociability, yet still small enough for members to know each other. The 'beau monde' can usefully be considered as one of many different 'types' of elite identity. As Francis M. L. Thompson persuasively argued, 'there was not one, unchanging set of aristocratic values. There were frivolous, extravagant, improvident, self-indulgent and immoral aristocrats…there were businesslike and entrepreneurial aristocrats…[there were] aristocrats who were neither industrial entrepreneurs…nor particularly extravagant or fast-living, because a high spending life in London society did not suit their disposition or their pocket.' 'The message is of horses for courses,' Thompson summarizes, 'the aristocracy sent out a range of different signals and which ones were picked up depended on the character and disposition of those who received them.' Francis M. L. Thompson, *Gentrification and the Enterprise Culture: Britain 1780–1980* (Oxford: Oxford University Press, 2001).

53 In comparison to the vast literature tackling other social groups, the configuration of elite status in the eighteenth century has been rather neglected. This is not to say that there has been an absence of interest in elite power. The 1980s, in particular, saw a flurry of interest in 'the elite' within eighteenth-century Britain. In his *Aristocratic Century: The Peerage of Eighteenth-Century England* (Cambridge: Cambridge University Press, 1984), John Cannon, for instance, labelled the eighteenth century the 'aristocratic century', arguing that the British aristocracy defended their ranks and retained their position far more successfully than their European counterparts. Closed to aspirants, the 'aristocracy' retained an oligarchic authority and character throughout the 1700s. Indeed, Cannon was so persuaded by the aristocracy's success in defending its exclusivity that he wondered whether a vociferous eighteenth-century rhetoric of social mobility was in fact a strategic device wielded to safeguard rather than challenge aristocratic power, an invented tradition of the eighteenth century that was repeated in subsequent centuries as the nobility's 'most potent weapon in defence of its own privileged position'. More controversially, Jonathan Clark wrote a polemical response to emerging work highlighting the 'modernising' nature of urban life, branding eighteenth-century England an *ancien régime* of traditional values and traditional hierarchies (J. C. D. Clark, *English Society 1688–1832: Ideology, Social Structure and Political Practice During the Ancien Regime,* Cambridge: Cambridge University Press, 1985; revised edn, 2000). In his account, monarchy, aristocracy, and the Church of England—not the middling sorts, commerce, liberty, and constitutional change—defined the period. A marked feature of 'elite' studies, however, is their reliance on comparatively rigid and formulaic definitions of status amongst the upper echelons of society. Lines were drawn, for instance, according to the size of an estate, yearly income, or strict membership of the peerage. Each individual's claim to such assets was measured independently and the individuals who met the necessary quantitative criteria were then taken to make up the group (whether framed as 'the peerage', the 'ruling elite', or 'the landed'). In stark contrast, historians studying communities lower down the social order have developed more fluid categories, emphasizing cultural indictors of status such as material display, social behaviour, and collective association. More subtle conceptions of what might constitute cultural definitions of social identity are particularly evident in the extensive literature on urban 'polite society' and 'middling sorts'. Generally speaking, many of the most influential eighteenth-century studies over the last twenty years have been primarily concerned with the ways in which a new urban and commercial culture, new forms of consumption, and new modes of sociability created a more inclusive culture that was open to, and exploited by, the untitled professional as well as the titled patrician. The 'urban renaissance', concludes historian Peter Borsay in his landmark study, provided 'the swelling middle tier of society with the means of entering the privileged

sphere of gentility' (Borsay, *Urban Renaissance*, 277–9, 282). For John Brewer, the creation of a 'cultivated public of sociable men' was one of the most marked developments of the period's new urban culture, a 'public' whose status was defined by personal qualities and not solely by hereditary rank. (Brewer, *Pleasures*, xvii–xviii). This blurring of divisions is not said to have eroded all forms of distinction across the social scale (as contemporaries feared), but to have stimulated new social and cultural definitions of status that were flexible enough to accommodate both a titled elite and an expanding sector of untitled professionals. In consequence, as Paul Langford explains, it is not so much that eighteenth-century Britain became 'a nation of gentry' but rather that its aspiring and strengthening middling ranks realigned the balance of power away from the traditional nobility and towards 'an increasingly dictatorial bourgeoisie' (Paul Langford, *Public Life*, 510). These established studies of eighteenth-century urbanization inform this book in a number of ways. The impact of a developing urban culture on perceptions of social status, the role played by material goods and consumer practices in mediating and projecting social position, the significant rise of public forms of commercial leisure, and the important development of an eighteenth-century print culture are all key features of canonical approaches that are, once again, revisited here. My intention, though, is to return to this well-mapped eighteenth-century terrain from a subtly different perspective. As a number of recent studies have highlighted, while the formation of a broadly middle-class identity has been thoroughly interrogated in the context of eighteenth-century urban development, the comparative responses of other social groups to the same transformative conditions have been subject to less sustained analysis. By recovering this elite culture, the study of the beau monde offered here explores the various ways in which social exclusivity was policed, projected, and maintained in a culture of urban publicity and ostensibly shared social practices. The book revisits the 'modernizing' forces of urban life that have so fascinated historians, but its principal and simplest aim is to examine their impact at the top, rather than in the middle, of the social scale.

54 Roach, *It*; Stephen Gundle, *Glamour: A History* (Oxford: Oxford University Press, 2009).

55 Stella Tillyard, 'Celebrity in Eighteenth-Century London', *History Today*, 55 (June 2005) and ' "Paths of Glory": Fame and the Public in Eighteenth-Century London', in Martin Postle (ed.), *Joshua Reynolds and the Creation of Celebrity* (London: Tate Publishing, 2005), 61–9; Michael Rosenthal, 'Public Reputation and Image Control in Late Eighteenth-Century Britain', *Visual Culture in Britain*, 7/2 (2006), 69–91.

56 Although the diversity of elite categories has not been fully examined, the emergence of such terminology can be seen as part of a broader preoccupation with how social status should be interpreted and defined. The 1700s were a time when a whole plethora of new social terms were coined. On the diversity

of social categories and descriptive phrases in circulation in the eighteenth century see, for example, Penelope J. Corfield, 'Class by Name and Number in Eighteenth-Century England', in Penelope J. Corfield (ed.), *Language, History and Class* (Oxford: Basil Blackwell, 1991), 101–30. For an accessible review of the historical debates surrounding the use of 'class' during the eighteenth century and a survey of contemporary constructions of the social hierarchy, see Roy Porter, *English Society in the Eighteenth Century* (Harmondsworth: Penguin, 1982), 48–98.

57 Theophilus Christian Esq, *The Fashionable World Displayed* (London, 1804), 2–4.

58 Quoted by Judith S. Lewis, *Sacred to Female Patriotism* (London: Routledge, 2003), 170.

59 Letter from Lady Hertford to her mother, London, 12 June 1724, in Helen Sard Hughes (ed.), *The Gentle Hertford: Her Life and Letters* (New York: Macmillan Co., 1940), 84.

60 For the cosmopolitan nature of the London elite and for attacks on their Frenchified nature in the second half of the century, see Gerald Newman, *The Rise of English Nationalism: A Cultural History 1740–1830* (New York: St Martins, 1997). For satirical obsession with the French influence over English fashions, see Diana Donald, *The Age of Caricature: Satirical Prints in the Age of George III* (London: Yale University Press, Paul Mellon Centre for Studies in British Art, 1996). On the role of French language in English elite culture, see Michele Cohen, *Fashioning Masculinity: National Identity and Language in the Eighteenth Century* (London: Routledge, 1996). For a broader view of the ways in which a concept of 'Britishness' was forged in opposition to perceptions of 'Frenchness', see Linda Colley, *Britons: Forging the Nation 1707–1837* (London: Yale University Press, 1992).

61 In her study of Victorian 'Society' and the London season, Lenore Davidoff argues that the political and social functions of London's high society were separated in the 1800s. As parliamentary activity became more professionalized and codified following the 1832 Reform Act, so 'Society' became more explicitly social and also more regimented in terms of its etiquette and organization than its eighteenth-century predecessor, the 'fashionable world'. See Leonore Davidoff, *The Best Circles: Society, Etiquette and the Season* (London: Croom Helm, 1973). Marjorie Morgan offers 1823 as the date when 'Society' first appeared in print. See Marjorie Morgan, *Manners, Morals and Class in England 1774–1858* (Basingstoke: Macmillan, 1994), 29.

62 See, for example, Donna T. Andrew, ' "Adultery à-la-mode": Privilege, the Law and Attitudes to Adultery 1770–1809', *History*, 82 (January 1997), 5–23.

63 Lewis, *Sacred to Female Patriotism*, chapter 6 'Reform Thyself', 159–90.

64 Archibald Alison, 'Hints to the Aristocracy: A Retrospect of Forty Years from the 1st of January 1834', *Blackwood's*, 35 (January 1834), 76; Jennifer Hall Witt, *Fashionable Acts: Opera and Elite Culture 1780–1880* (Durham, NH: University of New Hampshire, 2007), 138.

65 Terence Hanbury White, *The Age of Scandal: An Excursion Through a Minor Period* (London: Jonathan Cape, 1950).

66 Kathryn Hughes criticized the narrowing of biography to a few socialites and royal mistresses (the majority from the eighteenth century). Kathryn Hughes, 'The Death of Life Writing', *The Guardian*, Saturday 28 June 2008. See also, Hannah Greig, 'Sirens and Scandals', *History Today*, 58 (2008).

Chapter 1

1 See, for example, George Farquhar, *The Constant Couple; Or a Trip to the Jubilee* (1700), especially 19; *The Beau Monde or the Pleasures of St James's a New Ballad* (1730); *A View of the Beau Monde, or Memoirs of a Celebrated Coquetilla* (1731); Lord Chesterfield's analysis of a fashionable identity in *The World by Adam Fitz-Adam* (pseud.), no. 151 (20 November 1755); and *The Man of Pleasure's Pocket-Book of the Bon Vivant's Vade Mecum for the Year 1780* (1780), especially 144–5.

2 Fashion theory studies apply these core principles and have traditionally associated fashion as a concept with 'modernity' and mass consumption, rather than with longer historical processes. See Roland Barthes, *The Fashion System*, trans. Matthew Ward and Richard Howard (New York: Hill & Wang, 1985). Historians of eighteenth-century Britain have routinely flagged the importance of 'fashion' as a motivation behind changes in consumer practices, but in so doing imply that fashion as a concept operated and was interpreted in much the same way in the eighteenth century as it is today, namely as a quality associated with modishness. Roy Porter, for example, suggests that 'people did not merely acquire more household goods. Fashions changed and they invested in furnishings and ornaments that were lighter, more comfortable, more elegant or just simply newer.' Porter, *English Society in the Eighteenth Century*, 219. Fashion was often cited as key force behind social emulation in the demand-led economic model presented in work by Neil McKendrick and others: see McKendrick, Brewer, and Plumb (eds), *The Birth of a Consumer Society*. These studies were strongly influenced by Thorstein Veblen's now famous *Theory of the Leisure Class: An Economic Study of Institutions* (New York: Macmillan, 1899) but have since been significantly nuanced and countermanded by more recent histories of consumption that look beyond emulation. See, for example, Maxine Berg, 'New Commodities, Luxuries and their Consumers in Eighteenth-Century England', in Maxine Berg and Helen Clifford (eds), *Consumers and Luxury: Consumer Culture in Europe 1650–1850* (Manchester: Manchester University Press, 1999), 63–9; Styles and Vickery (eds), *Gender, Taste and Material Culture*. In many ways the history of fashion as a discipline is principally understood as equating to a history of dress. Although important work in dress has revealed much about the nature of clothed appearances and the value of clothing, there have been few attempts to develop a historicized definition of fashion as a concept, or

interrogate the developing and fluctuating discourse of fashion in the 1700s (in the same way that other key contemporary concepts of sociability, luxury and politeness, for example, have been approached through a history of ideas).

3 Adam Smith, *The Theory of Moral Sentiments* (1st edn, 1759, 1774), 92–3.

4 Charles Pigott, *The Rights of Nobles, consisting of extracts from Pigott's political dictionary* (1795).

5 Mary Barber, 'An Unanswerable Apology for the Rich', *Poems on Several Occasions* (1735).

6 Now held in the BL as Wentworth papers, Add. MS 22225–6. Additional Strafford manuscripts can be found under BL, Wentworth papers, Add. MS 22230–5. For more on the Countess of Strafford and her move into elite society, see Ingrid Tague, *Women of Quality: Accepting and Contesting Ideas of Femininity in England* (London: Boydell and Brewer, 2002), 141–2.

7 Throughout the first half of the eighteenth century there was real anxiety that James II and, later, his heirs might attempt to reclaim the throne. The anxiety was not without grounds, for Jacobites attempted two major invasions in 1714 and 1745 and many other plots and rumoured conspiracies fanned contemporary concerns about the threat posed by the exiled court. Daniel Szechi, *The Jacobites: Britain and Europe 1688 to 1788* (Manchester: Manchester University Press, 1994).

8 The family history and sequence of succession for the earldom of Strafford is especially complicated, with the title being created three times throughout English history. The first holder of the title, Thomas Wentworth, 1st Earl of Strafford, was created such in 1640. Already known as Baron Raby, an earldom pushed Thomas higher up the peerage hierarchy. Strafford was the name of the area of North Yorkshire where the family kept their seat, Wentworth Woodhouse. When Thomas Wentworth, 1st Earl of Strafford, was executed in 1641 his family were effectively stripped of the title. However, following the Restoration of the monarchy, his son William (who carried the inherited title 2nd Baron Raby) successfully regained the title in 1661 to become the 2nd Earl of Strafford. When William died without issue in 1695 the earldom became extinct but special privileges meant that the family's claim to the Raby baronetage could be inherited by a distant cousin, Thomas Wentworth, the subject of this chapter (and a grandson of the 1st Earl's younger brother). The death of the 2nd Earl split the title Baron Raby from the family estates, the former going to Thomas Wentworth, the latter bequeathed to Thomas Watson (a nephew of the 2nd Earl's wife). When Thomas Wentworth was rewarded for his diplomatic duties with a peerage promotion, the title Earl of Strafford was resurrected for his use and so Thomas officially became Thomas Wentworth, 1st Earl of Strafford (of the second creation). The circuitous route of the title through the family and the lack of inherited estate and funds to match the rank made Thomas's position especially tenuous. Thomas was himself succeeded by his son William, who became the 2nd Earl of Strafford (of the second creation). William

had no surviving children and so the title passed to a cousin, Frederick (3rd Earl of Strafford) but the title became extinct once more when Frederick died in 1799 without a successor. The Strafford title was recreated for a third time in the 1800s, as a vacant title bestowed on Field Marshal John Byng in 1835 (initially as Baron Strafford of the third creation and then, in 1843 as the 1st Earl of Strafford, third creation).

9 James J. Cartwright (ed.), *The Wentworth Papers 1705–39, Selected from the Private and Family Correspondence of Thomas Wentworth* (London: Wyman and Sons, 1883).

10 Disaffected, Strafford later threw in his lot with the Jacobites and was involved in the Atterbury plot (1721) that pledged armed support to the exiled James II with a view to restoring him to the throne. In 1722 Strafford was granted a Jacobite peerage and was raised to a dukedom by the Pretender. See Linda Colley, *In Defiance of Oligarchy: The Tory Party 1714–80* (Cambridge: Cambridge University Press, 1982), 182 and 198.

11 The remarkable exception to the aristocratic rule was number 16, which was occupied until the 1780s by the family of the carpenter who built it. Such was the square's social cachet that when the Duke of Ormonde moved to the square in 1782 his son congratulated him on the purchase, writing, 'how ill it would look now you are an English Duke to have no house there'. By 1721, six dukes, seven earls, a countess, and a baron lived there. See Sykes, *Private Palaces*, 45.

12 Sykes, *Private Palaces*, 45.

13 BL, Wentworth papers, Add. MS 22226, fo. 21, Countess of Strafford to the earl, 15 November 1711.

14 BL, Wentworth papers, Add. MS 22226, fo. 21, Countess of Strafford to the earl, 15 November 1711.

15 BL, Wentwirth papers, Add. MS 22226, fo. 22, Countess of Strafford to the earl, 28 October 1711.

16 BL, Wentworth papers, Add. MS 22226, fo. 135, Countess of Strafford to the earl, 8 April 1712.

17 Anon., *The Book of Gentility; or the Why and Because of Polite Society: By a member of 'The Beef Steak Club'* (1835), 33.

18 Gertrude Savile, diary entry for Monday 5 August 1728 in Saville (ed.), *Secret Comment*, 127.

19 Lewis Walpole Library, Yale, 'Household Book for Augusta, Dowager Princess of Wales: Liveries of Wax and Tallow Candles' (1751).

20 BL, Pelham papers, Add. MS 33159, Accompts [*sic*] of the Family of Pelham, 1555–1781.

21 Letter from Lady Anne Carew to Lady Coventry, February 1715, in Lady Newton (ed.), *The Lyme Letters 1660–1760* (London: William Heinemann, 1925), 281; quoted in Sykes, *Private Palaces*, 58; Beinecke Library, Yale, Osborn Shelves fc 80, Diary of Edward Piggott, reference to the expenditure of the late Duke of Bedford in diary entry for 25 June 1776.

22 BL, Wentworth papers, Add. MS 22226, fo. 181, Countess of Strafford to the earl, 23 July 1712.

23 BL, Wentworth papers, Add. MS 22226, fo. 195, Countess of Strafford to the earl, 15 August 1712. The reference is to Henry Bentinck, 2nd Earl of Portland, and his wife Elizabeth Noel. The Earl of Portland had succeeded his father in 1709 and he was soon to be elevated to a dukedom (1715).

24 BL, Wentworth papers, Add. MS 22226, fo. 203, Countess of Strafford to the earl, 29 August 1712. See Hannah Greig, 'Leading the Fashion: The Material Culture of London's Beau Monde', in Styles and Vickery (eds), *Gender, Taste and Material Culture* and Helen Jacobsen, 'Ambassadorial Plate of the Later Stuart Period and the Collection of the Earl of Strafford', *Journal of the History of Collections*, 19 (May 2007).

25 BL, Wentworth papers, Add. MS 22226 fo. 254 Countess of Strafford to the earl, 26 December 1712.

26 BL, Wentworth papers, Add. MS 22226, fo. 256 Countess of Strafford to the earl, 30 December 1712.

27 BL, Wentworth papers, Add. MS 22226 fo. 220 Countess of Strafford to the earl, 19 September 1712.

28 The richly moulded and gilded interior of Norfolk House from the 1750s, for example, has been interpreted as an architectural expression of political opposition (and alliance with the estranged Frederick, Prince of Wales), challenging the Palladianism favoured by Lord Burlington and other court favorites. See Desmond Fitzgerald, 'The Norfolk House Music Room', *V&A Museum Bulletin*, 2/1 (January 1966), 48.

29 It is difficult to impose strict party political labels on eighteenth-century politicians and their acquaintances. Throughout the century contemporaries used a range of terms, particularly 'independence', to describe their political persuasion. The Earl of Strafford claimed that he was 'of neither party called Wig [*sic*] or Tory'. However 'whig' is the label the Countess of Strafford herself applies to the Marlboroughs, and she distinguishes them from her own 'tory' allegiance. Consequently these labels have been retained here. For further details on the multiplicity of political factions between 1688 and 1800, see John Brewer, *Party Ideology and Population Politics at the Accession of George III* (Cambridge: Cambridge University Press, 1976); Tim Harris, *Party Politics under the Late Stuarts: Party Conflict in a Divided Society 1660–1715* (London: Longman, 1993); and John W. Derry, *Politics in the Age of Fox, Pitt and Liverpool: Continuity and Transformation* (Basingstoke: Palgrave, 2001).

30 For details of her encounter with the Duchess of Marlborough and daughter, see BL, Wentworth papers, Add. MS 22226, fo. 39, Countess of Strafford to the earl, 4 December 1711; for references to her acquaintance with the Duchess of Somerset, see Add. MS 22226, fo. 25, Countess of Strafford to the earl, 20

November 1711; and for Lady Masham, see Add. MS 22226, fo. 48, Countess of Strafford to the earl, [23] December 1711.

31 BRO, WPP, L30/44/333/166 Frederick Robinson, Stanmer, to Thomas Robinson, Madrid, 30 December 1778.

32 Diary of Lady Mary Campbell Coke, March 1767, in James Archibald Home (ed.), *The Letters and Journals of Lady Mary Coke*, vol. i (Edinburgh: D. Douglas, 1889), 247. Anne, Duchess of Grafton was the wife of Augustus Fitzroy, 3rd Duke of Grafton (the couple divorced in 1769). Margaret Cavendish-Bentinck, Duchess of Portland (1715–85), was the wife of William, 2nd Duke of Portland. Lady Elizabeth Montagu married Francis, 3rd Duke of Buccleuch (written in this extract as Buccleugh) on 2 May 1767.

33 Birmingham City Archive, Matthew Boulton papers, Letter Book MS 378/21/10.

34 Maria Edgeworth, 'Ennui', in *Tales of Fashionable Life* (1806), 18.

35 Edgeworth, 'Ennui', preface, iv.

36 Northumberland Record Office, Deleval Collection, NRO/650/D12 letter to Mrs Deleval from [J?] Hammond, Lincoln, 3 February 1753.

37 A stomacher was a decorated panel that fitted in the front part of a woman's formal dress, filling the gap between the side openings of a gown. It was often adorned with large pieces of jewellery.

38 Quoted in Diana Scarisbrick, *Jewellery in Britain 1066–1837* (Wilby: Michael Russell, 1994), 234. More recently, art historian Marcia Pointon has completed a detailed cultural history of precious gems (particularly diamonds). Marcia Pointon, *Brilliant Effects: A Cultural History of Gems Stones and Jewellery* (London: Yale University Press, 2010).

39 Natural History Museum Archives, SB fo. D6, Miscellanous papers of Dru Drury.

40 The Webb account books nestle anonymously amidst the diverse archives of the Chancery Court, suggesting a financial dispute eventually hit the business. Another unusual set of records are those of diamond merchants John and Nathaniel Cholmley, see Rosalind Bowden, 'The Letter Books of John and Nathaniel Cholmley', *North Yorkshire County Record Office Review* (2001), 6–57.

41 The National Archives (TNA), Chancery papers, Master Farrer's Exhibits, PRO C108/285 Webb v Ives, Ledgers 1735–57 and 1761–5.

42 See, for example, the trade directory compiled by Thomas Mortimer, *The Universal Directory* (1763) and newspapers such as: *The Daily Courant*, 26 October 1717 and 12 August 1718; *London Evening Post*, 6 June 1732; *Daily Advertiser*, 30 July 1744; *Gazetteer and New Daily Advertiser*, 6 August 1764; *London Evening Post*, 28 June 1773; *General Evening Post*, 16 November 1776.

43 Helen Clifford, *Silver in London: The Parker and Wakelin Partnership* (London: Yale University Press, 2004), 69.

44 TNA, Chancery papers, Master Farrer's Exhibits, PRO, C108/285, Webb v Ives, Ledger 1735–57.

45 TNA, Chancery papers, Master Farrer's Exhibits, PRO, C108/285, Webb v Ives, Ledger for 1761.

46 Diary of Lady Mary Campbell Coke, December 1774, in Home (ed.), *Lady Mary Coke*, vol. iv (Edinburgh, 1889), 544; BRO, WPP, L30/11/123/32, from Lady Mary Grey to Amabel, Lady Polwarth, 31 December 1774, 'I suppose Mama has told you of Mr Grenvilles being to be married to Miss Nugent...Lady Temple gives up her Jewels to the young Lady.'

47 BRO, WPP, L30/11/122/52, Jemima, Marchioness Grey to her daughter Amabel, Countess de Grey, 24 December 1773.

48 BRO, WPP, L30/11/123/18, Mary Grey to her sister Amabel, Countess de Grey, 13 December 1773; BRO, WPP, L30/14/188/7, Frederick Howard, 5th Earl of Carlisle, to Thomas Robinson, 2nd Lord Grantham, 14 January 1774.

49 *The Gentleman's Magazine*, 25 October 1731, 448.

50 Natural History Museum, Dru Drury papers, SB f D6, fo. 611.

51 BL, Wentworth papers, Add. MS 22226, fo. 77, Countess of Strafford to the earl, 25 January 1712.

52 BL, Wentworth papers, Add. MS 22226, fo. 56, Countess of Strafford to the earl, 31 December 1711.

53 BL, Wentworth papers, Add. MS 22226, fo. 369, Countess of Strafford to the earl, 28 November 1713.

54 BL, Wentworth papers, Add. MS 22226, fo. 365 Countess of Strafford to the earl, 22 November 1713.

55 BL, Blenheim (Marlborough) papers, Add. MS 61449, fo. 62, Duke of Bedford to Duchess of Marlborough, May 1725.

56 BL, Blenheim (Marlborough) papers, Add. MS 61449, fo. 64, Duke of Bedford to Duchess of Marlborough, May 1725.

57 Letter from Lady Sarah Cowper to Mary Dewes Port, 16 October 1768, in *The Autobiography and Correspondence of Mrs Delany*, ii. 499.

58 Recorded in her diary, 16 February 1716, published in Hon. Spencer Cowper (ed.), *Diary of Mary Countess Cowper Lady of the Bedchamber* (London: John Murray, 1864), 76.

59 Letter from Elizabeth Carter to Elizabeth Robinson Montagu, 31 May 1766, in *Letters from Mrs Elizabeth Carter to Mrs Montagu between the years 1755 and 1800*, vol. i (1817), 399.

60 6 July 1773, in Home (ed.), *Lady Mary Coke*, iv. 185.

61 BL, Wentworth papers, Add. MS 22226, fo. 263, Countess of Strafford to the earl, 9 January 1713; fo. 285, 3 February 1713.

62 The power of diamonds in communicating lineage and aristocratic title is also suggested by the extensive critical commentary targeting ostentatious shows of gems by newly rich nabobs returning from India. Often criticized as interlopers, nabobs' ready access to jewels appeared to challenge the alignment

between inherited wealth and elite status and the communication of power and networks through precious gems. On nabobs' jewellery, see Tillman W. Netchman, 'Nabobinas: Luxury, Gender and the Sexual Politics of British Imperialism in the Late Eighteenth Century', *Journal of Women's History*, 18 (Winter 2006), 8–30; Pointon, *Brilliant Effects*, chapter 6.

63 BRO, WPP, L30/14/333/91, from Frederick Robinson to Thomas Robinson, Whitehall, 4 May 1778.

Chapter 2

1 Hull University Library Archives (hereafter Hull), Papers of Bosville-MacDonald Family of Gunthwaite, Thorpe and Skye Collection. Evidence of repeated visits to London by Godfrey Bosville and his in-laws the Wentworths can be found in DDBM/32/7–9.

2 Hull, DDBM/32/9, Letter from Godfrey Bosville, London, to John Spencer at Cannon Hall, 28 January 1765.

3 With specific reference to 'mixing', see, for example, Peter Borsay, *The English Urban Renaissance: Culture and Society in the Provincial Town 1660–1770* (Oxford: Clarendon Press, 1991), 277–9; Roy Porter, *English Society in the Eighteenth Century*, 232 and *London: A Social History* (Cambridge, Mass.: Harvard University Press, 1998) 105; Paul Langford, *A Polite and Commercial People: England 1727–1783* (Oxford: Oxford University Press, 1992), 102; Terry Castle, *Masquerade and Civilization: Carnivalesque in Eighteenth-Century English Culture and Fiction* (Stanford, Calif.: Stanford University Press, 1986), 28. For a more extensive discussion of this historiographical interpretation see Hannah Greig, ' "All together and all distinct:" Sociability and Social Exclusivity in London's Pleasure Gardens, ca. 1740–1800', *Journal of British Studies*, 51/1 (January 2012), 50–75.

4 Drury Lane and Covent Garden had special and protected status as the only theatres recognized by royal patent. Their official duopoly was then consolidated by the 1737 Licensing Act. For details of the patent system and Licensing Act, see Joseph Donohue's erudite account in his introduction to *The Cambridge History of the British Theatre*, ii: *1660–1895*, ed. Joseph Donohue (Cambridge: Cambridge University Press, 2004), 4–37. As Jane Moody has demonstrated, these provisions did not, in effect, limit theatrical performances to the theatres royal, for a culture of 'illegitimate' theatre also thrived. Circumventing the provisions of the Act in inventive ways, a medley of amateur dramatics, burlesque performances, pantomime, comedies, and spoken plays formed a rich part of urban culture, encountered at fairs, on the street, and at all manner of small venues, some purpose built and some squatted by troupes for temporary shows. See Jane Moody, *Illegitimate Theatre in London 1770–1840* (Cambridge: Cambridge University Press, 2000).

5 The development of London's pleasure gardens has fascinated generations. The most comprehensive survey remains Warwick Wroth, *The London*

Pleasure Gardens (London, 1896). Vauxhall has drawn the most attention. Early studies include James Granville Southworth, *Vauxhall Gardens: A Chapter in Social History* (New York: Columbia University Press, 1941) and Walter Sidney Scott, *Green Retreats: The Story of Vauxhall Gardens, 1661–1859* (London: Odhams Press, 1955). More recent, and often cited, studies include Teri J. Edelstein (ed.), *Vauxhall Gardens* (New Haven: Yale University Press, 1983); David Solkin, *Painting for Money: The Visual Arts and the Public Sphere in Eighteenth-Century England* (London: Yale University Press, 1993), chapter 4 'Vauxhall Gardens or the Politics of Pleasure'; Ogborn, *Spaces of Modernity*, chapter 4 'The Pleasure Garden'; Peter de Bolla, *The Education of the Eye: Painting, Landscape and Architecture* (Palo Alto, Calif.: Stanford University Press, 2003), chapter 2 'Vauxhall Gardens: The Visibility of Visuality'; Jonathan Conlin, 'Vauxhall Revisited: The Afterlife of a London Pleasure Garden: 1770–1859', *Journal of British Studies*, 45/4 (2006), 718–43; Penelope Corfield, *Vauxhall and the Invention of the Urban Pleasure Garden* (London: History and Social Action Publications, 2008). The question of social mingling and the power of art at Vauxhall is also scrutinized by Gregory Nosan, 'Pavilions, Power and Patriotism: Garden Architecture at Vauxhall', in Michel Conan (ed.), *Bourgeois and Aristocratic Cultural Encounters in Garden Art 1550–1850* (Washington, DC: Dumbarton Oaks/Harvard University, 2002). See also Jonathan Conlin (ed.), *The Pleasure Garden, from Vauxhall to Coney Island* (Philadelphia: University of Pennsylvania Press, 2012). My thanks to Jonathan Conlin for sharing his introduction to this collection prior to publication and for his comments on work contained within this chapter.

6 See Borsay, *English Urban Renaissance*, 170 for an overview of the many pleasure gardens that developed in England. For Paris, see Jonathan Conlin, 'Vauxhall on the Boulevard: Pleasure Gardens in Paris and London, 1764–1784', *Urban History*, 35/1 (May 2008). Vauxhall's fame spread far, a 'Vauxhall pleasure and tea garden' was even established in 1862 in Dunedin, New Zealand by one Henry Charles Farley. See Ian Dougherty, *Dunedin's Notorious Victorian Pleasure Gardens: Vauxhall Gardens* (Dunedin: Saddle Hill Press, 2007).

7 David Coke and Alan Borg, *Vauxhall Gardens: A History* (London: Yale University Press, 2011), 20–3.

8 Solkin, *Painting for Money*, chapter 4 'Vauxhall Gardens or the Politics of Pleasure'.

9 As the mimic rather than the trendsetter, Ranelagh has been subject to less sustained historiographical attention than Vauxhall. Ranelagh is dealt with in Wroth's original survey, *The London Pleasure Gardens*, and also in John Timbs, *Clubs and Club Life in London* (London: Chatto and Windus, 1899). One of the few volumes to focus exclusively on Ranelagh is Mollie Sands, *Invitation to Ranelagh 1742–1803* (Sheffield: Westhouse, 1946). Notably, the collection of Ranelagh ephemera held in the British Library is also attributed to Mollie Sands, with the cover annotated with her name, see BL, 'A Collection of Prints and Printed Matter Concerning Ranelagh', L.R.282.b.7. Key studies of

eighteenth-century urban sociability also make brief reference to Ranelagh; see, for example, Amanda Vickery, *The Gentleman's Daughter: Women's Lives in Georgian England* (London: Yale University Press, 1998), 273–5 and Brewer, *Pleasures of the Imagination*, 66–9.

10 Horace Walpole to Sir Horace Mann, 26 May 1742, in Wilmarth Sheldon Lewis (ed.), *The Yale Editions of Horace Walpole's Correspondence*, vol. xvii (with Horace Mann, I) (New Haven: Yale University Press, 1954), 434.

11 Terry Castle's study remains the principal cultural history of the masquerade: Castle, *Masquerade and Civilisation*, see 6, 21, and 98 for references to masquerades at Vauxhall and Ranelagh. Both Miles Ogborn and David Solkin apply Castle's work to their detailed studies of Vauxhall, exploring the pleasure garden's culture of masquerade. See Ogborn, *Spaces of Modernity*, 128–33 and Solkin, *Painting for Money*, especially 135–9.

12 Ogborn, *Spaces of Modernity*, chapter 4 'The Pleasure Garden'.

13 *A Trip to Vauxhall or a General Satyr on the Times by Hercules MacSturdy of the County of Tiperary* (1737). See also Solkin's analysis of this poem in Solkin, *Painting for Money*, 121–4.

14 Anon. (attributed to Joseph Warton), *Ranelagh House: A Satire in Prose in the Manner of Monsieur Le Sage* (1747).

15 Solkin, *Painting for Money*, 123.

16 Langford, *Polite and Commercial People*, 101.

17 Dorothy Marshall, *Dr Johnson's London* (New York: Wiley, 1968), 161. Others who describe pleasure gardens in similar terms include: James van Horn Melton, who writes that London's pleasure gardens were places for a 'heterogeneous public' where 'people of all ranks congregated': Van Horn Melton, *Rise of the Public*, 169; Teri J. Edelstein, 'Vauxhall Gardens', in Boris Ford (ed.), *18th Century Britain: The Cambridge Cultural History*, 9 vols (Cambridge: Cambridge University Press, 1992), v. 203; Pierre Dubois, 'Resorts of Ambiguity: The Eighteenth-Century Pleasures Gardens, a "Bewitching Assemblage of Provocatives"', *Revue française de Civilisation Britannique*, 14, 2 (2007), 52–66. The extensive use of the 'mingling' metaphor is particularly striking and it can be found adopted and reiterated in an increasing spread of studies across disciplines. Indicative of the spread, compare, for example, Guiliana Bruno, *Atlas of Emotion: Journeys in Art, Architecture and Film* (London: Verso, 2002), 196 (where Bruno notes 'the shifting vistas of the gardens also included the mixing of social classes and sexes') and Tita Chico, *Designing Women: The Dressing Room in Eighteenth-Century English Literature and Culture* (Lewisburg, Pa.: Bucknell University Press, 2005), 205 (where Chico declares that Vauxhall was 'famous for its mixing of classes').

18 *Daily Post*, 21 June 1742.

19 *Daily Advertiser*, 23 May 1743.

20 *Westminster Journal or New Weekley Miscellany*, 31 August 1745.

21 Vauxhall Gardens Archive (VGA) Fiche 36, press cuttings 1732–1823, dated 1759 [unknown publication].

22 VGA, Fiche 36, press cuttings 1732–1823, dated 1759 and also BL, 'Collection of images and adverts relating to Ranelagh', 74/LR 282.b.7.

23 VGA, Fiche 2, Press cuttings 1732–1823, unknown newspaper clipping 1805. This particular advertisement may have been a satirical reference to rumours of a relationship between Marchioness Hertford and the Prince of Wales. The advert described a fireworks display to be held at the gardens as including a 'revolutionary shower of fire' and 'star of knighthood'.

24 *The Morning Post*, 10 June 1810.

25 Terry Castle makes a similar point with regard to the commercial masquerade, suggesting that the emphasis on 'elite' company was a marketing strategy. Castle, *Masquerade and Civilisation*, 27.

26 Gillian Russell has recently offered an alternative and more subtle reading of these puffs, suggesting that they might be approached as an attempt to commercialize the systems of patronage associated with elite sociability, and bring to 'public' sociability the same concern with interpersonal connection, gate-keeping, and patronage that marked 'private' sociability (or what Russell designates 'domiciliary sociability'). See Russell, *Women, Sociability and Theatre*, 11, and 17–37.

27 John Rylands Library University of Manchester, GB 133 Eng MS 1124, Travel Journals of Dorothy Richardson, III, Diary of Visit to London 1775. See journal entry for 14 July 1775.

28 GB 133 Eng MS 1124, Travel Journals of Dorothy Richardson, III, Diary of Visit to London 1775. Entry for 17 July 1775.

29 These particular attributions are given in John Riely, *Rowlandson's Drawings from the Paul Mellon Collection* (New Haven: Yale Centre for British Art, 1978), 5. Diana Donald has questioned the likenesses and argues that they might be better regarded as 'types' rather than portraits. See Donald, *The Age of Caricature*, 137. David Coke and Alan Borg have recently reaffirmed the attributions in Coke and Borg, *Vauxhall Gardens*, 238.

30 BL, Morgan Grenville papers, Add. MS 70964, Memorandum book of Marquess of Carnarvon, see entries for 22–9 May 1752. James Brydges, Marquess of Carnarvon (27 December 1731–29 September 1789), son of Henry Brydges, 2nd Duke of Chandos.

31 Huntington Library, Stowe papers, ST 108 v.2, Private Diary of Henry Brydges, 2nd Duke of Chandos. Henry Brydges was the second son of James Brydges, 1st Duke of Chandos, but, following his elder brother's death in 1727, he inherited the title from his father in 1744.

32 TNA, Chatham papers, PRO/30/8/12, fo. 227 Letter from William Pitt, London, to his mother, Lady Chatham, 13 June 1781.

33 See, for example, letter from Maria Josepha Holroyd Stanley, Baroness of Alderley, Portland Place, to Ann First, 14 May 1794, reprinted in J. H. Adeane (ed.), *The Girlhood of Maria Jospha Lady Stanley of Alderley, Recorded in the letters of a hundred years ago from 1776 to 1796* (1896), 281.

34 A 25 shilling fee was advertised in *The Daily Post*, 14 April 1741.
35 BL, Morgan Grenville papers, Add. MS 70964, Memorandum book of the Marquess of Carnarvon (1752).
36 National Library of Scotland, Sutherland papers Dep. 313/716, fo. 58, letter from Lady Sutherland to Lady Elgin, London, 17 September [no date].
37 Diary entry for May 1767, in Home (ed.), *Lady Mary Coke*, ii. 6.
38 BRO, WPP, L30/14/333/199, Frederick Robinson to Thomas Robinson, 20 April 1779.
39 Letter from Lady Louisa Stuart to Lady Caroline Dawson, Countess of Portarlington, 24 June 1784, in Mrs Godfrey Clark (ed.), *Gleanings from an Old Portfolio Containing Some Correspondence Between Lady Louisa Stuart and her Sister Caroline Countess of Portarlington and Other Friends and Relations*, 3 vols (Edinburgh, 1896), i. 254.
40 TNA, Leveson Gower papers, PRO 30/29/4/1, fo. 12, Letter from Elizabeth Herbert, Countess of Pembroke, Whitehall, to Lady Susan Stewart, 11 June [1765]. See also letter from Elizabeth Herbert, Countess of Pembroke to Lady Susan Stewart, Wilton House, 23 May [1763], fo. 5.
41 BRO, WPP, L30/11/123/56, Letter from Lady Mary Yorke to Amabel, Lady Polwarth, 28 June 1777, and L30/14/333/96, Letter from Frederick Robinson to Thomas Robinson, 19 May 1778.
42 Letters from Lady Harriot Pitt to her mother Hester, Lady Chatham 1 June 1781 and 13 June 1781, reprinted in Cuthbert Headlam (ed.), *The Letters of Lady Harriot Eliot 1766–1786* (Edinburgh: T. & A. Constable, 1914), 59, 61.
43 Conway to Walpole, 1 August 1758, in Lewis (ed.), *Walpole's Correspondence*, xxxvii. 557.
44 Letter from Lady Harriot Pitt to Hester, Lady Chatham, reprinted in Headlam (ed.), *The Letters of Lady Harriot Eliot*, 59.
45 Letter from Lady Harriot Pitt to Hester, Lady Chatham, 61.
46 VGA, Fiche 1.
47 Oliver Goldsmith, *The Citizen of the World* (1762), 203.
48 Horace Walpole to George Montagu, 27 May 1757, in Lewis (ed.), *Walpole's Correspondence*, ix. 207.
49 Somewhat surprisingly, Walpole's experience has been referenced in existing accounts in direct support of the 'melting pot' model of pleasure garden sociability, with Walpole's inclusion of 'Betty the fruit seller' in his description of the Petersham company claimed as evidence of the elite's willing engagement with a broad social mix. It is important to note, however, that Walpole presents Betty's participation as one of service. She is employed by Lady Caroline Petersham to wait on her party. Furthermore, and particularly significantly, when the party are ready to dine Walpole mentions that Petersham makes Betty dine at a separate table. According to Walpole's account: 'She [Lady Caroline Petersham] had brought Betty the fruit girl with hampers of

strawberries and cherries from Roger's, and made her wait upon us, and then made her sup by us at a little table.' If anything, Betty's participation in the Vauxhall jaunt was an additional dramatization of the group's manifest exclusivity. For the use of this same Walpole quote as evidence of 'mingling', see Solkin, *Painting for Money*, 124.

50 Diary entry for May 1767, in Home (ed.), *Lady Mary Coke*, ii. 7.

51 For box subscriptions and the division of the opera audience, see Hall Witt, *Fashionable Acts*, 55–81.

52 Diary entry for 17 May 1767, Home (ed.), *Lady Mary Coke*, i. 240.

53 Lady Sarah Bunbury to Lady Susan O'Brien, Barton, 9 January 1766, Countess of Ilchester and Lord Stavordale (eds), *The Life and Letters of Lady Sarah Lennox 1745–1826* (London: John Murray, 1901), 176.

54 Robert D. Hume, 'Theatres and Repertory', in *The Cambridge History of the British Theatre*, ii. 53–70. See also Brewer, *Pleasures of the Imagination*, chapters 8, 9, and 10, especially 325–30, 351–4, 362–4, 384–96.

55 The most comprehensive study of the King's Theatre and operatic culture in the second half of the century is Curtis Alexander Price, Judith Milhous, and Robert D. Hume, *Italian Opera in Late Eighteenth-Century London, i: The King's Theatre Haymarket 1778–1791* (Oxford: Oxford University Press, 1995). For the early eighteenth century, see Henrik Knif, *Gentlemen and Spectators: Studies in Journals, Opera and the Social Scene in Late Stuart London* (Helsinki: Finnish Historical Society, 1995). For the early nineteenth century, see Hall Witt, *Fashionable Acts*. Lady Mary Yorke commented 'I can hardly believe [the Opera] will really begin on Saturday tho they are advertised & Mr Gallini and the Creditors pretend they are reconciled.' BRO, WPP, L30/9/81/63, Mary Grey to Marchioness Grey, 27 November 1783.

56 Horace Walpole to Sir Horace Mann, 5 November 1741, in Lewis (ed.), *Walpole's Correspondence*, xvii. 190.

57 For the fortunes of the opera in the later decades, see Ian Woodfield, *Opera and Drama in Eighteenth-Century London: The King's Theatre, Garrick and the Business of Performance* (Cambridge: Cambridge University Press, 2001), which focuses on the 1770s.

58 *The Man of Pleasure's Pocket-Book or the Bon Vivant's Vade Mecum for the Year 1780* (1780), 124. Robert Hume puts the figures slightly lower for earlier decades, at 4*s.* for a place in the box, 2*s.* 6*d.* in the pit, 1*s.* 6*d.* for the first (lower) gallery, and 1*s.* for the upper gallery. Hume, 'Theatres and Repertory', 55.

59 *The Man of Pleasure's Pocket-Book*, 122. Hume cites pit and box prices at 10*s.* 6*d.* and gallery price at 5*s.*, 57.

60 Hume, 'Theatres and Repertory', 57. In a similar vein, writing for the later period, Baer notes 'no portion of the theatre in the early nineteenth century, not even the boxes, was the exclusive preserve of any social group. The patent theatres in this sense—while distinct—were not so very different from other forms or arenas of entertainment available in late Georgian London,

including summer theatres, fairs, pleasure gardens, or low theatres, where crowds of various composition saw a variety of performances.' See Marc Baer, *Theatre and Disorder in Late Georgian London* (Oxford: Oxford University Press, 1992), 167.

61 Theatres historians have long analysed the audience at plays, using different types of sources to illuminate the patchy official record. See, for example, Allardyce Nicoll, *The Garrick Stage: Theatres and Audience in the Eighteenth Century* (Manchester: Manchester University Press, 1980); Harry William Pedicord, *The Theatrical Public in the Time of Garrick* (Carbondale, Ill.: Southern Illinois University Press, 1966); and James J. Lynch, *Box, Pit and Gallery: Stage and Society in Johnson's London* (Berkeley and Los Angeles: University of California Press, 1953). Pedicord questioned the reach down the social scale, but more recent studies, such as Hume, Donohue, and Brewer, argue for a broader range and more socially mixed audience.

62 Manuscript copies of subscription lists survive for the early eighteenth century, although published versions do not appear until the 1780s (at the cost of 5s. per list). See Hall Witt, *Fashionable Acts*, 111 and appendix.

63 Carole Taylor, 'Italian Opera-going in London 1700–1745' (unpublished Ph.D. thesis, Syracuse University, 1991). Cited in Price, Milhous, and Hume (eds), *Italian Opera*, 9.

64 Hall Witt, *Fashionable Acts*, 114–16.

65 William Weber, 'Musical Culture and the Capital City', 78.

66 HallWitt, *Fashionable Acts*, 60.

67 William Lee, *The Plan of the Boxes at the Kings Theatre Hay-market with An Alphabetical List of the Subscribers for the Season 1797* (1797) and William Lee, *The Plan of the Boxes at the King's Theatre Haymarket with An Alphabetical List of the Subscribers for the Season 1807* (1807).

68 Suffolk Record Office, Bury St Edmunds Branch (SRO Bury), Grafton papers, HA 513/4/121–30, Diaries of Elizabeth, second wife of Augustus Henry, 3rd Duke of Grafton. She was born Elizabeth Wrottesley (1745–82), daughter of Sir Richard Wrottesley, Dean of Worcester.

69 BL, Barrington papers, Add. MS 73704, Viscount Barrington's engagement diary for 1777.

70 Huntington Library, Stowe Collection, ST vol 26, James Brydges, 1st Duke of Chandos, 'Journal of my daily activities', 1697–1702. BRO, WPP, L 31/129, Account books of Henry, 12th Earl of Kent (afterwards Duke of Kent), 1692–7.

71 Hall Witt, *Fashionable Acts*, 102–3.

72 Home (ed.), *Lady Mary Coke*, vol. i. For references to box seats, see i. 136, 144–5 and for reference to her correspondence with Lady Howe, see 146.

73 BRO, WPP, L30/9/61/46, from Mary Grantham to Marchioness Grey, Richmond, 26 September 1782; L30/9/81/47, 3 October 1782; L30/9/81/63,

27 November 1783. See also L30/11/122/213, Amabel, Lady Polwarth to Mary Grantham, Bath, 11 December 1783; and L30/9/81/64, Mary Grantham to Jemima, Marchioness Grey, 9 December 1793.

74 BRO, WPP, L30/11/240/187, from Mary Grantham to Lady Lucas (formerly Lady Polwarth), 22 December 1805.

75 BRO, WPP, L30/11/240/188, from Mary Grantham to Lady Lucas, 28 December 1805.

76 Birmingham University Library Special Collections, Lady Stafford's Letters 1774–1805, F 72. Letter from Lady Stafford, wife of Earl Gower, to Charlotte, wife of Henry Marquess of Worcester, Trentham, 1 December [1793].

77 Birmingham University Library, Stafford Letters, F 147, Lady Stafford to Charlotte, Lady Worcester, 5 September 1807. Her daughter Susan (1769–1838), the subject of the letter, was married to the 1st Earl of Harrowby.

78 BRO, WPP L30/11/240/184, from Mary Grantham to her sister Amabel, Lady Lucas, 7 December 1805; L30/11/240/187, from Mary Grantham to Lady Lucas, 22 December 1805; L30/11/240/188, from Mary Grantham to Lady Lucas, 28 December 1805.

79 BL, Blenheim (Marlborough) papers, Add. MS 61456, Letter from Lady Pembroke to the Duchess of Marlborough.

80 Diary entry for 26 March 1728, Saville (ed.), *Secret Comment*, 111.

81 Huntington Library, Stowe Collection, ST vol. xxvi, 'Journal of my daily activities', James Brydges 1st Duke of Chandos entries for 15 February 1697 and 29 January 1800. Consulting all of Brydges's diaries from 1697 to 1702 Knif counts 44 visits to the theatre or music meetings 'without [Brydges] once mentioning anything that was performed'. Knif, *Gentlemen and Spectators*, 209.

82 BL, Holland House papers, Add. MS 51415, fo. 211, Letter from Henry Fox to his wife Caroline, 27 January 1756.

83 BRO, WPP, L30/14/333/177, Frederick Robinson to Thomas Robinson, 2nd Lord Grantham, 9 Februrary 1779.

84 BRO (WPP) L30/11/123/41 Lady Mary Yorke to Amabel, Lady Polwarth, 7 November 1775.

85 TNA, Leveson Gower papers, PRO 30/29/4/1, from Lady Mary Coke to Lady Susan Stewart, 26 February 1780.

86 It is precisely such everyday social references that are often edited out of published collections of letters and diaries. Moreover, archive catalogues tend to list such correspondence under miscellaneous headings (Bedfordshire Record Office, for example, lists such social detail in the Grey correspondence as 'London chit chat').

87 BL, Wentworth papers, Add. MS 22226, fo. 113, Countess of Strafford to the earl, 28 March 1712.

88 BL, Wentworth papers, Add. MS 22226, fo. 48 Countess of Strafford to the earl, [no date].

89 SRO (Bury), Hervey Family Archive (HFA), Ickworth papers, 941/46/10, Lady Hervey to Lord Hervey, 26 April 1711.

90 Gillian Russell notes that although the Licensing Act of 1737 prevented political expressions on the stage, Georgian audiences nevertheless interpreted plays in a political light and the theatre was retained as an important politicized arena that incorporated a wide range of audience members and not just the elite. See Gillian Russell, *The Theatres of War: Performance, Politics and Society 1793–1815* (Oxford: Clarendon Press, 1995), 16–18.

91 Elaine Chalus, *Elite Women in English Political Life, c.1754–1790* (Oxford: Oxford University Press, 2005), chapter 3 'Women and Social Politics', 75–105.

92 Amanda Foreman, *Georgiana, Duchess of Devonshire* (London: Harper Collins, 1998), 140.

93 Richard, Lord Temple to William, Earl of Chatham, Sunday 4 June 1769, in Vere Birdwood (ed.), *So Dearly Loved, So Much Admired: Letters to Hester Pitt, Lady Chatham from her Relations and Friends 1744–1901* (London: HMSO, 1994), 21.

94 18 July 1769, Home (ed.), *Lady Mary Coke*, iii. 115.

95 On the power of women in the eighteenth-century theatre, see Felicity Nussbaum, *Rival Queens: Actresses, Performance and the Eighteenth Century* (Philadelphia: University of Pennsylvania Press, 2010) and Russell, *Women, Sociability and Theatre*.

96 TNA, Leveson Gower papers, PRO 30/29/4/1, fo. 12, Letter from Elizabeth Herbert, Countess of Pembroke, Whitehall, to Lady Susan Stewart, 11 June [1765]. Elizabeth, Countess of Pembroke (1737–1831), was born Lady Elizabeth Spencer, daughter of Charles Spencer, 3rd Duke of Marlborough. In 1756 she had married Henry Herbert, 10th Earl of Pembroke and 7th Earl of Montgomery (1734–94). See also S. Herbert (ed.), *Henry, Elizabeth and George, 1734–1780: Letters and Diaries of Henry, Tenth Earl of Pembroke and his Circle* (London: Jonathan Cape, 1939). Lady Susan Stewart (1742/3–1805) was the daughter of John Stewart, 6th Earl of Galloway. In 1768 she married politician Granville Leveson-Gower, 2nd Earl Gower (from 1786 1st Marquess of Stafford). For her involvement in politics, see Chalus, *Elite Women*.

97 SRO, Grafton papers, HA 513/4/121–30, Diaries of Elizabeth, second wife of Augustus Henry, 3rd Duke of Grafton. She was born Elizabeth Wrottesley (1745–82), daughter of Sir Richard Wrottesley, Dean of Worcester.

98 SRO, Grafton papers, HA513/4/121, diary of Elizabeth Duchess of Grafton, 1789. The regularity of her attendance at the opera suggests that she subscribed to a box. Published subscription lists show that the duchess was the principal subscriber to Opera box 41 in 1807. A subscription list for 1789 has not yet been identified.

99 For Duchess of Chandos's assemblies, see, for example, entries for Tues. 7 June 1791 and Tues. 14 June 1791. For Lady Horton's assembly, see Weds. 4 May and Weds. 11 May 1791.

100 BL, Barrington papers, Add. MS 73704–19, Engagement diaries 1777–92 of William Wildman Barrington, 2nd Viscount Barrington (1717–93).

101 BL, Egmont papers, Add. MS 47061, Journal of 1st Lord Egmont (March 1730/1 to May 1732).

102 Although not applied directly to the urban prestige system of London's beau monde, E. P. Thompson long ago flagged the centrality of the cultural and social performance of elite power, noting that 'once a social system has become "set" it does not need to be endorsed daily by exhibitions of power…what matters more is a continuing theatrical style', E. P. Thompson, 'Patrician Society, Plebeian Culture', *Journal of Social History*, 7 (Summer 1974), 389. Jennifer Hall Witt applies Thompson's model of a 'theatre of the great' to her analysis of fashionable opera culture in the late eighteenth and nineteenth centuries. See Hall Witt, *Fashionable Acts*, 16–17.

Chapter 3

1 www.oldbaileyonline.org, trial of William Harvey, theft (pickpocketing), 27 February 1751, t17510227-23.

2 Diary entry for 4 June 1794, in Peter Jupp (ed.), *The Letter-Journal of George Canning 1793–1795* (London: Royal Historical Society, 1991), 118.

3 *The Gentleman's Magazine*, March 1731, 122.

4 *The Gentleman's Magazine*, 18 January 1790, 80.

5 See, for example, *The Times*, 19 January 1792; *Bath Chronicle*, 22 January 1784; *Morning Herald*, 19 January 1788; *English Chronicle or Universal Evening Post*, 19 January 1790; *St James's Chronicle*, 27 February 1796; *General Evening Post*, 16 February 1797; *Telegraph*, 16 February 1797; *Whitehall Evening Post*, 23 July 1798; *Morning Post and Gazetteer*, 15 July 1798.

6 For example, BL, Blenheim (Marlborough) papers, Add. MS 61455, letter from Lady Frances Bathurst to the Duchess of Marlborough, Kensington, London, 20 October [1692]. Lady Frances Bathurst (née Apsley) was the wife of Sir Benjamin Bathurst, at that time treasurer to the household of Princess Anne (later Queen Anne).

7 BL, Wentworth papers, Add. MS 22256-7, letters from Anne, Countess of Strafford to Thomas Wentworth, 1st Earl of Strafford (second creation), 1711-36 and example, letter from Peter Wentworth to his brother Earl of Strafford, 12 January 1712, Cartwright, *The Wentworth Papers*, 247.

8 BL, Wentworth papers, Add. MS 22256, fo. 50, undated letter to Lady Anne Campbell (wife of William Wentworth, 2nd Earl of Strafford).

9 For example letter from Lady Hertford to Lord Beauchamp, 12 November 1742, in Hughes (ed.), *The Gentle Hertford*, 225.

10 For example, letter from Peter Wentworth to his brother Earl of Strafford of 12 January 1712, Cartwright (ed.), *The Wentworth Papers*, 247; BL, Egmont papers, Add. MS 47060–71, Journals of the first Lord Egmont 1730–47.

11 For example, letter dated 23 January 1773 reprinted in Birdwood (ed.), *So Dearly Loved, So Much Admired*, 110; BRO, WPP, L30/11/133/68, from Lady Mary Grey to her sister Amabel, Lady Polwarth, London, 20 January 1779.

12 More comprehensive studies of the Georgian courts include Robert O. Bucholz, *The Augustan Court: Queen Anne and the Decline of Court Culture* (Stanford, Calif.: Stanford University Press, 1993) and Hannah Smith, *The Georgian Monarchy* (Cambridge: Cambridge University Press, 2006).

13 Eveline Cruickshanks, *The Stuart Courts* (Stroud: Sutton, 2000), 10.

14 Simon Thurley, *Whitehall Palace: The Official Illustrated History* (2008) and *The Whitehall Palace Plan of 1670* (1998).

15 George Macaulay Trevelyan, *English Social History: A Survey of Six Centuries, Chaucer to Queen Victoria* (1st poublished 1945; Penguin, 1986), 338. Trevelyan's narrative and his conclusions have been widely quoted. See John M. Beattie, 'The Court of George I and English Politics, 1717–1720', *English Historical Review*, 81 (1966), 26; Bucholz, *Augustan Court*, 34.

16 Colley, *Britons*: chapter 5 'Monarchy' and Linda Colley, 'The Apotheosis of George III: Loyalty, Royalty and the British Nation 1760–1820', *Past and Present*, 102 (1984).

17 Hannah Smith, *Georgian Monarchy*. Additional revisionist studies include: Clarissa Campbell Orr, 'Queen Charlotte, "Scientific Queen"', in Campbell Orr (ed.), *Queenship in Britain* (Manchester: Manchester University Press, 2009), 236–66; David Watkin, *The Architect King: George III and the Culture of the Enlightenment* (London: Royal Collection, 2004); Jonathan Marsden (ed.), *The Wisdom of George the Third* (London: Royal Collection, 2005); Jane Roberts and Christopher Lloyd (eds), *George III and Queen Charlotte: Patronage, Collecting and Royal Taste* (London: Royal Collection, 2004).

18 Derek Hudson, *Kensington Palace* (London: Peter Davies, 1968), 6; Ephraim John Burford, *Royal St James's: Being a Story of Kings, Clubmen and Courtesans* (London: Hale, 1988), 17.

19 For the division between George I and the Prince of Wales (later George II), see Beattie, 'Court of George I', 26–37.

20 Davidoff, *Best Circles*, 14.

21 More detailed records survive for the nineteenth century and these have been used by Nancy Ellenberger to map the changing social status of those presented at court during Queen Victoria's reign. See Nancy W. Ellenberger, 'The Transformation of London "Society" at the End of Victoria's Reign: Evidence from Court Presentation Records', *Albion*, 22 (1990), 633–53.

22 BRO, WPP, L30/9/81/34, Mary Robinson to Jemima, Marchioness Grey, 21 January 1782.

23 BRO, WPP, L30/11/123/31, Lady Mary Grey to Amabel, Lady Polwarth, 17 December 1774.

24 Hampshire Record Office (HRO), 9M73/G835, London Diary of James Harris 1770.

25 BRO, WPP, L30/14/333/97, Frederick Robinson to Thomas Robinson, Whitehall, 22 May 1778.

26 Huntington Library, Stowe Manuscripts, ST vol. cix, vol. iii, Diaries James Brydges, 3rd Duke of Chandos.

27 *Original Weekly Journal*, 23 November 1717; *Post Boy*, 11 October 1722; *The Public Advertiser* reported that the royal family were based primarily at Windsor but stayed a few nights each week at Kensington to enable the queen to hold a St James's drawing room on Thursday and the king to host a *levée* for ministers each Friday morning (see, for example, *Public Advertiser*, 27 December 1790 and *Woodfall's Register*, 29 December 1790).

28 *Original Weekly Journal*, 23 November 1717.

29 *Post Boy*, 11 October 1722.

30 *Public Advertiser*, 27 December 1790; *Woodfall's Register*, 29 December 1790.

31 *Weekly Journal or British Gazetteer*, 2 June 1722, gave a full report of the progression of birthday celebrations: 'Monday being the Birth-Day of His Most Sacred Majesty King GEORGE, who then enter'd into the 63d year of his age…the Morning was usher'd with ringing of Bells, and at one o'clock the Guns on the Tower Wharf were fired to the Number of 62, being the exact Number of His Majesty's Years, after which they fired all round the Lines and Ramparts. There was a Drawing Room at Court crowded with a splendid Appearance of the Nobility and Foreign Ministers to compliment His Majesty, as did also their Royal Highnesses the Prince and Princess of Wales, and after the Birth-Day Song as usual, there was an illustrious Ball, at which were also present the Prince and Princess of Wales, so that the greatest Court was made, as has been seen in any Reign past.'

32 *Carlton House Magazine* reported that the company reconvened at 8 p.m. for the ball (which started at 9 p.m.). Twenty-two minuets danced in all, followed by one country dance (performed only by the 'first gentlemen' and 'ladies of the first rank'), *Carlton House Magazine* (1792), 83.

33 BRO, WPP, L30/9a/1/87, Jemima, Marchioness Grey to Mary Gregory, 1 December 1752.

34 Vickery, *Gentleman's Daughter*, 229–30.

35 William Matthews (ed.), *The Diary of Dudley Ryder 1715–1715* (London: Methuen & Co., 1939), See entries for 25 July 1715, 1 August 1715, 15 August 1715, 16 April 1716, 7 June 1716. Ryder's drawing room attendance was concentrated in the summer months, when the majority of the titled elite had returned to their country estates.

36 Letter from Josiah Wedgwood to John Wedgwood, reprinted in Katherine Euphemia Lady Farrar (ed.), *The Letters of Josiah Wedgwood*, i: *1762–1770* (Manchester: Manchester University Press, 1903), 38. The italicized emphasis is original to the letter.

37 This information is taken from Robert Bucholz's illuminating study: Robert O. Bucholz, 'Going to Court in 1700: A Visitor's Guide', *Court Historian*, 5/3 (December 2000), 191.

38 On 1 August for example he notes 'got an easy passage . . . by following another that went before me'. Diary entry for 1 August 1715, in Matthews (ed.), *Dudley Ryder Diary*, 66.

39 Ryder found access to the birthday court harder to secure. He notes that he was repulsed from court on his first attempt but later returned and gave a bribe to the guard to let him see the close of the ball. See diary entry for 30 October 1716, in Matthews (ed.), *Dudley Ryder Diary*, 356.

40 *Flying Post or the Weekly Medley*, 15 March 1729.

41 *St James's Chronicle*, 13 February 1762.

42 R. Brimley Johnson (ed.), *The Letters of Lady Louisa Stuart* (London: John Lane, 1926), 69.

43 BL, Althorp papers, Add. MS 75928, Lavinia, Countess Spencer to Earl Spencer, 19 April 1792.

44 BRO, L30/11/240/13, Mary Grantham to Amabel, Lady Lucas, 20 January 1781; Hon. Mrs H. Wyndham (ed.), *Correspondence of Sarah Spencer, Lady Lyttelton 1787–1870* (London: J. Murray, 1912), 2.

45 A useful survey of eighteenth-century fashion, including court dress, is offered in Jane Ashelford, *The Art of Dress* (London: National Trust, 2009). For more on the expensive fabrics used for court dress, see Jenny Lister, 'Twenty-Three Samples of Silks: Silks Worn by Queen Charlotte & the Princess at the Royal Birthday Balls 1791–1794', *Costume*, 37 (2003).

46 BL, Wentworth papers, Add. MS 22226, fo. 48, from the Countess of Strafford to the earl [1711].

47 National Register of Archives, Scotland, NRA(S) 2177, bundle 426, number 532, Accounts of the Duke and Duchess of Hamilton.

48 Noted by Lady Mary Coke, 13 January 1767, in Home (ed.), *Lady Mary Coke*, ii. 114. In comparison Lady Louisa Stuart suggested a gown for 'full dress' (worn to a private ball for example) might cost £24 whereas a court gown would cost over £70. Lady Louisa Stuart to Lady Portalington, 30 March 1789, in Johnson (ed.), *Letters of Lady Louisa Stuart*, 96.

49 Lady Louisa Stuart to Lady Portalington, 13 March 1787, in Johnson (ed.), *Letters of Lady Louisa Stuart*, 83.

50 In 1824, for example, Lady William Wynn noted that the Duchess of Argyll's dress was 'sometime exhibited at Milliners' before a court birthday, for which the train alone reputedly cost £200. See, Rachel Leighton (ed.), *Correspondence of Charlotte Grenville, Lady William Wynn and her Three Sons: Sir Watkin Williams Wynn, Bart., Rt Hon Charles William Wynn and Sir Henry Williams Wynn, GCH KCB 1795–1832* (London: John Murray, 1920), 312.

51 BL, Wentworth papers, Add. MS 22226, fo. 40 and fo. 42, Countess of Strafford to the earl, November to 11 December 1711.

52 See, for example, David Garrick to the Duke of Devonshire, Letter 191, 10 September 1757; Letter 210 4 September 1758; Letter 279, 15 December 1761, in David M. Little and George M. Kahrl (eds), *The Letters of David Garrick* (Oxford: Oxford University Press, 1963), 265, 286, and 347.

53 NLS, Sutherland MS Dep. 313/716, Correspondence of Mary, Countess of Sutherland (née Maxwell), Letter 13 from Lady Erskine to Mary, Countess of Sutherland (17 July 1761).

54 NLS, Sutherland MS Dep. 313/716, letter 11 from Lord Erskine to Lord Sutherland (8 August 1761).

55 BL, Wentworth papers, Add. MS 22228, fo. 322, from Ann Donelan (wife of James Donelan) to Lord Strafford, London, 13 October 1733; Mrs Rathborne (ed.), *Letters from Lady Jane Coke to her Friend Mrs Eyre at Derby 1747–1758* (London: Swann Sonnenschein, 1899), 123. In the 1830s, Henry Holland also describes attending a private event where court dresses were displayed, noting that he went first to St James's Park to see the procession of figures heading to court and then 'returned to the Bathursts where the young ladies came in their court dresses and looked very well'. See Earl of Ilchester (ed.), *Journal of Hon Henry Edward Fox afterwards Fourth and Last Lord Holland 1818–1830* (London, 1923). Journal entry for 23 April 1822, 113.

56 BL, Blenheim (Marlborough) papers, Add. MS 61456, fo. 66, letter from Frances, Countess of Scarborough to Sarah, Duchess of Marlborough [undated, *c*.1708–10].

57 BL, Wentworth papers, Add. MS 22226, fo. 145, letter from Countess of Strafford to the earl, 15 April 1712.

58 BL, Wentworth papers, Add. MS 22226, fo. 290, letter from the Countess of Strafford to the earl, February 1711/12.

59 Beattie, 'Court of George I', 206.

60 BL, Egmont Papers, Add. MS 47060, Journal of John Perceval, 1st Earl of Egmont, 12 March 1730.

61 Letter from Lord Bristol to Lady Bristol, Ickworth, 26 October 1716, in Sydenham H. A. Hervey (ed.), *Letter Books of John Hervey, 1st Earl of Bristol with Sir Thomas Hervey's Letters During Courtship and Poems During Widowhood*, i: *1651–1715* (Wells: Jackson, 1894), i. 34.

62 Peter Wentworth to the Earl of Strafford, London, 12 January 1712, reprinted in Cartwright (ed.), *The Wentworth Papers*, 247.

63 BL, Wentworth papers, Add. MS 22226, fo. 28, letter from the Countess of Strafford to the earl, London, February 1713.

64 BL, Wentworth papers, Add. MS 22226, fo. 28. Henry St John, First Viscount Bolingbroke (1678–1751), was Secretary of State between 1710 and 1714. At the date of the Countess of Strafford's letter he was in Paris negotiating terms of peace with France. 'Sir J. Hammond' is likely to be a reference to Anthony Hammond (1668–1738), who was deputy paymaster of British forces serving in Spain at this date. He was elected knight of the shire for Huntingdonshire

in 1695 and was married to Lady Jane Hammond, daughter of Sir Walter Clarges.

65 Peter Wentworth to his brother the Earl of Strafford, London, 12 January 1712, Cartwright (ed.), *The Wentworth Papers*, 247.

66 Bucholz, *Augustan Court*, 226. A description of the Marlborough incident is also treated by Bucholz; refer to 227–8 for details. Contemporary accounts reveal the widespread use of specific symbols to signal loyalty or opposition to royal houses. Mary Countess Cowper, for example, noted in her diary that, after 1714, some would wear 'green boughs' (oak leaves) in their hats on the anniversary of the Restoration, as a statement of opposition to the House of Hanover, and roses in buttonholes on the Pretender's birthday (the descendant of the exiled James II and the Stuart court). Supporters of the Protestant monarchy and the House of Hanover wore orange ribbons, to commemorate William of Orange on key dates associated with the Glorious Revolution. See entries for May 1716 in Charles Spencer Cowper (ed.), *Diary of Mary, Countess Cowper, Lady of the Bedchamber to the Princess of Wales 1714–1720* (1864), 107–10.

67 See, for example, BL, Egmont papers, Add. MS 47061, journal entry for 3 April 1730/1; BL, Add MS 47062, journal entry for 1 November 1732; BL, Add. MS 47064, journal entries for 21 January 1733/4 and 1 March 1733/4.

68 For a full study of Mary Delany's use of court clothing to signal her allegiance to the court, see Mark Laird and Alicia Weisberg-Roberts (eds), *Mrs Delany and her Circle* (New Haven: Yale University Press, 2009), chapters by Mark Laird, Clarissa Campbell Orr, Clare Browne, and Hannah Greig.

69 Lady Hertford to Lord Beauchamp, Sunday 12 November 1742, in Hughes (ed.), *The Gentle Hertford*, 225.

70 Diary entries for 21 and 24 January 1767 in Home (ed.), *Lady Mary Coke*, ii. 121–2.

71 Home (ed.), *Lady Mary Coke*, Thursday June 1773, 544. It is unclear what lay behind this attempt by the Duchess of Hamilton and Lady Susan Stewart to distort the information about Coke's court clothing. It seems likely that the rift may well have been driven by interpersonal rivalries between the Scottish noble families, rather than organized divisions between politicized factions. Nonetheless, the nuanced significance of whether court clothing was deemed new and fine or old and reused is underscored by this exchange.

72 James A. Home (ed.), *Lady Louisa Stuart, Selections from her Manuscripts* (New York: Harper Brothers, 1899), 187.

73 BRO, WPP, L30/11/122/287, Jemima, Marchioness Grey to her daughter Amabel, Lady Polwarth, Monday 19 February 1781.

74 *The Times*, 5 June 1789.

75 Lady Louisa Stuart to Lady Caroline Dawson, Countess of Portarlington, 30 March 1789, in Clark (ed.), *Gleanings from an Old Portfolio*, ii. 117.

76 *The World*, 18 April 1789.

77 *The Times*, 30 May 1789. Report repeated in *Felix Farley's Bristol Journal*, 6 June 1789.

78 Lady Strafford to George Leveson Gower, 12 February 1789, in Castalia Countess Granville (ed.), *Lord Granville Leveson Gower: First Earl Granville Private Correspondence 1781–1821* (London: John Muray, 1917), 12.

79 *The Times*, 19 January 1792.

80 *The Morning Chronicle*, 20 January 1795.

81 The advertisement noted that 'Mr Fox's birthday will be celebrated at the Crown and Anchor Tavern, the Strand, on Saturday 24th...tickets to be had of the stewards and at the Crown and Anchor bar.'

Chapter 4

1 BL, Wentworth papers, Add. MS 22226, fo. 21, Countess of Strafford to the earl, 15 November 1711.

2 BL, Wentworth papers, Add. MS 22226, fo. 21, Countess of Strafford to the earl, 15 November 1711.

3 On other occasions the Whigs also used rumours of the queen's poor health to cast doubt on the longevity of her reign. Bucholz, *Augustan Court*, 185–7.

4 Hoppit, *Land of Liberty?*, 304–5.

5 Philip Roberts (ed.), *The Diary of Sir David Hamilton, 1709–1714* (Oxford: Clarendon Press, 1975), 87 n. 145. Cited by Stuart Handley in 'Talbot, Charles, Duke of Shrewsbury (1660–1718)', *Oxford Dictionary of National Biography* (Oxford: Oxford University Press, 2004); online edn, January 2008 <http://www.oxforddnb.com.ezproxy.york.ac.uk/view/article/26922>, accessed 23 March 2013.

6 BL, Wentworth papers, Add. MS 22226, fo. 29, Countess of Strafford to the earl, 25 November 1711.

7 Bucholz, *Augustan Court*, 223.

8 Bucholz, *Augustan Court*, 223.

9 For an accessible but thorough summary of approaches to how the political culture of eighteenth-century Britain has been defined by historians, see Frank O'Gorman, *The Long Eighteenth Century: British Political and Social History 1688–1832* (London: Arnold, 1997). Broadly speaking, historians' current conceptions of eighteenth-century British political culture in the period result primarily from work that sought to overturn Sir Lewis Namier's longstanding characterization of politics as shaped entirely by interpersonal obligations (see online review by Peter Thomas of the influence of Namier's work on the subsequent shape of the field: Institute of Historical Research's 'Reviews in History', <www.history.ac.uk/reviews/review/32a.html>).

10 Such inherited privileges were specific to the English peerage. Once separate parliaments in Edinburgh and Dublin were dismantled (in 1707 and 1801 respectively), Scottish and Irish peers only had access to a restricted number of representative seats in Westminster to which they were chosen by election.

For more on the political relationship between, and comparative rights of, the English, Irish, and Scottish lords (and, eventually, British lords), see Julian Hoppit (ed.), *Parliaments, Nations and Identities in Britain and Ireland 1660–1850* (Manchester: Manchester University Press, 2003), especially 'Introduction' and chapter 5 'The Landed Interest and the National Interest 1660–1800'; and essays by Michael W. McCahill, 'The Scottish Peerage and the House of Lords in the Late Eighteenth Century' and 'Peerage Creations and the Changing Character of the British Nobility 1750–1850', both in Clyve Jones and David L. Jones (eds), *Peers, Politics and Power: The House of Lords 1603–1911* (London: Hambledon, 1986), chapter 12, 283–308, and chapter 14, 407–32.

11 The Duke of Portland's biographer, David Wilkinson, suggests that it would have been impossible for any cabinet to survive without the compliance of nobles. See David Wilkinson, *The Duke of Portland: Politics and Party in the Age of George III* (New York: Palgrave Macmillan, 2003), 2.

12 Quoted in John Field, *The Story of Parliament in the Palace of Westminster* (London: Politico's, 2002), 137.

13 Chalus, *Elite Women*, 7.

14 Hall Witt, *Fashionable Acts*, 14.

15 Francis M. L. Thompson calculated that by the end of the 1700s eight leading peers, making up a meagre 3 per cent of the Lords, controlled a minimum of 50 seats in the Commons between them (10 per cent of the entire House). John Cannon has found that between 1715 and 1785 peers in the Lords doubled the number of seats over which they had direct and longstanding control in the Commons, whilst Lewis Namier previously estimated that around 111 commons seats were under the influence of peers, rising to over 200 by the end of 1784. See Thompson, *English Landed Society*; John Cannon, 'The Isthmus Repaired: The Resurgence of the English Aristocracy 1660–1760', *Proceedings of the British Academy*, 68 (1982), 450; Cannon, *Aristocratic Century*, 105–7, and 112–13; Namier, *The Structure of Politics at the Accession of George III*, 148–9. Few historians would now characterize the political power brought by land ownership as absolute. Unquestionably there were a number of infamous 'rotten boroughs' and seats that were easily purchased, but it was more often the case that a landholder's right to 'choose' a parliamentary representative or promote a particular candidate was granted on the basis of complex reciprocal local relationships and patronage networks. Herman Wellenreuther persuasively argues that one reason that noble political influence proved so resilient throughout the century was not because the landowners enjoyed autocratic status but because they successfully met the local needs of voters. Herman Wellenreuther, 'The Political Role of the Nobility in Eighteenth-Century England', in Joseph Canning and Hermann Wellenreuther (eds), *Britain and Germany Compared: Nationality, Society and Nobility in the Eighteenth Century* (Gottingen: Wallstein, 2001), 99–140.

16 For an accessible history of parliament's evolution and its pre-1830s spatial organization, see Field, *The Story of Parliament*.

17 Elaine Chalus, 'Elite Women, Social Politics and the Political World of Late Eighteenth-Century England', *Historical Journal*, 43/3 (2000), 669–97.

18 Langford, *Public Life and Propertied Gentlemen*, 139; Peter Jupp, *The Governing of Britain 1688–1848: The Executive, the Parliament and the People* (London: Routledge, 2006), 35–7. Kathleen Wilson characterizes eighteenth-century political culture in comparable terms but in reference to a wider popular political culture rather than to the specific content of parliamentary business. 'Political consciousness', she argues, was 'forged as strikingly through the involvement of individuals in localized contests for power as through participation in national movements that aimed at ousting a minister or reforming the state.' Kathleen Wilson, *The Sense of the People: Politics, Culture and Imperialism in England, 1715–1785* (Cambridge: Cambridge University Press, 1998), 15.

19 Quote taken from Lewis, *Sacred to Female Patriotism*, 67. See also Elaine Chalus, ' "To serve my friends": Women and Political Patronage in Eighteenth-Century England', in Amanda Vickery (ed.), *Women, Privilege and Power: British Politics 1750 to the Present* (Cambridge: Cambridge University Press, 2001), 57–88.

20 Chalus, 'Elite Women, Social Politics'. The emphasis on interpersonal connections and influence in recent histories of elite women's political involvement has led some reviewers and critics to suggest this work represents a return to 'Namierite' political history, which emphasized personality at the expense of ideology. See Peter Mandler, 'Namier in Petticoats?', review no. 63, <https:www.history.ac.uk/reviews/review/63> Peter Mandler. Chalus addresses this criticism in Chalus, *Elite Women and English Political Life*, 11–12.

21 Chalus, 'Elite Women, Social Politics'.

22 Number 6 St James's Square was inherited by John, Lord Hervey (later Earl of Bristol) from his aunt in 1700. From that date he used it as his London residence. The house continued to be occupied by Hervey family descendants until 1955 (the longest single family tenure of any property in the square) when finally, and somewhat ironically, the family sold the house to the owners of number 5. St. James's Square: No. 6, *Survey of London: volumes 29 and 30: St James Westminster*, Part 1 (1960), 103–9. URL: <http://www.british-history.ac.uk/report.aspx?compid=40550>. Date accessed: 24 November 2011.

23 Character description taken from John Macky, *Memoirs of the Secret Services of J. Macky* (1733), cited by Philip Carter, 'Hervey, John, First Earl of Bristol (1665–1751)', *Oxford Dictionary of National Biography* (Oxford, 2004) <http://www.oxforddnb.com.ezproxy.york.ac.uk/view/article/1311>.

24 SRO (Bury), HFA, 941/46/10–11, Letters and verses between the Earl and Countess of Bristol 1695–1737.

25 Hervey described himself as 'Whigg' and routinely referred to his support for the Glorious Revolution and Protestant succession. See letter from John Hervey, Earl of Bristol, to his son, Lord Hervey, 18 August 1733, and letter from John Hervey, Earl of Bristol, Ickworth, to the Countess of Bristol, London, 29 October 1733, *Letter Books*, 99, 104. His promotion to 1st Earl of Bristol in 1714 was granted when George I acceded to the British throne, in recognition of his commitment to the Hanoverian crown. Eventually Hervey's steadfastness wavered and after 1718 he joined the Prince of Wales's political cohort when the court divided into competing units, and later opposed Walpole's government (a move that, as noted in the previous chapter, he and his wife initially masked through the judicious use of court dress).

26 Hervey recorded the dinner in his diary. See Syndenham H. J. Hervey (ed.), *The Diary of John Hervey, First Earl of Bristol with extracts from his book of expenses 1688–1742* (Wells: Jackson,1894), 55.

27 SRO (Bury), HFA, 941/46/10, Letters and verses between the Earl and Countess of Bristol, 1695–1737, Letter from Elizabeth Hervey (later Lord Hervey and then Earl of Bristol) to John Hervey at parliament house, 3 February 1795. Also reprinted in Hervey (ed.), *Letter Books*, i. 98. Marlborough's official post was Master-General of the Ordnance and Captain-General of the Army.

28 See, for example, SRO (Bury), HFA, 941/46/10, Letter from John Hervey to Elizabeth Felton (later Hervey), 20 July 1695, and Letter from John Hervey to Elizabeth Hervey, 9 April 1711.

29 Letter from John Hervey, Bury St Edmunds, to Elizabeth Hervey, London, 6 May 1702. See SRO (Bury), HFA 941/46/10, reprinted in Hervey (ed.), *Letter Books*, i. 163.

30 Chalus, *Elite Women*, 81–3.

31 BL, Wentworth papers, Add. MS 2226, fo. 151, Countess of Strafford to the earl, 25 April 1712.

32 SRO (Bury), HFA, 941/46/11, Elizabeth Hervey (now Countess of Bristol) to John Hervey (now Earl of Bristol), 18 May 1736.

33 In February 1712 she explained, 'the Whiggs to day has made a new story which is that you and L[or]d Privy Seal sends such different letters to ye Secretary of State that they did not know what to make of them & to the Queen sent an Express presently [to] tell you both she would receave no letter but what you had both signed together.' BL, Wentworth papers, Add. MS 22226, fo. 294, letter from Countess of Strafford to the earl, 15 February 1712.

34 For examples from the Countess of Strafford's correspondence see: for 'chatter chitter', letter dated 4 April 1712, BL, Wentworth papers, Add. MS 22226, fo. 129; for 'town' talk, see Add. MS 22226, fo. 25, letter of 20 November 1711, and Add. MS 2226, fo. 139, letter of 11 April 1712,; for 'scandall', see Add. MS 2226, fo. 25, letter of 20 November 1711, Add. MS 2226, fo. 27, letter of 25 November 1711, and Add. MS 2226, fo. 39, letter of 4 December 1711. For examples from Lady Hervey's correspondence see: for 'chit chat', SRO (Bury),

HFA, 941/46/10, letter of 2 May 1702, and Hervey (ed.), *Letter Books*, i. 158; for 'town' talk, see SRO (Bury), HFA, 941/46/10, letter dated 25 April 1696, and Hervey (ed.), *Letter Books*, i. 100; for 'scandal', see SRO (Bury), HFA, 941/46/10, letter dated 11 October 1722 and Hervey (ed.), *Letter Books*, ii. 243.

35 SRO (Bury), HFA, 941/46/10, letter from Elizabeth Hervey, London, to John Hervey, Newmarket, 25 April 1696; Hervey (ed.), *Letter Books*, i. 101.

36 SRO (Bury), HFA, 941/46/10, letter of 8 April 1697 and 1 May 1697; Hervey (ed.), *Letter Books*, i. 117, 120.

37 SRO (Bury), HFA, 941/46/10, letter of 25 April 1696; Hervey (ed.), *Letter Books*, i. 101.

38 SRO (Bury), HFA, 941/46/10, letter of 2 May 1702; Hervey (ed.), *Letter Books*, i. 158.

39 SRO (Bury), HFA, 941/46/10, letter of 7 May 1702; Hervey (ed.), *Letter Books*, i. 166.

40 SRO (Bury), HFA, 941/46/10, letter of 11 March 1707; Hervey (ed.), *Letter Books*, i. 231.

41 SRO (Bury), HFA, 941/46/10, letter of 5 April 1709; Hervey (ed.), *Letter Books*, i. 246.

42 SRO (Bury), HFA, 941/46/10, letter of 11 April 1713; Hervey (ed.), *Letter Books*, i. 355.

43 SRO (Bury), HFA, 941/46/10, letter of 14 April 1713; Hervey (ed.), *Letter Books*, i. 358.

44 SRO (Bury), HFA, 941/46/10, letter of 6 April 1716; Hervey (ed.), *Letter Books*, ii. 14.

45 SRO (Bury), HFA, 941/46/10, letter of 3 April 1712; Hervey (ed.), *Letter Books*, i. 321.

46 BL, Wentworth papers, Add. MS 22226, fo. 25, Countess of Strafford to the earl, 20 November 1711.

47 BL, Wentworth papers, Add. MS 22226, fo. 29, Countess of Strafford to the earl, 25 November 1711.

48 BL, Wentworth papers, Add. MS 22226, fo. 31, Countess of Strafford to the earl, 27 November 1711.

49 BL, Wentworth papers, Add. MS 22226, fo. 37, Countess of Strafford to the earl, 30 November 1711.

50 BL, Wentworth papers, Add. MS 22226, fo. 42, Countess of Strafford to the earl, 11 December 1711.

51 BL, Wentworth papers, Add. MS 22226, fo. 157, Countess of Strafford to the earl, 6 May 1712.

52 The Countess of Strafford's record of the invitation notes that she actually refused the invitation on grounds of being 'already ingag'd', an excuse also deployed by Lady Hervey (who promptly received a follow-up invitation from the tenacious Duchess of Shrewsbury for dinner and cards the following week). See SRO (Bury), HFA, 941/46/10, Elizabeth Hervey, London, to John Hervey, 24 April 1711; Hervey (ed.), *Letter Books*, i. 299.

53 Chalus, *Elite Women*.

54 BL, Hardwicke papers, Add. MS 35376, fos. 45 and 86, letters from Jemima, Marchioness Grey to her husband Philip Yorke (later 2nd Earl of Hardwicke), 16 January [n.d.] and 15 December [n.d.].

55 BRO, WPP, L30/91/1/148, letter from Jemima, Marchioness Grey to Lady Mary Gregory, 5 November 1756.

56 BL, Morley papers, Add. MS 48218, fo. 18, Anne Robinson, London, to Thomas Robinson [n.d. *c.* July 1766].

57 BL, Althorp papers, Add. MS 75926, Lavinia Countess Spencer, London, to Earl Spencer, 5 February 1783.

58 BL, Althorp papers, Add. MS 75926, Lavinia Countess Spencer, London, to Earl Spencer, 13 March 1783.

59 BL, Althorp papers, Add. MS 75928, Lavinia Countess Spencer to Earl Spencer, 26 February 1794.

60 Letter from Lady Harriot Eliot to Hester, Lady Chatham 11 Februrary 1786, in Headlam (ed.), *The Letters of Lady Harriot Eliot*, 132.

61 BL, Althorp papers, Add. MS 75926, Lavinia Countess Spencer to Earl Spencer, 14 March 1783.

62 *Lady's Magazine*, April 1771.

63 For example, BRO, WPP, L30/14/139, letters from Augustus Henry Fitzroy, 3rd Duke of Grafton; L30/14/140 letters, from Earl Fitzwilliam; L30/14/145 Letters from William Forrester; L30/14/188, letters from Frederick Howard, 5th Earl Carlisle; L30/14/226 Letters from Thomas Lockhart.

64 BRO, WPP, L30/14/333/191, Frederick Robinson to Thomas Robinson, 2nd Baron Grantham, 26 March 1779.

65 BL, Althorp papers, Add. MS 75670, fo. 101, George Villiers to Lady Spencer, London 26 March 1764.

66 Letter to Hester, Lady Chatham from Lady Harriot Eliot, London, 11 February 1786 in Headlam (ed.), *The Letters of Lady Harriot Eliot*, 130.

67 Lady Mary Coke, diary entry for March 1767, in Home (ed.), *Lady Mary Coke*, i. 178.

68 Diary entry for 6 April 1767, in Home (ed.), *Lady Mary Coke*, i. 201.

69 BRO, WPP, L31/108, Memoirs of 2nd Lord Grantham, entry dated 16 October 1761.

70 Chalus, *Elite Women*, 684.

71 Recorded in Lady Hertford's journal, 15 February 1742, in Hughes (ed.), *The Gentle Hertford*, 209.

72 Hampshire Record Office (HRO), 9M73/G835-44, London diaries and account book 1770–80.

73 HRO, 9M73/G754, Conversations in London February to March 1770; 9M73/G762 Memorandums in London November 1775 to June 1776; 9M73/G764, Stories and Facts while in London during the spring of the year 1777.

74 HRO, 9M73/G840, London diary November 1775 to June 1776 with accounts.

75 HRO, 9M73/G762, Memorandums in London November 1775 to June 1776.

76 HRO, 9M73/G840, London diary November 1776–June 1777.

77 HRO, 9M73/G764, 'Stories and facts while in London during the Spring of the year 1777'.

Chapter 5

1 Quote taken from a tribute written by Daniel Pulteney and the Earl of Chesterfield to Lady Hervey, *c*.1720, on the occasion of her marriage: 'So perfect a beau and a bell | As when Hervey the handsome was wedded | To the beautiful Molly Lapell...So pow'rful her charms, and so moving | They would warm an old monk in his cell | Should the Pope himself ever go roaming | He would follow dear Molly Lapell.' Reprinted John Heneage Jesse, *George Selwyn and his Contemporaries with Memoirs and Notes*, 4 vols (London: Richard Bentley, 1843), i. 214.

2 *Morning Post and Daily Advertiser*, 2 October 1776.

3 *London Chronicle*, 3–5 September 1776.

4 Matthew Prior, *The Female Phaeton* (1718); BRO, WPP, L30/11/123/78, Lady Mary Grey to Amabel, Lady Polwarth, 5 March 1780 and also L30/11/123/79, Lady Mary Grey to Amabel, Lady Polwarth, 15 March 1780.

5 Horace Bleackley, *The Story of a Beautiful Duchess* (London: John Lane, 1907); Alexander Meyrick Broadley, *The Beautiful Lady Craven* (London: John Lane, 1914); and John Fyvie, *Wits, Beaux and Beauties of the Georgian Era* (London: John Lane, 1909).

6 Francette Pacteau, *The Symptom of Beauty* (London: Reaktion, 1994), 14.

7 Naomi Wolf, *The Beauty Myth: How Images of Beauty are Used Against Women* (London: Chatto and Windus, 1990), 10.

8 Thorough, yet, accessible studies of aesthetic traditions and theory are offered by James Kirwan, *Beauty* (Manchester: Manchester University Press, 1999); Paul Guyer, *Values of Beauty: Historical Essays in Aesthetics* (Cambridge: Cambridge University Press, 2005); Elizabeth Prettejohn, *Beauty and Art: 1750–2000* (Oxford: Oxford University Press, 2005). On beauty as a political construction, see Pierre Bourdieu, *Distinction: A Social Critique of the Judgment of Taste* (London: Routledge and Kegan Paul, 1984); Diana Maltz, *British Aestheticism and the Urban Working Classes 1870–1900: Beauty for the People* (Basingstoke: Palgrave Macmillan, 2006); Ruth Livesey, *Socialism, Sex and the Culture of Aestheticism in Britain 1880–1914* (Oxford: Oxford University Press, 2007). A further recent feminist critique can be found in Peg Zeglin Brand (ed.), *Beauty Matters* (Bloomington, Ind.: Indiana University Press, 2000).

9 Robert W. Jones, *Gender and the Formation of Taste in Eighteenth-Century Britain: The Analysis of Beauty* (Cambridge: Cambridge University Press, 1998); Prettejohn, *Beauty and Art*; Annie Richardson, 'From the Moral Mound to the Material Maze: Hogarth's *Analysis of Beauty*', in Maxine Berg and Elizabeth Eger (eds), *Luxury in the Eighteenth Century: Debates, Desires and Delectable Goods* (Basingstoke: Palgrave Macmillan, 2003).

10 *Beauty and Proportion: A Poem* (1733), 4.

11 Jones, *Gender and the Formation of Taste*.

12 *Beauty and Proportion: A Poem*, 5, 7–8.

13 William Hogarth, *The Analysis of Beauty*, ed. with introduction and notes Ronald Paulson (New Haven: Yale University Press, 1997), 18.

14 Hogarth, *Analysis*, 35.

15 Hogarth, *Analysis*, 65–6.

16 *The Ladies Magazine* (April 1772).

17 *Dictionary of Love* (1795), 20.

18 Le Camus's *Abdeker* offered eighteenth-century readers a detailed guide to the preparation and application of cosmetics, A. Le Camus, *Abdeker, or the Art of Preserving Beauty* (1754). For a history of cosmetics and further details of eighteenth-century beauty products and routines, see Fenja Gunn, *The Artificial Face: A History of Cosmetics* (Newton Abbot: David and Charles, 1973), 109–29; Neville Williams, *Powder and Paint: A History of the Englishwoman's Toilet, Elizabeth I–Elizabeth II* (London: Longmans, Green and Co., 1957), 38–75; Aileen Ribeiro, *The Female Face in the Tate's British Collection 1569–1876* (London: The Gallery, 1987), 3–6.

19 A fashionable woman would often host gatherings whilst she was at her 'toilette'. To be invited into a dressing room and be present whilst a woman was at her 'toilette' served as an indication of a privileged connection. This practice is satirized by Hogarth in the third painting of his series *Marriage-a-la-Mode*. See also *The Ladies Dressing-Room Unlock'd; and her Toilette Spread* (1700). Examples of fashionable women hosting 'toilettes' are given in Williams, *Powder*, 57–60.

20 *The Connoisseur* noted that 'the vigils of the card-table have spoiled many a good face', *The Connoisseur* for 12 December 1754, 46, 272. An example of the perceived links between 'beauty' and 'luxury' is offered in *The Lady's Toilette* (1808), 33–4. For the notion of artificial 'beauty' as a 'French curse', see *The World* for 2 January 1755, 209. 'Foreign arts' and the association between make-up and a corruptive, immoral French influence is also explicit in *Beauty: A Poetical Essay* (1766). Many earlier tracts also denounced the use of make-up as irreligious. See, for example, *A Discourse of Beauty, in Point of Conscience between Two Ladies* (1692).

21 *The World*, 2 January 1755, 213.

22 Ilchester and Stavordale (eds), *Lady Sarah Lennox*, 182.

23 Diary of Lady Mary Coke, 1766 in Home (ed.), *Lady Mary Coke*, i. 61. The rumoured marriage never took place. Miss Sackville eventually married Sackville Tufton, 7th Earl of Thanet, a year later. Sir Francis Molyneux died unmarried.

24 BRO, WPP, L30/9a/6/79, Jemima, Marchioness Grey to Catherine Talbot, 25 April 1752.

25 Letter from Horace Walpole to Sir Horace Mann, 31 August 1751, in Lewis (ed.), *Walpole's Letters* xx. 272.

26 Letter from Horace Walpole to Sir Horace Mann, 18 June 1751, in Lewis (ed.), *Walpole's Letters*, xx. 258.

27 Letter from Mary Delany to Mrs Dewes, 22 February 1755, in Lady Llanover (ed.), *The Autobiography and Correspondence of Mrs Delany*, 2 vols (London: Richard Bentley, 1862), 335.

28 Jones, *Gender and the Formation of Taste*, 134–6.

29 Horace Walpole to Sir Horace Mann, 28 October 1752, in Lewis (ed.), *Walpole's Letters*, xx. 338.

30 Jones, *Gender and the Formation of Taste*, 131–2.

31 Jesse, *George Selwyn*, 114.

32 Jesse, *George Selwyn*, 115.

33 Fanny Burney to Mrs Delany, quoted in Hugh Stokes, *The Devonshire House Circle* (London: Herbert Jenkins, 1917), 75.

34 *London Chronicle*, 3–5 September 1776.

35 *Morning Post and Daily Advertiser*, 2 October 1776.

36 *The Man of Pleasure's Pocket-Book or the Bon Vivant's Vade Mecum, for the year 1780, being the Universal Companion in every Line of Taste Gallantry and Haut Ton* (1780).

37 *Gazetteer and New Daily Advertiser*, 14 June 1793; *Woodfall's Register*, June 1793.

38 Stella Tillyard, *Aristocrats: Caroline, Emily, Louisa and Sarah Lennox 1740–1832* (London: Vintage, 1995), 121–2.

39 Tillyard, *Aristocrats*, 171.

40 Colwyn Edward Vulliamy, *Aspasia: The Life and Letters of Mary Granville, Mrs Delany 1700–1788* (London: Geoffrey Bles, 1935), 86. The Duchess of Queensbury was 42 when Mrs Delany celebrated her 'beauty' in these terms, suggesting that the association between 'beauty' and 'airs' enabled the accolade to be attributed to women regardless of age. Even when the Duchess was 76 Mrs Delany still maintained her to be 'beautiful'.

41 Edmund Morris (ed.), *The Letters of Mary Lepel, Lady Hervey* (1821), xi.

42 Lord Chesterfield to his son, 22 October 1750, in David Roberts (ed.), *Lord Chesterfield's Letters* (Oxford: Oxford University Press, 1998), 207.

43 Robert Halsband (ed.), *The Complete Letters of Lady Mary Wortley Montagu*, 3 vols (Oxford: Clarendon Press, 1965–7), ii. 67; Lady Constance Charlotte Elisa Russell, *Three Generations of Fascinating Women and Other Sketches from Family History* (London: Longmans & Co., 1904), 180.

44 *Dr. Johnson's English Dictionary* (London, 1799), vol. i.

45 *Morning Post and Daily Advertiser*, 2 October 1776.

46 *Gazeteer and New Daily Advertiser*, 14 June 1793; *Woodfall's Register*, June 1793.

47 *London Chronicle*, 3–5 September 1776.

48 *The Man of Pleasure's Pocket-Book or the Bon Vivant's Vade Mecum, for the year 1780, being the Universal Companion in every Line of Taste Gallantry and Haut Ton* (1780).

Chapter 6

1 Theophilus Christian Esq (pseud.) [John Owen], *The Fashionable World Displayed* (1804), 12–13. John Owen (1766–1822) was the son of a London jeweller who became a curate and secretary of the British and Foreign Bible Society. He published a number of religious and moral tracts. His daughter married William Wilberforce.

2 Daniel Defoe, *Roxana: The Fortunate Mistress* (1724; Oxford: Oxford University Press, 2008); Frances Burney, *Evelina: Or the History of Young Lady's Entrance into the World* (1778; Oxford: Oxford University Press, 2008).

3 Anon., *A View of the Beau Monde: or, Memoirs of Celebrated Coquetilla. A real History in which is interspersed the amours of several persons of quality and distinction. By a person of distinction* (1731).

4 N. Dralloc, *The Life and Extraordinary Adventures of James Molesworth Hobart, alias Henry Griffin, alias Lord Massey, the Newmarket Duke of Ormond etc* (1794); *Old Bailey Proceedings Online* December 1792, trial of Henry Griffin, t17921215-121; *Old Bailey Proceedings Online* April 1723, trial of Alexander Day, t17230424-43.

5 Extract from letter written by Lady Charlotte Campbell, reprinted in John Douglas Sutherland Campbell, Duke of Argyll (ed.), *Intimate Society Letters of the Eighteenth Century*, 2 vols (London: Stanley Paul & Co., 1910), ii. 655, quoted by Hall Witt, *Fashionable Acts*, 60. For example, in 1738, the Earl of Bristol demanded that his youngest son end his 'inexcusable folly' and 'extravagancies' of London life. Rather than keeping himself and his wife 'in the fashion', the Earl demanded that the family instead retired 'to some cheap country'. SRO (Bury), HFA, 941/46/11, Earl of Bristol to Rt. Hon. Henry Hervey, 21 June 1738.

6 See, for example, diary entry for September 1721 in Saville (ed.), *Secret Comment*, 2.

7 Since then the V&A has acquired some pieces, including a silver gilt dish and ewer purchased from a Sotheby's sale in 1963. In November 2010, an export bar was placed on a silver cistern that had formed part of the Strafford service and was being sold through Sotheby's. With support from heritage and art funds this important piece was acquired by Temple Newsam House in October 2011.

8 Diary of Lady Mary Campbell Coke for July 1768, in Home (ed.), *Lady Mary Coke*, ii. 440.

9 Home (ed.), *Lady Mary Coke*, iii. 495.

10 Home (ed.), *Lady Mary Coke*, iii. 495.

11 Tillyard, *Aristocrats*, 263–88.

12 Diary of Lady Mary Campbell Coke for February 1769, Home (ed.), *Lady Mary Coke*, iii. 495.

13 Tillyard, *Aristocrats*, 263–88.

14 Tillyard, *Aristocrats*, 288–9. Only many years later, when she was completely alone on the estate, did she venture to invite her close friend Lady Susan

O'Brien to visit her there. See Sarah Lennox to Susan O'Brien, 20 November 1777, in Ilchester and Stavordale (eds), *Lady Sarah Lennox*, i. 259.

15 Lady Sarah Lennox to Lady Susan O'Brien, 14 May 1781, in Ilchester and Stavordale (eds), *Lady Sarah Lennox*, i. 323.

16 Tillyard, *Aristocrats*, 291.

17 Lady Sarah Lennox to Lady Susan O'Brien, November 1778, in Ilchester and Stavordale (eds), *Lady Sarah Lennox*, 278.

18 Lady Susan O'Brien to Lady Sarah Lennox, May 1781, in Ilchester and Stavordale (eds), *Lady Sarah Lennox*, ii. 12–13.

19 Lady Sarah Napier to Lady Susan O'Brien, 25 March 1783, in Ilchester and Stavordale (eds), *Lady Sarah Lennox*, ii. 34.

20 Tillyard, *Aristocrats*. She was reputed to have had affairs with Frederick Howard, 5th Earl of Carlisle, and Armand-Louis de Gontaut, Duc de Lauzun. See Rosemary Richey, 'Napier, Lady Sarah (1745–1826)', *Oxford Dictionary of National Biography* (Oxford: Oxford University Press, 2004); online edn, January 2008.

21 Tillyard, *Aristocrats*.

22 *Whitehall Evening Post or London Intelligencer*, London, 17–19 January 1769.

23 Newspapers often reported the extravagant attire worn by Derby and his servants. For example, 'Lord Derby's Coachman and Footmen with their red Feathers, and Flame-coloured Silk Stockings looked like so many Male figurantes taken from behind the Scenes of the Opera House.' *St James's Chronicle or the British Evening Post*, 3–5 June 1777.

24 Extensive reports of the spectacle and its cost were widely circulated in the press. There was some suggestion that the information was fed to the papers by Stanley himself. See, for example, *General Evening Post*, London, 9–11 June 1774; *St James's Chronicle or the British Evening Post*, London, 9–11 June 1774; *London Evening Post*, London, 11–14 June 1774; *Gazetteer and New Daily Advertiser*, London, 13 June 1774; *General Evening Post*, London, 14–16 June 1774. Some contemporaries clearly felt the extravagant celebrations were bordering on the ridiculous. 'The company at the *fête champêtre*,' noted Elizabeth Carter, 'were exceedingly amused by their entertainment…But there was a strange kind of exhibition, in compliment to Lady B[etty] H[amilton], which I find was thought absurd and indelicate; so poor Lord Stanley, with all his cost and trouble, has proved, like many others "*dedecorum pretiosus emptor*." I hear, however, that he denies having any share himself in the contrivance of the druid and the epithalamium.' Letter from Elizabeth Carter to Elizabeth Robinson Montagu, 21 June 1774.

25 Bleackley, *Beautiful Duchess*, 254.

26 BRO, WPP, L30/14/333/96, Frederick Robinson to Thomas Robinson, 19 May 1778.

27 BRO, WPP, L30/14/333/150, Frederick Robinson to Thomas Robinson, 8 December 1778.

28 Lady Sarah Lennox to Lady Susan O'Brien, February 1779, in Ilchester and Stavordale (eds), *Lady Sarah Lennox*, 290–1.
29 BRO, WPP, L30/11/122/186, Jemima, Marchioness Grey to Amabel, Lady Polwarth, 25 December 1778.
30 Newspaper reports suggest that she went first to Switzerland, and later to Austria and Italy. See, for example, *Morning Post and Daily Advertiser*, London, 3 June 1780; *Public Advertiser*, London, 14 February 1782; *Morning Herald and Daily Advertiser*, London, 8 May 1782; *Whitehall Evening Post*, 7 January 1783.
31 'Lady Derby since her return to England has resided with her mother, the Duchess of Argyle, near Windsor, many attempts have been made to bring about a reconciliation between her ladyship and the Earl, which have hitherto been rendered ineffectual by Mrs A-d for whom his lordship has so great a consideration and so violent a fondness.' *Morning Post and Daily Advertiser*, 4 August 1779.
32 TNA, Leveson Gower papers, PRO 30/29/4/1, fo. 37, from Lady Mary Coke to Lady Susan Stewart, 26 February 1780.
33 BRO, WPP, L30/11/123/78, Jemima, Marchioness Grey to her daughter, 6 March 1780.
34 Reprinted in Bleackley, *Beautiful Duchess*, 282.
35 *Public Advertiser*, 12 January 1783.
36 *Morning Herald and Daily Advertiser*, 18 January 1783; *Public Advertiser*, 18 January 1783.
37 *General Evening Post*, London, 22 May 1783; *Morning Post and Daily Advertiser*, 30 June 1783; *Public Advertiser*, 2 July 1783.
38 *Morning Herald and Daily Advertiser*, 12 April 1784.
39 BL, Althorp papers, Add. MS 75610, Caroline Howe to Lady Spencer, 10 April 1764.
40 BL, Althorp papers, Add. MS 75670, George Villiers to Lady Spencer, 10 April 1764.
41 BL, Althorp papers, Add. MS 75670, George Villiers to Lady Spencer, 10 April 1764.
42 Tillyard, *Aristocrats*, 187–8.
43 BL, Holland House papers, Add. MS 51360, 'The Journal of Lady Susan O'Brien' (1770–1810).
44 'The Journal of Lady Susan O'Brien'. See diary entries for 1810 where Lady O'Brien sets out her disappointment with London and explains the move to Kent. Many entries relating to time spent in London reveal their discomfort, for example on 30 January 1801 she noted 'much of this month has been unpleasant—we feel our circumstances disagreeably'.
45 Lady Spencer to Georgiana, Duchess of Devonshire, 19 October 1798, in Earl of Bessborough (ed.), *Georgiana: Extracts from the Correspondence of Georgiana, Duchess of Devonshire* (London: Murray, 1955), 202.

46 The Tory Duchess of Gordon took her place as London's 'leading political hostess', see Foreman, *Georgiana*, 296.
47 The following details are taken from *Old Bailey Proceedings Online*, April 1723, trial of Alexander Day, t17230424-43 and William Jackson, *The New and complete Newgate calendar, or, villainy displayed in all its branches* (1795), i. 326.
48 *London Journal*, 16 March 1723. The case was widely reported. See also *Daily Post*, 11 March 1723; *Daily Journal*, 29 April 1723; *British Journal*, 4 May 1723; *Weekly Journal or Saturday's Post*, 4 May 1723.
49 *Daily Journal*, 15 May 1723; *British Journal*, 18 May 1723; *Evening Post*, 18 May 1723; *London Journal*, 18 May 1723.
50 *London Journal*, 20 December 1729.
51 The details of Hobart's history are taken from N. Dralloc, *The Life and Extraordinary Adventures of James Molesworth Hobart, alias Henry Griffin, alias Lord Massey, the Newmarket Duke of Ormond etc* (1794) and *Old Bailey Proceedings Online*, December 1792, trial of Henry Griffin, t17921215-121.
52 Of course, there is always the possibility that these newspapers refer to Hobart masquerading as 'Lord Massey' rather than to the real Lord Massy. Further research would be required to track Massy's actual movements but visits to Bath and London would seem likely for an unmarried young heir who had recently succeeded to an estate and was perhaps scouting the marriage market.
53 Detailed descriptions of Hobart's attire appeared in notices printed by the bank in the newspapers, offering a reward of £40 for information about the criminal. See, for example, *Morning Post and Daily Advertiser*, 20 October 1791.
54 *London Chronicle*, 17 November 1791.
55 *Lloyds Evening Post*, 10 October 1791.
56 *Morning Chronicle*, 12 October 1791.
57 *St James's Chronicle or the British Evening Post*, 3 November 1791.
58 'The History of Hubbard, Lord Massey etc', in *Anecdotes, bon mots, traits, stratagems, and biographical sketches of the most remarkably highwaymen, swindlers and other daring adventurers* (1797).
59 *St James's Chronicle or the British Evening Post*, 14 February 1793.

Conclusion

1 *The World*, 151, 20 November 1755, 51.
2 Lewis, *Sacred to Female Patriotism*, 191.
3 Edward P. Thompson, 'Patrician Society, Plebeian Culture', *Journal of Social History*, 7 (Summer 1974), 389.
4 Leslie Mitchell, for example, describes 'le monde' as essentially 'a hermetically sealed world of close friendships' consisting exclusively of Fox's friends and supporters. Leslie Mitchell, *Charles James Fox* (Oxford: Oxford University

Press, 1992), 94. For more on the late eighteenth-century Whigs as the leaders of fashionable society, see Leslie Mitchell, *Whig World: 1760-1837* (London: Hambledon, 2005); Foreman, *Georgiana*, especially 22-62; P. Mandler, *Aristocratic Government in the Age of Reform: Whigs and Liberals, 1830-1852* (Oxford: Oxford University Press, 1990), 13, 16-22.

5 Davidoff, *Best Circles*.
6 Davidoff, *Best Circles*, 19.
7 Marjorie Morgan, *Manners, Morals and Class in England 1774-1858* (Basingstoke: Macmillan, 1994), 19.
8 Hall Witt, *Fashionable Acts*, 230-1.
9 Jonathan Conlin, 'Vauxhall Revisited: The Afterlife of a London Pleasure Garden', *Journal of British Studies*, 45/4 (2006), 718-43.
10 Davidoff, *Best Circles*, 26-8.
11 Morgan, *Manners Morals and Class*, 27-30.
12 Nancy W. Ellenberger, 'The Transformation of London "Society" during Victoria's Reign: Evidence from the Court Presentation Records', *Albion* (Winter 1990), 633-53.
13 Morgan, *Manners Morals and Class*, 29.

Appendix

1 In a survey of thirty dictionaries published between 1700 and 1830, only five included 'beau monde'.
2 Samuel Johnson, *A Dictionary of the English Language*, 2 vols (1755).
3 *The World*, 101, 5 December 1754 (1823).
4 Johnson, *A Dictionary of the English Language*.
5 *Barclays Universal Dictionary* (1800). Webster's Dictionary aimed at an American market followed suit with a similar emphasis on high rank, although more broadly defined, listing 'fashion' as 'genteel life or good breeding' and 'genteel company'. Noah Webster, *An American Dictionary of the English Language* (5th edn, 1830).
6 Webster, *An American Dictionary of the English Language*.
7 Delarivier Manley, *Letters from Mrs Manley* (1696), 12.
8 Colley Cibber, *Loves Last Shift, or, The Fool in Fashion: A Comdey: as it is acted at the Theatre Royal by his Majestys Servants* (1696), Act II, Scene 1, 21.
9 Sir George Etherege, *The Man of Mode, or Sir Fopling Flutter A Comedy: Acted at the Duke's Theatre* (1676), 51; Mary Pix, *The Beau Defeated, or The Lucky Younger Brother A Comedy As it is Now Acted by His Majesty's Servants at the New Theatre in Lincolns Inn Fields* (1700). For specific use of 'beau monde' in these places see, Etherege, *Man of Mode*, 51.
10 Cynthia Wall, *The Literary and Cultural Spaces of Restoration London* (Cambridge: Cambridge University Press, 1998).
11 For example, Samuel Foote, *Taste* (1752) and *The Maid of Bath* (1772); Richard Brinsley Sheridan, *The Rivals* (1775), *A Trip to Scarborough* (1777), and *The*

School for Scandal (1777); Hannah Cowley, *Who's The Dupe?* (1779); David Garrick, *The Male Coquette or Seventeen Fifty Seven* (1757), *Bon Ton or High Life Above Stairs* (1775).

12 In *The Rivals* Fag says to Coachman, 'What the devil do you do with a wig Thomas? None of the London Whips of any Ton wear wigs now.' See Sheridan, *The Rivals*, 9. In *A Trip to Scarborough* Berinthia (played by Elizabeth Farren) says of Miss Hoyden (played by Frances Abington), 'And I doubt not [she] will soon distinguish herself in the Beau Monde.' See Sheridan, *A Trip to Scarborough*, 67.

13 Although of course it featured extensively in George Colman's prologue.

14 Garrick, *Bon Ton*, 22.

15 Russell, *Women, Sociability and Theatre*, 119–52, 195–7, 202.

16 Henry Carey, *The Beau monde: Or, the pleasures of St James's', Poems on Several Occasions* (1729). See also a later reprint, *Blunderella or the Impertinent, a Tale to Which is Added The Beau Monde or the Pleasures of St. James's a New Ballad* (1730).

17 Carey, *The Beau Monde*, 11.

18 Captain Cockade (pseud.), *The Important Triflers: A Satire Set Forth in a Journal of Pastimes a -la-Mode Among Young People of Fashion in the Spring-Season of the Year, and Address'd as a Trifle to the Polite Ladies in Town and to the Beau Monde in General* (1748).

19 *A Sketch of the Beau Monde inscribed to Charles Hastings Esq* (1764). Other examples include W. Kendrick, *The Town: A Satire* (1748) and *The Vices of the Town: A Satire* (1747).

20 Both 'The Ton' and 'Haut Ton' are bound together in Anon., *The Ton: Anecdotes Chit Chat and on Dits; Dedicated to All the Gossips* (1819).

21 'Haut Ton' in *The Ton* (1819), 14.

22 Carey (reputedly the illegitimate son of George Savile, Marquess of Halifax), poet and songwriter working in the 1720s and 1730s. He regularly composed music and lyrics for ballad operas performed at Drury Lane, some of which enjoyed long runs and considerable popular success. Indeed, we can presume that his poem *Beau Monde* was intended as a sung ballad. Yet precisely where or when it was performed (and even if it was ever performed), and how the emphases of the poem were modulated when sung, remain unclear.

23 Richard Steele, *The Tatler: The Lucubrations of Isaac Bickerstaff*, 4 vols (1709–11); D. F. Bond (ed.), *The Spectator 1711–1712*, 5 vols (Oxford: Oxford University Press, 1965).

24 In issue 490 of the *Spectator*, for instance, fashion was deemed responsible for the decline of marital values and disharmony between negligent husbands and wives. 'It is certain', 'Mr Spectator' reflected, 'that the greater Part of the Evils attending to this condition of Life [breakdown of marriage] arises from Fashion.' In contrast, the essay continued, for 'all persons who

have made good sense the rule of action, marriage is described as the state of capable of the highest human Felicity'. *The Spectator*, 490, 22 September 1712.

25 *The Spectator*, 14, 16 March 1711.

26 *The World*, 1/1.

27 *The World by AdamFitzAdam*, 95, 24 October 1754.

28 *The Connoisseur*, 44, 28 November 1754, 262.

29 *The Connoisseur*, 99, 18 December 1755, 210.

30 *Adventurer*, 1/35, 6 March 1753, 205.

31 Frances Burney, *Evelina: Or, the History of Young Lady's Entrance into the World* (1778).

32 Francis Coventry, *The History of Pompey the Little: Or, The Life and Adventures of a Lap-Dog* (1751; 1800) 98.

33 Cindy McCreery, 'Keeping up with the Bon Ton: The Tete-a-Tete Series in the *Town and Country Magazine*', in Barker and Chalus, *Gender*, 207–29; Marilyn Morris, 'Marital Litigation and English Tabloid Journalism: Crim Con in *The Bon Ton* (1791–1796)', *Journal for Eighteenth-Century Studies*, 28/1 (October 2008).

34 *The Fashionable Magazine or Lady's and Gentleman's Monthly Recorder or New Fashions Being a Compleat Universal Repository of Taste, Elegance, and Novelty for Both Sexes* (1786).

35 *Le Beau Monde or Literary and Fashionable Magazine* (1806–8).

36 Russell, *Women Sociability and Theatre*, 203.

37 BRO, WPP, L 30/14/138/8, Earl of Ossory to Thomas Robinson, 25 June 1778. Suggestively, John Tobin's comedy *The Faro Table: Or, The Guardians* was written in the 1790s but not performed at Drury Lane because one of its characters, Lady Nightshade was known to be a caricature of Lady Sarah Archer. The play was only eventually staged after Tobin's death in 1816. See Gillian Russell, 'Faro's Daughters: Female Gamesters, Politics and the Discourse of Finance in 1790s Britain', *Eighteenth-Century Studies* (2000), 33.

38 *The Morning Post*, 22 January 1785; *London Courant*, 11 February 1782.

39 Georgiana Cavendish, Duchess of Devonshire, *The Sylph: A Novel in 2 Volumes* (1779).

40 Foreman, *Georgiana*, 59.

41 Lady Anne Hamilton, *The Epics of the Ton* (1807). Her inclusion of a poem targeting 'L H' (Lady Hamilton), the authoress herself, failed to prevent her identity eventually being revealed.

42 Quoted in Alison Adburgham, *Silver Fork Society: Fashionable Life and Literature from 1814 to 1840* (London: Constable, 1983), 26.

43 Letter from Lady Holland to Mrs Creevey, 21 May 1816, in Right Hon. Sir Herbert Maxwell (ed.), *The Creevey Papers: A Selection from the Correspondence and Diaries of the Late Thomas Creevey MP*, 2 vols (London: John Murray, 1904), i. 254.

44 Marianne Spencer Hudson, *Almack's: A Novel*, 3 vols (1826); Charlotte Campbell Bury, *The Exclusives* (1830).

45 *A Key to the Royal Novel The Exclusives* (1830).

46 Lord Raby (later Earl of Stafford) to Brigadier General Cadogan (who fought triumphantly alongside the Duke of Marlborough at the Battle of Bleinheim) (24 February 1705), in James J. Cartwright (ed.), *The Wentworth Papers 1705–1709* (London: Wyman and Sons, 1883), 15.

47 Letter from Lady Mary Pierrepoint Wortley Montagu to Frances Pierrepoint, 1724, in Lord Wharncliffe (ed.), *The Letters and Works of Lady Mary Wortley Montagu*, vol. ii (London: R. Bentley, 1837), 163.

48 BRO, WPP, L30/11/123/41, Lady Mary Grey to Amabel, Lady Polwarth, Richmond, 7 November 1775.

49 BRO, WPP, L30/14/333/189, Frederick Robinson to Thomas Robinson, 2nd Baron Grantham, 19 March 1779.

50 Letter from Lady Bute to Lady Carlow, London, 13 January 1785, in Clark (ed.), *Gleanings from an Old Portfolio*, ii. 2; W. H. Dixon (ed.), *Lady Morgan's Memoirs: Autobiography, Diaries and Correspondence*, 2 vols (1862), ii. 200; Letter from Lady Sarah Napier and Lady Susan O'Brien, London, 8 August 1782, in Ilchester and Stavordale (eds), *Lady Sarah Lennox*, ii. 23; Thomas Creevey to Miss Ord, 3 May 1822, in Maxwell (ed.), *The Creevey Papers*, ii. 37.

51 Letter from Horace Walpole to Henry Seymour Conway, London, 31 October 1741, in Lewis (ed.), *Walpole's Correspondence*, xxxvii. 114.

52 For Lady Charlotte Bury, a ball was of the 'highest fashion' when populated by nobles: 'A great ball' she noted in 1810, 'Dukes of Portland, Beaufort, Earl Harrowby etc.' A. Francis Steuart (ed.), *The Diary of a Lady in Waiting by Lady Charlotte Bury, being the Diary illustrative of the times of George the 4th*, i (London: John Lane, 1908), 3.

53 Letter from Lady Harriet Cavendish to Lady Georgina Morpeth, [March 1807], in Sir George Leveson Gower and Iris Palmer (eds), *Hary-O: The Letters of Lady Harriet Cavendish, 1769–1809* (London: John Murray, 1940), 183.

54 Letter from Mary Granville Pendarves Delany to Mary Dewes Port, 23 April 1767, Sarah Chuancey Woolsey (ed.), *The Autobiography and Correspondence of Mrs Delany* (1879), ii. 118.

55 Diary of Lady Mary Campbell Coke, 23 February 1767, in Home (ed.), *Lady Mary Coke*, i. 153.

56 BL, Althorp papers, Add. MS 756000, Letter from Lavinia, Countess Spencer to Georgiana, Dowager Countess, London, 23 May 1800.

57 Diary entry for 17 December 1810 in Steuart (ed.), *Lady Charlotte Bury*, 24.

58 Birdwood (ed.), *So Dearly Loved, So Much Admired*, 2.

59 Letter from Mrs Bradshaw to Henrietta Howard, Countess of Suffolk, April 1720, in J. W. Croker (ed.), *Letters to and from Henrietta Howard, Countess of*

Suffolk, and her second husband the Hon George Berkeley; from 1712–1767 (London: John Murray, 1824), i. 49.

60 Letter from Frances Boscawen to Admiral Boscawen, London, 11 December 1747, in Cecil Aspinall-Oglander (ed.), *Admiral's Wife: Being the Life and Letters of the Hon. Mrs Edward Boscawen from 1719 to 1761* (London: Longman's, 1940), 64–5.

SELECT BIBLIOGRAPHY

Manuscripts
This list gives the location of manuscript collections consulted. In the case of very large collections, I have indicated the most relevant subsections. Full references and folio numbers relating to individual documents cited in the text can be found in the endnotes.

(i) National Archives
British Library, London
Add. MS 61997: Theatre Royal Account Book: Account book of John Dunstall, recording purchasers of seats in the boxes, pit, and galleries of the Theatre Royal, Covent Garden, 1756.

Althorp papers, especially:
Add. MS 75348: Account book of money received and spent, kept by Peter Flournoys, steward of Charles Spencer, 3rd Earl of Sunderland, covering household and personal expenses, May 1705–May 1707.
Add. MS 75358: Correspondence and papers of Richard Boyle, 3rd Earl of Burlington, 1721–41.
Add. MS 75575–97: Letters to Lady Spencer from her son, George John, 2nd Earl Spencer, 1764–1814.
Add. MS 75598–600: Letters to Lady Spencer from her daughter-in-law, Lavinia, wife of George John, 2nd Earl Spencer, 1780–1813.
Add. MS 75609: Letters from Lady Spencer to her husband, John, 1st Earl Spencer, with a diary of the days following his death, [1769?]–1783.
Add. MS 75610–67: Correspondence of Lady Spencer with Caroline, wife of John Howe, and sister of Richard, 1st Earl Howe, 1759–1814.
Add. MS 75669–82: Letters to Lady Spencer from George Bussy Villiers, 4th Earl of Jersey, 1759–1804.
Add. MS 75686: Correspondence of Lord and Lady Spencer, 1761–99.
Add. MS 75689: Letters to Lady Spencer concerning politics, from Richard Rigby, MP, and others, 1777–88.
Add. MS 75690: Letters to Lady Spencer, annotated by her 'Cavendishes. Politicks, &c', 1779–88.

Add. MS 75691: Letters from Lady Spencer to Theadora Cowper, 1754–1801.

Add. MS 75770: Rates, taxes, repairs, and furniture for Spencer House, St James's, and St James's Place, 1772–5.

Add. MS 75926–38: Letters to George, 2nd Earl Spencer from his wife, Lavinia, Countess Spencer, 1781–1830.

Add. MS 76316–28: Diaries of Lord Spencer, 1788–1806.

Add. MS 77981: Letters, bills, etc., relating to alterations to Spencer House, 1791–1847.

Add. MS 78026: Inventories of the furniture, household goods, and paintings at Althorp.

Add. MS 78031: Valuation of the contents of Spencer House and Wimbledon House, with an inventory of plate, 1834.

Barrington papers:

Add. MS 73703: Account book showing Lord Barrington's personal expenditure, 1766–70.

Add. MS 73704: Viscount Barrington's engagement diary for 1777.

Blenheim papers, especially:

Add. MS 61357: Correspondence, particularly with Sir Christopher Wren and his son, accounts, estimates, and narratives of the duchess, relating to the building and furnishing of Marlborough House, 1710–15.

Add. MS 61427–31: Correspondence and papers of Sarah, Duchess of Marlborough: Correspondence with her husband, John, 1st Duke of Marlborough, [1676?]–1715.

Add. MS 61427–56: Correspondence and papers of Sarah, Duchess of Marlborough: Family correspondence.

Add. MS 61473: Inventory of the tapestries, pictures, furniture, linen, plate, and other contents, at Blenheim Palace and Marlborough House.

Dropmore Papers, especially:

Add. MS 69285: Letters and papers of Robert Pitt and his wife Harriet Pitt, 1705–36.

Add. MS 69389: Letters to Charles Russell from his sister Fanny, woman of the bedchamber to Princess Amelia, 1743–7, and Letters to Mary Russell from Mary, Lady Talbot, mostly relating to her separation from William, Earl Talbot, 1744–63.

Egmont papers:

Add. MS 47060–71: Journals of the 1st Lord Egmont, 1730–47.

Hardwicke papers:

Add. MS 35376: Letters from Jemima, Marchioness Grey, to her husband Philip, 2nd Earl of Hardwicke, 1744–83.

Hertford papers:
Egerton MS 3263 (Eg 3263): Letters from Francis Charles, afterwards 3rd Marquess of Hertford, to his wife, 1803–23.

Holland House papers:
Add. MS 51414–16: Correspondence of 1st Lord Holland with his wife, Georgina Caroline, 1744–67.
Add. MS 51950: Holland House dinner-books, 1799–1845.
Add. MS 51360: 'The Journal of Lady Susan O'Brien' (1770–1810).

Lamb (Melbourne) papers:
Add. MS 45546–7: Correspondence of Lady Melbourne, 1805–22.

Morley papers:
Add. MS 48218: Miscellaneous family papers and correspondence of family of Parker, Barons Boringdon and Earls of Morley, of Saltram, 1648–1811.

Morgan Grenville papers, especially:
Add. MS 70963: Miscellaneous papers relating to the Grenville family, 1752–1879.
Add. MS 70964: Memorandum Book of James Brydges, Marquess of Carnarvon and later 3rd Duke of Chandos, 1752.
Add. MS 70965–82: Engagement diaries or pocket books of Lord Carnarvon, Anne Eliza, his second wife, and of their daughter Anne Elizabeth, Lady Temple and later Marchioness and Duchess of Buckingham and Chandos, [1781–1823].
Add. MS. 70992: Correspondence of the first Duke and Duchess of Buckingham and Chandos.

Newcastle papers:
Add. MS 33073–8: Correspondence between the Duke and Duchess of Newcastle, 1714–68.
Add. MS 33159: Duke of Newcastle's house-keeping and personal expenses 1764–6.

Pelham papers:
Add. MS 33159: Accompts [*sic*] of the Family of Pelham, 1555–1781.

Palmerston papers:
Add. MS 59852: Pocket-book journal of Lady Palmerston, 1791.

Portland papers:
Add. MS 70137: Account book of Sir Edward Harley, 1696–8.
Add. MS 70348: Portland papers, Account book of Elizabeth Harley, 1687–8 and of Martha Hutchins (née Harley) 1692, 1703–15, 1687–1715.

Add. MS 70350: Account book of Robert, 1st Earl of Oxford, 1723-4.
Add. MS 70465: Accounts of the 2nd Earl and Countess of Oxford, 1719-32.

Wentworth papers, especially:
Add. MS 22225: Letters of Isabella, Lady Wentworth to her son Thomas Wentworth, Earl of Strafford, 1707-29.
Add. MS 22226: Letters of Anne, Countess of Strafford, to her husband the Earl of Strafford, 1711-36.
Add. MS 22227: Letters of Peter Wentworth and Juliana his wife to the Earl of Strafford, 1706/7-1737.
Add. MS 22228-9: Miscellaneous family correspondence of the Earl of Strafford, 1707-38.
Add. MS 22257: Miscellaneous bills and accounts of Thomas and William Wentworth, Earls of Strafford, 1695-1791.
Add. MS 31145: Family correspondence of Lord Strafford, 1692-1739.
Add. MS 31150: Official and private correspondence and papers of Thomas Wentworth, Lord Raby and Earl of Strafford, 1689-1714.
Add. MS 63471: Private accounts 1703-33.
Add. MS 63474: Houses at St James's Square.

Seymour papers:
Add. MS 23728: Letters of Frances Seymour, Countess of Hertford and Duchess of Somerset, to Henrietta Knight, Lady Luxborough 1742-54.

The National Archives (TNA), Kew
Chancery Papers, Master's Exhibits:
C107/60, Master Senior's Exhibits, Woolley v. Hall, 1743-61 (includes papers and account books of Christopher Hall, carriage maker of Long Acre).
C 107/67, Master Senior's Exhibits Jackson v West, 1729-86 (includes household bills and day and account books for Holkham Hall, Norfolk).
C107/149, Master Senior's Exhibits, Cornelys v Fermor, 1760-1 (includes papers of Mrs Cornelys, manager of balls and concerts, of Soho Square).
C108/215, Master Farrer's Exhibits, Waters v Taylor, 1792-1814 (account books and lists of subscribers for King's Theatre, Haymarket).
C 108/284, Master Farrer's Exhibits, Webb v Ives, 1717-91 (includes jeweller's account books and inventories).

Family papers:
Leveson-Gower papers, especially:
PRO 30/29/1/14-17: Correspondence of 2nd Earl Gower and 1st Marquess of Stafford.

PRO 30/29/4/1–55: Correspondence of Lady Susan Stewart, Countess Gower and Marchioness of Stafford.

PRO 30/29/17/6: Correspondence of Henrietta Elizabeth, Countess Granville, to her grandmother, Georgiana, Countess Spencer.

Chatham papers, especially:

PRO 30/8/1–5: Correspondence of William Pitt, 1st Earl of Chatham, and Lady Hester (Grenville) his wife.

PRO 30/8/7–9: Letters of Lady Chatham.

PRO 30/8/11–12: Letters of William Pitt Junior, to his father and mother.

PRO/30/8/62: Letters of Earl Temple, to his sister Lady Chatham.

The National Art Library, V&A Museum

Garrick papers:

86.KK.42: Manuscript accounts of Chippendale Haig & Co for the furnishing of David Garrick's house in the Adelphi, 1771–2.

86.NN.4 (i): Bills and receipts relating to transactions by Mr and Mrs Garrick with various tradesmen, 1762–94.

86.NN.4 (ii): Inventories originally made in 1779 of the household furniture, pictures, etc. belonging to David Garrick.

86.ZZ.125: Bills for furniture, fabric, decorating etc., 1766–1818.

PC 4/3 no 5: Bills submitted by Henry Shepherd to David Garrick for various domestic items in silver 1774.

The National Library of Scotland, Edinburgh

Mure Family of Caldwell papers:

MS 4943–56: Correspondence of Elizabeth, Duchess of Hamilton.

Dukes of Hamilton papers:

MS 8286: Letters and estate papers.

MS 16714: Letters and estate papers.

MS 17612: Marriage contract of the Duchess of Hamilton and Hon. John Campbell.

Sutherland papers, especially:

Dep. 313/501: Bundle of papers of Jean Wemyss (Countess of Sutherland) including correspondence and legal papers, 1637–98.

Dep. 313/513–14 and 517–18: Miscellaneous accounts of the 15th Earl of Sutherland.

Dep. 313/545: Letters of Frances, Countess of Sutherland, to the 15th Earl, 1727–8.

Dep. 313/572–3: Correspondence of Lord and Lady Strathnaver.

Dep. 313/624: Memoranda book for Lady Strathnaver, 1750–1.

Dep. 313/716: Correspondence of Mary, Countess of Sutherland, 1760–5.

Dep. 313/740-3: General correspondence of the duchess-countess, 1789–1826 (originals now moved to Staffordshire Record Office).

Dep. 313/744: Correspondence of the duchess-countess and Frances, Lady Douglas, 1790–1811 n.d.

National Records of Scotland, Edinburgh
NRA(S) 2177: Miscellaneous papers of the Duke and Duchess of Hamilton (bundle 426, bundle 1442, bundle 2123-5, bundle 2874).

Natural History Museum Archives
SB f. D6: Miscellaneous papers of Dru Drury.

(ii) Local Archives
Bedfordshire and Luton Records and Archives, Bedford
Wrest Park [Lucas] Archive, especially,
L30/9/3/1-116: Letters of Lady Anson.

L30/9/24/1-41: Letters from Lady (Elizabeth) Carpenter (née Petty) to Marchioness Grey.

L30/9a/3-9: Letters of Jemima, Marchioness Grey to Catherine Talbot.

L30/11/121/1-41: Letters of Amabel, Lady Lucas, to her mother Jemima, Marchioness Grey.

L30/11/240: Correspondence between Amabel, Lady Lucas, Countess de Grey (1751–1833), and Mary Jemima Robinson, Baroness Grantham (1756–1830).

L30/13/12: Correspondence between Mary Jemima Robinson, Baroness Grantham (1756–1830), and Amabel, Lady Lucas, Countess de Grey (1751–1833).

L30/14: Correspondence of Thomas Robinson, 2nd Baron Grantham.

L30/15: Correspondence of Frederick Robinson.

L31/122: Account book (probably of Mary Baroness Lucas wife of 11th Earl of Kent, 1694/5).

L31/129: Account book of Henry, 12th Earl (afterwards Duke of Kent).

L31/133-43: Bills for Jemima, Marchioness Grey.

L31/225/1-2: Miscellaneous town and country bills.

L31/340/22: Miscellaneous poems.

Whitbread papers:
W3932/1-29: Diaries of Samuel Whitebread.

Orlebar papers:
OR2071/378-9: Letters from Gertrude, Duchess of Bedford, to Richard Orlebar.
OR2071/234: Rhyming letter from Lady Buck.

Birmingham University Library, Birmingham
GB 150 STA: Lady Stafford's letters 1774–1805.

Birmingham City Archives and Heritage Service, Birmingham
Archives of Soho (Matthew Boulton papers), especially
MS 378/21/10–11: Boulton scale and letter book.
MS 3782/1/14: Letter book 1782–6.
MS 3782/1/9: Letter book 1770–3.
MS 3782/8: Private books and correspondence.
MS 3782/12: Correspondence and papers of Matthew Boulton.
MS 3782/14/63: London House account books.
MS 3782/16/1: Correspondence of Mrs Ann Boulton 1759–81.

Brynmor Jones Library, University of Hull
DDBM/32/7: Letters to and from Diana Bosville.
DDBM/32/8: Letters to and from Godfrey Bosville.

Derbyshire Record Office
Wilmot Horton of Catton papers:
D1355/C3020–9: Sir R. Wilmot correspondence.
D3155 M/C3780–830: Wilmot Horton of Catton papers: correspondence.
D3155/WH 2176: Prospectus for the improvement of the fashionable circles (1827).

Fitzherbert family papers:
D239/E5099: Inventory of jewels purchased for Lady Fitzherbert at her marriage
    and to continue as heirlooms, 1791.

Essex County Record Office (Chelmsford Branch)
Orsett Hall Estate papers:
T/B 357/34: Diary of Lady Caroline Montagu (daughter of the Duke of Buccleuch),
    1803.

Guildhall Library, London
Guildhall MS 5643A: Holmes and Pyke, Coachbuilders day book 1792–7.
Guildhall MS 31621: Accounts of Thomas Blossom, coachbuilder 1808–14.

Hampshire Record Office, Winchester
Carnavon of Highclere papers:
75M91/A1: Letters from 1st Countess of Carnavon to the 1st earl, 1798.
75M91/A4: Letters from their daughter, Lady Frances Herbert.

Malmesbury papers:
9M73/G835–45: London diaries of James Harris, 1770–80.
9M73/G343: Letters of Susannah, 4th Countess of Shaftesbury, daughter of 3rd
    Earl of Gainsborough, 1735–57.
1M44/13–15: Account books of Viscountess Wallingford.

Hertfordshire Archives & Local Studies, Hertford
Panshanger papers, especially:
D/EP F 53–57: General correspondence of William 1st Earl Cowper.
D/EP F 71–9: Diaries of 1st Earl Cowper 1711–22.
D/EP F 243–4: Pocket book diaries of 2nd Earl Cowper 1752 and 1753.
D/EP F 249: General correspondence of 2nd Earl Cowper.
D/EP F 252: Family correspondence of 2nd Earl Cowper.
D/EP F 193: Correspondence between Lord Cowper and Mary Countess Cowper 1706–23.
D/EP F 194: Family correspondence of Lady Cowper.
D/EP F 203: General correspondence to Lady Cowper.

Huntingdon Library and Archives, Huntingdon
Montagu papers, especially:
DDM10/3/1–46: Letters to Millicent Sparrow (later Duchess of Manchester) 1817–22.
DDM10a/4: Letters to Millicent Sparrow 1813–20.
DDM10b/32: Manuscript notebook by Susan, Duchess of Manchester (1827), regarding her separation from the duke in 1813.
DDM21b/8: Political letters.
DDM53/1: Letters regarding the Duchess of Manchester's settlement (1795).

John Rylands Library, University of Manchester
R93692: Dorothy Richardson's journals 1770–5.

Kent History and Library Centre, Maidstone
Pratt papers
U840 C3/1–25: Letters from Sir Charles Pratt to his daughter Frances Pratt (later Lady Frances Stewart, Countess and Marchioness of Londonderry).
U840 C 7/1–19: Letters from Charles Pratt to his daughter Lady Elizabeth.
U80 C 4/1–11: Letters from Charles Pratt to Robert Stewart, later Earl and Marquess of Londonderry, his son-in-law.
U 840 C 490/1–2: Lady Frances Stewart to her brother Sir John Jeffreys.

Sackville of Knole papers
U 269 C 161: Letters to Lady Sackville 1746–80.
U 269 A14/1–4: Account books kept by Arabella Diana, Duchess of Dorset, 1798–1802.

Leicester Record Office
DG7/4/12a: Diaries of Louisa, Countess of Pomfret 1748.

London Metropolitan Archives
Villiers papers:
Acc. 510/104: Bills of Lord Villiers.
Acc. 510/157–90: General correspondence of William, 3rd Earl of Jersey, and Anne, Countess of Jersey 1733–50.
Acc. 510/191–234: Letters of Hon. Thomas Villiers to his brother, 3rd Earl of Jersey.
Acc. 510/273–332: Family correspondence of 5th Earl and Countess of Jersey and their children, 1793–1847.
Acc. 510/371–454: Various people to Lady Jersey in chronological order 1812–33.
Acc. 510/536–88: Letters to 5th Lady Jersey.
Acc. 510/589–602: Miscellaneous letters and notes.
Acc. 1128/103/1–16: Bills for Lady Harriet Villier's trousseau, 1806.
Acc. 1128/204–5: Subscription books for Almack's, 1836.
Acc 1128/248/1–16: Visiting cards.

Nottinghamshire Archives, Nottingham
DD/SR 212/10–11: Diaries of Gertrude Savile 1711–22.

North London Collegiate School
STB Box 2 (3): Letter book of Cassandra Brydges, Duchess of Chandos, 1713–35.

Royal Holloway College, Bedford Library
Vauxhall Gardens Archive: Microfiches 1–79 from Lambeth Council.

Southwark Local Studies Library
Account books of Ann, Lady Rose of Walworth, 1797–1807.
Diary of Ms De Crespigny from 1809.

Suffolk Record Office (Bury St Edmunds Branch)
Grafton papers:
HA513/4/51–80: Correspondence relating to separation of 3rd Duke of Grafton with first wife Anne 1764–5.
HA 513/4/121–30: Diaries of Elizabeth, second wife of Augustus Henry, 3rd Duke of Grafton, 1787–1812.

Hervey papers:
941/46/10–11: Letters and verses between the Earl and Countess of Bristol, 1695–1737.
941/46/4: Verses on Isabella Carr Hervey (1689–1711).
941/46/7: An imperfect sketch of Lord Bristol's character collected from several authors by the Countess of Bristol (n.d.).

941/47: Papers and correspondence of John, Lord Hervey (1696–1743).
941/50/1: Letters from Mary, Lady Hervey, to Augustus John, 3rd Earl of Bristol.

(iii) International Archives
Beinecke Library, Yale University
Osborn Collection:
d. 73: Journal of Lady Champion de Crespigny (Mary Clarke), 1750–1812.
fc. 1101/2: Letter books to Charlotte (Dyve) Clayton, Lady Sundon, 1713–31.
fc. 80: Diary of Edward Pigott, 1775–6.

Huntington Library, California
Stowe Collection, Stowe Volumes
ST vol. 26 (vols 1–2): James Brydges, 1st Duke of Chandos, Journal of my daily activities, 16 January–19 May 1697–1702.
ST vol. 44: James Brydges, 1st Duke of Chandos, Instructions to his servants at Canons, Middlesex, 1721.
ST vol. 83: James Brydges, 1st Duke of Chandos, Inventories, plans, dimensions, 1725.
ST vol. 108 (vols 1–10): Henry Brydges, 2nd Duke of Chandos, Diaries 1732–71.
ST vol. 109 (vols 1–4): James Brydges, 3rd Duke of Chandos, Diaries 1751–88.
ST vol. 153: Sir Richard Temple, London house book 1688–91.
ST vol. 440: Robert Craggs, 1st Earl Nugent, London receipt book, 1768–72.
ST vol. 458: Household accounts London furniture repair book.

Stowe Collection, Brydges
STB Box 28 (33): James Brydges, 3rd Duke of Chandos, to Lydia Catherine Brydges, Duchess of Chandos, *c*.1748.
STB Box 2 (3): Letter book, Cassandra Brydges, Duchess of Chandos, 1713–35.

Lewis Walpole library, Yale University
Manuscript letters from Lady Elizabeth Laura Waldegrave to Anne Clement.
Household book for household of Augusta, Dowager Princess of Wales (1751).
Manuscript account book of George, first Marquess Townshend [1724–1807].

Published Primary Material
(i) Published letters and diaries
E. and F. Anson (eds), *Mary Hamilton; afterwards Mrs John Dickenson, at court and at home from letters and diaries* (1925).
Cecil Aspinall-Oglander (ed.), *Admiral's Wife: Being the Life and Letters of the Hon. Mrs Edward Boscawen from 1719 to 1761* (London: Longman's, 1940).
Earl of Bessborough (ed.), *Georgiana: Extracts from the Correspondence of Georgiana, Duchess of Devonshire* (London: Murray, 1955).

Vere Birdwood (ed.), *So Dearly Loved, So Much Admired: Letters to Hester Pitt, Lady Chatham from her Relations and Friends 1744–1801* (London: HMSO, 1994).

John Douglas Sutherland Campbell, Duke of Argyll (ed.), *Intimate Society Letters of the Eighteenth Century*, 2 vols (London: Stanley Paul & Co., 1910).

James J. Cartwright (ed.), *The Wentworth Papers 1705–1709* (London: Wyman and Sons, 1883).

Mrs Godfrey Clark (ed.), *Gleanings from an Old Portfolio Containing Some Correspondence Between Lady Louisa Stuart and her Sister Caroline Countess of Portarlington and Other Friends and Relations*, 3 vols (Edinburgh, 1896).

Hon. Spencer Cowper (ed.), *Diary of Mary Countess Cowper Lady of the Bedchamber* (London: John Murray, 1864).

J. W. Croker (ed.), *Letters to and from Henrietta Howard, Countess of Suffolk, and her second husband the Hon George Berkeley; from 1712–1767* (London: John Murray, 1824).

William Hepworth Dixon (ed.), *Lady Morgan's Memoirs: Autobiography, Diaries and Correspondence*, 2 vols (London: W. H. Allen, 1862).

Katherine Euphemia Lady Farrer (ed.), *The Letters of Josiah Wedgwood*, i: *1762–1770* (Manchester: E. J. Morten [for] the Trustees of the Wedgwood Museum, 1973).

Sir George Leveson Gower and Iris Palmer (eds), *Hary-O: The Letters of Lady Harriet Cavendish, 1769–1809* (London: John Murray, 1940).

Castalia Countess Granville (ed.), *Lord Granville Leveson Gower: First Earl Granville Private Correspondence 1781–1821* (London: Murray, 1917).

James Greig (ed.), *The Diaries of a Duchess: Extracts from the Diaries of the First Duchess of Northumberland 1716–1776* (London: Hodder and Stoughton, 1926).

Lord Grenville (ed.), *Letters Written by the late Earl of Chatham [William Pitt] to his Nephew Thomas Pitt* (London: T. Payne, 1804).

Cuthbert Headlam (ed.), *The Letters of Lady Harriot Eliot 1766–1786* (Edinburgh: T. & A. Constable, 1914).

S. Herbert (ed.), *Henry, Elizabeth and George, 1734–1780: Letters and Diaries of Henry, Tenth Earl of Pembroke and his Circle* (London: Jonathan Cape, 1939).

Syndenham H. J. Hervey (ed.), *The Diary of John Hervey, First Earl of Bristol with extracts from his book of expenses 1688–1742* (Wells: Jackson, 1894).

Sydenham H. J. Hervey (ed.), *Letter Books of John Hervey, 1st Earl of Bristol with Sir Thomas Hervey's Letters During Courtship and Poems During Widowhood*, i: *1651–1715* (Wells: Jackson, 1894).

J. A. Home (ed.), *The Letters and Journals of Lady Mary Coke*, 4 vols (Edinburgh: David Douglas, 1889).

Helen Sard Hughes (ed.), *The Gentle Hertford: Her Life and Letters* (New York: Macmillan Co., 1940).

Countess of Ilchester and Lord Stavordale (eds), *The Life and Letters of Lady Sarah Lennox 1745–1826* (London: John Murray, 1901).

Earl of Ilchester (ed.), *Journal of Hon Henry Edward Fox afterwards Fourth and Last Lord Holland 1818–1830* (London: Thornton Butterworth, 1923).

John Heneage Jesse, *George Selwyn and his Contemporaries with Memoirs and Notes*, 4 vols (London: Richard Bentley, 1843).

Peter Jupp (ed.), *The Letter-Journal of George Canning 1793–1795* (London: Royal Historical Society, 1991).

J. W. Kaye (ed.), *Autobiography of Miss Cornelia Knight Lady Companion to the Princess Charlotte of Wales with extracts from her journals and anecdote books*, 2 vols (1861).

Rachel Leighton (ed.), *Correspondence of Charlotte Grenville, Lady William Wynn and her three sons: Sir Watkin Williams Wynn, Bart., Rt Hon Charles William Wynn and Sir Henry Williams Wynn, GCH KCB 1795–1832* (London: John Murray, 1920).

W. S. Lewis (ed,), *The Yale Edition of Horace Walpole's Correspondence*, 48 vols (New Haven: Yale University Press, 1937–83).

David M. Little and George M. Kahrl (eds), *The Letters of David Garrick* (Oxford: Oxford University Press, 1963).

Lady Llanover (ed.), *The Autobiography and Correspondence of Mrs Delany*, 2 vols (London: Richard Bentley, 1862).

William Matthews (ed.), *The Diary of Dudley Ryder 1715–1715* (London: Methuen & Co., 1939).

Herbert Maxwell (ed.), *The Creevey Papers: A Selection from the Correspondence and Diaries of the Late Thomas Creevey MP*, 2 vols (London: John Murray, 1904).

Right Hon. Sir Herbert Maxwell (ed.), *The Creevey Papers: A Selection from the Correspondence and Diaries of the Late Thomas Creevey MP*, 2 vols (London: John Murray, 1904).

Edmund Morris (ed.), *The Letters of Mary Lepel, Lady Hervey* (1821).

Lady Newton (ed.), *The Lyme Letters 1660–1760* (London: William Heinemann, 1925).

Mrs Rathborne (ed.), *Letters from Lady Jane Coke to her Friend Mrs Eyre at Derby 1747–1758* (London: Swann Sonnenschein, 1899).

P. Roberts (ed.), *The Diary of Sir David Hamilton, 1709–1714* (Oxford: Clarendon Press, 1975).

L. G. Robinson (ed.), *Letters of Dorothea, Princess Lieven During her Residence in London 1812–1834* (London: Longmans and Co., 1902).

Samuel Henry Romilly (ed.), *Letters to 'Ivy' from the First Earl of Dudley* (London: Longmans, Green 1905).

A. Saville (ed.) *Secret Comment: The Diaries of Gertrude Savile, 1721–1757* (Kingsbridge: Kingsbridge History Society, 1997).

Francis Steuart (ed.), *The Diary of a Lady in Waiting by Lady Charlotte Bury, being the Diary Illustrative of the Times of George the 4th*, vol. i (London: John Lane, 1908).

Virginia Surtees (ed.), *A Second Self: The Letters of Harriet Granville, 1810–45* (Norwich: Michael Russell, 1990).

Colwyn Edward Vulliamy (ed.), *Aspasia: The Life and Letters of Mary Granville, Mrs Delany 1700–1788* (London: Geoffrey Bles, 1935).

Lord Wharncliffe (ed.), *The Letters and Works of Lady Mary Wortley Montagu* (London: R. Bentley, 1837).

Hon. Mrs H. Wyndham (ed.), *Correspondence of Sarah Spencer, Lady Lyttelton 1787–1870* (1912).

(ii) Historical Manuscripts Commission (HMC) Reports

HMC Supplementary Report on the Manuscripts of his Grace the Duke of Hamilton (HMSO, 1932).

The Manuscripts of the Duke of Beaufort, KG the Earl of Donoughmore and others, HMC 12th Report, Appendix Part IX (HMSO, 1891).

The Manuscripts of the Duke of Portland at Welbeck, vol. iv (HMSO, 1897).

The Manuscripts and Correspondence of James, First Earl of Charlemont, vol. i 1745–83, HMC 12th Report, Appendix Part X (HMSO, 1891).

The Manuscripts of the Earl of Cowper at Melbourne Hall, Derbyshire, vol. ii, HMC 12th Report, Appendix Part II (HMSO, 1888).

The Manuscripts of Earl of Dartmouth, vol. ii, HMC 14th Report, Appendix Part X (HMSO, 1895).

The Manuscripts of the Duke of Rutland Preserved at Belvoir Castle, vol. ii.

HMC 12th Report, Appendix Part 5 (HMSO, 1905).

(iii) Microfilmed Collections

Aristocratic Women: The Social, Political and Cultural History of Rich and Powerful Women, Part 1 (Correspondence of Jemima, Marchioness Grey and her Circle).

Aristocratic Women: The Social, Political and Cultural History of Rich and Powerful Women, Part 2 (Correspondence and Diaries of Charlotte Georgiana, Lady Bedingfeld).

(iv) Newspapers and Periodicals

Bell's Weekly Messenger (1796–1800).

Daily Post (1719–46).

Daily Advertiser (1731–96).

Le Beau Monde or Literary and Fashionable Magazine (1806–8).

London Chronicle (1757–1800).

Morning Herald (1780–1800).

Morning Post (1773–1810).

Records of Fashion and Court Elegance by Mrs Fiske (1809–12).

The Connoisseur (1754–56).

The Fashionable Magazine or Lady's and Gentleman's Monthly Recorder or New Fashions Being a Compleat Universal Repository of Taste, Elegance, and Novelty for Both Sexes (1786).

The Lady's Magazine (1770–1837).
The St James's Chronicle (1761–1800).
The Times (1785–1800).
The World (1753–56).
Westminster Journal or New Weekley Miscellany (1742–59).
Whitehall Evening Post (1746–1800).
Woodfall's Register (1789–93).

(v) Other (place of publication London unless otherwise stated)

R. Ackermann, *The Repository of the Arts, Literature, Commerce, Manufactures, Fashions and Politics* (1810–22).

Anon., *A Discourse of Beauty, in Point of Conscience between Two Ladies* (1692).

Anon., *A View of the Beau Monde: or, Memoirs of Celebrated Coquetilla. A real History in which is interspersed the amours of several persons of quality and distinction. By a person of distinction* (1731).

Anon., *Beauty and Proportion: A Poem* (1733).

Anon., *A Trip to Vauxhall or a General Satyr on the Times by Hercules MacSturdy of the County of Tiperary* (1737).

Anon. (attributed to Joseph Warton), *Ranelagh House: A Satire in Prose in the Manner of Monsieur Le Sage* (1747).

Anon., *Court and city calendar, or gentleman's register for the year 1762* (1762).

Anon., *A Sketch of the Beau Monde inscribed to Charles Hastings Esq* (1764).

Anon., *Beauty: A Poetical Essay* (1766).

Anon., *The Man of Pleasure's Pocket-Book or the Bon Vivant's Vade Mecum, for the year 1780, being the Universal Companion in every Line of Taste Gallantry and Haut Ton* (1780).

Anon., *Ambulator, or a pocket companion in a tour round London within the circuit of twenty five miles* (1793).

Anon., *A Dictionary of the English Language with an alphabetical account of the heathen deities; and a list of the cities, towns and boroughs and remarkable villages in England and Wales* (1794).

Anon., *Dictionary of Love* (1795).

Anon., *Anecdotes, bon mots, traits, stratagems, and biographical sketches of the most remarkably highwaymen, swindlers and other daring adventurers* (1797).

Anon., *The Ton: Anecdotes Chit Chat and on Dits; Dedicated to All the Gossips* (1819).

Anon., *Fashion and Folly illustrated in a series of twenty one humorous coloured engravings by William Heath* (1822).

Anon., *The Necessary Qualifications of a Man of Fashion* (1823).

Anon., *The Book of Gentility; or the Why and Because of Polite Society: By a member of 'The Beef Steak Club'* (1835).

Mary Barber, 'An Unanswerable Apology for the Rich', *Poems on Several Occasions* (1735).

Barclays Universal Dictionary (1800).

Jon Bee, Esq (pseud.) *Slang: A Dictionary of the Turf &c* (1823).

Book of Fashion: Being a Digest of the Axioms of the Celebrated Joseph Brummell (1832).

P. Boyle, *Boyle's fashionable court and country guide and town visiting directory* (1803).

Frances Burney, *Evelina: Or, the History of Young Lady's Entrance into the World* (1778).

Lady Charlotte Bury, *The Exclusives*, 3 vols (1830).

Henry Carey, *The Beau monde: Or, the pleasures of St James's', Poems on Several Occasions* (1729).

Henry Carey, *Blunderella or the Impertinent, a Tale to Which is Added The Beau Monde or the Pleasures of St. James's a New Ballad* (1730).

Cavendish, Georgiana, Duchess of Devonshire, *The Sylph: A Novel in 2 Volumes* (1779).

Theophilus Christian Esq (pseud.) [John Owen], *The Fashionable World Displayed* (1804).

Colley Cibber, *Loves Last Shift, or, The Fool in Fashion: A Comedy: as it is acted at the Theatre Royal by his Majestys Servants* (1696).

Captain Cockade (pseud.), *The Important Triflers: A Satire Set Forth in a Journal of Pastimes a-la-Mode Among Young People of Fashion in the Spring-Season of the Year, and Address'd as a Trifle to the Polite Ladies in Town and to the Beau Monde in General* (1748).

Francis Coventry, *The History of Pompey the Little: Or, The Life and Adventures of a Lap-Dog* (1751).

Hannah Cowley, *Who's The Dupe?* (1779).

Daniel Defoe, *Roxana: The Fortunate Mistress* (1724; Oxford: Oxford University Press, 2008).

N. Dralloc, *The Life and Extraordinary Adventures of James Molesworth Hobart, alias Henry Griffin, alias Lord Massey, the Newmarket Duke of Ormond etc* (1794).

Maria Edgeworth, *Tales of Fashionable Life* (1806).

George Etherege, *The Man of Mode, or Sir Fopling Flutter A Comedy: Acted at the Duke's Theatre* (1676).

Samuel Foote, *Taste* (1752).

Samuel Foote, *The Maid of Bath* (1772).

Henry Fox, *A New Dictionary in French and English containing all the French words now in use, with their different acceptations, properly explained in English according to the genuine spirit of both languages* (1769).

David Garrick, *The Male Coquette or Seventeen Fifty Seven* (1757).

David Garrick, *Bon Ton or High Life Above Stairs* (1775).

Catherine Frances Gore, *Women as they are, or the Manners of the Day* (1830).

Elizabeth Gunning, *The Man of Fashion: A Tale of Modern Times in 2 volumes by the late Miss Gunning* (London, 1815).

Lady Anne Hamilton, *The Epics of the Ton or the Glories of the Great World in 2 books* (1807).

William Hazlitt, *Table Talk or Original Essays on Men and Manners* (1821–2).

Marianne Spencer Stanhope Hudson, *Almacks: A Novel in 3 volumes* (1827).

William Jackson, *The New and complete Newgate calendar, or, villainy displayed in all its branches* (1795).

Samuel Johnson, *A Dictionary of the English Language*, 2 vols (1755).

William Lee, *The Plan of the Boxes at the Kings Theatre Hay-market with An Alphabetical List of the Subscribers for the Season 1797* (1797).

William Lee, *The Plan of the Boxes at the Kings Theatre Hay-market with An Alphabetical List of the Subscribers for the Season 1807* (1807).

Percival Leigh, *Fiddle Faddle Fashion Book and beau monde a la francaise: enriched with numerous highly coloured figures of lady-like gentlemen* (London, 1840).

Charles Pigott, *The Rights of Nobles, consisting of extracts from Pigott's political dictionary* (1795).

Mary Pix, *The Beau Defeated, or The Lucky Younger Brother A Comedy As it is Now Acted by His Majesty's Servants at the New Theatre in Lincolns Inn Fields* (1700).

Matthew Prior, *The Female Phaeton* (1718).

Richard Brinsley Sheridan, *The Rivals* (1775).

Richard Brinsley Sheridan, *The School for Scandal* (1777).

Richard Brinsley Sheridan, *A Trip to Scarborough* (1777).

Adam Smith, *The Theory of Moral Sentiments* (1st edn, 1759, 1774).

Tobias Smollet, *The Expedition of Humphrey Clinker* (1st published 1771; Oxford, Oxford University Press, 2009).

Noah Webster, *An American Dictionary of the English Language* (5th edn, New York, 1830).

Harriette Wilson, *Harriette Wilson's memoirs of herself and others* (1825).

Secondary
(i) Books

Alison Adburgham, *Silver Fork Society: Fashionable Life and Literature from 1814 to 1840* (London: Constable, 1983).

Dana Arnold, *Re-Presenting the Metropolis: Architecture, Urban Experience and Social Life in London, 1800–1840* (Aldershot: Ashgate, 2000).

Jane Ashelford, *The Art of Dress: Clothes and Society 1500–1914* (London: National Trust, 2009).

Marc Baer, *Theatre and Disorder in Late Georgian London* (Oxford: Oxford University Press, 1992).

Hannah Barker, *Newspapers, Politics and English Society 1695–1855* (London: Longman, 2000).

Hannah Barker and Elaine Chalus, *Gender in Eighteenth-Century England: Roles, Representations and Responsibilities* (Harlow: Longman, 1997).

Roland Barthes, *The Fashion System*, trans. Matthew Ward and Richard Howard (New York: Hill & Wang, 1985).

John Maurice Beattie, *The English Court in the Reign of George I* (Cambridge: Cambridge University Press, 1967).

John V. Beckett, *The Aristocracy in England 1660–1914* (Oxford: Basil Blackwell, 1986).

Maxine Berg, *Luxury and Pleasure in Eighteenth-Century Britain* (Oxford: Oxford University Press, 2005).

Maxine Berg and Helen Clifford (eds), *Consumers and Luxury: Consumer Culture in Europe 1650–1850* (Manchester: Manchester University Press, 1999).

Maxine Berg and Elizabeth Eger (eds), *Luxury in the Eighteenth Century: Debates, Desires and Delectable Goods* (Basingstoke: Palgrave Macmillan, 2003).

Ann Bermingham and John Brewer (eds), *The Consumption of Culture 1600–1800: Object, Image and Text* (London: Routledge, 1995).

Timothy C. W. Blanning, *The Culture of Power and the Power of Culture: Old Regime Europe 1660–1789* (Oxford: Oxford University Press, 2003).

Horace Bleackley, *The Story of a Beautiful Duchess* (London: John Lane, 1907).

Peter de Bolla, *The Education of the Eye: Painting, Landscape and Architecture* (Palo Alto, Calif.: Stanford University Press, 2003).

Peter Borsay, *The English Urban Renaissance: Culture and Society in the Provincial Town 1660–1770* (Oxford: Clarendon Press, 1991).

Pierre Bourdieu, *Distinction: A Social Critique of the Judgment of Taste* (1984).

John Brewer, *Party Ideology and Population Politics at the Accession of George III* (Cambridge: Cambridge University Press, 1976).

John Brewer, *The Sinews of Power: War, Money and the English State 1688–1783* (New York: Routledge, 1989).

John Brewer, *Pleasures of the Imagination: English Culture in the Eighteenth Century* (London: Harper Collins, 2000).

John Brewer and Roy Porter (eds), *Consumption and the World of Goods: Consumption and Culture in the Seventeenth and Eighteenth Centuries* (London: Routledge, 1994).

John Brewer and Susan Staves (eds), *Early Modern Conceptions of Property* (London: Routledge, 1995).

Alexander Meyrick Broadley, *The Beautiful Lady Craven* (London: John Lane, 1914).

Robert O. Bucholz, *The Augustan Court: Queen Anne and the Decline of Court Culture* (Stanford, Calif.: Stanford University Press, 1993).

Anne Buck, *Dress in Eighteenth-Century England* (London: B. T. Batsford, 1979).

Ephraim John Burford, *Royal St James's: Being a Story of Kings, Clubmen and Courtesans* (London: Hale, 1988).

M. L. Bush, *The English Aristocracy: A Comparative Synthesis* (Manchester: Manchester University Press, 1984).

David Cannadine, *Aspects of Aristocracy: Grandeur and Decline in Modern Britain* (London: Penguin, 1995).

David Cannadine, *Decline and Fall of the British Aristocracy* (New Haven: Yale University Press, 1996).

Joseph Canning and Hermann Wellenreuther (eds), *Britain and Germany Compared: Nationality, Society and Nobility in the Eighteenth Century* (Gottingen: Wallstein, 2001).

John Cannon, *Aristocratic Century: The Peerage of Eighteenth-Century England* (Cambridge: Cambridge University Press, 1984).

Philip Carter, *Men and the Emergence of Polite Society, Britain 1660–1800* (London: Longman, 2001).

Terry Castle, *Masquerade and Civilization: Carnivalesque in Eighteenth-Century English Culture and Fiction* (Stanford, Calif.: Stanford University Press, 1986).

Elaine Chalus, *Elite Women in English Political Life, c.1754–1790* (Oxford: Oxford University Press, 2005).

Edwin Beresford Chancellor, *The Private Palaces of London Past and Present* (London: Keegan, Paul and Co., 1908).

Edwin Beresford Chancellor, *The Pleasure Haunts of London during Four Centuries* (1925).

Jonathan C. D. Clark, *English Society 1688–1832: Ideology, Social Structure and Political Practice During the Ancien Regime* (Cambridge: Cambridge University Press, 1985; revised edn, 2000).

John T. Cliffe, *The World of the Country House in Seventeenth-Century England* (London: Yale University Press, 1999).

Helen Clifford, *Silver in London: The Parker and Wakelin Partnership* (London: Yale University Press, 2004).

Michele Cohen, *Fashioning Masculinity: National Identity and Language in the Eighteenth Century* (London: Routledge, 1996).

David Coke and Alan Borg, *Vauxhall Gardens: A History* (London: Yale University Press, 2011).

Linda Colley, *In Defiance of Oligarchy: The Tory Party 1714–80* (Cambridge: Cambridge University Press, 1982).

Linda Colley, *Britons: Forging the Nation 1707–1837* (London: Yale University Press, 1992).

Penelope J. Corfield, 'Class by Name and Number in Eighteenth-Century England', in Penelope J. Corfield (ed.), *Language, History and Class* (Oxford: Basil Blackwell, 1991), 101–30.

Penelope J. Corfield, *Vauxhall and the Invention of the Urban Pleasure Garden* (London: History and Social Action Publications, 2008).

Brian Cowan, 'Public Spaces, Knowledge and Sociability', in Frank Trentmann (ed.), *Oxford Handbook of History of Consumption* (Oxford: Oxford University Press, 2012).

Michael Curtin, *Propriety and Position: A Study of Victorian Manners* (London: Garland Publishing, 1987).

Leonore Davidoff, *The Best Circles: Women and Society in Victorian England* (London: Croom Helm, 1973).

Leonore Davidoff and Catherine Hall, *Family Fortunes, Men and Women of the English Middle Class 1780–1850* (London: Routledge, 1987).

John W. Derry, *Politics in the Age of Fox, Pitt and Liverpool: Continuity and Transformation* (Basingstoke: Palgrave, 2001).

Diana Donald, *The Age of Caricature: Satirical Prints in the Age of George III* (London: Yale University Press, Paul Mellon Centre for Studies in British Art, 1996).

Peter Earle, *The Making of the English Middle Class: Business, Society and Family Life in London 1660–1730* (London: Methuen, 1989).

Teri J. Edelstein (ed.), *Vauxhall Gardens* (New Haven: Yale University Press, 1983).

Norbert Elias, *The Civilizing Process: Sociogenetic and Psychogenetic Investigations* (Oxford: Blackwell, rev. edn, 1994).

Norbert Elias, *The Court Society* (Oxford: Oxford University Press, 1983).

Boris Ford (ed.), *18th Century Britain: The Cambridge Cultural History*, 9 vols (Cambridge: Cambridge University Press, 1992).

Amanda Foreman, *Georgiana, Duchess of Devonshire* (London: Harper Collins, 1998).

John Fyvie, *Wits, Beaux and Beauties of the Georgian Era* (London: John Lane, 1909).

Mark Girouard, *Life in the English Country House: A Social and Architectural History* (London: Yale University Press, 1st published 1978; new edn, 1994).

Amanda Goodrich, *Debating England's Aristocracy in the 1790s: Pamphlets, Polemics and Political Ideas* (London: Boydell and Brewer, 2005).

Harriet Guest, *Small Change: Women, Learning and Patriotism 1750–1810* (London: University of Chicago Press, 2000).

Stephen Gundle, *Glamour: A History* (Oxford: Oxford University Press, 2009).

Fenja Gunn, *The Artificial Face: A History of Cosmetics* (Newton Abbot: David and Charles, 1973).

Paul Guyer, *Values of Beauty: Historical Essays in Aesthetics* (Cambridge: Cambridge University Press, 2005).

Frances Harris, *A Passion for Government: The Life of Sarah, Duchess of Marlborough* (Oxford: Clarendon, 1991).

Tim Harris, *Party Politics under the Late Stuarts: Party Conflict in a Divided Society 1660–1715* (London: Longman, 1993).

Tim Harris, *Revolution: The Great Crisis of the British Monarchy 1685–1720* (London: Penguin, 2007).

Felicity Heal, *Hospitality in Early Modern England* (Oxford: Oxford University Press, 1990).

Julian Hoppit, *A Land of Liberty? England 1689–1727* (Oxford: Oxford University Press, 2002).

Julian Hoppit (ed.), *Parliaments, Nations and Identities in Britain and Ireland 1660–1850* (Manchester: Manchester University Press, 2003).

Margaret Hunt, *The Middling Sort: Commerce, Gender and the Family in England, 1680–1780* (Berkeley and London: University of California Press, 1996).

Jonathan I. Israel (ed.), *The Anglo-Dutch Moment: Essays on the Glorious Revolution and its Global Impact* (Cambridge: Cambridge University Press, 1991).

Muriel Jaeger, *Before Victoria: Changing Standards and Behaviour 1787–1837* (London: Chatto and Windus, 1956).

Philip Jenkins, *The Making of a Ruling Class: The Glamorgan Gentry 1640–1790* (Cambridge: Cambridge University Press, 2002).

Clyve Jones and David L. Jones (eds), *Peers, Politics and Power: The House of Lords 1603–1911* (London: Hambledon, 1986).

Gareth Stedman Jones, *Languages of Class: Studies in Working Class History, 1832–1982* (Cambridge: Cambridge University Press, 1983).

Robert W. Jones, *Gender and the Formation of Taste in Eighteenth-Century Britain: The Analysis of Beauty* (Cambridge: Cambridge University Press, 1998).

Peter Jupp, *The Governing of Britain 1688–1848: The Executive, Parliament and the People* (London: Routledge, 2006).

Heidi Kaufmann and Chris Fauke (eds), *An Uncomfortable Authority: Maria Edgeworth and her Contexts* (Newark, NJ: University of Delaware Press, 2004).

Matthew J. Kinservik, *Sex, Scandal and Celebrity in Late Eighteenth-Century England* (Basingstoke: Palgrave, 2007).

James Kirwan, *Beauty* (Manchester: Manchester University Press, 1999).

Lawrence Klein, *Shaftesbury and the Culture of Politeness: Moral Discourse and Cultural Politics in Early Eighteenth-Century England* (Cambridge: Cambridge University Press, 1994).

Henrik Knif, *Gentlemen and Spectators: Studies in Journals, Opera and the Social Scene in Late Stuart London* (Helsinki: Finnish Historical Society, 1995).

David Kuchta, *The Three-Piece Suit and Modern Masculinity: England, 1550–1850* (London: University of California Press, 2002).

Mark Laird and Alicia Weisberg-Roberts (eds), *Mrs Delany and her Circle* (New Haven: Yale University Press, 2009).

Paul Langford, *Public Life and Propertied Englishmen, 1689–1798* (Oxford: Clarendon, 1991).

Paul Langford, *A Polite and Commercial People: England 1727–1783* (Oxford: Oxford University Press, 1992).

Judith Schneid Lewis, *In the Family Way: Childbearing in the British Aristocracy 1760–1860* (New Brunswick, NJ: Rutgers University Press, 1986).

Judith Schneid Lewis, *Sacred to Female Patriotism* (London: Routledge, 2003).

James J. Lynch, *Box, Pit and Gallery: Stage and Society in Johnson's London* (Berkeley and Los Angeles: University of California Press, 1953).

Cindy McCreery, *The Satirical Gaze: Prints of Women in Late Eighteenth-Century England* (Oxford: Clarendon, 2004).

Neil McKendrick, John Brewer, and J. H. Plumb (eds), *The Birth of a Consumer Society: The Commercialization of Eighteenth-Century England* (London: Europa, 1982).

Simon McVeigh, *Concert Life in London from Mozart and Haydn* (Cambridge: Cambridge University Press, 1993).

Erin Mackie (ed.), *The Commerce of Everyday Life: Selections from the Tatler and Spectator* (London: Macmillan, 1997).

Erin Mackie, *Market a la Mode: Fashion, Commodity and Gender in The Tatler and The Spectator* (Baltimore: Johns Hopkins University Press, 1997).

Peter Mandler, *Aristocratic Government in the Age of Reform: Whigs and Liberals, 1830–1852* (Oxford: Clarendon, 1990).

Peter Mandler, *The Fall and Rise of the Stately Home* (London: Yale University Press, 1997).

James van Horn Melton, *The Rise of the Public in Enlightenment Europe* (Cambridge: Cambridge University Press, 2001).

George E. Mingay, *English Landed Society in the Eighteenth Century* (London: Routledge, 1963).

Jane Moody, *Illegitimate Theatre in London 1770–1840* (Cambridge: Cambridge University Press, 2000).

Marjorie Morgan, *Manners, Morals and Class in England 1774–1858* (Basingstoke: Macmillan, 1994).

Gerald Newman, *The Rise of English Nationalism: A Cultural History 1740–1830* (New York: St Martins, 1997).

Allardyce Nicoll, *The Garrick Stage: Theatres and Audience in the Eighteenth Century* (Manchester: Manchester University Press, 1980).

Felicity Nussbaum, *Rival Queens: Actresses, Performance and the Eighteenth Century* (Philadelphia: University of Pennsylvania Press, 2010).

Miles Ogborn, *Spaces of Modernity: London's Geographies 1680–1780* (NewYork: Guilford Press, 1998).

Frank O'Gorman, 'Eighteenth-Century England as an *Ancien Regime*', in Stephen Taylor, Richard Connors, and Clyve Jones (eds), *Hanoverian Britain and Empire: Essays in Memory of Philip Lawson* (Woodbridge: Boydell Press, 1998), 23–36. Clarissa Campbell Orr (ed.), *Queenship in Britain* (Manchester: Manchester University Press, 2009).

Francette Pacteau, *The Symptom of Beauty* (London: Reaktion, 1994).

William Pedicord, *The Theatrical Public in the Time of Garrick* (Carbondale, Ill.: Southern Illinois University Press, 1966).

Steven Pincus, *1688: The First Modern Revolution* (New Haven: Yale University Press, 2009).

Marcia Pointon, *Brilliant Effects: A Cultural History of Gems Stones and Jewellery* (London: Yale University Press, 2010).

Marcia Pointon, *Hanging the Head: Portraiture and Social Formation in Eighteenth-Century England* (New Haven: Yale University Press, 1993).

Marcia Pointon, *Strategies for Showing: Women, Possessions and Representation in English Visual Culture 1650–1800* (Oxford: Oxford University Press, 1997).

Roy Porter, *English Society in the Eighteenth Century* (Harmondsworth: Penguin, 1982).

Roy Porter, *London: A Social History* (Cambridge, Mass.: Harvard University Press, 1998).

Martin Postle (ed.), *Joshua Reynolds and the Creation of Celebrity* (London: Tate Publishing, 2005).

Elizabeth Prettejohn, *Beauty and Art: 1750–2000* (Oxford: Oxford University Press, 2005).

Curtis Alexander Price, Judith Milhous, and Robert D. Hume, *Italian Opera in Late Eighteenth-Century London*, i: *The King's Theatre Haymarket 1778–1791* (Oxford: Oxford University Press, 1995).

Kate Retford, *The Art of Domestic Life: Family Portraiture in Eighteenth-Century England* (New Haven: Yale University Press, 2006).

Kimberley D. Reynolds, *Aristocratic Women and Political Society in Victorian Britain* (Oxford: Oxford University Press, 1998).

Aileen Ribeiro, *Dress and Morality* (London: Batsford, 1986).

Aileen Ribeiro, *The Female Face in the Tate's British Collection 1569–1876* (London: The Gallery, 1987).

Aileen Ribeiro, *The Art of Dress: Fashion in England and France, 1750–1820* (New Haven: Yale University Press, 1995).

Aileen Ribeiro, *Facing Beauty: Painted Women and Cosmetic Art* (London: Yale University Press, 2011).

John Riley, *Rowlandson's Drawings from the Paul Mellon Collection* (New Haven: Yale Centre for British Art, 1978).

Joseph Roach, *It* (Chicago: University of Michigan Press, 2007).

Jane Roberts and Christopher Lloyd (eds), *George III and Queen Charlotte: Patronage, Collecting and Royal Taste* (London: Royal Collection, 2004).

Daniel Roche, *The Culture of Clothing: Dress and Fashion in the 'Ancien Regime'*, trans. J. Birrell (Cambridge: Cambridge University Press, 1989).

George F. E. Rudé, *Hanoverian London: 1714–1808* (London: Sutton Publishing, 2003).

Gillian Russell, *The Theatres of War: Performance, Politics and Society 1793–1815* (Oxford: Clarendon Press, 1995).

Gillian Russell, *Women, Sociability and Theatre in Georgian London* (Cambridge: Cambridge University Press, 2007).

Gillian Russell and Clara Tuite (eds), *Romantic Sociability: Social Networks and Literary Culture in Britain 1770–1840* (Cambridge: Cambridge University Press, 2002).

Mollie Sands, *Invitation to Ranelagh 1742–1803* (London: J. Westhouse, 1946).

John Sekora, *Luxury: The Concept in Western Thought, Eden to Smollett* (1977).

Kevin Sharpe, *Remapping Early Modern England: The Culture of Seventeenth-Century Politics* (Cambridge: Cambridge University Press, 2000).

Francis H. W Sheppard (ed.), *Survey of London, Volumes 29 and 30: St James's Westminster part 1*, 78–81 and *Survey of London, Volumes 29 and 30: St James's Westminster part 2* (London: English Heritage, 1960).

David S. Shields, *Civil Tongues and Polite Letters in British America* (Chapel Hill, NC: University of North Carolina Press, 1997).

John Smail, *The Origins of Middle-Class Culture: Halifax, Yorkshire 1660–1780* (Ithaca, NY: Cornell University Press, 1994).

Hannah Smith, *The Georgian Monarchy* (Cambridge: Cambridge University Press, 2006).

Woodruff D. Smith, *Consumption and the Making of Respectability 1600–1800* (London: Routledge, 2002).

R. Malcolm Smuts, *Court Culture and the Origins of a Royalist Tradition in Early Stuart England* (Philadelphia: University of Pennsylvania Press, 1999).

Michael Snodin and John Styles (eds), *Design and the Decorative Arts: Britain 1500–1800* (London: V&A Publications, 2001).

David Solkin, *Painting for Money: The Visual Arts and the Public Sphere in Eighteenth-Century England* (London: Yale University Press, 1993).

Patricia Meyer Spacks, *Gossip* (New York: Alfred A. Knopf, 1985).

William Arthur Speck, *Reluctant Revolutionaries: Englishmen and the Revolution of 1688* (Oxford: Oxford University Press, 1988).

Rachel Stewart, *The Town House in Georgian London* (London: Yale University Press, Paul Mellon Centre, 2009).

Hugh Stokes, *The Devonshire House Circle* (London: Herbert Jenkins, 1917).

Lawrence Stone, 'The Residential Development of the West End of London in the Seventeenth Century', in Barbara C. Malament (ed.), *After the Reformation: Essays in Honor of J. H. Hexter* (Manchester: Manchester University Press, 1980), 167–214.

Lawrence Stone and Jeanne C. Fawtier Stone, *An Open Elite? England 1540–1880* (Oxford: Clarendon, 1986).

Christopher Storrs (ed.), *The Fiscal-Military State in Eighteenth-Century Europe: Essays in Honour of P. G. M Dickinson* (Farnham: Ashgate, 2009).

John Styles, *Dress of the People: Everyday Fashion in Eighteenth-Century England* (London: Yale University Press, 2007).

John Styles and Amanda Vickery (eds), *Gender, Taste and Material Culture in Britain and North America 1700–1830* (London: Yale University Press, 2007).

John Summerson, *Georgian London* (London: Pimlico, 1st published 1962; revised edn, 1991).

Christopher Simon Sykes, *Private Palaces: Life in the Great London Houses* (London: Chatto and Windus, 1985).

Daniel Szechi, *The Jacobites: Britain and Europe 1688 to 1788* (Manchester: Manchester University Press, 1994).

Ingrid Tague, *Women of Quality: Accepting and Contesting Ideas of Femininity in England* (London: Boydell and Brewer, 2002).

Edward P. Thompson, *The Making of the English Working Class* (Harmondsworth: Penguin, 3rd edn, 1980).

Edward P. Thompson, *Customs in Common: Studies in Traditional Popular Culture* (Merlin Press, 1991).

Francis M. L. Thompson, *English Landed Society in the Nineteenth Century* (London: Routledge, 1961).

Francis M. L. Thompson, *Gentrification and the Enterprise Culture: Britain 1780–1980* (Oxford: Oxford University Press, 2001).

Stella Tillyard, *Aristocrats: Caroline, Emily, Louisa and Sarah Lennox 1740–1832* (1995).

John Timbs, *Clubs and Club Life in London* (London: Chatto and Windus, 1899).

Edward Vallance, *The Glorious Revolution: 1688 and Britain's Fight for Liberty* (London: Abacus, 2006).

Thorstein Veblen, *Theory of the Leisure Class: An Economic Study of Institutions* (New York: Macmillan, 1899).

Amanda Vickery, *The Gentleman's Daughter: Women's Lives in Georgian England* (London: Yale University Press, 1998).

Amanda Vickery (ed.), *Women, Privilege and Power: British Politics 1750 to the Present* (Cambridge: Cambridge University Press, 2001).

Amanda Vickery, *Behind Closed Doors: At Home in Georgian England* (London: Yale University Press, 2009).

Dror Wahrman, *Imagining the Middle Class: The Political Representation of Class in Britain c.1780–1840* (Cambridge: Cambridge University Press, 1992).

Cynthia Wall, *The Literary and Cultural Spaces of Restoration London* (Cambridge: Cambridge University Press, 1998).

E. A. Wasson, *Born To Rule: British Political Elites* (Stroud: Sutton, 2000).

Rachel Weil, *Political Passions Gender, the Family and Political Argument in England 1680–1714* (Manchester: Manchester University Press, 1999).

Terence Hanbury White, *The Age of Scandal: An Excursion Through a Minor Period* (London: Jonathan Cape, 1950).

Susan Whyman, *Sociability and Power in Late-Stuart England: The Cultural World of the Verneys 1660–1720* (Oxford: Oxford University Press, 1999).

David Wilkinson, *The Duke of Portland: Politics and Party in the Age of George III* (New York: Palgrave Macmillan, 2003).

Jennifer Hall Witt, *Fashionable Acts: Opera and Elite Culture 1780–1880* (Durham, NH: University of New Hampshire, 2007).

Naomi Wolf, *The Beauty Myth: How Images of Beauty are Used Against Women* (London: Chatto and Windus, 1990).

Susan Wollenberg and Simon McVeigh (eds), *Concert Life in Eighteenth-Century Britain* (Aldershot: Ashgate, 2004).

Ian Woodfield, *Opera and Drama in Eighteenth-Century London: The King's Theatre, Garrick and the Business of Performance* (Cambridge: Cambridge University Press, 2001).

Warwick Wroth, *The London Pleasure Gardens* (London, 1896).

Articles

Donna T. Andrew, ' "Adultery à-la-mode": Privilege, the Law and Attitudes to Adultery 1770–1809', *History*, 82 (January 1997), 5–23.

Peter J. Atkins, 'The Spatial Configuration of Class Solidarity in London's West End 1792–1939', *Urban History*, 17 (1990).

John M. Beattie, 'The Court of George I and English Politics 1717–1720', *English Historical Review*, 81 (January 1966), 26–37.

'The Beautiful Miss Gunnings', *Cornhill Magazine*, 16 (1867), 418–31.

R. M. Bleackley, 'The Beautiful Misses Gunning', *Connoisseur: An Illustrated Magazine for Collectors*, 12 (1905).

Rosalind Bowden 'The Letter Books of John and Nathaniel Cholmley', *North Yorkshire County Record Office Review* (2001), 6–57.

Robert O. Bucholz, 'Going to Court in 1700: A Visitor's Guide', *Court Historian*, 5/3 (2000), 181–215.

John Cannon, 'The Isthmus Repaired: The Resurgence of the English Aristocracy 1660–1760', *Proceedings of the British Academy*, 68 (1982).

Elaine Chalus, 'Elite Women, Social Politics and the Political World of Late Eighteenth-Century England', *Historical Journal*, 43/3 (2000), 669–97.

'Chaperons and Leaders of Fashion I–III', *Court Journal and Gazette of the Fashionable World, Politics, Literature and the Arts* (August 1845), 849–50.

Jonathan Conlin, 'Vauxhall Revisited: The Afterlife of a London Pleasure Garden: 1770–1859', *Journal of British Studies*, 45/4 (2006), 718–43.

Jonathan Conlin, 'Vauxhall on the Boulevard: Pleasure Gardens in Paris and London, 1764–1784', *Urban History*, 35/1 (May 2008).

Penelope J. Corfield, 'Class by Name and Number in Eighteenth-Century Britain', *History*, 72 (1987), 38–61.

Brian Cowan, 'What was Masculine about the Public Sphere? Gender and the Coffeehouse Milieu in Post-Restoration England', *History Workshop Journal*, 51 (2001), 127–57.

Diana Donald, ' "Mr Deputy Dumpling and Family": Satirical Images of the City Merchant in Eighteenth-Century England', *Burlington Magazine*, 131 (1989), 755–63.

Pierre Dubois, 'Resorts of Ambiguity: The Eighteenth-Century Pleasure Garden, a "Bewitching Assemblage of Provocatives" ', *Revue française de Civilisation Britannique*, 14, 2 (2007), 52–66.

Nancy W. Ellenberger, 'The Transformation of London "Society" at the End of Victoria's Reign: Evidence from the Court Presentation Records', *Albion*, 22/4 (1990), 633–53.

F. J. Fisher, 'The Development of London as Centre of Conspicuous Consumption in the Sixteenth and Seventeenth Centuries', *Transactions of the Royal Historical Society*, 30 (4th series, 1948), 37–50.

D. Fitzgerald, 'The Norfolk House Music Room', *V&A Museum Bulletin*, 2/1 (January 1966).

Hannah Greig, '"All together and all distinct": Public Sociability and Social Exclusivity in London's Pleasure Gardens ca. 1740–1800', *Journal of British Studies*, 51/1 (January 2012), 50–75.

Benjamin Heller, 'The "Mene Peuple" and the Polite Spectator: The Individual in the Crowd at Eighteenth-Century London Fairs', *Past and Present*, 2/1 (August 2010).

Helen Jacobsen, 'Ambassadorial Plate of the Later Stuart Period and the Collection of the Earl of Strafford', *Journal of the History of Collections*, 19/1 (May 2007).

C. Jones, 'The Life of a London Peer in the Reign of Anne', *London Journal*, 16 (1991), 140–55.

Lawrence Klein, 'Politeness and the Interpretation of the Eighteenth Century', *Historical Journal*, 45/4 (2002), 869–98.

Jenny Lister, 'Twenty-Three Samples of Silks: Silks Worn by Queen Charlotte & the Princess at the Royal Birthday Balls 1791–1794', *Costume*, 37 (2003).

J. N. McCord Jnr., 'Taming the Female Politician in Early Eighteenth-Century England: John Bull versus Lady Jersey', *Journal of Women's History*, 13/4 (2002), 30–52.

Marilyn Morris, 'Marital Litigation and English Tabloid Journalism: Crim Con in *The Bon Ton* (1791–1796)', *Journal for Eighteenth-Century Studies*, 28/1 (October 2008).

Tillman W. Netchman, 'Nabobinas: Luxury, Gender and the Sexual Politics of British Imperialism in the Late Eighteenth Century', *Journal of Women's History*, 18/4 (Winter 2006), 8–30.

Arthur Oswald, 'Norfolk House, St James's Square: The Town House of the Duke of Norfolk', *Country Life* (25 December 1937), 604–60.

Michael Rosenthal, 'Public Reputation and Image Control in Late Eighteenth-Century Britain', *Visual Culture in Britain*, 7/2 (2006), 69–91.

Gillian Russell, 'Faro's Daughters: Female Gamesters, Politics and the Discourse of Finance in 1790s Britain', *Eighteenth-Century Studies*, 33/4 (2000), 481–504.

Leonard D. Schwarz, 'Social Class and Social Geography: The Middle Classes in London at the End of the Eighteenth Century', *Social History*, 7 (1982), 167–85.

Elmer Edgar Stoll, 'The *Beau Monde* at the Restoration', *Modern Language Notes*, November/49 (1934), 425–32.

E. P. Thompson, 'Patrician Society, Plebeian Culture', *Journal of Social History*, 7 (Summer 1974), 382–405.

E. P. Thompson, 'Eighteenth-Century English Society: Class Struggle without Class', *Social History*, 3 (1978), 133–65.

Stella Tillyard, 'Celebrity in Eighteenth-Century London', *History Today*, 55/6 (June 2005).

Amanda Vickery, 'Golden Age to Separate Spheres?', *Historical Journal*, 36 (1993), 383–414.

Elias A. Wasson, 'The House of Commons, 1660–1945: Parliamentary Families and the Political Elite', *English Historical Review*, 106 (1991), 635–51.

E. A. Wrigley, 'A Simple Model of London's Importance in Changing English Society and Economy, 1650–1750', *Past and Present*, 37 (July 1967), 44–70.

INDEX

Page numbers in italic indicate illustrations

335